THE OXFORD BOOK OF
AUSTRALIAN
Letters

THE OXFORD BOOK OF
AUSTRALIAN
Letters

Edited by
BRENDA NIALL AND
JOHN THOMPSON

with PAMELA WILLIAMS

Melbourne
OXFORD UNIVERSITY PRESS
Oxford Auckland New York

OXFORD UNIVERSITY PRESS AUSTRALIA

Oxford   New York
Athens   Auckland   Bangkok
Bogotá   Buenos Aires   Calcutta
Cape Town   Chennai   Dar es Salaam   Delhi
Florence   Hong Kong   Istanbul   Karachi
Kuala Lumpur   Madrid   Melbourne
Mexico City   Mumbai   Nairobi   Paris   Port Moresby
São Paolo   Singapore   Taipei   Tokyo   Toronto   Warsaw

and associated companies in
Berlin   Ibadan

OXFORD is a trade mark of Oxford University Press

National Library of Australia
Cataloguing-in-Publication data:

The Oxford book of Australian letters.

ISBN 0 19 553985 0.

1. Australian letters.   I. Niall, Brenda, 1930– . II.
Thompson, John (John Robert), 1947– .

A826.008

Typeset by Desktop Concepts Pty. Ltd., Melbourne
Printed by Kyodo Printing Co. Pty Ltd., Singapore
Published by Oxford University Press,
253 Normanby Road, South Melbourne, Australia

Contents

Editors' Acknowledgments

Many people in Australia and overseas have assisted in the making of this anthology of Australian letters. While the choices we have made represent our own taste, enthusiasms and predilections, as editors we owe much to others: to scholars in several fields, but especially historians and biographers; to colleagues and friends; to librarians and archivists; and to many private custodians of letters who willingly offered us access to material which can still touch an emotional nerve.

Not all of the letters which came into our hands could be used, but their availability gave us a stronger sense of the range and variety of Australian letter writing. In some cases, the people we thank here have provided us with other kinds of help—ideas, suggestions, the loan of material, research assistance, the perusal and identification of material in collections we could not visit and, in three notable instances, the preparation of authoritative transcriptions of letters. We are especially grateful to Sally Anne Hasluck in Western Australia for providing us with access to the private letters of her parents-in-law and in giving us information which set those letters into their family context, to Patricia McKeown in Tasmania for her transcription of the George Meredith letter and to Patrick O'Neill in Canberra for the help he gave us with the pair of letters written by Walter Richardson and Mary Bailey and for the preparation from their difficult handwriting of usable transcriptions. In England, Sara Joynes gave valuable practical assistance and very kindly located material which might otherwise have been inaccessible to us.

But our greatest debt is to the writers of the letters themselves, the majority of them unwitting contributors to an anthology which is intended to celebrate a tradition of Australian letter writing as it has been practised and enjoyed for more than two centuries. Their letters, and the many others we looked at, have taken us deep into the private worlds of individuals and families. For that we are grateful as we are conscious also of a sense of privilege and trust.

For help of many different kinds we thank: Michael Ackland; Richard Allen; Sally Anderson; Giovanni Andreoni; Leigh Astbury; Thea Astley; Philip Ayres; Elaine Barry; Jan Bassett; Carol Beaumont; Carmel Bird; Lissant Bolton; Tim Bowden; Phyllis Boyd; Veronica Brady; Ian Britain; Penelope Buckley; Janine Burke; Wally Caruana; Betty Churcher; Axel Clark; Dymphna Clark; Mary Ryllis Clark; Graeme Clarke; Jessie Deakin Clarke; Peter Cochrane; Kay Cole; Alan Croker; Robert Crossley; Christopher Cunneen; Tim Curnow; Sue Dadswell; Rodney Davidson; Graeme Davison; Maryanne Dever; Desmond Digby; Rosemary Dobson; Kay Dreyfus; Derek Drinkwater; John Dunlop; Victoria Emery;

Marjorie Esson; Raymond Evans; Carole Ferrier; Peter Fitzpatrick; Nancy Robinson Flannery; Helen Garner; Ron Gilchrist; Anna Gray; Peter Groves; Gideon Haigh; Marion Halligan; Janie Hampton; Judith Deakin Harley; Margaret Harris; John Harwood; Nicholas Hasluck; Janet Hay; Heather Henderson; Margaret Henty; Paul Hetherington; Katie Holmes; Donald Horne; Ken Inglis; Ian Jones; Nicholas Jose; Guy Joyce; Beverley Keats; Brendon Kelson; Brian Kiernan; Garry Kinnane; Lou Klepac; Peter Kocan; Greg Kratzman; Harry Laing; Karen Lamb; Diane Langmore; Elizabeth Lawson; Margaret Le Mire; Susan Lever; Kate Llewellyn; Mary Lord; Phillip Lynch; Derek McDonnell; Humphrey McQueen; Aliki Mahon; David Marr; Tony Marshall; Alan Martin; Mandy Martin; Norma Martin; Richenda Martin; Ray Mathew; J.D. Merralls; Barbara Miechel; Harry M. Miller; Val and Betty Miller; Jan Minchin; Barbara Mobbs; Alastair Morrison; Ann Moyal; Douglas Muecke; John Mulvaney; Dame Elisabeth Murdoch; Angela Neustatter; Vasiliki Nihas; Maev O'Collins; Terence O'Neill; Teresa Pagliaro; Andy Palmer; Barbara Perry; Moira Peters; Philippa Poole; Cassandra Pybus; Marian Quartly; Kerry Reid; John Rickard; Michael Roe; Philippa Ryan; Kay Saunders; Jessie Serle; Phyllis Simons; Bob Simpson; F. B. Smith; Fern Smith; Bruce Steele; John Stapledon; Christopher Steinwedel; Dame Joan Sutherland; Ian Templeman; Chris Tiffin; Marjorie Tipping; Glen Tomasetti; Barbara Wall; Jennifer Wallace; Jonathan Wantrup; Elizabeth Webby; Nadia Wheatley; Ursula Whiteside; E. G. Whitlam; Marie Wood; Marguerita Wu; Barry York; Sir John Young.

Our debt to librarians and archivists is substantial. In the public domain they are the custodians of the letters, diaries and other records which are the raw materials of history. For the knowledge and skills of these dedicated professional men and women we are especially grateful. In particular, we want to thank the following: at the Alexander Turnbull Library in the National Library of New Zealand, Margaret Calder and Kirsty Smith; at the Archives Office of Tasmania, Robyn Eastley; at the Australian Archives in Canberra and in the Northern Territory Regional Office, Maggie Shapley and Katherine Goodwin; at the Australian Defence Force Academy in Canberra, Marie-Louise Ayres; at the Australian War Memorial in Canberra, Elizabeth Dracoulis, Carmel McInerny, Paul Mansfield and Tim Roberts; at the Barr Smith Library, University of Adelaide, Susan Woodburn; at the Beinecke Rare Book and Manuscript Library at Yale University, Vincent Giroud; at the Grainger Museum in the University of Melbourne, Alessandro Servadei; at the Harry Ransom Humanities Research Center, The University of Texas at Austin, Cliff Farrington; at the La Trobe Library, State Library of Victoria, Dianne Reilly, Gerard Hayes (who gave inspired assistance) and Jock Murphy; at the Monash University Library, the Rare Books Librarian Richard Overell was especially helpful; at the National Library of Australia, Graeme Powell, Valerie Helson, Dawn Melhuish and Paula Waring; at the Powerhouse Museum in Sydney, the archivist Helen Yoxhall; at the Public Records Office of Western Australia, Chris Coggin; at the Royal Historical Society of Victoria, the Honorary Librarian, Barbara Nixon; at the Queensland State Archives, Lee McGregor; at the State Library of New South Wales, where the staff were generous beyond words, Margy Burn, James Andrighetti, Paul Brunton and Warwick Hirst; and at the University of Melbourne Archives, Cecily Close and her staff.

We acknowledge with gratitude the support of the English Department, Monash University, the National Library of Australia and, in particular, the encouragement of the Director-General Warren Horton and the Assistant Director-General (Collections and Reader Services), Jan Fullerton and the financial support of the Australian Research Council. To Pamela Williams, our research assistant, who prepared an impeccable manuscript we are especially grateful: as editors, our burden was greatly eased by her prompt, capable and efficient support. To Peter Rose at Oxford University Press we extend particular thanks. The commissioning of this anthology rested with him and he has taken an active and lively interest in the discoveries we made along the way. His support and encouragement have meant a great deal.

INTRODUCTION

The death of the novel has been predicted many times and it has not come about. The death of the letter sounds more likely. Threatened by the telephone, is it now being finished off by faxes and e-mail? Perhaps it is, although there is a good case for e-mail as a new form of letter writing, a conversation less formal than the pen and paper method, and much quicker in transmission.

What have we gained; what is being lost? E-mail is quicker but letters last longer. Those written by the famous survive in library and archival collections and are essential for biographers and historians. Others are kept among family papers and cherished for their testimony of past lives.

Part of the meaning of the letter depends on the way it is transmitted. The formalities of elegantly spaced and folded pages establish a mood quite different from that of a hasty scrawl, with crossings out and missing words. It used to be thought impolite to type a private letter; the individuality of handwriting was part of the one-to-one transaction. As distinctive as a fingerprint, it announces the sender as surely as the signature.

Not so long ago the Australian postman, in blue serge uniform, went on suburban rounds on a bicycle, escorted by a posse of neighbourhood dogs, and blowing his whistle as he made each letter-box drop. Now it's the sound of a motor-bike and a quick glimpse of an orange crash helmet. In Britain a sharp click of brass on brass is still the signal, as the post falls through the front door slot on to the carpet. The postman's rounds have been checked by time and motion studies: no chance now for the cup of tea or even the shout of 'Nothing today!'

It would be hard to match the intensity of the ritual observed by early settlers in Australia. Everything stopped at the sight of a ship coming in to Sydney Harbour, or through the Heads to Melbourne. Watkin Tench describes the arrival of the *Lady Juliana*, months overdue, in June 1790. Driving rain and wild seas had the watchers in agony at the ship's possible danger. Some could not wait; they boarded the ship from a rowing boat:

> 'Letters, letters!' was the cry. They were produced and torn open in trembling agitation. News burst on us like meridian splendour on a blind man. We were overwhelmed with it, public, private, general and particular.[1]

It took days to assimilate so much news. King George III had gone mad and been restored to sanity. The 'wonderful and unexpected' French Revolution was a year old. The world had changed, and ink and paper proved it, reporting events which had become history.

Letters to and from Australia, endangered by storm and shipwreck, slow and uncertain in delivery, had a powerful impact because of the long wait with fears and hopes held in check. 'News from Home' was a set-piece in nineteenth-century paintings. Usually, it's bad news: a grizzled drover or prospector holds the fatal letter, while his mate stands by ready to commiserate on the loss of a wife or child.

Letters of separation stem inevitably from the Australian experience. Those unused to writing made heroic efforts. The strain shows, in punctuation marks scattered at random and much guesswork in spelling. Yet the letter's burden is carried by the force of emotion, the need to talk when talking isn't possible. Often, such letters make the more correct and literary production seem artificial.

Notions of correctness used to dominate the 'how to write a letter' part of the Australian school curriculum. One mysterious prescription ruled: 'Do not talk about yourself in the first paragraph': this was a warning against too much concern with the self. There were firm distinctions in the proper ways to begin and sign off. Spontaneity was not encouraged.

Yet the best letters always broke the rules. Joseph Furphy to Miles Franklin begins with 'My matchless Miles'. Edward ('Weary') Dunlop signed off to his future wife with 'Goodnight adorable'. Addresses can be expressive: the ominous 'Somewhere in France' of First World War letters; the casually evocative 'On the track' or 'Back o' Bourke'; or in a Northern Territorian's vagueness about time and place: 'March (Something) 1918' from 'Kelly Yard on the road from Wave Hill to Katherine'.

Biographers need letters, not necessarily to disclose events, but to get close to the feelings of a period, to understand how the subject appeared to others. Matters of tone, characteristic ways of expressing the self: these are lost in narrative, and they don't necessarily come through even in autobiography. Because autobiography is tethered to the time of its writing, and the notion of self that then prevails, it may be less revealing than a bundle of letters written at intervals in a life span.

In her biography of the poet Sylvia Plath, Janet Malcolm claims that letters are 'the biographer's only conduit to unmediated experience'. Everything else, Malcolm says, is 'stale, hashed over, told and retold, dubious, inauthentic, suspect'.[2] Perhaps so, but isn't the letter mediated too?

Some letters seem to present an unedited self, but the act of writing itself brings reflection. And some consciously set out to dramatise the self for the recipient. Patrick White's letters are works of art. Knowing that they would be read by posterity, he urged his correspondents to frustrate biographers by burning every scrap. Yet he must also have known that this would not be done. Nor was it: thousands of White's letters survived. White eventually authorised David Marr to use them in his celebrated biography, and they were later published as a separate volume.

Mediated or not, letters are the best material biographers have. In Malcolm's phrase, they give the 'sense of life retrieved'. They give intimacy; a sense of what it was like to know the writing self. And even when there is a strong element of theatre in the letter, it's revealing to discern the ways in which the author chose to dramatise the self for others.

Letters express a relationship. They differ in tone and mood depending on the closeness to or distance from the person addressed. Martin Boyd's sharp, irascible letters to his publisher are quite different from the passionate protests against British bombing of German cities which he directed to the Archbishop of Canterbury in 1943. And these are different again from the affectionate, informal, gossipy letters he sent his friends. So, while none of these is unmediated experience, their cumulative effect gives a strong sense of personality and voice.

When this anthology was commissioned it was suggested that it might serve in some measure as 'a personal, oblique history of Australia'. It was also felt that such an anthology would fill a surprising gap on the Australian shelf. Although volumes of collected letters have appeared — notably those of Mary Gilmore, Henry Lawson, Joseph Furphy and Patrick White — there has so far been no wide-ranging historical collection.

Our collection was to be eclectic: its choices made not simply from the correspondence of the famous, not from writers only, nor from those most practised in self-expression. Among those whose letters we searched out were public figures, politicians and journalists, explorers and sports people, judges, scientists, painters and musicians. We set out also to represent those who made no special mark on history, but whose letters illuminated in some personal way a particular aspect of the national experience.

Among these we include the letters of pioneer women and men, prompted by separation from home to express their sense of strangeness and dislocation and to make intelligible their bewildering new experiences. Among these we find examples of a distinctive genre: the letter-diary, written in instalments over a period of time, and completed only when a ship carrying outward mail was due to sail. Such letters give the texture of daily life as well as a strong sense of personality. They enable modern readers to see Australia through the eyes of those who found the land alien and harsh; they can also bring surprises in showing how adaptable our forebears were.

Some letters were simply too long for our purposes. We had to make difficult choices in which the shorter letters (still lengthy enough) took privilege. We did, however, include a few which exceeded our notional word limit. George Meredith's letter to his wife seemed a worthwhile exception, not only because it comes from a well-known Tasmanian pioneer, but for its unexpectedly free expression of sexual passion.

We looked for letters from and about indigenous Australians whose lives were so abruptly and permanently changed by European settlement. Here the range of choice was limited, but some poignant and revealing ones have been found. Especially moving is the mid-twentieth century appeal of W. Bray to the Northern Territory's Protector of Aborigines against the removal of his children. 'It would not be fair to us, the loss of them. Also not fair to them, the loss of their parents, causing crying and fretting'.

Such letters, like those of the early settlers, are beyond question part of the Australian experience. We have, however, used the term 'Australian' in a broad sense to represent letters which have a strong Australian association, such as those written by the English scientist Charles Darwin, who visited Australia in the 1830s, or sharp-eyed observers like the actors Charles and Ellen Kean, on tour in the 1860s, or Beatrice and Sidney Webb taking the national pulse in the 1890s. Other choices say something about the spread of Australian influence in the wider world.

Among letters from Australians abroad we include some from the famous, others perhaps unknown or forgotten. The painter Adelaide Ironside, writing from Italy in 1860, makes a strong assertion of independence and ambition when she disdains an offer of financial help from Sydney patrons. Decades later, Nellie Melba reports on her American tour, in an intriguing mixture of naiveté and shrewdness.

One notable group of letters comes from men and women at war; from the Gallipoli Peninsula on the day of the Anzac landing in 1915, from an enchanted respite in Greece in the immediate aftermath of the fighting in Turkey, from a hospital in Egypt and from the horrors of the trenches in France. Equally expressive and moving are letters written by wives and mothers in the Second World War. Ethel Turner writes exultantly when, after long months of doubt, she learns that her son is alive in a Japanese prison camp. May Sands keeps writing, stubbornly, optimistically, long after her son is reported missing, until the official letter puts an end to hope.

In some war letters and in other selections we have been able to present both sides of a correspondence. A sense of the letter as dialogue is strong in the letters between Agnes Miller, writing from Sydney throughout the First World War, and her future husband Olaf Stapledon in Flanders with the Friends' Ambulance Unit. This exchange also calls into question the easy use of categories such as 'war letters' or 'love letters': these are both.

Others fall more readily into categories, although their voices are varied and distinctive. The 1850s courtship letters of Walter and Mary Richardson (who were to be the parents of novelist Henry Handel Richardson) are full of hope as they plan their marriage. Her diffidence contrasts with his reflectiveness and confidence. Against them place two letters written years apart by Vance and Nettie Palmer, partners in marriage and in Australian literary and cultural life. Vance's ardent courtship letter of 1912 stands in striking contrast with his wife's painful, even abject, plea for love's renewal after years of marriage.

As with love and war, themes of love and death are intertwined. Herbert Brookes writes three weeks after the death of his young wife, directly addressing his 'Angel Lover' in a letter which was then sealed in a tin box, to be kept all his life. Hilda Dale's expression of grief at the death of her husband is sent to her friend Katharine Susannah Prichard, but it reads as a desperate assertion to herself of his continuing life, so long as she can hold him in memory.

We have tried to represent as many as possible of the very different ways in which the letter has been used. Some letters interweave public and private concerns: others focus on the inner life of the writer and the personal connection with the recipient. We have chosen examples of the letter to the editor, intended for as wide a readership as possible. Official letters from government files, which reflect a policy rather than a person, hint nevertheless at private misfortunes. A testimonial letter vouching for the capacity of Robert O'Hara Burke to lead a team of explorers has an added dimension of irony because we know his fate.

Time brings other ironies. Lord Dudley, advising his successor Lord Denman how best to endure his term as Governor-General, expressed the certainties of his time and class. Dudley's list of colonial deficiencies and crudities was written in all earnestness: today it reads as comedy, even parody.

An anthology of 200 letters culled from a seemingly limitless pool brings obvious problems of choice and balance. There were other difficulties. From the outset we were committed to publishing complete texts, with only very minor corrections to the original spelling and punctuation. As far as possible we wanted to give our readers the full flavour of the original. Some elements, of course, are missing: the idiosyncrasies of handwriting, the quality of paper and ink, the stamp and postmark, which are all part of the letter's ceremony. We omitted addresses, solely for reasons of space.

The decision not to abridge brought its own problems. Some letters contain wonderfully expressive passages, but lapse into banality or obscure private reference. We decided that if a letter required too much annotation to make its meaning clear, then in the anthologist's sense it failed an important test. We have provided some brief notes to give context and illuminate puzzling references, but whenever it seemed that the reader's access would be too much impeded we thought it best to make a different choice.

We have pondered questions of balance. The letters most easily found in public collections or in published form are those of the famous or the historically significant. Understandably, novelists and poets are eloquent and assured writers of letters. But it was never our intention to set up a canon of the 'best' Australian letters. We have looked for variety of tone and mood and have not put our chosen letters through tests of correctness or even fluency. Some very modest letters have earned a place for their natural quirkiness or for the tangential glimpse they provide of a larger Australian story.

Two letters written to Mrs Jeannie Gunn are worlds apart in style and provenance, yet it would be hard to give preference to either. Lord Kintore, a former Governor of South Australia, writes from the heart of London's clubland to express his pleasure in Gunn's *We of the Never Never*. Graceful and courteous, this is a letter of great charm. A second letter to Mrs Gunn comes from an unknown Northern Territorian who had once worked on the Gunns' station: 'I laid down in my camp & read it again, and in my fancy I lived the old days over again …' This writer sounds the note of the Australian balladists, while Kintore's urbanity is of his time and class, essentially British. In putting the two letters side by side we hope that readers will find pleasure in the contrasting styles.

In looking through the collection we have wondered whether there were not too many sombre or tragic letters in proportion to the rest. Yet this may be inevitable. Comic, frivolous occasional letters are less likely to be kept than those that mark solemn or tragic experiences. Certain letters demand to be written: those that break bad news or try to comfort the bereaved. There are happy, forward-looking love letters, and we have included some of these. Yet the happiest lovers are together; they don't need to write. Even in the buoyant love letters of Edward Dunlop to his future wife there is the shadow of war and our own knowledge of ordeals to come.

Looking for joyous letters, it would be hard to do better than those of Arthur Streeton in which a painter's eye brings moments of existence into vibrant life. His Sydney Harbour is 'all glowing and oriental … little steamers puffing hard and skipping over the blue water clouds of smoke … & over all the bright harmony the warm palpitating sky of the Sunny South'. Streeton is one of many who respond eloquently to the Australian landscape. Percy Grainger is another: 'Dear mother, dont neglect to take a chew at young gum leaves sometimes'. D.H. Lawrence evokes a sense of place in letters which also reflect on the Australian temperament: 'no inside life of any sort, just a long lapse and drift'.

With letters as numerous and brilliant as those of Percy Grainger or Patrick White we faced a new problem of choice. Was it essential to look for the one most characteristic of the writer — if indeed that could be done — or should we give priority to the qualities of each individual text, leaving its author out of mind? If we had luck enough to find a hitherto unpublished letter, did that add to its merits? Was Patrick White, 'the Slasher' as he called himself, to be preferred to PW in gentle mood? With White, as with a number of other prolific writers, we allowed ourselves more than one letter. We gained extra value by choosing from White the only example of a long tradition of childhood: the letter to Father Christmas.

All things being more or less equal, it made sense to choose two late letters from Gwen Harwood, since a selection of her early letters has been published (*Blessed City*, 1990). Out of Harwood's abundance there could be no question of finding 'the best'; so many beckoned, and all of them of extraordinary quality. The two finally chosen show how she could make the most of the small ceremonies of her quiet life in Hobart. They are letters of friendship, unassuming comic masterpieces.

It was not a determinant of choice but it was a bonus to find that a good letter had been written in unusual circumstances. The proposal of marriage written by Patrick McMahon Glynn has great charm and verve. Writing from the floor of the New South Wales Legislative Assembly, during the Australasian Federal Convention of 1897–98, Glynn 'put the question' to his future wife while the politician William Lyne 'within a yard of me [was] pouring on the too-thinly protected top of my head, a niagra of figures'. Less eloquent than Glynn but a vivid letter in its own right, a 1916 account of life in the trenches is unusual in being part of a long correspondence between two people who never met. It was initiated when Wilson Tong put his name and regimental number in a bottle amd threw it overboard from his troop ship; a young girl found it when it was washed up on Phillip Island.

A search for 200 Australian letters from countless possibilities might seem as brave an enterprise as posting a letter in a bottle from a ship at sea. We have been helped in many ways. The first debt is to biographies in which quoted extracts from letters put us on the track to the originals. Often the biographers themselves have helped us to find the best examples. Other works of scholarship, and other scholars, offered useful leads.

We heard from friends about collections of private papers which might hold treasures. Sometimes we were fortunate in being approached by the owners of letters when our project became known. We have a major debt to libraries and to manuscript librarians and archivists for suggesting places to look, or even looking on our behalf for an exceptional letter in a collection. Some lucky guesses have paid dividends: a hunch that someone would have written good letters, or that a certain event must have been well described by some observer.

Many of the letters in this collection are published here for the first time. Others have appeared in scholarly editions or popular anthologies. Where possible we have located and checked the original manuscript. Some readers may recognise familiar letters in slightly different, or longer, versions. A letter from pioneer Rachel Henning, for example, was published in an abridged form: we have restored the full text, as we have done with a letter from the artist Joy Hester. In cases where the original has been lost, we reproduce what seems the most reliable transcript.

Like most anthologists, we debated the merits of the chronological approach as against a thematic arrangement. The more closely we studied our material, the more dissatisfied we became with divisions which too often seemed arbitrary. Love and war were indissolubly linked; letters of friendship could also be political letters. To what category should we assign a bishop's account of a sea voyage which describes in comic detail the difficulties of conducting a religious service in stormy weather as the ship lurched and rolled? A chronological ordering gave historical perspective and context, suggesting unobtrusively some developments in Australian society while letting the reader, unprompted, see changes in language and modes of address. Our only departure from chronology occurs when we have chosen more than one letter from the same author, or when letter and reply have been included. Here it seemed best to group or pair the letters.

The period of this anthology covers the rise and decline of the letter. When the first Europeans came to Australia, letter writing was a privilege from which many were excluded. To write and receive letters was a matter of course only for the literate and the well-to-do. Unless the letter was paid for in advance by a Member of Parliament or someone in a position to provide a frank, the recipient would be put to expense. The cost was determined by the number of pages: hence the habit of 'crossing' the pages so as to get double value. Jane Austen's novel *Mansfield Park* (1814) illustrates the costliness of postage in the overwhelming gratitude of heroine Fanny Price when her letter to her midshipman brother is franked by her rich uncle.

In Britain, penny postage in 1840 and delivery by rail instead of stage coach brought letter writing within the means of many more. Australia's gold-rush immigrants in the 1850s had developed the habit of keeping in touch by letter; and they were used to prompt deliveries. In Australia they endured delays and dangers: the long sea journeys; coaches lurching over bush roads, risky missions with mailbags on horseback over flooded rivers.

From the mid nineteenth century until the 1950s the letter was of central importance in countless Australian lives. Not only were letters eagerly awaited and read with the most intense emotion, they were cherished by the recipients and passed on to their descendants. The notion of a bundle of letters retrieved from an ancient trunk or unvisited attic makes a powerful appeal to the imagination. This is not simply a matter of access to history. Usually written with only one reader in mind, the letter discloses inner worlds, affirms the feelings and gives first-hand testimony of experience. Even when the ink has faded the spark of authentic life remains.

Telegrams for major events and the telephone for everyday conversations of life gradually displaced the letter in the early twentieth century. Whether fax and e-mail should be seen as marking a further stage in decline, or as a means of revival, is still in debate as this century ends. The new forms of conversation are rather like the letter in the late eighteenth century in being available only to the privileged, technologically equipped, minority. Will there be a breakthrough as dramatic as penny postage, bringing electronic communication within general easy reach, as much a matter of course as the telephone?

The last three items in this anthology show that fax and e-mail conversations can be as vibrant and personal as any exchange of letters. Unlike the telephone call, they can be converted into permanent form. We see them as offering continuity as well as change; and if indeed the letter is in terminal decline, these new modes of conversation give a generation unused to letter writing many of the uses and delights of the earlier form.

NOTE ON THE TEXTS

As far as possible we have reproduced these letters as they were written, without editorial intervention. Many have been transcribed from the handwritten originals, whose spelling and punctuation remain uncorrected. Occasionally, defeated by the handwriting, we have inserted 'illegible' in square brackets. None of the letters has been abridged. Where ellipses occur, they belong to the original, in which they have been used as a form of punctuation. In working from typewritten originals we have corrected some obvious typographical mistakes. When letters have been located in published versions we have made every effort to check the original text. In cases where it has not been possible to sight the original we have used the most reliable scholarly editions.

The headnotes and footnotes are intended to give the reader basic information for the understanding of each letter. Because some of our writers are virtually unknown it was not always possible to find biographical information. The footnotes are not designed to be comprehensive. They identify persons and places mentioned in the texts only where such information is available and thought to be helpful in reading the letter. Preference has been given to Australian references, on the grounds that sources on major international figures are more readily found. Thus, a note on painter Russell Drysdale is supplied while Rembrandt and Monet are assumed not to need identification.

1   Watkin Tench, in Tim Flannery (ed.), *1788. Comprising a Narrative of the Expedition to Botany Bay and A Complete Account of the Settlement at Port Jackson*, Text Publishing, Melbourne, 1996, p. 127.
2   Janet Malcolm, *The Silent Woman*, Picador/Pan Macmillan Australia, 1994, p. 111.

James Cook

Captain James Cook (1728–79) completed his first journey around the world in HMS Endeavour in the years 1768–71, during which he circumnavigated New Zealand and charted the east coast of Australia. Writing from London, Cook tells his traveller's tale to the man to whom he had been apprenticed before joining the Royal Navy in 1755.

1. To John Walker, 13 September 1771

Sir

In my last I gave you some account of my Voyage as far as the South Sea Islands the remainder shall be the subject of this letter. What I mean by the South Sea islands are those which lay within and about the Tropicks, they are in general small; Georges Island, which is only about 33 Leagues in circuit is one of the largest. the Inhabitants of this Island gave us an account and the names of 130 Islands laying in these Seas. they are of two kinds very low or very mountainous, the low Islands are such as are call'd Keys in the West Indies, that is mostly shoals, ledges of Rock &c. the chief produce of the firm land is Coaco-nutts. these and fish with which all these Islands abound are the chief support of the Inhabitants. The mountainous parts of the High Islands are in general dry and barren, and as it were burnt up with the sun. but all these Islands are skirted round with a border of low land, which is firtile and pleasant to a very high degree, being well clothed with various sorts of fruit trees which nature hath planted here for the use of the happy natives. These people may be said to be exempted from the curse of our fore fathers scarce can it be said that they earn thier bread with the sweat of thier brows, benevolent nature hath not only provided them with necessarys but many of the luxuries of life; Loaves of Bread or at least what serves as a most excellent substitute growes here in a manner spontaneously upon trees, besides a great many other fruits and roots, and the Sea Coasts are well stored with a vast variety of excellent fish; they have only three species of tame animal Hogs, Dogs, and Fowles, all of which they eat. Dogs we learnt from them also to eat, and there were but few among us who did not think that a South Sea Dog eat as well as English Lamb. Was I to give a full description of these Islands the Manners and Customs of the Inhabitants &c it would far exceed the bounds of a letter. I must therefore quit these Terrestial Paradises in order to follow the Course of our Voyage. In the beginning of Augst 1769 we quited the Tropical Regions and steer'd to the South-ward in the midst of the South Sea, to the height of 40° without meeting with any land or the least visible signs of any, we then steer'd to the westward between the Latitude of 30° and 40° untill we fell in with the East Coast of New Zeland a very small part of the west coast of which was first discoverd by Tasman in 1642, but he never once set foot upon it. this country was thought to be a part of the Southern Continent, but I found it to be two Large Islands both of which I circumnavigated in the space of Six Months. they extend from the Latitude of 34° South to 47 1/2° South, and are together nearly as big as great Britain. It is a hilly Mountainous Country, but rich and firtile, especially the northern parts, where it is also well Inhabited. The Inhabitants of this Country are a strong well made active people, rather above the common size, they are of a very dark brown Colour with long black hair, they are also a brave warlike people with sentiments void of treachery, their arms are Spears, Clubs, Halbarts, Battle-Axes, darts and stones, they live in Strong held or fortified Towns built in well chose situations and according to art. We had frequent skirmishes with them, always where we were not known, our fire arms gave us the Superiority. at first some of them were kill'd, but we at last learnt how to manage them without taking away their lives, and when once Peace was settled they ever after were our very good friends. These people speake the same Language as the people of the South Sea Islands we had before visited tho distant from them many hundred Leagues and of whom they have not the least knowledge or of any other people whatever; their chief food is Fish and firn roots, they have too, in places large plantations of Potatoies, such as we have in the West Indies and likewise yamms &ca. Land animals they have none either wild or tame except Dogs which they breed for food. This Country produceth a grass plant like Flags of the nature of Hemp or Flax but superior in quality to either. of this the natives make clothing, Lines, Netts &ca. The men very often go naked with only a narrow belt about their wastes, the women on the contrary never appear naked. Their Government, Religion, notions of the creation of the world, Mankind &ca are much the same as the natives of the South Sea Islands—

We left this Country on the 1st Apl 1770 and steer'd for New Holland all the East part of which remain'd undiscover'd, my design being to fall in with the Southern part call'd Van Diemens Land, but the winds forced me to the northward of it about 40 Leagues, so that we fell in with the Land in the Latitude of 38° South. I explored the Coast of This Country / which I call'd New South Wales / to its northern extremity, in the doing of which we were many times in great danger of loosing the Ship, once we lay 23 hours upon a Ledge of Rocks, was obliged to throw our Guns and many of our stores over board, received very much damage in her bottom but by a fortunate circumstance got her into Port and repair'd her—great part of this coast is cover'd by Islands and Sholes, which made the exploring exceeding dangerous even to a very great degree. We sailed upon this Coast near 400 Leagues by the Lead without ever once having a Leadsman out of the Chains, with sometimes one two and three boats a head to direct us, and yet with all this precaution we were very often obliged to anchor with all sails standing to prevent running a shore, we at last surmounted all difficulties and got into the India Sea by a passage intirely new—

The East Coast of new Holland or what I call new South Wales extends for 38° South to 10 1/2°. if new Holland can be call'd an Island it is by far the greatest in the known world. the Interior part of this immense tract of land is not attall known what borders upon the sea Coast is a mixture of Firtile and Barren land. the Soil in general is of a loose sandy nature. The Natives of this Country are not numerous. They are of a very dark brown or Chocolate [colour] with lank black hair, they are under the common size and seem to be a timerous inoffensive race of Men. they spoke a very different Language to any we had met with. Men women and children go wholy naked. it is said of our first parents that after they had eat of the forbidden fruit they saw themselves naked and were ashamed: these people are naked and are not ashamed; they live chiefly on Fish and wild Fowle and such other articles as the land naturly produceth, for they do not cultivate one foot of it. These people may truly be said to be in the pure state of Nature and may appear to some to be the most wretched upon Earth; but in reality they are far more happier than we Europeans being wholly unacquainted not only with the superfluous but with any of the necessary conveniences so much sought after in Europe they are happy in not knowing the use of them. They live in a Tranquility which is not disturb'd by the inequality of condition. the Earth and Sea of their own accord furnishes them with all things necessary for life; they covet not magnificent Houses Household-stuff &ca. they sleep as sound in a small hovel or even in the open as the King in His Pallace on a Bed of down—

After quiting new Holland we steer'd for the Coast of New Guinea where we landed but once then made the Best of our way to Batavia and in our way touch'd at an Island partly under The Dutch East India Company, here we got plenty of refreshments which was very exceptable we arrived at Batavia in Octr all in good health and high spirits [illegible] thought all our hardships at an end but Providence thought proper to order it otherwise, the repairs the ship wanted caused a delay of near 10 weeks in which time we contracted sickness that here and on our passage to the Cape of Good Hope carried of a bove thirty of my people, the remainder of the Voyage was attended with no material circumstance.—If any intresting circumstances should occur to me that I have omited, will hereafter you acquaint you with it. I however expect that my Lords Commissioners of the Admiralty will very soon publish the whole voyage, Charts &ca. Another Voyage is thought of with two Ships which if it take place I believe the command will be confer'd upon me—if their is anything that I can inform you in regard to my late voyage I shall take a pleasure in doing it, and believe me to be your obliged Servt:

JAMS: COOK

New South Wales] it was not until 22 August 1770, when he had passed into the Torres Strait and landed at what is now Possession Island, that Cook claimed possession of the whole of the eastern coast in the name of King George III. He had called it first New Wales but later changed the name to New South Wales   publish the whole voyage] the first published account, the so-called Hawkesworth's Edition, appeared in London in 1773

GEORGE WORGAN

George Bouchier Worgan (1757–1838), surgeon, sailed in the First Fleet on board HMS Sirius. He brought with him a piano, probably the first such instrument to come to Australia. In a lively and spirited letter to his brother, Worgan gives one of the more generous early accounts of the Aboriginal inhabitants of the area around Port Jackson.

2. TO RICHARD WORGAN, 12 JUNE 1788

DEAR RICHARD

I think I hear You saying, "Where the D—ce is Sydney Cove Port Jackson?" and see You whirling the Letter about to find out the Name of the Scribe: Perhaps You have taken up Salmons Gazetteer, if so, pray spare your Labour, and attend to Me for half an Hour—We sailed from the *Cape of Good Hope* on the 12th of November 1787—As that was the last civilised Country We should touch at, in our Passage to *Botany Bay* We provided ourselves with every Article, necessary for the forming a civilised Colony, Live Stock, consisting of Bulls, Cows, Horses, Mares, Colts, Hogs, Goats, Fowls and other living Creatures by Pairs. We likewise, procured a vast Number of Plants, Seeds & other Garden articles, such as Orange, Lime, Lemon, Quince Apple, Pear Trees, in a Word, every Vegetable Production that the Cape afforded. Thus Equipped, each Ship like another Noah's Ark, away we steered for *Botany Bay*, and after a tolerably pleasant Voyage of 10 Weeks & 2 Days *Governour Phillip*, had the Satisfaction to see the whole of his little Fleet safe at Anchor in the said *Bay*.

As we were sailing in We saw 8 or 10 of the Natives, sitting on the Rocks on the South Shore, and as the Ships bordered pretty near thereto, we could hear them hollow, and observe them talking to one another very earnestly, at the same time pointing towards the Ships; they were of a black reddish sooty Colour, entirely naked, walked very upright, and each of them had long Spears and a short Stick in their hands; soon after the Ships had anchored, the Indians went up into the Wood, lit a Fire, and sat Around about it, as unconcerned (apparently) as tho' nothing had occurred to them. Two Boats from the *Sirius*, were now Manned and armed, and the *Governor*, accompanied by Captn. Hunter, and several other Officers, went towards the Shore, where they had seen the Natives, who perceiving the Boats making towards the Beach, came out of the Wood, and walked along, some distance from the Water-side, but immediately on the Boats landing, they scampered up into the Woods again, with great Precipitation. On this, the Governor, advised, that we should seem quite indifferent about them, and this apparent Indifference had a good Effect, for they very soon appeared in sight of Us, When, the Governor held up some Beads, Red Cloth & other Bawbles and made signs for them to advance, but they still were exceedingly shy & timid, and would not be enticed by our allurements; which the Governor perceiving, He shewed them his Musket, then laid it on the Ground, advancing singly towards them, they now seeing that He had nothing in his Hands like a Weapon, one of ye oldest of the Natives gave his Spears to a younger, and approached to meet the Governor, but not without discovering manifest tokens of Fear, and distrust, making signs for the things to be laid on the Ground which, the *Governor* complying with, He advanced, tooke them up, and went back to his Companions; Another, came forth and wanted some of the same kind of Presents, which, were given to Him by the same Method, at length, after various Methods to impress them with the Belief that We meant them no harm, they suffered Us to come up to them, and after making them all presents, which they received with much the same kind of Pleasure, which Children shew at such Bawbles, just looking at them, then holding out their Hands for more, some laughing heartily, and jumping extravagantly; they began to shew a Confidence, and became very familiar, and curious about our Cloaths, feeling the Coat, Waistcoat, and even the Shirt and on seeing one of the Gentlemen pull off his Hat, they all set up a loud Hoop, one was curious enough to take hold of a Gentlemans Hair that was cued, and called to his Companions to look at it, this was the occasion of another loud Hoop, accompanied with other Emotions of Astonishment. In a Word, they seemed pretty well divested of their Fears, and became very funny Fellows.

They suffered the Sailors to dress them with different coloured Papers, and Fools-Caps, which pleased them mightily, the strange contrast these Decorations made with their black Complexion brought strongly to my Mind, the Chimney-Sweepers in London on a May-Day.—They were all Men & Boys in this Tribe.

I should have told You, that the Governor, left the *Sirius* soon after we sailed from the *Cape of Good Hope*; and Embarked on Board the *Supply Brig* & Gave up the Command of ye Convoy to Captn. Hunter, in order that he might proceed on before the main Body of the Fleet, but he arrived in Botany Bay, only two Days before Us. In this Time, He had obtained an Intercourse or two, with some Natives on the *North Shore*, but, as the Means which he took to gain their Confidence, and effect a Parley, were much the same as those, I have given you an account of, I shall only mention a few singular Circumstances that occurred in these Intercourses. The *Supply Brig*, arrived in ye *Bay* about 2 °Clk in the Afternoon of ye 18th January and at 4 °Clk, The Governor, attended by several Officers, went in two armed Boats towards a part of the Shore where, 6 of the Natives, were, and had been sitting the whole time the *Supply* was entering the Bay, looking and pointing at Her with great Earnestness; When the Boats had approached pretty near this Spot, two of the Natives got up, and came close to the Waters-Edge, making Motions, pointing to another part of the Shore and talking very fast & loud, seemingly, as if the Part to which they pointed, was better landing for the Boats, they could not however, discern any thing unfriendly, or threatening in the Signs and Motions which the Natives made.—Accordingly the Boats coasted along the Shore in a Direction for the Place, to which, they had been directed, the Natives following on the Beach. In the mean Time, the Governor, or somebody in his Boat, made Signs that they wanted Water, this they signified by putting a Hat over the Side of the Boat and seeming to take up some of the salt Water put it to his Mouth, the Natives, immediately, understood this Sign and with great Willingness to Oblige, pointed to the Westward, and walked that Way, apparently with an Intention to show their Visitors the very Spot. The Boats steered towards the Place, and soon discovered the Run of fresh Water, opposite to which, they landed, and tasting it found it to be very good. The Natives had stopped about 30 Yards from ye Place where the Boat landed, to whom, the Gentlemen made signs of thanks for their friendly Information, at the same time offering Presents, and doing everything they could think of, to make them lay aside their Fears and advance towards them, but this point was gained only, by the Methods that I have mentioned: and when they did venture to come and take the things out of the Governor's & the other Gentlemen's Hands, it was with evident Signs of Fear, the Gentlemen now having distributed all their Presents among them, returned on Board.

Thus, was our first Intercourse obtained, with these *Children of Nature.*—About 12 of the Natives appeared the next Morning, on the Shore opposite to the *Supply*, they had a Dog with them, (something of the Fox Species); The Governor and the same Gentlemen that were of his Party Yesterday went on Shore, and very soon came to a Parley with them, there were some of their Acquaintances among the Number, and these advanced first (leaving their Spears with their Companions who remained behind at a little Distance) as they had done Yesterday; They all of them in a short time became Confident, Familiar & *vastly funny* took anything that was offered them, holding out their Hands and making Signs for many things that they saw, laughed when we laughed, jumped extravagantly, and grunted by way of Music, & Repeated many Words & Phrases after Us. The Gentlemen having passed about an hour with them, returned on Board, but could not induce any of the Natives to accompany them there. A Part of Us made an Excursion up an Arm in the North part of the *Bay*, where we had not been long landed before we discovered among the Bushes a Tribe of the Natives, who at first did not discover such an inoffensive & friendly Disposition, as those I have spoke of, above; for these rude, unsociable Fellows, immediately threw a Lance, which fell very near one of the Sailors, and stuck several Inches in the Ground, we returned the Compliment by firing a Musket over their Heads, on which I thought they would have broken their Necks with running away from Us. About an hour after, we, in our Ramble, fell in with them again, they stood still, but seemed ready for another Start. One of Us, now laid down the Musket and advanced towards them singly, holding out some Bawbles, and making Signs of Peace; In a little time they began to gain Confidence, and two of them approached to meet the Gentlemen who held out the Presents, the Introduction being amicably settled, they all joined Us, and took the Trinkets we offered them; The same Emotions of Pleasure, Astonishment, Curiosity & Timidity, appeared in these poor Creatures, as had been observed in our first Acquaintances—There were some Old and young Women in this Tribe, whom the Men seemed very jealous & careful of, keeping them at Distance behind some young Men, who were armed with Spears, Clubs & Shields, apparently as a Guard to them. We could see these curious *Evites* peeping though the Bushes at Us, and we made signs to the Men, who were still with Us, that We wished to give some Trinkets to the Women, on which, One of the Husbands, or Relations (as we supposed) hollowed to them in an authoritative Tone, and one of these Wood-Nymphs (as naked as Eve before she knew Shame) obeyed and came up to Us; when; we presented her with a Bracelet of blue Beads for her obliging Acquiescence; She was extremely shy & timid, suffering Us, very reluctantly, even to touch Her; Indeed, it must be merely from the Curiosity, to see how they would behave, on an Attempt to be familiar with them, that one would be induced to touch one of Them, for they are Ugly to Disgust, in their Countenances and stink of Fish-Oil & Smoke, *most sweetly.*—I must not omit mentioning a very singular Curiosity among the Men here, arising from a Doubt of what Sex we are, for from our not having, like themselves, long Beards, and not seeing when they open our Shirt-Bosoms (which they do very roughly and without any Ceremony) the usual distinguishing Characteristics of Women, they start Back with Amazement, and give a Hum! with a significant look, implying. What kind of Creatures are these?!—As it was not possible for Us to satisfy their Inquisitiveness in this Particular, by the simple Words. *Yes* or *No*, We had Recourse to the Evidence of *Ocular Demonstration*, which made them laugh, jump & Skip in an extravagant Manner.—In a Tribe of these funny, curious Fellows, One of them, after having had His Curiosity gratified by this mode of Conviction, went into the Wood, and presently came forth again, jumping & laughing with a Bunch of broad Leaves tied before Him, by Way of a Fig-leaf Veil.— Before we took our leave of the Tribe that threw the Lance; they endeavoured to convince Us, that it was not thrown by general Consent, and one of them severely reprimanded the Man who threw it, and several of them struck him, but more to shew Us their Disapprobation of what he had done, than as a Punishment for it.

During our stay at *Botany Bay*, the *Governor* had made himself well acquainted with the Situation of the Land Nature of the Soil etc. etc. which he not finding so Eligible, as he could Wish, for the Purpose of forming a Settlement, He determined, before he fixed on it, to visit an Inlet on the Coast, about 12 Miles to the Northward of this *Bay* which, our great Circumnavigator, *Captn. Cook*, discovered, and named, (in honour of one of the then Commissioners of the Navy) *Port Jackson* accordingly, the Governor, attended by a Number of Officers went in 3 Boats, on this Expedition, and the third day, they returned, gave it as their Opinion, that *Port Jackson* was one of the most spacious and safe Harbours in the known World, and said they had already fixed on a Spot, on which the Settlement was to be formed. In Consequence of this Success, the Idea was entirely given up, of establishing a Colony at *Botany Bay*, and three days after, the Wind favouring our Designs, the Fleet sailed for *Port Jackson* and in the Evening of the Day of our Departure, We arrived, and anchored in one of the many beautiful Coves which it Contains, which *Cove* Sir, the *Governor* has (in honour of *Lord Sydney*), named *Sydney Cove*.

Though the Description given by the Gentlemen who first, visited this *Port* was truly luxuriant, and wore the air of Exaggeration, Yet they had by no means done its Beauties and Conveniences Justice, for as an Harbour, None, that has hitherto been described, equals it in Spaciousness and Safety. the Land forms a Number of pleasant

Coves in most of which 6 or 7 Ships may lie secured to the Trees on Shore. It contains likewise a Number of small Islands, which are covered with Trees and a variety of Herbage, all which appears to be Evergreens. The Whole, (in a Word) exhibits a Variety of Romantic Views, all thrown together into sweet Confusion by the careless hand of Nature. Well, Dear Dick, now I have brought you all the way to *Sydney Cove*, I must tell you what we have done, since our arrival in these Seas, & in this Port—what we are doing, what has happened etc. etc.

On the Evening of our Arrival (26th January 1788) The Governor & a Number of the Officers assembled on Shore where, they Displayed the British Flag and each Officer with a Heart, glowing with Loyalty drank his Majesty's Health and Success to the Colony. The next Day, all the Artificers & an 100 of the Convicts were landed, carrying with them the necessary Utensils for clearing the Ground and felling the Trees. By the Evening, they were able to pitch a Number of Tents and some Officers and private Soldiers slept on shore that Evening. In the Interval of that time and the Date of this Letter, the principal Business has been the clearing of Land, cutting, Grubbing and burning down Trees, sawing up Timber & Plank for Building, making Bricks, hewing Stone, Erecting temporary Store-houses, a Building for an Hospital, another for an Observatory, Enclosing Farms & Gardens, making temporary Huts, and many other Conveniences towards the establishing of a Colony.

A small Settlement has been established on an Island, which is about a Fort-night's sail from this place, and named by Captn. Cook *Norfolk Island*, the Intention of this Settlement I believe, is on account of the fine Pine Trees, of wh. the Island is full, and to try what the Soil will produce.

We have discovered an Island in these Seas, never before seen by our Navigators, We have named it, *Lord Howe's Island*. It affords Turtle in the Summer Season, and the *Supply Brig*, brought away 18 very fine Ones, on which, we feasted most luxuriously, it also, abounds with Birds of the Dove Species, which are so stupid, as to suffer us to take them off the Bushes with our Hands. As this Island is not above 4 or 5 Days sails from Port Jackson, we hope, to have Turtle Feasts frequently: if this be the Case, I suppose We shall have a Shipload of Aldermen coming out to New South Wales.

As I mean to annex to this Letter, a kind of Journal of each Day's Transaction and Occurrences, I shall pass over many things in this Narrative, and enter immediately on a rough Sketch of the Country of New South Wales, its Inhabitants etc. etc. as far, at least, as We have been able to learn. *Botany Bay*, *Port Jackson*, and another Inlet (8 Miles to the Northward of *Port Jackson*, which Captn. Cook calls *Broken Bay*,) lie between the Latitudes of 35° & 40° South. This Part of the Coast (which is as much as we have been near enough, to judge of) is moderately high and regular, forming small Ridges, Plains, easy ascents and descents. It is pretty generally clothed with Trees and Herbage Inland; The Shore is rocky and bold, forming many bluff Heads, and overhanging Precipices. On approaching the Land which forms *Botany Bay* (but I shall speak more particularly to that which forms *Port Jackson*) It suggests to the Imagination Ideas of luxuriant Vegetation and rural Scenery, consisting of gentle risings & Depressions, beautifully clothed with variety of Verdures of Evergreens, forming dense Thickets, & lofty Trees appearing above these again, and now & then a pleasant checquered Glade opens to your View.— Here, a romantic rocky, craggy Precipice over which, a little purling stream makes a Cascade—There, a soft vivid-green, shady Lawn attracts your Eye: Such are the prepossessing Appearances which the Country that forms *Port Jackson* presents successively to your View as You sail along it.

Happy were it for the Colony, if these Appearances did not prove so delusive as upon a nearer Examination they are found to do; For though We meet with, in many parts, a fine black Soil, luxuriantly covered with Grass, & the Trees at 30 or 40 Yards distant from each other, so as to resemble Meadow Land, yet these Spots are frequently interrup. in their Extent by either a rocky, or a sandy, or a Swampy Surface crowded with large Trees, and almost impenetrable from Brush-wood which, being the Case, it will necessarily require much Time and Labour to cultivate any considerable Space of Land together. To be sure in our Excursions Inland, which I believe have not exceeded 30 or 40 Miles in any Direction, we have met with a great Extent of Park-like Country, and the Trees of a moderate Size & at a moderate distance from each other, the Soil, apparently, fitted to produce any kind of Grain and clothed with extraordinarily luxuriant Grass, but from its Situation, and the Quantity of Wood, though in a moderate Quantity in Comparison with that in other Parts. It is the general Opinion here, that it would be a great Length of Time, and require a vast Number of Cultivators to render it fit to produce Grain enough to supply a small Colony. About 50 Miles to the West, and North West Inland, there appears to be some mountainous Country and from our having seen Smoke on it, now & then, We are led to suppose that it is Inhabited. The Governor intends to visit these Mountains shortly, and I have his permission to accompany Him in this Excursion, but I don't think, he will go, before he has discharged, and despatched all the Ships for England.

the Governor] Arthur Phillip (1738–1814), naval officer and first governor of New South Wales
Captn. Hunter] John Hunter (1737–1821), later Admiral and second governor of New South Wales

ARTHUR PHILLIP

Arthur Phillip (1738–1814) was a naval officer and the founding governor of New South Wales. Here he writes to Sir Joseph Banks (1743–1820), the naturalist and patron of science who sailed with Cook on his first circumnavigation of the globe 1768–71, which included landfalls on the Australian east coast. He became the acknowledged authority on New South Wales and maintained an intense interest in its flora and fauna. Phillip's letter to Banks is one of the earliest private letters to survive from the cradle period of European settlement in Australia.

3.   To Joseph Banks, 2 July 1788

Dear Sir,

I have the pleasure of sending you some Seeds & would gladly have sent a larger quantity, but the person employed, either neglected collecting them at the proper time, or we were too late in the Season. In the Kanguroo which is stuffed, not to alarm Lady Banks, you will observe the feet to be different to what is described in your voyage. These Animals are very numerous, but after being fired at grow very shy. The Stones w.ch I send on account of the appearance of Metal & the Ochre, were found in the bed of a river, which in the rainy Season runs thro' a Slate quarry. The Slate, is according to the information of a Slater, not fitt for any use as it is rotten & will not split, for the Skin of a Bird which I send to Ld Sydney may merit your attention, it differs from the Ostrich & from the Emu. I have seen several but it is very difficult to get within shot of them. Black Swans are seen frequently but only one has been killed. The situation of the Penis in the Kangurroo appears to me uncommon, between the Anus & the Testicles, & very close to the former. This Animal grows to a great size, one has been killed that weighed very near to Two hundred weight, & one was found dead in the Woods, the Tail of which I have, that measures Eighteen inches in circumference. The procuring Shelter & Security for ourselves & provisions has giving full employment, but I have made some excursions in order to examine the Country around us, the difficulty of which you, My Dear Sir, can form a just Idea of. inland there is a Country in w.ch the Timber grows as you observed about Botany Bay, at such a Distance that the Ground may be Cultivated with little trouble, but our situation does not permit us to go from the Cove in which I have fix'd the Settlement. The carrying Stores & Provisions inland, a single days journey would be impossible. Mr Nepean will tell you my reason for settling here, & such particulars respecting the Country as I have been able to inform him of. The Natives are far more numerous than I expected to find them. I have seen two hundred & twelve men in one Cove near Botany Bay, & reckon fifteen hundred in Botany bay, this Port & Broken bay (a good harbour) including those who live on the intermediate Coast. I have traced them thirty miles in land & having seen Smoke on Lansdown Hills, which are fifty miles in land, there cannot be the least doubt but that there are Inhabitants in interior parts of the Country.

almost all the men wanting the front tooth in the upper Jaw (which is pulled out) & most of the Women wanting the two first joints of the little finger on the left hand, are circumstances not observed in your voyage. I have seen a female Child of five years of Age that had lost the two Joints, & I have seen young Children whose fingers were perfect. I have likewise seen two Women with Child, & one Old Woman who had not suffered the operation, so that it is not in my power at present, to say at what Age it is performed, or on what account. We have unfortunately lost all our Cows & a party is just returned after being out eight days, they say that they saw a very large Lake, or river, of fresh water & w.ch I shall visit as soon as the Ships have sailed.

I have taken the liberty of saying that if Lord Sydney or Mr Nepean wish any Seeds you will let them have them. a good Botanist in this Country would find full employment, unfortunately I have not even a good Gardner. The flowering Shrubs & Trees of which I have sent seeds, grow in light black mould, & appear to thrive equally well in a Sandy & very Stony Ground. In a few months I hope to be able to attend a little more to the Natives, with whose customs & manners I wish much to acquainted. They are now much distressed for food, few fish are caught & I am told that many of them appear on the Beach where the Boats go to haul the Seins, very weak & anxious to get the small fish, of which they make no account in the Summer nor can we give them much assistance as very few fish are now caught, & we have many sick. These people never come amongst us, tho' they have several times gone along with the Sirius, but when I, or anyone that is known, go down the Harbour, they join us very readily. Mons.r La Perouse having been obliged to fire on them & the bad behaviour of some of our people, have made them avoid us more than when we first came, & which they have reveng'd by killing three of the Convicts. one was found with four spears in him, one of which had entered at the back and the point appeared below the breast bone. They throw these spears with great force. a few plants are put into some Spirits of Wine & there are a few dried plants.

You will, Sir, be so obliging as to make my Compliments acceptable to Lady Banks & to the Ladys of your family. The hurry in which I write you will excuse & do me the honor of believing me with great esteem

DEAR SIR/YOUR OBLIGED/& MOST OBEDIENT/HUMBLE SERVANT/A. PHILLIP

Ld Sydney] Thomas Townshend, 1st Viscount Sydney (1733–1800), English statesman and, in 1788, Secretary for the Home Department, which then dealt with colonial affairs   Mr Nepean] Evan Nepean (1752–1822), under-secretary of state in the Home Department, in which post he was concerned in the arrangements for the administration of New South Wales

With a number of like-minded men in England, including the Marquis of Lansdowne (1737–1805), Phillip was committed to the free trade ideology of Adam Smith, author of An Inquiry into the Nature and Causes of the Wealth of Nations *(1776), now acknowledged to have been a factor in the larger strategic thinking which influenced the establishment of the Australian colony.*

4. TO WILLIAM PETTY, 2ND EARL OF SHELBURNE, MARQUIS OF LANSDOWNE, 3 JULY 1788

MY LORD

As I was unwilling to trouble Your Lordship with letters that could only contain assurances of Respect, I defer'd writing till I arrived in this Country, the few extracts from my journal, is all the information I am able to give your Lordship, at present, of the Natives; who never come to us & with whom I have never been able to remain but a very short time. The Rains now fall very heavy & many of the Natives find it difficult to support themselves, as few fish are caught. I shall be able to give a better account of the Country when I have visited Lansdowne Hills—they form part of a Range of Mountains that appear to be fifty Miles in land & on which I have in alate excursion seen Smoke, which, with my having traced the Natives Thirty Miles towards these Hills, leaves no doubt but that there are Inhabitants in the interior parts of the Country. I thought these Hills worthy the Name I have giving them, and at the foot of which I flatter my self that I shall find a River, that communicates with the Sea, at no great distance from port Jackson, which I have preferd to Botany bay as affording a more eligible Situation for the Colony, & being with out exception the finest Harbour in the World. My reason for thinking there must be a large river, is the having found pools of water which did not appear to be formed in the Rainy Season. The want of time prevented of tracing them to their Source.

The Woods by which we are surrounded are not removed but with a labour of which no Idea can be formed, & unfortunately the Timber is only fit for fire wood, & I was obliged to fix on this Spot, on account of Water which in the dry Season is scarce, as here are not any runs of fresh water but what are drains from the Marshes, form'd in the Rainy Season. Botany bay, offerd no Security for large Ships, here a Thousand Sail of the Line may ride in the most perfect Security.

The clearing the ground will be a Work of time & it will be four Years at least, before this Colony will be able to support it self, & perhaps no Country in the World affords less assistance to first Settlers. Still, My Lord, I think that perseverance will answer evry purpose proposed by Government, & that this Country will hereafter be a most Valuable acquisition to Great Britain from its situation.

It has been my determination from the time I landed, never to fire on the Natives, but in a case of absolute necessity, & I have been so fortunate as to have avoided it hitherto. I think they deserve a better Character than what they will receive from Mons.ʳ La Perouse, who was under the disagreeable necessity of firing on them, I think better of them from having been more with them. They do not in my opinion want personal Courage, they very readily place a confidence & are, I believe, strictly honest among themselves.

Most of the Men wanting the right front tooth in the Upper Jaw, & most of the Women wanting the first & second joints of the little finger of the left hand, are circumstances not observed in Capt. Cooks Voyage

Your Lordship will I hope do me the justice to believe me fully sensible of the polite attention I receiv'd when leaving England, & permit me the honor of subscribing my self with the greatest Respect & esteem

MY LORD/YOUR LORDSHIPS/OBLIGED & MOST OBEDIENT/HUMBLE SERVANT/A PHILLIP

Lansdowne Hills] part of the Blue Mountains west of Sydney   La Perouse] Jean-François De Galaup La Pérouse (1741–88), French navigator who landed at Botany Bay in January 1788, two days after Phillip had sailed to Port Jackson

MARY REIBEY

Mary Reibey (née Haydock) (1777–1855) arrived in Sydney on the convict transport the Royal Admiral *on 7 October 1792. She was fifteen years old and determined already to make the best of her situation. A fortunate marriage followed but there is no doubt that Reibey's prosperity derived as much from her own efforts and her strong character as it did from the thriving business inherited from Thomas Reibey in 1811. This letter, written on arrival to her aunt in Lancashire, is one of the earliest surviving letters by an Australian convict.*

5.   TO PENELOPE HOPE, 8 OCTOBER 1792

MY DEAR AUNT

We arrived here on the 7th and I hope it will answer better than we expected for I write this on Board of ship but it looks a pleasant place—Enough we shall but have 4 pair of trowser to make a week and we shall have one pound of rice a week and 4 pound of pork besides Greens and other Vegetarbles the tell me I am for life wich The Governor told me I was but for 7 years wich Grives me very much to think of it but I will watch every oppertunity to Get away in too or 3 years. But I will make my self as happy as I Can In my Present and unhappy situation. I will Give you Futher satisfaction when I Get there and is setted. I am well and hearty as ever I was in my life I Desire you will answer me by some ship that is Coming and lett me know how the Children is and all inquireing frinds. So I must Conclude because we are in a hurry to go a shore remember My Love to my sister and aunt Wamsley and My Cousens. So no more at pressent from your Dutifull neice Mary Haydock. Mr Scot Took 2 Ginnues of me and said he would Get me My Libberty with my sister has been very ungrat To me so I must never see you again.

Eliza Marsden

Eliza Marsden (1772–1835) arrived in New South Wales in 1794 with her husband the Reverend Samuel Marsden (1764–1838), assistant to the settlement's first chaplain Richard Johnson. Although this letter to friends in England stresses her isolation, she had established a friendship with Elizabeth Macarthur who, like the Marsdens, lived at Parramatta.

6. To Mary Stokes, 1 May 1796

Dear Madam

Your kind favour dated March 10th 1795 we received November 6th 95, but find myself at a loss in what manner to express myself: your good wishes & kind remembrance merit my warmest gratitude & that is the only tribute I can pay to your goodness. I long for an opportunity of conversing with you face to face. this would enable me to open my mind more fully than I can now do with paper & ink; but whether I shall ever be indulged with that privilege or no, is still in the dark womb of Providence. We seem in our present situation to be almost totally cut-off from all connexion with the world, especially the virtuous part of it. Old England is no more than like a pleasing dream; when I think of it, it appears to have no existence but in my own imagination. I feel as if I had once conversed with friends united in love by some Spirit; some faint remembrance of those pleasures still remain, & I cannot but flatter myself with some distant hope that it will again be with me as in months past.

Had we only a few pious friends to pass away an hour with it would render this colony more tolerable. The want of a place for public worship is still to be regretted. We have not one at Parramatta, nor any likely to be. So little attention being paid to the Ministers makes religion appear contemptible: sometimes Mr Marsden preaches in a convict's hut; sometimes in a place appropriated for corn; & at times does not know where he is to perform it—which often makes him quite uneasy, & puts him out of temper both with the place & people. With respect to myself I enjoy both my health & spirits pretty well, equally as well as when in England.

I thank you for your kind attention to my daughter; the book you sent her I hope she will live to benefit by. She can now talk pretty well, & is an entertaining companion to a fond Mother, whose feelings you will readily excuse. I have also a little native boy who takes up part of my attention—He is about six years old & now begins to read English & wait at table, & hope at some future period he may be a useful member of society. He has no inclination to go among the natives, & has quite forgot their manners.

Present my best respects to Mr Stokes, Miss Stokes, & Master Edward, & tell him we often talk of him when we are eating melons. The seeds of which he was so kind as to give me with wishing you every blessing in this life, I remain dear Madam Yrs

Eliza Marsden.

Mr M. gives you a line, but two ships sail together … we divide the letters.

ELIZABETH MACARTHUR

The wife of Captain John Macarthur of the New South Wales Corps (1767–1834), Elizabeth Macarthur (1767?–1850) arrived in the colony in 1790. One of the first of the more privileged class of settlers to envisage a future for her children in the new world, she was closely involved in the daily work of Elizabeth Farm on the Parramatta River where the Macarthurs' flock of Spanish merino sheep, imported in 1797, was to become celebrated.

7. TO BRIDGET KINGDON, 1 SEPTEMBER 1799

Once again, my much loved friend, it is permitted me to sit down under a conviction that the letter I am about to write will be received by you with pleasure. By the Capture of a Ship off the Coast of Brazil we were left without any direct intelligence from Europe for twelve months. We firmly believed that a revolution or some National Calamity had befallen Great Britain, & that we should be left altogether to ourselves, until things at home had resumed some degree of order, & the tempest a little subsided. These fears however have by a late arrival proved without foundation.

This Country possesses numerous advantages to persons holding appointments under Government; It seems the only part of the Globe where quiet is to be expected. We enjoy here one of the finest climates in the world. The necessaries of life are abundant, & a fruitful soil affords us many luxuries. Nothing induces me to wish for a change but the difficulty of educating our children, & were it otherwise it would be unjust towards them to confine them to so narrow a society. My desire is that they may see a little more of the world, & better learn to appreciate this retirement. Such as it is. The little creatures all speak of going home to England with rapture—My dear Edward almost quitted me without a tear. They have early imbibed an idea that England is the seat of happiness & delight, that it contains all that can be gratifying to their senses, & that of course they are there to possess all they desire. It would be difficult to undeceive young people bred up in so secluded a situation, if they had not an opportunity given them of convincing themselves. But hereafter I shall much wonder if some of them make not this place the object of their choice. By the date of this letter you will see that we still reside on our Farm at Parramatta—a native name signifying the head of a river, which it is.

The town extends one mile in length from the landing place, & is terminated by the Government House which is built on an Eminence named Rose Hill. Our Farm, which contains from four to five hundred acres, is bounded on three sides by Water. This is particularly convenient. We have at this time, about one hundred & twenty acres in wheat, all in a promising state. Our Gardens with fruit & vegetables are extensive & produce abundantly. It is now Spring, & the Eye is delighted with a most beautiful variegated landscape—Almonds, Apricots, Pear and Apple Trees are in full bloom. The native shrubs are also in flower, & the whole Country gives a grateful perfume. There is a very good Carriage road new made from hence to Sydney, which by land is distant about fourteen miles; & another from this to the river Hawkesbury, which is about twenty miles from hence in a direct line across the Country. Parramatta is a central position between both. I have once visited the Hawkesbury & made the journey on horseback. The road is through an uninterrupted wood, with the exception of the village of Toongabie, a farm of Government, & one or two others which we distinguish by the name of Greenlands, on account of the fine grass, & there being a few trees compared with the other parts of the Country, which is occasionally brushy & more or less covered with underwood. The greater part of the country is like an English Park, & the trees give to it the appearance of a Wilderness or shrubbery, commonly attached to the habitations of people of fortune, filled with a variety of native plants placed in a wild irregular manner. I was at the Hawkesbury three days. It is a noble fresh water river, taking its rise in a precipitous range of mountains, that it has hitherto been impossible to pass. Many attempts have been made altho' in vain. I spent an entire day on this river, going in a boat to a beautiful spot, named by the late Governor Richmond Hill, high & overlooking a great extent of Country. On one side are those stupendous barriers to which I have alluded, rising as it were, immediately above your head; below the river itself, still & unruffled—out of sight is heard a Waterfall whose distant murmurs add awfulness to the scene. I could have spent more time here, but we were not without apprehensions of being interrupted by the Natives, as about that time they were very troublesome, & had killed many white people on the banks of the river. The soil in the valley of this river is most productive; & greatly superior to any that has been tilled in this Country, which has induced numbers to settle there, but having no vessels, there is at present much difficulty in transporting the produce to Sydney. Our stock of cattle is large, we have now Fifty head, a dozen Horses, & about a thousand Sheep. You may conclude from this that we kill mutton, but hitherto we have not been so extravagant. Next year, Mr Macarthur tells me, we may begin. I have a very good Dairy, & in general make a sufficiency of Butter to supply the Family, but it is at present so great an object to rear the calves, that we are careful not to rob them of too much milk—We use our Horses both for pleasure & profit—they alternately run in the Chaise or Cart.

Mr Macarthur has also set a plough at work—the first which has been used in this country, & it is drawn sometimes by oxen, & at others by Horses. The ground was before tilled with the hoe. These details, I am sensible, have no other interest than as far as they serve to show the progressive state of this yet infant settlement.

Mr Macarthur once superintended the Agricul.l concerns of the Government, but since the arrival of Governor Hunter he has declined further interference.

By the kindness of the Commanding Officer of the Reg.t we are permitted to reside here, & there being a good road, as I have before observed, to Sydney, Mr M. is enabled to attend to all his duties at Head Quarters, altho' at times upon very short notice. Myself or one or more of the Children occasionally accompany him. As the distance is convenient our stay is prolonged as business or pleasure require, or we return the same day, but as our Family is large we do not choose to be long absent from home together.

Mr Macarthur has frequently in his Employment thirty or forty people whom we pay weekly for their labour. Eight are employed as Stock keepers, & in the Garden, Stables & House five more, besides women servants, these we both feed & clothe, or at least we furnish them with the means of providing clothes for themselves. We have but two men fed at the expense of the Crown, altho' there are persons who contrive to get twenty or more, which the Governor does not or will not notice.

You will wonder how a return is made for the daily expense which it must appear to you we incur. In the first place some thousands of persons are fed from the public Stores—perhaps between three & four thousand, all of whom were formerly supplied with flour from England to meet the demand for Bread. But since so many individuals have cleared Farms, & have thereby been enabled to raise a great quantity of grain in the Country, which at present time is purchased by the Commissary at 10/- a bushel, & issued for what are termed rations—or the proportionate quantity due to each person instead of Flour. In payment for which the Commissary issues a receipt approved of by the Government. These receipts pass current here as Coin & are taken by Masters of Ships & other adventurers who come to these Ports with Merchandize for sale. When any number of these have been accumulated in the hands of individuals, they are returned to the Commissary who gives a Bill on the Treasury in England for them. These Bills amount to thirty or forty thousand Pounds annually. How long Govt may continue so expensive a plan it would be difficult to foresee. Pigs are bought upon the same system, as would also Sheep & Cattle, if their numbers would admit of their being killed. Beef might be sold at 4/- if not 5/- the lb. A good Horse is worth £140 to £150. Be it ever so bad it never sells for less than £100. A Cow is valued at about £80. An English cow that was the property of Colonel Grose sold for £100. From this statement you will perceive that those persons who took early precautions to raise live Stock have at present singular advantages.

We fatten & kill a great number of Hogs in the year, which enables us to feed a large establishment of servants. These labourers are such as have been Convicts, & whose time of transportation had expired. They then cease to be fed at the expense of Government, & employ themselves as they please. Some endeavour to procure a passage home to England; some become Settlers, & others hire themseves out for labour. They demand an Enormous price, seldom less than 4 or 5 shillings a day. For such as have many in their employment it becomes necessary to keep on hand large supplies of such articles as are most needed by these people for shops there are none—The Officers in the Colony with a few others possessed of money or credit in England unite together & purchase the cargoes of such Vessels as repair to this Country from various Quarters. Two or more are chosen from the number to bargain for the Cargo offered for sale which is then divided amongst them, in proportion to the amount of their subscriptions. This arrangement prevents monopoly, & the imposition that would otherwise be practised by Masters of Ships. These details which may seem prolix are necessary to shew you the mode in which we are, in our infant condition, compelled to proceed.

I have had the misfortune to lose a sweet Boy of eleven months old who died very suddenly by an illness occasioned by teething. The other three Elizabeth John & Mary are well. I have lately been made very happy by learning the safe arrival of Edward in England.

We often remember & talk over in the evening the hospitalities which we have both received in Bridgerule Vicarage & happy shall I be if it is ever permitted me to mark my remembrance more strongly than is expressed in these lines.

If you are in the habit of visiting the Whitstone family I pray that you will kindly remember me to them. The benevolence of the Major's heart will dispose him to rejoice at the success which has attended us, & that the activity which was very early discernable in the mind of Mr Macarthur has had a field for advantageous exertion.

How is it my dearest friend that you are still single—Are you difficult to please, or has the War left you so few Bachelors from amongst whom to choose. But suffer me to offer you a piece of advice—abate a few of your scruples & marry—I offer in myself an instance that it is not always with all our wise foreseeings, those marriages which promise most or least happiness, prove in their result such as our friends may predict. Few of mine I am certain when I married thought that either of us had taken a prudent step. I was considered indolent & inactive; Mr Macarthur too proud & haughty for our humble fortune or expectations, & yet you see how bountifully Providence has dealt with us.

At this time I can truly say no two people on earth can be happier than we are. In Mr Macarthur's society I experience the tenderest affection of a Husband who is instructive & cheerful as a companion. He is an indulgent Father, beloved as a Master, & universally respected for the integrity of his Character. Judge then my friend if I ought not to consider myself a happy woman.

I have hitherto in all my letters to my friends forborne to mention Mr Macarthur's name lest it might appear in me too ostentatious. Whenever you marry, look out for good sense in a husband. You would never be happy with a person inferior to yourself in point of understanding. So much my early recollection of you & of your character bids me say.

E.M

by the date of this letter] the date has been read as 1 September 1795, but the evidence favors 1799 since the arrival of Governor Hunter] Hunter arrived in September 1795

George Harris

George Prideaux Harris (1774–1810) was one of the founders of Hobart Town in Van Diemen's Land (Tasmania). As Deputy Surveyor-General of New South Wales, his task from 1804 was to explore new country, survey land grants and, as a magistrate, contribute to the maintenance of law and order in a frontier outpost. The long intervals between the writing and the receiving of letters highlighted for this first generation of settlers a sense of isolation, even abandonment, which could, however, be replaced by euphoria when the mails eventually arrived. In letters to his brother Henry (Harry) Barham Harris (1777–1807) and his mother Dorothy Prideaux Harris (1747–8?– 1827), George Harris gives voice to these extremes of feeling.

8. To Henry Harris, 8 August 1804

My dear Harry

I never in my whole life experienced so much disappointment & vexation than this Week has given me—Two Ships have arrived from England (the Coromandel & Experiment) by which Every Officer in the Colony has recd. Letters & Newspapers &c from his friends, except myself—but for me, not one individual friend has had the kindness to send me a single line or token that they at all remember me—I cannot therefore but conclude I am forgotten or not worth notice. For it is impossible that those Ships could have sailed, without its being publickly known, else how shod. other persons friends send them large pacquets.

I have not neglected those at home so—I have written from Teneriffe—Rio de Janeiro—Port Phillip twice—& from this place three times. I am so much hurt at this coolness & inattention, that I could almost resolve never to write to England again whilst I stay here—

Be good enough to get the inclosed Letters forwarded./Believe me Yours afftely./G.P. Harris

9. To Dorothy Harris, 12 October 1805

About three Months since by the arrival of a sea Whaler from Pt. Jackson I had the inexpressible happiness to hear from my dearest Mother & other friends for the first time, since leaving them, going on now for 3 Years! I need not say the joy I felt at the receipt of the valuable Pacquet, more especially to find that you were all in as good health & happy as when I left you—The anxious hours I had passed daily looking for some tidings, was fully repaid by the pleasing Intelligence I received tho I almost dreaded to open them least I might find in so long a time that I had lost some dear & valued friend—but thank God it was not the case & I hope I shall ever receive such welcome news—

The last date of your Letters were in Octr. 1804 & some as far back as August & Septr. 1803—so that I think I must have received all you had written to that time—as there were abt. 24 of them—John & Tom did not write—which I am sorry for as I should wish always to hear from every one of you—I had several Letters from Harry, but from Nancy—what a delightful packet!! I have hardly read all the volumes thro yet—I shall thank her for them—as well as my little dears Dolly & Mary—but I forget; the former by this time is I suppose Mrs R … R(?) … lly! but of that more by & by—I have also to thank my kind & worthy friend Comyns for his very friendly Letter—I shall write him a very long letter & wish it was in my power to send him some Curiosities by this Conveyance—but I have met with a great Misfortune in having a large Case of Birds (some capital ones) abt. 100 in number totally destroyed by a nest of large ants eating into it unknown to me—Not a feather was left on them—Nancy & Mr. Comyns write me to preserve them in Spirits, but they could not know the scarcity of that Article—but Adieu to this subject, which I wonder how I got into when I have one so much more interesting to talk about—

My dearest mother I have to beg pardon of you for doing something without your leave, but for the life of me I could not help it—I followed Harrys example without knowing of it & that very day 12 Months—*married*? Yes, my dearest Mother & what is more enjoy *the most perfect happiness* My sweet little Girl is one of the most ameanable Disposition I ever met with—and her affectionate attachment to me is such as must render my life devoted to her happiness in return—You will naturally expect and have a right to know who your new daughter in law is—She *was* Miss Ann Jane Hobbes; her Father was a brave Officer in the Navy (a Lieut.) who died shortly before she left England & a Brother also a Lt. in the Navy was killed in Egypt. there were then the Mother, 4 Daughters and a younger Son—The Eldest married Mr. Hopley who was appointed one of the Surgeons of this place, and Mrs. Hobbs having only the widows pension, was persuaded to follow her Daughter here with the rest of her family They came passengers with me in the Ocean where I first got acquainted—and here at Hobart Town had the happiness to call Ann Jane the 3rd daughter mine To use Harry's words "I might perhaps have got a *richer* but I could not have got a *better* Wife"—for young as she is (not 18) I'll be bound to say there is not many double her age that understand more of Domestic Management—She often reminds me [of] my Dr. Mother *when I see her* so busily employed about Household affairs—I will give you a sketch of her Person—she is about the middle size, well formed, fine blue eyes & brown hair & is altogether a fine woman—I may consider myself as peculiarly happy in having the fortune to gain the heart of one calculated for my comfort in every point of view & whom with pride I can call by the name of *Wife*—otherwise I should have perhaps followed the example of most others here, who having only convicts about them for Servants have been induced to take temporary ones but thank God I have escaped that rock & got safe into the Harbour of happiness—And now my dearest Mother my beloved Ann Jane joins me in begging your blessing on us, which I am sure you will not withhold, for I make no doubt you will feel as happy in hearing from me that I am—as I do in assuring you of it—your motherly affection for me has ever been such as to convince me of it.

But now I suppose you will wish to know a little in what manner we go on here—I can assure with respect to general comforts very badly indeed—I have not yet had a house to live in (except one I have rented)—nothing but Canvas in all weathers—What I am now in is a miserable Hovel a Ground floor of 2 Rooms about the size of a Nutshell—2 Windows—1 Door—1 Chimney—& thatched—& for this I pay at the rate of 50£ pr. ann—without any Garden or Land belong. to it and very little probability of getting into a better for Govr. Collins has not paid the least attention to the wants of his Officers in this respect—Only one Officer has yet had a House built him—all the rest have either been obliged to build for themselves or else to hire houses or live in Marques tho God knows he has had time enough to do it since he had built *elegant houses* for *Convicts*, where the *Wife* was a *favorite*—Times are very much altered here for the worse—everything is most abominably dear & in some instances we pay 500 pr Cent on the English Goods—particularly Shoes—Broad Cloths—Hats etc etc and some times cannot get them for love or Money—

We have lately & are now almost in a state of starvation having been on the allowance of 4 lb bread, 2 lb Pork per man pr week, owing to not having had any supplies from Sydney, but as we have such abundance of Kanguroo here we can never *want*—from 2 to 3000 [lbs] weight a week having been turned into the Store by the Officers at 1/- pr lb. which has considerably helped us on. We are in daily expectation of a Ship from Sydney or England with Supplies which will be a delightful occurrence for us—I have however notwithstanding all these difficulties being getting a house under weigh & hope shortly to be in one I can call my own without obligations to any one —

I have got about 1 Acre of Wheat in this Year (which considering is doing wonders)—My stock consists of 1 Cow & Calf—1 Ram 2 Ewes—2 Ewe Lambs 1 He Goat—4 females 2 female Kids—4 Geese—10 Goslings—[?] fowls—Besides which I have a pack of Kangaroo Dogs as good as any in the whole Country—namely Lagger, Weasel, Lion, Boatswain, Brindle etc etc—& with those Dogs I scarcely ever go or send out (for I have two Huntsmen) but get 3 4 5 or sometimes 8 Kangaroos in a day or two—Some of the Kanguroo stand 6 feet high & weigh from 100 to 130 or 150 lbs & fight the dogs most desperately so as sometimes to kill them & very frequently to wound them sadly—Sometimes we get Emus, a large Bird (Species of the Ostrich) which are hunted in the same manner as Kanguroo & make a worse resistance They frequently weigh 80 or 90 lb. & run (for they cannot fly) amazingly swift, so that the swiftest greyhound can scarcely get up with them—They are much coarser food than the Kangaroo, which when young, is nearly as good as Venison—it only wants fat—Kangaroo hunting, fishing & shooting are the only recreations we have at this place—there is no society—I cannot visit *with* my wife most of my brother Officers because they have female Companions—we seldom therefore visit except to Captn. Sladdens (Marines) who is married—or in her family, who are the only females she can associate with—this with the very great Dearth of every kind of News for there is none (except the daily account of Robberies during the Night) unless on the arrival of a Ship makes the place extremely dull & very unlike Old England— Books are also a very scarce article and the few there are have been read over & over again Therefore every little trifle—newspaper—handbill or anything that comes from England is valuable & interesting—I must beg of you to save all pamphlets—Newspapers—Handbills—Murders, Dying Speeches—Calendars &c &c & send them to Harry for me. I have sent him a list of Books &c I wish to have sent out—I am in great measure deprived of my favorite amusement—Drawing, having used or lost most of my paints, & expended all my drawing & other papers which is a great drawback on me, no such article as either to be got in the Colony—

I am very much obliged to you for the Flower Seeds which I shall take care & put in our Garden & hope you will send me some more—If you can send some Gooseberry, Raspberry, Currant Seeds—Plumb & Cherry Stones—Acorns ripe, Thornberrys or any thing of that kind I think they would thrive well—In return I will this year collect flower & tree seeds from this place—it is too early yet being only the commencement of Spring, but there are some beautiful shrubs & flowers here *quite new* at home—

Could I have an opportunity of sending by a Ship *direct* from this place to England, I could make up a Box of little things for you & wd. send a few of the Beautiful Parroquet we have here, was there any one I could trust to take care of them & deliver them alive— but the Ships that have come to this Port are either gone on the Whalefishing for 12 or 18 mos. or else to Port Jackson, and as I know no one there, things might lie & spoil long before an opportunity offered to send them. I expect that Captn. Bristow of the Ocean Whaler will return here from Norfolk Island in about 3 Months & then I shall be able to make up a Package for you and my friend Comyns which I am daily collecting —

I was very sorry to hear of poor old Mrs. Bradfords Death, she was a good old lady & I shall always respect her Memory—

I have now my Dearest Mother written you a long letter, and as I have several more to write by the same Conveyance, I must beg you will remember me most affectionately to every friend of which I have so many that I shall not particularize one but include them all together—Mrs. Hobbs my Mother in law begs I will say all that is kind for her tho unknown & hopes we may all one day meet together—My Ann Jane joins me in every thing affectionate & dutiful—Believe me ever my dear Mother while I have breath

YOUR TRULY AFFT. SON/GEO. PRIDEAUX HARRIS

Comyns] a friend of George Harris in his native Exeter and a collector of natural history specimens Miss Ann Hobbes] Ann (1784–1862) married Harris on 15 February 1805 at New Town, near Hobart. She married secondly George Weston Gunning and is buried in the Gunning family vault at Richmond, Tasmania   my favourite amusement—Drawing] Harris had some ability in drawing, sketching and draughtsmanship, which he applied to his interest in natural history. Examples of his work are held in the collections of the State Library of New South Wales and the National Library of Australia.

George Meredith

George Meredith (1777–1856) emigrated to Van Diemen's Land in 1820, and was a pioneer settler on the east coast. Before Meredith left Britain his first wife, Sarah, died giving birth to her sixth child. Eight months later George Meredith married a former servant, Mary or Maria Evans (1795–1842), by whom he already had one son. Although the marriage appears to have been happy, Meredith was conscious of Maria's lack of education, and was unwilling to take her into Hobart society until she acquired some of the social graces of her predecessor.

10. To Maria Meredith, 21 April 1826

My ever dear and beloved Wife

When the sloop *again* arrives on your shores & you do *not* see *one* appear, I know full well how *greatly* you will *feel* disappointed, and what will *add* to your vexation will be the knowledge that the Gang of Whalers are sent down to erase that care and anxiety — which I ought to have in my own person entirely relieved you from—and most devoutly do I wish that instead of this *Letter* being put into your *hand* your *fond and faithful Husband* could glide into *your Arms*.

For the moment, my dear M, your heart will droop, but it will be but for the moment, reflexion and the Conviction of what you *know* to be my feelings and wishes, on this, as on every other occasion of our separation from one another, will *again* raise your Spirits, and your mind will be *satisfied* that I am doing what is *right* although at the expence of our *present mutual* happiness.

If you could doubt my *Constancy* or my *love*, or that my prolonged stay was attributable to my *indifference* for the Society or person of an affectionate, devoted wife, or my *inclination* for the pleasures of a world *without* you. Then my love you *might* indulge in grief & be unhappy. But sensible as you are by *years* of experience, & never *failing proofs* of the *truest love* that my heart is *wholly* & solely *yours* and that so far from being attracted by the allurements of *worldly* pleasures, or mere *selfish* gratification, that *you* are all the world to me, and that I really *enjoy* no pleasures in which *you* do not *participate*. I repeat, my poor Girl, that all these considerations must cheer up your Spirits and induce you to sooth the feelings of *fervent* disappointment by *pleasurable anticipations* & if you still need further consolation, I offer it in the declaration that it is my sincerest hope & wish that our next meeting may be to *part no more*, this is my Consolation. Think as I do upon those many *many* happy hours we had heretofore enjoyed together and promise yourself—as I do—years of happiness yet to come, how we *have* met in all the ardour of more *youthful* love. I need not say, but I can most happily appeal to my own heart as well as yours, to testify that we still meet with as much *affection* as we ever did, perhaps we are not propelled by the influence of youthful passions, or transported by those almost delirious pleasures which the fullness of nature once led us into, but are not our enjoyments more *satisfying* to the *mind* and our mutual desire towards each other as strong (if not so ardent) and as sincere as true Affection & personal fondness can make it. Separate from the influence of the Grosser passions of our natures, what Constant, unvaried proof of love do we not manifest, *and* is not the *lover* and husband shown to be *still* combined in *all* my attentions by day and by Night, are you not my ever Welcome Companion by day, whenever you *Can* be so, & do I partake even the most trifling enjoyment in which I am not *anxious* that *you* should participate. Then at night, when you *receive* me in your *Arms*, what *abatement* of *affection* can you perceive, do I not sink into your *soft embrace* with *delight*, rest fondling on your *bosom* and *press* upon your *lips reiterated Kisses*. I repeat my dearest M, that *without* mixing up the grosser passions of nature, do I not thus delight in your fond Embrace, fondle, & press & kiss and *prove* how *much* I *still love you*. You, in your turn, my Dear, endeavour to rival all my affection, you would, if possible, through all my daily avocations be ever at my side, to partake my Cares & add to my pleasures. Your personal appearance it is your aim to make *Conformable* to my *wish* and *attractive* to my *Eyes* & your manners and conduct pleasing to me, instructive to all, & I *almost* say with the Poet—*Grace was in all steps, heaven in her Eye*, and in *every gesture, dignity, and love*. Thus through the day you move the Mother and Mistress of the family, but *retired* within the sacred precincts of our *Chamber-of-love* the studied demeanour of the dignified matron gives way to all the *feelings & fondness* of the *Wife*. Of a wife enjoying all the fullness of a doating Husbands love and whose *every thought & wish* is to *prove* to him how dearly she prizes it. Skreen[d] from view, whilst o'er your person falls the limped water & then enfolded in a snow white robe, forth you come—like another Venus from the waves—& then you *hasten* to our humble Couch there to *receive & bless* the *partner* of your *bed and heart*. No maiden Coyness now restrains your love but knowing *every* wish & thought of mine, you *prove* yourself *all* that a loving wife should be, *my Queen of Love, what* these endearments *are*—how *varied* by *you* to *draw* my fond Caresses forth—I need not say. I *feel* them all, & approve the increasing affection which *prompts* them. The mere gratifications of passion, that momentary impulse which *alone* actuates *too many* Seldom *endures* or *terminates our long & happy embraces*, your Arms are my shelter from worldly cares, your sweet bosom my pillow of love, & your fond Kisses my solace & delight, how often does oblivious Sleep overtake us lock[d] in each others Arms, & when again we wake how constantly do we renew the wished embrace. If *you* first wake, you stretch your Circling arms to draw me to you and with sweetest kisses call my Senses to the *enjoyment* of your fond *caresses*. If *I* perchance shall first renew the powers of the mind, my hand *instinctively* is moved to *replace* my loss and wander over all your soft form, as though to know that *all* my treasures safe, and then again, I fold you in my *Close* embrace & so we kiss and fondly with *mutual* feelings, mutual wishes, & *this* is *real love*. *This* is the *bodies worship* enjoined in the marriage vows, it is the wifes due to receive, the husbands duty to pay, happy the man who can so pay this worship with the same feelings that I do and doubly happy the woman who can attract by her person and preserve by her fond endearments, that worship *perfect to herself* as you do. I have said this much of the *duties* enjoined by wedlock & to place both our personal fondness and our written Confession upon a *just* ground—for it is said that *such* subjects *so* discussed may lead to demoralize the female mind & excite improper & immodest thought and ideas. Not so, my M, between *you* and *I*. The happiness we enjoy with *each other*, this *confidential* exchange of thoughts this expression of *mutual* feelings & wishes, tends to *bind us* still more *indissolubly* to each other, the mind becomes associated with Corporeal feelings & so habituated are we to these love Scenes, *mutually excited, mutually enjoyed*, that should the impulses of Nature raise up any idea of a sensual kind, it is associated with that beloved object to whom *alone* extends the wish or *thought* of *gratification*, & I will, now I have gone *so* far, add that a prudent, *reflecting* owes it to herself & her *own* happiness to *render herself* by *all & every* means the *sole* & most *attractive* object to her husband & by a constant *study* of his *wishes* and the practice of those little unexpressible misteries of love, to give a *zest* to the pleasure & enhance those blissful enjoyments, so as to make him *return* to *her* Embrace with increased delight, even *should* he ever be guilty of momentary *incontinence*. How many *indifferent* Couples would *thus* have been happy ones. You and I, my dearest M, never required these little aids & what might have been considered the artifices of love in other women, have been with you the spontaneous effusion of unbounded affection & a never ceasing wish to be *every thing* woman *can* be to her Husband, and fear not that I shall be to you less kind, less Constant, less fond than I ever have been. When I behold a form more beautiful than usual, I think of my youthful Maria. When I chance to gaze upon a desplay of those charms which sometimes must attract the Eyes toward virgin loveliness, still I think of a *youthful* Maria, and the Comparison is always favorable to her once *too* attractive person. And when I observe more than usual affection & happiness in any married couple, I *then* think of *home & you* and when I *return* to your *opening Arms*, & resign *myself* to your *fond Embraces*, I feel that *our* happiness is Complete, whatever may be the fate of others, and here, my dear wife, let me beseech you, if ever one thought arises in your mind, either to check our present state of mutual happiness, *or* calculated to confirm or increase it, breath it forth. Sometimes, things *will* occur to occasion a painful impression in the mind, & *sometimes* I know that I am hasty. Always tell me your thoughts & guard me from what I *wish* to have Corrected. I never can behold a Tear in your *Eyes* without *pain*, nor can I ever receive one of your fond, affectionate Kisses without *pleasure*. If then we ever *should* think differently upon any subject, or that I should give way to any hasty conduct or expression toward you, Kiss me & tell me of it.

It is now past One o clock, the Sloop sails in the morning and I have things still to procure & my *general* letter to write, & yet I hardly know how to part with you yet. As the Sloop will not return, I know not how, or when I am to receive any long & anxiously expected letters unless Charles or any man could be spared. If you really *wish* that, Pugh should leave immediately, you may send *him* up as a messenger & I will arrange with Lakeland to keep him or perhaps the Sergt. *would* send up a Soldier to learn if any Commands are to be sent down to his party, now that all the Bushrangers are taken. You *see* how *much* I *desire* to *hear* from you. I have often told you how I indulge in retrospective thoughts, tell me *which* of the Scenes and incidents in the story of the Capt. & Maria *you* most *delighted* to *think* upon, & which you suppose *I do*, and give *your* thoughts and reflexions upon the subject of *this*, and if *you* think we ought *not* to indulge in these little *Confidential effusions of love*, I wish you to *practice* the *forming & delivering opinions* upon *various* subjects & what you write. When you have leisure, *Write neatly*. I wish you could imitate Sarahs hand, & her style and uniformity. Some of your letters are round, some sharp, some short, some lengthy—You *have* improved both in *language* and *writing*—but I would have *my* Maria *perfect* in *everything*. The Ladies in Hobart Town *must* be *envious* of your *personal superiority*. I wish them to be made sensible of your Mental attainments also. But I will not say more on this head. Take *care* of your *health* tell me how *everything* goes on. I cannot dream of you but I *think* of you *hourly* and *anxiously* with all the fond feelings & unceasing desire of a Lover as well as,

YOUR FAITHFUL & AFFECTIONATE HUSBAND./G MEREDITH

when the sloop arrives on your shores] Meredith's property at Swansea, on the western shore of Oyster Bay, was accessible by sea from Hobart   Charles] Charles Meredith, son of George and Sarah Meredith and husband of writer Louisa Anne Meredith   Sarah's hand] a reference to the ladylike handwriting of Meredith's first wife

GEORGIANA MOLLOY

In 1829 Georgiana Molloy (1805–1842) migrated with her husband Captain John Molloy to the newly established Crown colony of Western Australia. Her letter to a life-long friend in Scotland expressed her loneliness as well as the privations of pioneer life. Later she found pleasure in the native flora: by sending plants and seeds to British horticulturist John Mangles she made a major contribution to their study and cultivation.

11.   TO MARGARET DUNLOP, 12 JANUARY 1833

MY BELOVED MAGGIE,

I received your and dear Mary Ker's letters of September 1831, in October 1832. You do us an injustice to censure us for a moment for not writing and thinking of you. Never a day passes that we do not speak of you; and, as I have all along told you, so few vessels call at this port except to barely supply us with provisions, that we have not frequent opportunities of sending. Besides, I always hesitate to send a single letter, knowing the expense thereof.

We have all been quite well since writing. In November Molloy went to the Swan on business, where he remained a month, and was brought back in H.M.S. *Imogene* by Captain Blackwood, from whose name this river is called. He is a very nice gentlemanly man and connected with the Grahams of Netherby.

Molloy again went last Monday to view his large grant of land on the Vasse—a most pleasing country and answering with truth to the description given of its park-like appearance, with long waving grass, and abounding also in kangaroos.

In the interim a vessel has been in, which has given me not only my own, but Jack's letters to write—which I am almost unable to do—as at the beginning of the week I was confined to bed from over-exertion. For in truth, Maggie, I have not time to say my prayers as I ought—I must unbosom myself to you, my dear girl, which I have never done—but this life is too much both for dear Molloy and myself. And what I lament is that, in his decline of life, he will have to lead a much more laborious life than he did in one and twenty years' service. He does not despair, but I never knew or heard of anyone having his losses to bear—but who would?

May God have mercy on us and poor little Sabina Dunlop who is remarkably well. As I lay in bed on Monday she all at once got up and began to walk. She came to my bedside and said 'Mam, Mam'. She keeps going backwards and forwards the whole day long with something for me. Never cries, though I dip her in a tub of water. She is a great blessing. I need not blush to tell you I am, of necessity, my own nursery-maid.

By this I write to Mary and Mrs Caldecott. I have had seven letters of Molloy's relating to business to answer, besides my own correspondence, to weigh out rations, attend to baby; and, although needlework of every kind both for her, Molloy, myself and servant is required, I have not touched a needle for this week. I am now exhausted and the day uncommonly hot. I told you how it would be: I should have to take in washing and Jack carry home the clean clothes in a swill. The last of this has not yet happened, but between ourselves, dear Maggie, the first is no uncommon occurrence, but time will show. What goes to my heart is that dear Molloy has so much exertion bodily and mentally, but I am repaid with interest when any part I can perform eases his burden. The Lord is good and has shown Himself to us in many wonderful instances, but we are sadly forgetful of His Love and bounty amid the hurried concerns of this life.

Oh! my loved 'sister'! I cannot contain myself when I think of the past. I never, never trust myself to think of all we have said to one another. What is all this about Irving and the super-natural gifts and strange tongues? Please tell me. My head aches. I have all the clothes to put away from the wash; baby to put to bed; make tea and drink it without milk as they shot our cow for a trespass; read prayers and go to bed besides sending off this tableful of letters. I wish I had you here to help me. What golden dreams we used to have about your coming to stay with me! How would you like to be three years in a place without a female of your own rank to speak to or be with you whatever happened?

Sabina has just toddled in, hiding her little face in her hand in play. She is sometimes so lively she is neither 'to hand nor to bin', as James Angus would express it. My kind love to Robert and accept the same with unabated affection from your sincerely attached sister,

GEORGIANA MOLLOY

P.S. Mr P. Salmon would not look at poor worn-out Mrs Molloy. The thistle seed never came up; please send me some more quite new. G.M.

Mary Ker] a sister of Margaret Dunlop   the Swan] the Swan River   Captain Blackwood] the naval commander for whom the Blackwood River was named   the Vasse] Captain Molloy took up land on the Vasse River, north of Augusta where he first settled   Sabina Dunlop] the Molloys' eldest surviving child, b. 1831

JOHN BEDE POLDING

John Bede Polding OSB (1794–1877), of the Catholic Benedictine congregation at Downside Abbey, England, was appointed Bishop of New Holland in 1834 and Archbishop of Sydney in 1842. This letter to the Prior of Downside reports on his voyage out in the company of several other Benedictines, with whom he began missionary work from Sydney in 1835.

12.   TO LUKE BERNARD BARBER, 3 MAY 1835

MY DEAR MR. BARBER

I had not time to write to you to mention the day of our departure from L'pool—to thank you & my dear good Sisters at Salford for their many kindnesses to me. Of course you would hear of it in due Season. We have now commenced our 6th week and the time has passed quite as pleasantly as I could have anticipated, except as regards some circumstances of which you will hear at a later date. The weather is extremely hot—the thermometer stands at 85 in the shade. We enjoy nevertheless a breeze which is very refreshing I cannot say I am much incommoded by the heat, but poor Bede Sumner is quite in a melting mood, & Mr. Cotham is not much better. We are all quite well & in excellent health &—for which God be praised. Quite united amongst ourselves & on good terms with our fellow passengers. We live in some sense Conventualiter. We meet three times each day for Office; have our meditation and Spiritual lecture together. I have commenced a course of Moral Theology with the young men; and the priests and myself hold a conference on the Sacr^{ts} three times each week. Tuesday and Thursday are half recreation days. Such is our present course of life, which we commenced as soon as we recovered from sea sickness and have never interrupted one day. We received the Holy Comm^n for the first time on Maundy Thursday, and again on Easter Sunday. I proposed saying Mass on that great festival, but the water was so rough we could not meet except for Office. To my shame I must say, I am as much inclined to laugh when I ought to be serious, by sea as by land: indeed, more so. Such queer things do sometimes happen. For instance, I was giving the blessing at Prime on Easter Sunday, and just as I said the word *disponat* the Ship gave a lurch and seated me on the floor of my cabin. Bede was thrown to the side opposite to that on which he was sitting, and no sooner there than another lurch sent him back to his first position.

Then we are so curiously habited. I, of course, am dressed *à l'ordinaire*—but of the rest, one in jockey coat, another without or else panting like expiring oysters. I celebrated Mass last Sunday and again today assisted by the Priests. Thus assisted, there is small risk. I am sure you would enjoy the voyage extremely. The Captn is extremely civil & kind—our provisions hitherto as good as could be expected. The quantity of water is somewhat restricted—we have each half a pint for washing and by the time we reach Sydney I shall be enabled to wash in a thimblefull—I am slung up each night in a thing called a Cott. It swings about 2ft from the ceiling. How I should like to see you try to ride this most skittish horse. It goes to and fro like the pendulum of a Clock for a quarter of an hour after you are in, but the danger is in getting in or of either going over or tumbling out. I have had two accidents. At one time the ropes at the feet broke & another those at the head—down I came & only hurt my toe. We have not had any stormy weather—the ocean generally presents a wild melancholy spread of water, monotonous as a whole, tho each individual part is in motion. We passed in sight of Antonio, one of the Cape Verd Islands, the only land we have seen ever since we bade adieu to Cape Clear. We have not observed many fish. Two or three whales, and some binitos—one was speared two days since and we [had] it for dinner. Gregory, who lives in the same Cabin with me, saw yesterday a Shark astern. We hope to catch one shortly. It is delightful to witness the Shoals of flying fish about the size of a herring which sometimes take a course thro the air to avoid their enemies. One came into the Cabin of a Passenger. I hope all are quite well. Do write to me a long letter—direct Sydney, New S.W.

Something is paid with the letter—8d. in London. How is the arbitration going on? I do not think I shall have time to write so fully to Downside as I could wish—please therefore to send this letter and also mention to the President with our united respects and love and wish all that is kind to our good Sisters. My hand is shaking with the heat and the motion of the vessel is so great I am afraid you will scarcely make out this,

EVER MOST AFFLY YR CONFRERE/+ J.B. POLDING

Prime] the service of communal prayer each morning   *disponat*] order, dispose   *à l'ordinaire*] as usual

---

In letters from Sydney to his cousin 'Hep' (the Reverend T.P. Heptonstall OSB) at Down-side Abbey, Polding wrote informally, allusively, humorously. Heptonstall acted as Pold-ing's agent, sending out whatever might be needed in the Australian community.

13.   TO THOMAS PAULINUS HEPTONSTALL, 19 JUNE 1849

Feast of Dame Juliana who pinned me to her apron 46 years ago.

MY DEAR HEP,

Just rec^d your January despatch by ship with queer name. I think you will not complain again of the paucity of my letters. They come thick and long, don't they? As for Papers—the *Chronicle* is dead and of course can't send he. Then the *Herald* contains nuffin worth nowin. Well, now I think of it, I will send you the *Advocate*—a weekly—

Your Papers serve one purpose—You have news to the 9th of March—and your January and February Papers are not yet in. Much interest when they do come—well, I reads and thinks [?]. Now tell me, have you made enquiries at War Office? about Daniel? Would you call at 35 Golden Square and enquire if the Vicar Gener. has ascertained whether a wife I wrote about be dead or alive. I can never get answers on these subjects. So *you have killed Dr Walsh*, Ah, you Lunnuners! R.I.P. Have you received a desire of mine to remit some two or three pounds to Dr Murray. Hope so. Be sure you let me have the "acquits"—for my good name for honesty is sadly pulled about of late.

Do you recollect Jesson's Brass Band? Well, we have one. First rate, I assure you, but we want Music proper for it. Be so good as to send two or three copies of *Music arranged for Brass Bands by Cocks*. It comes out monthly. I think I saw it advertised in Jerrold. I want, I tell you again, some works on Architecture. There is one entitled *Parish Churches*—Another by T. & W. Brandon. Hansom's specifications do not suit us.

We have had a small to do about the Convicts sent out. The big and little folks were all in a splutter. A Vote of Censure on the Gubner—a turn out for Earl Grey. What think you of that Master?—Great fools they made of themselves—Poor Connolly! I never thought well of the man. He attended me at Mass & seemed to know little about his business, but what has the fellow to do in the Court of Arches? Let him go to Rome and take his wife if she be there. The Bishop thank God continues to improve in health. I expect him down in Sydney next week. I enclose a scrap of a Note, the first I have received from him since his resuscitation. It was a near go, I assure you—had not my clothes off for many nights—was quite in my own true and real vocation. Night Caps not Mitres were meant for me—ahem! At all events he is himself once again—God and his B. Virgin Mother be praised for the same—shall write again shortly. C. Fransoni won't complain, I guess, I do not write often enough.

Ever most affly,/J.B.P., Sydneien
Write on my part a line to Rev. N. Davis or Mother and Downside

Dame Juliana] St Juliana Falconieri   As for Papers] the Sydney newspapers sent to England by Polding   Dr Murray] the Archbishop of Dublin   a vote of censure on the 'Gubner'] Sir Charles FitzRoy (1796–1858), Governor of New South Wales, faced protests in June 1849 against the landing of a convict ship in Sydney   Poor Conolly] Rev Philip Conolly of Van Diemen's Land was at odds with Polding   The Bishop] Dr Davis, Bishop of Maitland, was Polding's Coadjutor   C. Fransoni] Cardinal Fransoni, Prefect of the Congregation of Propaganda Fide, Rome

CHARLES DARWIN

The young Charles Robert Darwin (1809–1882) held the post of naturalist (1831–36) in HMS Beagle *on a survey voyage which took him to Australia. His theories on evolution and natural selection were influenced in part by his scientific observations in this country. King (1791–1856), hydrographer and a Fellow of the Royal Society, was the son of Philip Gidley King (1758–1808), third Governor of New South Wales.*

14. TO PHILLIP PARKER KING, 21 JANUARY 1836

MY DEAR SIR

I arrived here yesterday evening, certainly alive, but half roasted with the intense heat.— If my horses do not fail, I shall reach Dunheved on Sunday evening & if you are at home, shall have much pleasure in staying with you the ensuing day.—I have seen nothing remarkable in the Geology or indeed I may add in anything else: It appears to me, very singular, how very uniform the character of the scenery remains, in so many miles of country. At Mr Walker's Farm I staid one day, & went out Kangaroo hunting, but had not the good fortune even to see one. In the evening however, we went with a gun in pursuit of the Platypi & actually killed one.— I consider it a great feat, to be in at the death of so wonderful an animal.— I shall take advantage of your note of introduction to Mr Hughes & sleep there tomorrow night: if I should hear of anything remarkable in rocks of the neighbouring mountains I might be delayed there one day, in which case I should not reach Dunheved till Monday evening.—

BELIEVE ME, DEAR SIR/VERY SINCERELY YOURS./CHARLES DARWIN.

arrived here] at Bathurst, New South Wales

Although Darwin did not return to Australia after his brief sojourn in the country in the 1830s, in later life he expressed pride in what he called his 'adopted country'. To the botanist Sir Joseph Hooker (1817–1911), author of Flora Tasmaniae *(1855–60), he confided that emigration to Tasmania was his castle in the air.*

15. TO CATHERINE DARWIN, 14 FEBRUARY 1836

MY DEAR CATHERINE

I am determined to begin a letter to you, although I am sadly puzzled, as you may see by the length of the date, to know what to write about. I presume you will have received, some few days before this, my letter from Sydney.—We arrived here after a six days passage, & have now been here 10.—Tomorrow morning we Sail for King George Sound.—1800 miles of most Stormy Sea.—Heaven protect & fortify my poor Stomach.—All on board like this place better than Sydney—the uncultivated parts here have the same aspect as there; but from the climate being damper, the Gardens, full of luxuriant vegetables & fine corn fields, delightfully resemble England.—

To a person not particularly attached to any particular kind, (such as literary, scientific &c,) of society, & bringing out his family, it is a most admirable place of emigration. With care & a very small capital, he is sure soon to gain a competence, & may, if he likes, die Wealthy.—No doubt in New S. Wales, a man will sooner be possessed of an income of thousands per annum. But I do not think he would be a gainer in comfort.—There is a better class of Society. Here, there are no Convicts driving in their carriages, & revelling in Wealth.—Really the system of emigration is excellent for poor Gentlemen.—You would be astonished to know what pleasant society there is here. I dined yesterday at the Attorney General's, where, amongst a small party of his most intimate friends he got up an excellent concert of first rate Italian Music. The house large, beautifully furnished; dinner most elegant with *respectable*! (although of course all Convicts) Servants.—A Short time before, they gave a fancy Ball, at which 113 people were present. .—At another very pleasant house, where I dined, they told me, at their last dancing party, 96 was the number.—Is not this astonishing in so remote a part of the world?—

It is necessary to leave England, & see distant Colonies, of various nations, to know what wonderful people the English are.—It is rather an interesting feature in our Voyage, seeing so many of the distant English Colonies.—Falklands Island, (the lowest in the scale), 3 parts of Australia: Is^d of France, the Cape.—St Helena, & Ascencion—My reason tells me, I ought to enjoy all this; but I confess I never see a Merchant vessel start for England, without a most dangerous inclination to bolt.—It is a most true & grievous fact, that the last four months appear to me [as] long, as the two previous years, at which ra[te] I have yet to remain out four years longer.—There never was a Ship, so full of home-sick heroes, as the Beagle.—We ought all to be ashamed of ourselves: What is five years, compared to the Soldier's & Civilian's, whom I most heartily pity, life in India?— If a person is obliged to leave friends & country, he had much better come out to these countries & turn farmer. He will not then return home, on half pay, & with a pallid face.—Several of our Officers are seriously considering the all important subject, which sounds from one end of the Colony to the other, of Wool.

My Father will be glad to hear, that my prophetic warning in my last letter, has turned out false.— Not making any expedition, I have not required any money.—

Give my love to my dear Father I often think of his kindness to me in allowing me to come this voyage—indeed, in what part of my life can I think otherwise.—

Good bye my dear Katty. I have nothing worth writing about, as you may see,— Thank Heaven, it is an unquestioned fact that months weeks & days will pass away, although they may travel like most arrant Sluggards. If we all live, we shall meet in Autumn.

YOUR AFFECTIONATE BROTHER/CHARLES DARWIN.—

Catherine] Emily Catherine Darwin (1810–66), his sister

CHARLES JOSEPH LA TROBE

Melbourne was a four-year-old settlement when Charles Joseph La Trobe (1801–1875) took up his duties as Superintendent of the Port Phillip District in 1839. Until its separation from New South Wales in 1851, Port Phillip was under the jurisdiction of the Governor, Sir George Gipps (1791–1847) in Sydney; this letter is the first in a correspondence in which a personal friendship developed while official matters were discussed.

16. TO GEORGE GIPPS, 19 OCTOBER 1839

MY DEAR SIR GEORGE,

The first scene of the first act of the drama is over. The welcome which the good people of this portion of your territories gave me, was as the papers would say *enthusiastic*: that is to say, the grave amongst them got up grave addresses & received grave answers—the gay made bonfires, put lights in their casements & fired off fowling pieces:—& the lower class got jovially drunk & were fined—all in my honor.

The second scene has now commenced. The newspapers (I understand for I have not had time to read them) begin to give me a great deal of very excellent advice—every man in the street thinks (as I must now have rested sufficiently from the fatigues of the voyage) that it would be both improper & impolitic to pass the door of my temporary office without stopping to do business with 'His Honor'. One steps in to ask after my health & how I like Australia Felix—another to request I would give him a government appointment: a third to inoculate me with his opinion on some subject of public interest. Official men have all some arrears of one kind or another to fetch up: having modestly kept them in the back ground till *'His Honor' should arrive*: so that I am led to suppose that every body within the District (the Hentys' from Portland Bay even have been at me) thinks that he does the state good service in assailing me: & all this at a time when I have neither a roof over my head, nor a single shelf upon which I may arrange my papers. However, I do not complain, on the contrary I take it as a matter of course that I must pass through this ordeal in common with other honorable men. They will soon find that the lemon has been squeezed so often that there is no longer any juice in it, & then I hope to have a quiet life. A quiet life it may be, but I have no idea that it will be an idle one. I am sure you will give me time to recollect myself & to get to understand my business, & then I will send you a full report of what is doing & what is to be done in this part of the Colony. I have found Capt. Lonsdale a truly excellent, worthy, intelligent man & one to whose opinion I am bound to listen with respect & deference. From no other official here, were I so necessitated, dare I seek for perfectly unbiassed opinions as to many matters connected with this District; for all, as might be expected, have entered more or less into the speculations of the time, with the exception of Lonsdale, whose self denial, & regard to the moral ascendency which one, filling his station in the community ought to be possessed of, rather than to his worldly advantage I consider worthy of the highest respect & praise: I am sure you will appreciate it.

As to my own private arrangts.—they are soon stated. Upon my arrival here, I fixed upon a suitable spot in the Government paddock, next to that in which Capn L resides & took measures to put up my portable cottage & whatever offices were indispensably necessary. I know that I am there on sufferance & not of right, & that whenever circumstances may oblige you to tell me to remove I must do so at all risks. Nevertheless I have been obliged to spend so much even in putting up these temporary erections (for such they must be called) from the exorbitant price of labour (10/- to 14/- per diem) & materials, that this alone would make me unwilling to move for some time unless it were necessary. But, other considerations impel me to ask you to sanction my remaining where I am proposing to live, till the public good or other circumstances require my removal, & that is my utter inability to cope with the speculators of this town in buying land within any reasonable distance, and my determination to seek from you no advantage or indulgence in selecting & purchasing what might suit me, beyond what you might accord to any other. Were there no land fever in the District, & were land selling in a natural way: plentiful as it is, there might have been no impropriety in my asking you to sanction my purchasing a given plot of ground conveniently situated at an evaluation: or to allow it to be put up to auction at one of the land sales that I might become the purchaser—& none in your yielding [?] to my request. But as matters are, I can do neither with propriety and so little hope have I of procuring land at present within a few miles of the town at any reasonable rate, that I have taken measures to dispose of my permanent House which I expect daily from England, even before it arrives, as, to keep it warehoused here is out of the question—I believe the position I have chosen is not likely to interfere with any one. The paddock is railed in, & is part of that reserve which was set apart by Sir Richard Bourke's orders for the use of Govt cattle & horses. The mounted police have their barrack in one corner of it & I have modestly placed my cottage &c near another.

Mrs. La Trobe is well, thank God, in the midst of all our discomfort & confusion for we have not yet been able to get in to our quarters. She requests me to present her kind regards to Lady Gipps to whom I beg to offer my respects.

I have written to you, my dear Sir George, sans façon, as I believe I have your permission, & as your uniform friendly & open intercourse with me in Sydney encourages me to do—I do not wish to inflict a correspondence à la Robinson upon you (he has opened a terrible file fire upon me, of which more another opportunity) but shall have great pleasure in writing to you occasionally

& AM EVER/MY DEAR SIR GEORGE/YOUR VERY FAITHFULLY/CHARLES JOS. LA TROBE

the Hentys] the Henty family had settled in Portland in 1834   Lonsdale] Captain William Lonsdale (1799–1864), Police Magistrate at Melbourne, had been in virtual charge of the settlement until La Trobe's arrival   the Government paddock] the area between what is now the central business district and Punt Road–Hoddle Street   my portable cottage] La Trobe paid for his prefabricated house, Jolimont, and for the land on which it was put up.   Sir Richard Bourke] Gipps' predecessor as Governor of New South Wales   à la Robinson] George Augustus Robinson (1791–1866), Chief Protector of Aborigines in Port Phillip, known for his wordy correspondence

Henry Parkes

Henry Parkes (1815–96), the future knight, five times Premier of New South Wales and 'Federation Father' arrived in Sydney in 1839. He formed a bleak view of the prospects to be offered by life in Australia, and was in no doubt of the country's 'wickedness'.

17. To 'Friends', 1 May 1840

My Dear Friends,

This is a duty I ought to have performed months ago, and you will think harshly of me for this neglect. I have no excuse to plead, save that I was unwilling to sadden your hearts with a tale of misery. I waited from day to day, and from month to month, hoping to be able to give a cheering account of this country, but it is a sad one I write at last. I have been disappointed in all my expectations of Australia, except as to its wickedness; for it is far more wicked than I had conceived it possible for any place to be, or than it is possible for me to describe to you in England. We came to anchor in Sydney harbour on the morning of the 25th July, 1839, my dear wife having become the mother of a little girl on the 23rd, when we were a few hours' sailing clear of Bass's Strait. Our little blue-eyed ocean child gets on very well, and is now, of course, more than nine months old. I thank God for this blessing.

> "He moves in a mysterious way
> His wonders to perform,"

or this sweet one of ours could never have out-lived the many ills which every day of its short life hath brought. I had but two or three shillings when we got to Sydney, and the first news that came on board was that the 4lb. loaf was selling at half-a-crown! and everything proportionately dear. There was no place for the emigrants to go to till such time as they could engage with masters, or otherwise provide for themselves. When they left the ship they had to do as best they could. Poor Clarinda in her weak state had no one to do the least thing for her, not even dress her baby, or make her bed; and in a few days she was obliged to go on shore, with her new-born infant in her arms, and to walk a mile across the town of Sydney to the miserable place I had been able to provide for her as a home, which was a little low, dirty, unfurnished room, without a fire place, at five shillings per week rent. When she sat down, within these wretched walls, overwhelmed with fatigue, on a box which I had brought with us from the ship I had but threepence in the world, and no employment. For more than two weeks I kept beating about Sydney for work, during which time I sold one thing and another from our little stock for support. At length, being completely starved out, I engaged as a common labourer with Sir John Jamison, Kt., M.C., to go about thirty-six miles up the country. Sir John agreed to give me £25 for the year, with a ration and half of food. This amounted to weekly:—

10$\frac{1}{2}$ lbs. beef—sometimes unfit to eat.

10$\frac{1}{2}$ lbs. rice—of the worst imaginable quality.

6$\frac{3}{4}$ lbs. flour—half made up of ground rice.

2 lbs. sugar—good-tasted brown.

$\frac{1}{4}$ lb. tea—inferior

$\frac{1}{4}$ lb. soap—not enough to wash our hands.

2 figs of tobacco—useless to me.

This was what we had to live upon, and not a leaf of a vegetable or a drop of milk beyond this. For the first four months we had no other bed than a sheet of bark off a box tree, and an old door, laid on two cross pieces of wood, covered over with a few articles of clothing. The hut appointed for us to live in was a very poor one. The morning sunshine, the noon-tide shower, and the white moonlight of midnight, gushed in upon us alike. You will, perhaps, think had you been with us, you would have had a few vegetables at any rate, for you would have made a bit of garden, and cultivated them for yourselves; but you would have done no such thing! The slave-masters of New South Wales require their servants to work for them from sunrise till sunset, and will not allow them to have gardens, lest they should steal a half-hour's time to work in them. I should mention that our boxes, coming up from Sydney on Sir John's dray, were broken open, and almost everything worth carrying away was stolen. I made this at first a very grave complaint, but only got laughed at for my pains, and told that was nothing. During the time I was at Sir John's, I was employed mostly in a vineyard consisting of sixteen acres of land. I was there during the vintage season, and left just as we had done wine-making in the middle of last February, having been in his service six months. This estate of Sir John's is named 'Regentville,' and is situated about three miles from the small town of Penrith, on the bank of the Nepean River, and about the same distance from the first range of the Blue Mountains. I have been in Sydney now better than two months, part of which time I worked in a large ironmongery store in George-street, which was founded by Macdonald, who now resides, I believe, at Birmingham. I am at the present time at work for Messrs. Russell Bros., engineers and brassfounders, Queen's Place, George-street. I get five shillings per day, finishing brass work; good brassfounders get 7s. 6d. and 8s. a day, I think I could get plenty of light turning to do, and a good price for it, if I had a lathe, which I will try to get before long. I am very unsettled at present on account of ill-health. This brass business does not suit me at all—have not been able to do any work for the last week. I think I shall be obliged to go into the country again. As soon as I get settled I will write and arrange with you how you may forward a few things which I should like to get from England as soon as I can remit the money. In the meantime, be pleased to write immediately, and let us know how all our dear friends have fared since we left home, I hope well. Address, Mr. Henry Parkes, ivory turner, at the General Post Office, Sydney, New South Wales. You must pay the land postage, or the letters will not be sent with the mails on board ship. Send me some newspapers, and write on the wrappers of them 'newspaper only.' Send me all the news you can. I have seen but one person since I have been in this colony, whom I had any knowledge of in England; that was————, who was transported about two years ago, from Moseley-street. I saw him once—met him in Sydney—he was then staying in the hands of Government at the new prison at Woolloomooloo. For the encouragement of any at home who think of emigrating, I ought to add that I have not seen one single individual who came out with me in the *Strathfieldsaye* but most heartily wishes himself back at home. Mr. Isaac Aaron, who lived in Deritend, is practising in this colony as a surgeon, at Raymond Terrace, on the River Hunter.

WITH MY HEART'S PRAYERS FOR YOU ALL,/I REMAIN,/H. PARKES

P.S.—Wages in Sydney at the present time are about as follow—good workmen :—

	£	s.	d.		£	s.	d.	
Smiths ...	2	0	0	to	2	10	0	per week.
Engineers ...	2	2	0	"	3	0	0	"
Carpenters ...	2	0	0	"	2	10	0	"
Masons ...	2	0	0	"	2	8	0	"
Compositors ...	2	10	0	"	3	0	0	"
Turners ...	1	10	0	"	1	16	0	"
House painters ...	1	16	0	"	2	8	0	"
Other mechanics about the same.								
Labourers ...	1	4	0	"	1	10	0	"

You might get as good a house in Birmingham for 2s. 6d. per week when I left as you can get in Sydney for 15s. per week.

Clarinda sends her love and best wishes to her dear parents, with which I unite my own. Tell my own dear father and mother, if—as I trust—they are both alive, that they are seldom absent from my thoughts. Give my love to my dear nephews Thomas and William. Tell James I am not sorry he did not come out here with us, though I think he might have done as well as most. I will give you some general account of this country in my next, which you may expect in a month or two after the receipt of this, and I hope my next account of my own progress will be more satisfactory. Tell John Varney I would advise him by no means to come to this colony. Tell him to write.

my dear wife] Parkes married his first wife, Clarinda, daughter of John Varney, butcher, 11 July 1836. She died in 1888   Sir John Jamison] Jamison (1776–1844), physician, landowner and constitutional reformer   Regentville] built 1825 and named in honour of George IV, the former Prince Regent   Messrs. Russell Bros.] foundry business established by the Russell brothers, Peter, Robert and John, in Queen's Square on Sydney's Tank Stream. Peter Nicol Russell (1816–1905) made substantial benefactions to the University of Sydney   ivory turner] in 1845 Parkes set himself up as an ivory turner and importer of fancy goods. The business failed in the 1850s, one of the many financial disasters to befall him.

WILLIAM WESTGARTH

The Edinburgh-born William Westgarth (1815–89) achieved success in colonial Victoria as a merchant, financier, politician and historian. He arrived in the infant town of Melbourne on 13 December 1840. Over forty years later he wrote his Personal Recollections of Early Melbourne & Victoria, *described by Geoffrey Serle as 'one of the very best of Australian pioneer reminiscences'.*

18. TO CHRISTIAN WESTGARTH, 24–25 DECEMBER 1840

MY DEAR MOTHER

My last letter was to Anne, dated I think on the 19th which I sent by the overland mail to Sydney, and as there is some chance of a vessel sailing from this soon with wool for London I write this to be ready. The weather has been very variable, as it always is here in Spring and the beginning of Summer. Today it blows so strong from the north that we cannot get ashore. The wind from the north at this time blows as from a furnace, and the thermometer now stands at 86°, at 2 p.m. 91°, tho; we are 2 miles from land. I have better prospects for selling my Goods than I had thought. Though the Melbourne people grumble about having too many things on hand, they still give good prices for wine. I expect 50 per cent on some very fine Dutch Cheese and will sell a few casks of Port Wine very well.

I will write uncle George a long business letter soon. Mr. & Mrs. Jamieson sailed for Sydney a week ago. Glengarry, who was in the Perfect with his family, was taken great notice of here, and it is hoped he will finally settle at Port Phillip. We have a number of highly respectable people here, and the Melbourne folks are very gay. Ladies come into the city for the shopping, and dandies occasionally glimmer forth, parading in the sunshine; but the grand bent of all is the making of money, and I do think some is to be made here. We will get away in 3 or 4 days, and I am longing to get back from Sydney, and commence operations.

I had my first bushranging expedition the other day and I could not help wishing it would be the last, at least in that style. Richard Alexander has a small brick-work three miles up the country, and we agreed to pay it a visit after business hours. At 11 p.m. we accordingly set off. It had been raining a few hours before, and very soon after we set off, it recommenced, and not in a very lax manner. After stumbling against stumps of trees & logs lying in all directions, our first mishap was encountering the ground work operations for several buildings at the outskirts of the town, where we plotted about for several minutes unable to find the way either out or in. At length we emerged, and returned to town to find what R.A. considered a more certain route. This found, we again pursued our journey. It was quite dark, and anything for a road we were constantly losing from its indistinctness. Our eyes were always on the watch for logs & stumps of trees, which had fortunately an extra darkness at a few feet distance. There was a large paddock or fence, which we were first to come upon, and then take bearings for the hut we were bound to; but the paddock had four sides, and the want of light made it difficult to distinguish the right one. In short after reaching the paddock and groping about in a maze, paddock and all left behind and lost, we lay down about ½ past one under shelter of the slanting stump of an old tree, the rain pouring worse than ever, and the tree making the water meet below and fall upon us in an ever placid stream. These things are thought little of here; an umbrella covered our heads and R.A. was soon snoring as loud as if in a down bed. A cold wind which began soon after roused us both, and after an hour's refreshment we again started. Just as we had gained our feet we perceived a light, and making for it, heard the welcome sound of dogs. "Who does this place belong to", cried R.A.? "Why, it belongs to me" retorted an indignant voice within. It turned out, however, that R. knew him, but he had no accommodation, and recommended us with many kind words to continue our journey, as the hut was not far off. This accordingly we did, and after another hour's wandering and losing our way, at length we reached the welcome hut about 4 in the morning and got comfortably to bed. Next morning they shot some parroquets and other birds, which are numerous up there, and some black trout were caught in the Yarra, which tasted very well when fried. The country up there is really beautiful only rather uncouth, and the River both broad and deep—30 feet deep indeed, except at the sea, where there is a bar.

25th.   This is Christmas day, and all the shops shut. I learn that a vessel, the Lord Saumurez, will leave this for London on the 28th, and I will send this by it. I have called several times on Dr. Patrick, Mr. Copland's friend, who is a very pleasant man. He has come to town for some time at present, but has a station 80 or 100 miles to the North, where Thos. Copland also is, at least not far off, & in partnership with another, doing well. I have not yet heard of John Dunsmure. The Hardies of Leith are settled near Geelong about 35 miles S.W. of this. I must carry on W. M. Kenn's letters to Hobartown or Sydney, as the communications are very rare here with Adelaide. Today the weather is very cool and pleasant with a strong southerly wind—thermr. about 69° at the highest, which shews how suddenly changeable the climate is at this time of the year. Business is so constantly before your eyes here, that you feel very impatient lingering over mere news; however you must not think I will the less enjoy those from Edinr. When this reaches you, I suppose you will be thinking about going to some country quarters. A gentleman here takes his family to the beach about 3 miles off, for the bathing, & pitches a tent wherever he likes, there being no lodgings. Every night that there is a strong north wind, we see "the Bush" on fire, and last night there was a burning about ¼ of a mile long a few miles from the town, which illuminated the heavens like a fine darkish sunset. The lightening was also amazingly vivid. Nature is seen here in many respects on a grand scale. Numerous curious shells, insects, fish, Birds etc. are to be gathered; but I must get somewhat settled before I can reacquire my taste for these things. I have not seen any snakes; but ants are most numerous both in town & country, covering the roads in millions. One kind, the horse ant, is of a tile colour, an inch long, & ferocious & bloodthirsty. I am told also of spiders with bodies like a walnut, & 6 or 8 legs 3 inches long, centipedes larger than men's fingers etc. etc. but nobody fears all these wonders of creation, and "the root of all evil" prevents a due attention being bestowed on them.

I intend writing Marg^t. and Rd. and hope they have written me ere this.

Give my best love to my Father and all at home, and to all friends. I remain,

My dear Mother,/Your affectionate son,/W. Westgarth

RICHARD BOWLER

At the age of only 16 or 17, Richard Bowler of Brill in Buckinghamshire was transported to Tasmania on the ship Malabar. *Assigned as a farm labourer, he worked in various country districts until pardoned in 1840. His life in Australia is recorded in a handful of letters, innocent of punctuation, and some lines of doggerel verse written mainly to his brother John, a clockmaker in Brill. In twenty-two years in Tasmania, Richard appears to have received only four letters from his family in England.*

19. To John Bowler, 1 January 1841

Dear Mother Brother, Sisters to your Husbands Wife & children all likewise to all Relations & Inquiring friends I address these few lines to you hoping to find you all well as it leaves me at present I think it very Strange I have not received a single letter from any of you this last three years I have wrote to you John three letters you expected according to my information to you I should have been in England two years ago but the regulations of the Government often alter and that was the only reason But I am happy to inform you that I have now received my free pardon in this Colony but I have now to wait for her Majesty's pleasure which I expect about next Christmas Then I shall be my own Master once more which [h]as not been the like this twenty years Dear Brother I expect if I should hear from you I shall hear you are Married but I am Single yet and likely to remain so

Dear Brother I hope you will answer this letter and inform me all particulars Give my love to My Mother if she his living and if she his Dead I hope the Lord will rest her Soul I should much like to see the old lady once more and if living should God spare my life I will My love to you Brother & your children & if a wife to her likewise altho perhaps a stranger Likewise to My Sister Ann Newton & her Husband Likewise to My Sister Elizabeth her husband & family Likewise to My Uncle Aunt & all my cousins Likewise to Wm. & Grace Burgess & all their family and their familys to them that are married and good luck may attend them that are single and every one of you and not forgetting myself at the same time Brother should I not get any answer to this you will not hear from me any more till you see me Not forgetting My poor Sister Mary husband & children So I must conclude with saying I remain your affectionate Son & Brother & Uncle to many faces I never seen

Richard Bowler

In 1821 all on the 11th May
From Aylesbury Castle we set out
To Woolwich went straight way
On board of the ship Justitia the[y] placed us for a time
Our irons being light our usage being kind
We was there one Month when the ship she did come down
And taken one hundred & seventy to Vandiemens Land was bound
It was on fifteen day of June when the Malabar did sail
There was many a rosy looking man & many a one look pale
By being parted from our Native land & our friends we held so Dear
But we like[h]eroes cheer our hearts and on the Ocean steer'd
We had a pleasant voyage 17 weeks & 5 days
Then we reached our Destination & to you I [illegible]
Through wind & rains we did engage & braved their chilling [illegible]
On the 26th of October 1821 we landed in Hobart Town
In the Island called Vandiemens Land
Some of us were assigned & some to Government
According to our Descriptions so was our employment
For many a year I was assigned as you the truth shall know
But now I am a free man My liberty I hold
I hope my lines you will excuse as I have been so bold
And a better story I will tell when I reach my Native Home
So success to Liberty
RICHD. BOWLER

Justitia] a convict hulk on which Bowler was held before sailing to Australia

CHARLES SYMMONS

Soon after his arrival in the colony in January 1841, John Hutt (1795–1880) expressed concern that Aborigines, who did not understand the system of British law, were tried, not by their peers, but by white men. He therefore recommended the establishment of the position of Protector of Natives. Some settlers thought Hutt too lenient, but the report of Protector Charles Symmons suggests tight control and self-congratulation.

20. TO JOHN HUTT, GOVERNOR OF WESTERN AUSTRALIA, 30 JUNE 1841

SIR,—

Enclosed is my Quarterly Diary of matters connected with the Aborigines in my District, which I have the honor of submitting for His Excellency's information.

In perusing it, His Excellency will, I trust, feel gratified at observing that while the period which it comprises has passed over unmarked by any serious outrage on the part of the native population, the efforts of the authorities in the apprehension of some old and recent offenders have been eminently successful. With but one exception, not a native over whom any serious charge is impending is at this moment at large; a fact which argues well both for the general peaceable demeanour of the Aborigines and the efficiency of the police. To the energy and activity of Mr. Drummond, the Superintendent of Police, much of these results must be attributed; and His Excellency has no reason to regret having selected so efficient an agent in all matters connected with the bush as the individual above alluded to.

Nor must the efficacy and usefulness of our Native Constables be wholly overlooked. On several late occasions have they apprehended and brought in offenders who, from their knowledge of the intricacies of the bush have defied the efforts of the legal authorities. It argues much for our influence over these uncivilized men that, untempted by any large reward, they can thus be induced voluntarily to act in direct opposition to men not only of their own colour, habits, and dispositions, but not unfrequently their very blood-relations.

Amongst people so notorious as the Aborigines of Western Australia in avenging all injuries real or imaginary, we might suppose that men whose duty must necessarily render them obnoxious to their comrades would not long remain unpunished, but it is remarkable that on occasions when the native constables have come into collision with the sable brethren, in the exercise of their official duties, their peculiar costume and character have invested them with a protecting power and permitted them to insult the prejudices and oppose the passions of the many, not only with impunity but generally with most satisfactory results. This amongst a people owning no chief—a literally pure democracy—is only another proof of the halo of protection shed around the native when supposed to be supported by the authority and influence of the white man.

The native children of both sexes domiciliated with the inhabitants of Perth continue to give general satisfaction, and their usefulness increases in proportion to the length of their service.

The unfavorable state of the weather has frustrated several attempts I have made to visit the Convict Establishment at Rottnest, but I have the satisfaction of informing His Excellency of the healthy state of the prisoners, and the general satisfactory working of the system adopted by the Superintendent.

Rottnest probably, from its insulated position, and the consequent ignorance of the Aborigines relative to its interior arrangements, is shrouded by such undefined terrors in the minds of the native population as to prove one of the most efficient preventives of crime, and the severest possible punishment on its commission.

I consider the prison on Rottnest as one of the most powerful engines which the Colonial Government wields (rather in *terrorem* than in point of fact) over the Aborigines of Western Australia.

As Protector, and consequently interested in all plans for the amelioration of the native condition, I may be allowed to express my gratification at a late order in the

Government Gazette, whereby His Excellency offers gratuities to all such employers as can produce a certificate of having efficiently instructed a native in the operations of a farm, or any handicraft trade. If duly carried out in the spirit of the regulation, no plan would appear better devised for eventually breaking down the barrier which at present intervenes between the settler and the Aborigines. Once prevail upon the adult savage to domiciliate himself for a lengthened period under our roofs, a gradual appreciation of the comforts and luxuries of our civilization will naturally creep upon him, together with a consequent disgust of, and inability to return to his former precarious and desultory mode of life.

I HAVE THE HONOR TO REMAIN,/SIR,/YOUR VERY OB'D'T SERVANT,/
CHARLES SYMMONS/PROTECTOR OF NATIVES

Native Constables] Hutt recommended that the 'best-behaved and most intelligent' Aborigines be chosen for this work   Rottnest] the isolation of Rottnest Island gave added severity to a conviction

JOHN HENRY HOWITT

The eldest son of one of Melbourne's first settlers, medical practitioner and botanist Dr Godfrey Howitt, John Henry Howitt (1831–43) was eleven years old when he sent this letter-diary to his twelve-year-old cousin Alfred in England. The Howitts had left Britain in the vain hope that their son's health would benefit from the change.

21. TO ALFRED HOWITT, 1 MARCH 1842

MARCH 1ST

My dear Alfred Are you alive and well this and fifty other things I want to know about you; Anna Mary's letters to Mamma did not say one syllable about you, I never thought I could have been so angry with Anna Mary who was so kind to me at Esher and in London I felt very much inclined to wish her letters into the candle I hope she will never again forget to write about you and I will forgive her this once. And I think you deserve a scold too, for you promised you would write to me as soon as you were at Heidelburg and give me a long account of its famous castle Mamma has often told me when I wanted something to do to begin you a Journal but I thought I would wait till your letter came but I am at last tired of waiting. To day is very hot the thermometer 96 in the shade just the heat that suits me: I was very poorly all last winter and kept almost entirely to the sofa but the hot weather has at last began to do me good. though I do not sit out of doors as I did last summer I get plenty of fresh air for we keep all our windows and doors open

4TH   Our dear little Charlie has many times been ill, he is cutting teeth; now he is lying quite still on Mamma's lap and takes very little notice of us so different to when he was well. oh what a fat merry little creature he then was; he has never been so ill before and Papa is very much afraid he will not get better. I dont know what we should do without him he is such a very sweet entertaining little creature

13TH   When I began this journal I had no idea I should have such a sorrowful subject to write about Our darling little Charlie died on the 9th at 5 in the morning He is buried in the garden. I shall put this by till we feel cheerful again

17TH   I have had such a pleasant drive to day, down to the Beach. the very sight of the sea did me good, it was extremely green with just the tops of the waves tiped with foam. many ships, schooners, &c were lying at anchor at Williams Town. 3 miles beyond the Manlius was in quarantine the Pathfinder with many of her sails set was tacking out of the bay; the Corsair steamer from Launceston was coming up some boats close to us were pulling out to sea and famously they were rocked up and down It was altogether a beautiful sight I did long to be on board the Pathfinder for I believe another journey would do me good

18TH   Willie and Edith go to school now to Mrs Stevenson from ½ past 9 till 3 and they like it very much Willie is reading Markhams History of England which have been very favourite books of mine He is a much better accountant than I am but that does not say much for him I had intended to learn Latin on the voyage but I have not begun yet in good earnest. I have no doubt you would think us all great dunces.

21ST   to day the thermometer is 70 the sun is very bright and there is a most gentle breeze I am sure you would think this a most pleasant country.

12TH APRIL   I have been staying 3 weeks at the Plenty with Mamma and came home yesterday I enjoyed it exceedingly, all but the drive there and back which shook me too much. Uncle Robert made me a little carriage to ride in, and took me several short drives in it. I went to see some trees that Willie had felled when he was there as thick as himself which he had made a famous boast of. Uncle Robert has a very nice garden it is down in a flat you go to it by a zig zag walk; his vines were 14 feet high They have abundance of Melons The pigs are regulary fed on them while we were there the dray and 4 bullocks brought up a load out of the garden, for the rats had taken a fancy to them there. The bell birds sing all day long at the Plenty I like to hear them much better than the laughing jack-asses I read The Talisman, Old Mortality, and Ivanhoe while I was there which delighted me exceedingly and I am now reading Quentin Durward As we came home we called at the Yarra to see Uncle Richard. The river winds there very prettily I had just a peep into the cottage but it did not look very clean I assure you Mamma got out but I took my very notes sitting in the carriage

29th All the talk lately has been about the Bushrangers who live in the Plenty district, the first there have been in Australia Felix. they are a party of 4 well armed and mounted, who have robbed more than thirty stations beside highway robbery, but their reign of terror did not last more than a week. they commit their daring deeds in broad day light would you not think it extremely pleasant to be bailed up in a corner with some one standing over you with a pistol threatening you with instant death if you stired; this they do while the other bushrangers ransack the hut of what they want and then are off to the next station. Two parties of gentlemen and a few of the mounted police went in pursuit of them one of the party 5 in number at last got on their track and at Mr. Hunter's the bushrangers were interrupted just as they were going to sit down to a break-fast of roast ducks The gentlemen of the house haveing been ordered from table to make way for their superiors When they saw the party in search of them they called out to stand to your arms men they then rushed out and fired a volley but in retreating to the hut the ringleader got separated from the rest and after a very desperate resistance 3 of the gentlemen haveing been wounded the man was shot in self defence The other 3 after fireing 60 shots at last surrendered and are brought in for trial. Uncle's escaped a visit from these Bushrangers and only heard of them the night before they were taken

29 Edith has been a week at Brighton and is to stay 2 more. it is by the sea side. There is a nice firm beach. I dare say she will be fonder of runing about on the beach than attending to her lessons though Miss Ascham a lineal descendant of Roger Ascham is the teacher at Mrs Were's. Little Johny Were is a very funny boy he says he does so wish he was married his Mamma is so cross to him. he is only four years old.

May. I have had a very nice ship sent me it is not half complete in the rigging I have been very busy putting Main Mizen and fore top gallant masts, flying jibboom, main fore and sprit sail yards, and in a few weeks I shall make it a complete model full rigged ship. It was made by a sailor who had not time to finish it. the length is two feet six. it is a 4 gun ship Melbourne people are very fond of keeping birthdays the children went yesterday into the country to celebrate one and they had a famous romp at hiding seek among the bushes. They went and returned in a tax cart and were in such high spirits. Edward intends to be a Doctor and Mrs Palmer told him she would have him when she was ill to cure her and he is quite set up about it I read the papers every morning there is generally some good fun in them such curious police reports The Police Magistrate is very peremptory, so his name is a bye word here. "I'll Major St John you" Judge Willis is very quarrelsome in one case a little Lawyer who had the boldness to address him was frightened out of his senses by haveing thundered in his ear "who are you" "down sir, down sir I say" and with this the little Man rushed out of Court upsetting every one in his way. so Tipstaff was not summoned to take him out. Even Teddy stands a little in awe of Judge Willis and Big Chin, Mr La Trobe's messenger. But Judge Willis is a very good man though he is so cross sometimes. Willie, Edith and Edward join me in dear love to you Claude and Charlton and to Anna Mary

YOUR VERY AFFECTIONATE COUSIN/JOHN HENRY HOWITT

Anna Mary] Anna Mary Howitt, sister of Alfred   Heidelburg] Alfred had been at school in Heidel-berg, Germany   dear little Charlie] Charles Howitt, brother of John Henry   Willie and Edith] William and Edith Howitt, brother and sister of John Henry   Uncle Robert] Robert Bakewell, brother of John Henry's mother Phoebe Howitt   Uncle Richard] Richard Howitt (1799–1870) farmed in Heidelberg, Victoria, 1840–44 and after his return to Britain wrote out his frustrations in *Impressions of Australia Felix* (1845)   The Police Magistrate] Major Frederick Berkeley St John had a stormy career, which involved charges of bribery and corruption   Judge Willis] The Hon. John Walpole Willis (1793–1877), first resident judge of the Port Phillip District   Mr La Trobe] the Superintendent of Port Phillip, C.J. La Trobe (see Letter 16)

ALFRED WILLIAM HOWITT

Alfred Howitt (1813–1908), son of writers William and Mary Howitt, came to Victoria in search of gold in 1852. The venture failed but he spent the rest of his life in Australia. He worked as a police magistrate in Gippsland; he took part in the search for the ill-fated explorers Burke and Wills; and he was an influential thinker and writer in the field of anthropology and natural science. This letter to his sister Anna Mary Howitt expresses his doubts as to whether his talents are best fulfilled in Victoria, in India, or in a return to his family in Britain.

22. TO ANNA MARY HOWITT, 9 JUNE 1855

MY DEAREST ANNIE

I wrote in great haste by the Boomerang the other day and I dare say you would be all no little surprised by it but I hope that now you do not think me quite unadaptable— I have very long considered the matter over and have spoken to one or two people about it all have come to the decision that it is the best thing I can do. It has been a very severe trial giving up all ideas of going home for at least several years but from what my sister says in her letter about things at home being so depressed by the [war?] and the very bad state of colonial commercial affairs I have thought it only right to stay and try to do something here and I think that with a little money to start up as a farmer in a humble way and not being afraid of work I might manage pretty well after a time. I am very sick of doing nothing and all this uncertainty often makes me very low spirited. I see people all about doing capitally but dont seem to see my own way clear—I dont want to spend my life with a lash as an overseer and yet without a foundation one wont build even the smallest house. However if you think that I had better return home I will do so directly I hear from you— till then I shall try and get something agricultural to do so that I may at all events learn something, but it is so difficult to find for a few months just what one wants how happy it would be if we were all quietly settled down on some pleasant place here—all of us I mean—I am sure my father and Charlton must often long for the splendid weather we have here. If it were not for you dear ones I could adopt Victoria for my home without a pang—the country is improving and people expect that all things will be in a more healthy state before long. Metalled roads have been made up to most of the diggings, bridges built and everywhere land is being enclosed, the stride made in this respect during the last twelve months has been immense. I think you must pretty well understand my [illegible] and that I am quite ready to do whatever you may in consideration think best. I have never heard a word from Austin which in itself would have prevented my going to Madras. If I returned home I do not see what I could do there and as for being any one's clerk I would a thousand times rather turn bullock driver and be my own master. However if nothing else could be done I should not mind taking any appointment in some part of the world—I should be quite indifferent Borneo or anywhere, but I would rather either return to stay in England—with those I love but in that being out of the question remain here and turn tiller of the soil—I was at Toorak the other evening at the birthday ball and a queer affair it was as you will see by the papers—colonial swipes in common earthenware jugs and small decanters of horrible stuff supposed to be wine on the suppertable, then with Eau sucret and such like constituted the drinkables—no not drinkables for no one was able to do more than taste them—parched with thirst I drank part of a glass of swipes and felt as if I had taken some indescribable physic—I never tasted such a flavour and the wine was excruciating—the covered approach to the hall door from which the carriages set people down was illuminated with tallow candles in tin lanthorns and two sentries kept watch over the haystack lest common men might appropriate the vice regal hay to plebeian horses. Having made my bow to their excellencies I joined some people I knew in watching the various modes of making bows and the whalebone inclinations of their excellencies. The queerest object there was Mrs Chisholm a perfect guy with her unfortunate miserable of a husband with her. Neither Sir Charles nor Lady Hotham danced with anyone and only the last dance with each other and behaved in such an extraordinary manner to their guests that everyone is disgusted. Sir Charles is more universally hated here than I really believe, any colonial governor that ever lived. However I had a very pleasant evening despite the supper as I knew a great many people there and had dancing to any amount. I went outside an omnibus taken by the officers—the only seat I could get up to the eleventh hour and a very messy and noisy omnibus full it was with a lot of little boys running after us hurahing at the redcoats and goldlace inside. I dare say you will see all about the ball from the papers which have been full of absurd things about—some of them tolerable clever—I have half an idea of collecting the Hotham Anecdotes for Joe with explanatory notes—they are endless and most ludicrous and many of them not all to their credit.

I should fancy that Sir Charles must feel 'considerable mean' now but he doesn't seem to be—though he was received with a shout of 'swipes' the other day. He says he does not care on his own account but that he is sorry for Lady Hotham who spent a fortnight in trying to please the Victorians. Murphy was so chaffed about his "Murphys entry" that he is said to have started for his station at Colbinabin the day after the party—I hope you admire the picture at the beginning I think it is very natural. I choose to believe it very early morning just before sunrise when one of the travellers has got up to see that all is right and make up the fire. The two others are curled up to get a little warm before they wake up and there is a hazy kind of look about the country that reminds me of an early morning before sunrise. Remember me very affectionately to Joe and tell Joe particularly that I shall write very soon to him but that I have not felt up to writing any more than I was absolutely obliged to—I shall write a good gossiping letter to all next time. With dearest love believe me dearest Annie

VERY AFFEC YOURS/AWH

Charlton] Charlton Howitt, brother of Alfred, who took part in the goldfields enterprise but returned to Britain with William Howitt   Toorak at the birthday ball] an annual event arranged by the Governor of Victoria, Sir Charles Hotham (1806–55), whose official residence was then Toorak House   picture at the beginning] a sketch by Howitt precedes his letter.   Joe] Joe Todhunter, family friend of the Howitts

Ludwig Leichhardt

The naturalist and explorer Wilhelm Friedrich Ludwig Leichhardt (1813–48) was born in Trebatsch, Prussia, and arrived in Australia in 1842 keen to explore the inland. He made a number of journeys, sometimes unaccompanied, including one to the Moreton Bay District in 1843. His work as an explorer and as a man of science was highly regarded in Australia and internationally. In 1848, Leichhardt and his party disappeared without trace in an attempt to cross the continent from east to west. The charming qualities of his correspondence are demonstrated in Marcel Aurousseau's translation.

23. To Sophie Leichhardt, 27 June 1843

Dearest Mother

I can now tell you that I have already made long journeys in this colony—I've seen a great deal and I've been through a great deal. I've often been quite alone, on the tops of mountains or in the remoteness of the bush, and, as I lay by my fire at night, wrapped up in my blanket, my thoughts would lead me back to you, and to the rest of the family, so far away over there, at home. But your son is having a wonderful time. Poor though he is, he's doing his best to cope with circumstances and whenever the prospect has been gloomy somebody has offered a helping hand. Think of a young farmer in jacket and trousers, riding a small black horse, with a roll of blankets and a satchel strapped across the saddle, with a heavy hammer hanging from the pommel and a lighter one in his pocket, and you'll have a fair idea of what your good son looks like as he goes riding through the Australian forests. Often my only companion, apart from the horse, is a white pointer. When it's important to keep moving, and the country is not very interesting, I make as much as 5–6 German miles a day. But if the country is interesting I halt, give my horse a spell, and go wandering about, observing and collecting anything worth while. The settlers on the whole are very hospitable. Most of them are young, unmarried men, with 500 to 1500 head of horned cattle, and are trying to increase their herds as fast as they can. The stations are about four miles apart, and consist of no more than a few slab huts, but they give adequate protection from wind and weather in such a mild climate as this.—Some of the cattle are fine beasts though, and I never ate better beef or saw fatter animals during my journeys in Europe.—Other parts of the country are covered with flocks of sheep. There are thousands and thousands of sheep on the hills of New England and the plains of the Darling Downs. These districts are particularly well suited for sheep, which can there be run in flocks of 2 to 3 thousand beasts—a great advantage, considering the high wages paid to shepherds. These fellows get from 140 to 190 rix dollars a year. Don't forget, though, that they find necessities correspondingly dear. In the interior of the colony meat is the staple diet. On sheep and cattle stations they eat no other meat but beef or mutton, with a kind of unleavened bread called damper. It's made from well kneaded dough baked in the hot ashes. They drink unheard of quantities of tea, and a billy can of tea appears at all meals—breakfast, dinner and supper. It seems to take the place of soup. Although pumpkins do well here and are very floury, they're seldom eaten. Even though people can have just as much meat as they can possibly eat, and they eat nearly 2 lbs each a day (they're allowed 12 lbs a week), they don't, on the other hand, get the vegetables that you all enjoy so much at home. Potatoes and cabbages are luxuries because the heat of Summer so often kills the plants. I have met several Germans, and am glad to say that Germans are generally liked here because they work hard and are modest in their demands. They quickly manage to become independent. Some of those I met were thought of highly as shepherds. Another was a wine grower. Here at Moreton Bay I'm living with the German Mission. It consists of good, zealous people who have been sorely tried in their most disappointing efforts to convert the blacks. They are all married and now number 7 families with 22 well-behaved children. I feel very contented here among them, because their simple goodness is something one encounters far too seldom in this colony.—Although the blacks show little inclination to accept Christianity or to bother about religious matters, many of them are highly intelligent and very astute. This is most evident with children who have been removed from their parents when very young and have then been taught apart. The little clans, however, are dying out, and in many instances clans that were once 100 strong can now muster only 2 or 3 individuals. In some places they cause the settlers great loss by spearing cattle or by driving sheep away and killing shepherds.—About 8 years ago there was a ship wrecked 100 miles or so farther North, which had some bullocks on board. One of them swam ashore, where he waxed fat on virgin pastures. The blacks, who had never seen so huge a creature before, were wonder struck. They came from near and far to gaze at the unknown monster, and many a plan was forged for his undoing. But whenever they approached him the bullock charged, and scattered them. At length the whites appeared on the scene. They understood the ponderous wonder, and it fell to their first shot. It was extraordinarily fat, and one gentleman who tried a steak from the carcase was never tired of telling how deliciously tender it was.

I can't remember if I told you that my own life was once in danger when I was attacked by a wild bullock. I was alone in the forest, and I dodged behind a tree just in time to save myself. He went for me several times so I dealt him a blow with my hammer, which seemed to take the fight out of him, and I darted back from tree to tree.—It meant the loss of the hammer, which I had carried through France, Italy and Switzerland—but better that than my life, of course.—

My health is as good as, if not better than ever. Yet people tell me that I'm looking older—and the grey hairs are coming faster. I might not have stood the hardships of travel so well had I not always held to a clean respect for my body and striven to honour the training which I owe to my good old mother. If you were fond of the boy and the youth who sometimes gave you a lot of trouble—though he never really meant to—you'd rejoice even more in the man, who has come slowly through to a calmer state of mind yet wants to retain the glad heart of childhood.—Let us hope that we shall meet again under the same old sky. Until then and thereafter may God grant you health and happiness. How I long for news of you all—and perhaps there's a letter waiting for me in Sydney. Regular postal services, however, do not extend into the interior from Sydney, and, as I am constantly moving on, letters can't be forwarded to me. Still, I might hear from you this very day, as a steamer has just arrived at Moreton Bay from Sydney and I expect letters from my friend by it. I'm fortunate in having found a really staunch friend in this country, who supports me to the limits of his ability. It's as if he were William's deputy, providentially sent out here ahead of me when William decided not to come. And not even from my brotherly William have I had any news for a long time. I'm sending him this letter, just the same, so that he can forward it to you.—Well, Mother, good-bye for now, and give my love to the rest of the family.

YOUR AFFECTIONATE SON/LUDWIG

William] William Alleyne Nicholson (d. 1853), a student friend of Leichhardt in England. It had been planned that William would accompany Leichhardt to Australia but family obligation forced him to remain behind.

ELIZA [BATMAN] WILLOUGHBY

By her first marriage to John Batman (1801–39), one of the founders of Melbourne, Eliza (c. 1804–1852), a former convict, had seven daughters and one son, John Charles. After Batman's death, Eliza married his former clerk John Willoughby. In 1844 her son was drowned in the Yarra River, after which Eliza left Willoughby and lived restlessly and unhappily until 1852, when she was beaten to death in a brawl in Geelong.

24. TO ELIZABETH BATMAN, 30 JANUARY 1845

MY DEAR ELIZABETH

I am sure you were much distressed when you heard of the Death of your dear brother I wrote a hurried letter to your Aunt acquainting her of the sad event and also sent a newspaper with the particulars—it seems that he was catching some small fishes which are left by the tide among the stones at the falls and in getting up in haste one of stones he was standing on gave way and he was immediately carried away a considerable distance by the current into the middle of the *unlucky Yarrow Yarra* and before any assistance could be procured my lovely boy had sunk, every effort was made to get the body but to no purpose until next morning when several of the blacks dived in different parts of the River and were successful in finding him—oh my dear child had you but have seen him you would never have forgotten his countenance no person would have thought he was dead he looked as if he was in a quiet sleep with a heavenly smile on his sweet face I am almost heart broken when I think of him and believe me Elizabeth all my happiness in the world is *buried in the grave with him I loved him to excess*—the only thing that reconciles me to this Bereavement is that I am sure that he is now in heaven the Lord has taken him from the evil to come he gave him to me and he has in the order of his divine will taken him from me and blessed be his holy name I send you a piece of his hair which I cut of myself before he was put into the coffin he was buried Very Respectfully Several Gentlemen attended they wore white Bands and scarfs he was carried in a hearse and about one hundred and fifty children followed carrying flowers in their hands which they threw over his grave he was buried in the Vault with his Father and placed on the top of his coffin which looked as fresh and as new as the first day it was placed there altho six years have nearly elapsed since the unfortunate occurrence—Lucy has been living with Mrs Soloman for some time and intends to remain until they return from VD Land they go over in the next Shamrock the wax candles Lucy has now in her possession they are very good give my Affectionate Love to my sister and Mr Stevens and accept the same

YOUR AFFECTIONATE BUT AFFLICTED/MOTHER

DENIS PRENDERGAST

This frank and tender letter of homosexual love survives from the Tasmanian penal settle-ment of the 1840s. Prendergast, under sentence of death for murder, accepts his fate with equanimity.

25. TO HIS LOVER, 1846

DEAR LOVER,

I hope you wont forget me when i am far away and all my bones is moldered away I have not closed an eye since i have lost sight of you your precious sight was always a welcome and loving charming spectacle. Dear Jack I value Death nothing but it is in leaving you my dear behind and no one to look after you But I hope you will beware of the delusive of man. the only thing that grieves me love is when i think of the pleasant nights we have had together. I hope you wont fall in love with no other man when i am dead I remain your True and loving affectionate Lover.

DENIS PRENDERGAST

CHRISTINA CUNINGHAME

Christina Cuninghame arrived in Sydney in 1839, with her brothers, Archibald and John, and her sister Sarah. Some months later Archibald took up land in the Port Phillip District, where his sisters joined him. John Cuninghame managed the Wanregarwan run, on the Goulburn River, near the present town of Molesworth, and Christina kept house for him. The Cuninghames' cousin Agnes Cochran-Patrick of Ayrshire, Scotland, was a crucial link with home.

26. To Agnes Patrick, 22 October 1851

MY DEAREST NAN

As I wrote to you only six weeks ago, I should not so soon have taken up my pen, but I had since a nice letter from dear Janet, and I know not her address to reply so I must enclose my answer to your care; her accounts of her health and happiness are most pleasing, and she was just arrived in London to see the Great Exhibition! for which I certainly much envy her; I do hope you may also get a peep of the wonderful sight, and tell me the impression it makes on you; as to the wonders you would see there, I should never expect you to describe *them*, as I am sure a large volume would be needful, but I should like much to hear from some one what feelings so wonderful a scene excited; it appears to me that *bewilderment* would be the first thing. I have not much news since I wrote, except that the weather is now beautiful, and in consequence the *gold frenzy* has burst forth now in full force, and we are about to be left without either cook or nurse, as all the servants have got their heads perfectly turned, and even those who cannot go to dig for themselves, go off in the idea that they will make fortunes of wages elsewhere, rating their value so high, and getting so insolent that for my part I would rather cook than have them but I am told this state of things will not last long, and by and bye crowds are sure to come to the gold from home & elsewhere and they will find themselves disappointed, at least all who are not fit for *very hard* work. One man lately was smothered in the hole he was digging, and others narrowly escaped; they have each just 8 feet square, & in these little spaces dig perhaps twenty feet down so imagine the risk but they all get too much excited to mind; many gentlemen are there, others go just for a few days to see the strange scene, which they say at the principal diggings is very exciting, one person said he did not think the great Exhibition could be more extraordinary!! Then they have such difficulty in getting all the necessaries of life collected in the bush for such crowds; fancy one man pushing a wheelbarrow with a 200 lb bag of flour *70 miles!* This really occurred; others carry their goods & chattels in little carts drawn by dogs and all [?], as they cannot get drays & Bullocks enough to furnish them and the roads have been shocking Baby has been very well since I wrote last but I am afraid Sarah will find it one great burden to take the entire charge of him his nurse leaves tomorrow, with her husband who has been cook; they are a Nasty ill tempered, Mischievous pair and *he* is every way a useless servant but *she* was very useful to the baby, and Sarah is much annoyed at losing her; for my part I think that if others may [be] got, they would be a good riddance. I shall have to do all the kitchen work with the help of a *Black* woman the only useful one of her tribe who is fortunately here at present; we still have a washer-woman, but she and her husband also leave in three weeks for the *diggings*. I do hope we shall get another before that, as I can do nothing about washing. Sarah and her husband went to Kilmore, a township fifty miles off, last week, in search of servants, but without success, and Mr Wrey has had an illness in consequence of the ride; he is however well again. We have had such a houseful of gentlemen for eight days. We have sold 500 head of cattle to a Young Swiss, a Mr Castella[?] and he and others are here collecting them; I hope it will be over tomorrow morning for it causes a terrible bustle and stops all other work, it is fortunate it has been before any servants leave Now I must say goodbye as I cannot cross more on this thin paper. With kind regards to your gudeman, and many loves from us all to you and your little chicks

BELIEVE ME DEAREST AGNES,/YOUR AFFECT^E COUSIN/CHRISTINA

Baby] George (b. 1851), son of Christina's sister Sarah who married George Bourchier Wrey
Mr Castella] probably Paul de Castella of Yering Station, Yarra Valley

ROBERT SHEGOG

Robert Hamilton Shegog (1815–1905) arrived in Port Phillip from Ireland in 1849. Before trying his luck at the diggings in 1851 he was a cabinet maker in Albert Street, Collingwood. His letter, urging emigration to Australia, was copied and circulated in his home district around Clontibret, Co. Monaghan, and in Westport, Co. Mayo, where his brother lived.

27. TO HIS FAMILY, 25 DECEMBER 1851

DEAR MOTHER, BROTHERS AND SISTERS,

We are quite well, hoping this will find ye all likewise. Dear Mother we are now 70 miles from home at the Goldmines, there is about 800 men at the diggings. I am getting at the very least £12 per week to my own Share, there is the three in our party and we all dig the hole first and then we wash, one rocks the cradle and the other beals [bails] in the water, and another draws the stuff to be washed, the cradle is just like a childs cradle with a wire cive [sieve] on the top, which we wash the earth in what lies in the bottom that we take in a tin dish and washes, Sometimes we get one ounce and sometimes more, the gold is £3 per oz, and sometimes we get 2 or 4 oz in the day, it is £3-17s in England. Dear Brothers I would advise you all to come out, and my brother-in-law, for I think you could do well out here. There is poor boys come out here in the same vessel with me that is independant just with this gold work. I would like to see John and William and

George and in fact you all if my mother was aggreable, to come and if not let George leave the place with Sinclair and send him money for paying in it [the rent] and if not come on and if you prefer wheeling earth on the bracklagh hills, to gold here, you may stay, but if not <u>come on like men.</u> You need not fear the sea, for it is not half as dangerous as going to America, and if you come put your name down for emigration to Port Phillip, and when you land in the bay write to Mr. Bell, Grocer, Newtown, or come on and inquire for him and you will not go astray, for he is a Brother-in-Law of mine. You can get out on a free passage, as well as a paid one, and be thought of as much as if you had paid it 10 times, Dear Mother, I hope you will have spent as happy a Christmas day as I have, one of us went down into the hole and got 6 oz of pure gold. Dear Brother, come out here for I think you could not do better than come, for if you were working until you be old men you could not do as well as you could do here in one twelve month, or in two years you would be independant. Dear Mother if you could bring out some flour and some butter and ham or two of Bacon and some tea and sugar and some Baking Soda and bring plenty of Shoes and boots, and if the girls come they need not bring any dresses, they are as cheap here as at home, but the girls might bring 5 or 4 pairs of boots and Shoes. They might bring my wife three or four pair of fine ones and I will pay them. Get ones with lether straps across the toe of them, they should be a middling large size 4 or 5's and dont forget a fether bed for me, put it in the bottom of your chest. Give my love to all inquiring friends, John McFarland could do well here, my wife and Sarah Jane hoping to see ye,

Yours Truly/R.H. [Robert] Shegog.

P.S. The gold is for seven years in these mountains, it is for 30 miles around here, when ye come ashore dress yourselves well and neat.

Copied at Ayle, this 22nd day of May 1852.

William Clay.

JOHN NEWCOME

John Newcome comes down to us in history as an unknown representative of the immigrants who poured into Australia in the 1850s to try their luck on the Victorian goldfields. He seems to have been well educated and remarkably accepting of the difficult and not always rewarding experiences of life on the 'diggings'. His letter to a friend in Adelaide is written from Forest Creek (Castlemaine).

28. To Jonas Sly, February 1853

Dear Jonas,

Worse and worse! No gold yet, but a superabundance of calamities. My mother anticipated for me invitations to the Commissioner. I have not been honoured with any such communication from his Worship, but, nevertheless was very abruptly introduced to him the other day. Walking along despondingly, with my hands in my pockets—the only articles I have to put in them—I suddenly found myself surrounded by three or four men in plain clothes, but with muskets on their shoulders, & saw at a short distance an additional dozen of armed Policemen, with twenty or thirty captive Diggers under their charge. I was asked for my licence & having none was added to the motley assemblage. We were immediately marched off to the Commissioner's camp, our numbers increasing as we proceeded. Several individuals were fined five Pounds & made to pay the Licence fee for the current month. Three, of whom your unfortunate humble servant was one, having no money, were tied to trees, & comforted with the assurance of being made to work on the roads. After I had been exposed for about three hours to the gaze & jeers of passersby, a stout, Johnbullish looking man, who said his party were short of a hand, proposed that he should pay my fine, & that I should work on hire until my wages might enable me to repay the loan & purchase tools, when, if he & his mates should like me, I might perhaps join their party. To this proposal I gladly assented.

On arriving at my deliverer's tent I believe I astonished him by my wonderful dexterity with knife & fork. Damper & skinny mutton disappeared with a celerity which would have done credit to a turkey or roast-pig. A fast of ten hours is, I find, a wonderful stimulant to the digestive organs. I fear my host augured from my expertness with the light implements of the table, equal efficiency with the heavier ones, the pick & shovel. If so, he is by this time undeceived.

It was, of course, agreeable to be saved the degradation of compulsory labour on the public roads; but my present life is scarcely less miserable. I am cook to the establishment. Think of that, Jonas, cook! Would not you like to see me getting dinner ready? No, you would not. Cynic as you are, you would yet pity me. Could you see me, at early dawn, bearing homewards on my shoulder a side of mutton, limp & reeking from the slaughter, yet covered with the living spawn of those abominable blue-bottles, which, with the characteristic go-ahead instincts appertaining to new Colonies, find their way into existence without undergoing the ceremony of being hatched—could you see me cutting up the flabby mass into clumsy junks on the stump of a tree, & then frying the said junks in the open air, a blast of hot wind now & again carrying the fire from beneath the pan &, at the same instant, peppering the meat abundantly with dust—could you see these things, Jonas, I am sure you would abandon your habitual sarcastic grin, & sigh at my unhappy condition.

A stone might have wept could it have seen me attempting my first damper. Probably you have been long enough in Australia to know what this kind of bread is. It is a flat unleavened cake consisting of flour, water, & a little salt. Here, they make them as big as cart-wheels, to save time. They are usually baked in hot ashes, but sometimes a camp-oven is used.

On the morning after I joined them, my mates on proceeding to their work told me to make a damper for dinner—a big one, & big enough it was before I had done with it. Sometimes it was too stiff & required water; then it was too thin, & required flour; till our largest washing dish would scarcely contain it. Sometimes it stuck to my fingers like bird-lime, & became altogether unmanageable. By hook or by crook, however, I got it into the ashes; & only got it out again just as the party returned from work. Their ill-breeding on the occasion was abominable. They laughed at sight of the damper as if it was the first they had seen. True, it was by no means a picturesque or an ornamental object. It should have been round, but its shape accorded with no known figure. The edges ressembled more a cross-cut saw with broken teeth than anything else which occurs to me. Its thickness was very unequal, & its colour varied in places from black to dirty white. Some parts were burnt & others required frying. Still, it was a damper, & what better could they have expected.

The worst of it was that Jackson, a low cross-grained fellow, who is always snarling at me, calling me cockney, dandy &c, chanced to get a piece in which a few ingredients not originally contemplated had found a place. For instance, he spat out, at intervals, a rusty nail, two buttons, & three teeth of an old comb. Of course this was very unpleasant, but how can such things be avoided where accommodations are so scanty!

You see, Jonas, making the damper was not the worst of the matter, for I had to eat part of it after it was made, or go without bread. When the damper was baked I thought my cooking miseries were over till another should be wanted. Alas! not so. Yesterday being Sunday my mates started immediately after breakfast on a prospecting tour. Before leaving, they desired me to make a plum-duff for dinner, the ingredients for which had been procured the previous evening. I asked them where they kept their pudding-cloth, at which they laughed heartily, & told me I must find or make one. I found it much more easy to mix pudding than to knead damper, but what to do for a cloth I knew not. Blankets were too large, my pocket-handkerchief too small; we had but one towel amongst us, & that was in frequent use. What was to be done? To dispense with the envelope altogether would have been productive of porridge, instead of pudding. A lucky thought struck me—one of my stockings would just contain the duff. Into the stocking therefore it went instanter. A recital of what I had to endure when I set the stuffed & smoking stocking before my mates at dinner time (for the pudding stuck so to the cotton that I could not pull it off) would horrify you. The ungrateful rascals roared, stamped, swore & called me all the synonyms of dandy & fool to be found in or out of the dictionary. No doubt there was something strange in beholding what appeared to be a man's leg smoking on the board, but the queerness of the thing speedily disappeared, for when Jackson separated the foot part by amputating just above the ankle, the upper portion as far as the knee made a very respectable approximation to the shape of a roll pudding. Besides, my mode of treatment had no perceptible influence on the flavor.

When not engaged in cooking I am obliged to work like a negro but I must postpone a narrative of my working miseries to a future day.

No Post letter yet, therefore no cash—Jonas! What is to become of your unhappy friend

JOHN NEWCOME?

FRANK ROGERS

In 1853, stimulated by the Victorian gold discoveries, American initiative established the coaching firm of Cobb & Co., which quickly achieved domination of the Australian transport industry until it was eventually displaced by rail. The service was famous for the skill and popularity of its drivers, many of whom were Americans selected in preference to local men because of their experience in handling large teams of horses. One of them, Frank Rogers, wrote a colourful account of his early impressions of Australia to an unnamed niece at home.

29. To 'My dear Neice', 31 December 1854 – 1 January 1855

My dear Neice

Yours of July 16th was received with others Dec 22nd and I assure you it pleased me much for I did not expect it. I will try and answer it to the very letter. In the first place we never have had what you call a Fog we have the rainey and the dry season. The rainey season commenced about the middle of April and ended in September. We commenced Stageing the 11th of October and have had only two storms sence and one of them was the day before yesterday it lasted about 4 hours and came down by the bucketsfull.

You say Fruit is scarce in Lynn, but if you were here you would say 'Lynn folks had a plenty' even if they had none. All our fruit comes from Van diemans land 600 miles. I have paid 75 cents a pound for cherries and [illegible] that 1/6 or about 37 cents for a fresh cucumber and 25 cents per pound for apples which was none of the best. You can travel 300 miles and not see a fruit tree not original this is a great country for comfort and ease where grows nothing but Possums Kangaroos and Gum Trees. I have seen about 200 Kangaroos in one drove some of them seven feet high and what is more Ive eat them and considered the finest flavoured meat I ever eat. As to the manners and customs of the people you must know the People are from all nations China included. and of all grades from the Gentleman with his Fifty thousand a year, down to the pauper pensioner who can hardly get his mutton and damper some make money, others lose it. But the most independent are the Yankees. those that dont like the country curse it and leave for California or some other place where a White Man is as good as a Nigger. There is one thing certain the americans get credit for their enterprise here. When they first came they found a cool reception among some classes but that class were mostly convicts, Old Lags and Ticket of Leave men. As to the manners of the people I must say they are rather hoy esk[?] everybody is for himself and the old gentleman for them all.

Jan 1st 1855

The folks with whom I board at Caliban are of the real Old English stamp, I like them very much. It seems like boarding with Mr Hunting as they have a daughter about

[57]

18 years old and she plays the piano and sings first rate. I have been teaching her card drawing etc for amusement.

The Hotel at Keiler Plains is rather different here the folks think more of a mans shilling than they do of him, when I stop here I generally go to sleep for the reason there is nothing to keep awake for.

I am glad you took so much interest in Helen. I hope James will give her as good advantages as you have got. You ask about Agriculture thriveing. There is but very little here at present owing to the high price of land, and the want of water, water in this country is very scarce. People in citys have to buy it out of carts, at the rate of one dollar and fifty cents for 150 gallons.

You say your a great horsewoman, hope you wont get hurt but if you were here I would soon show you how we do it. Perhaps you worl like to know how we drive. I'll tell you. Each driver drives 40 miles and has 8 teams to do it some 4 horses and some 6 horses. My rout is from Keilor Plains to caliban over the worst road I ever saw. The Black Forest is the worst, just immygeing a man driveing a 6 horse Coach from the High Rock over the range of hills, through the woods between trees and stumps, over rocks etc and you have a slight idea of our driveing in this country. I have to drive at the rate of 16 miles per hour over some parts, but in the Forrest which is 9 miles long it takes me one and a half hours to get through. In other parts we go at the rate of 10 & 12 according to the road. It is something never attempted in this country to go from Castlemaine to Melbourne in one day but we have done it in 9 hours, and now we have 2 oppositions but none can come up to our time for the simple reason they have got English instead of Yankee drivers and they dare not follow us. Think not I'm boasting but we have had more Presents and more compluments than all the drivers in Australia, and well do we deserve them for we do what they dare not, nor could if they dared. Tell Robert I am glad he is doing well it is my worst wish to anybody and should I chance to drop in to his shop unawares I hope he will ask me to take a cigar and walk into his loafing room. Tell Helen God willing I shall come back to see her tell Mother and Grandmother I often think of them although I do not write. Give my respects to all inquireing and believe me still to have some love for you I remain

YOUR UNCLE FRANK

You must excuse me from writeing more for when I arrived at Keilor Plains, after the Ostler unhooked the horses they all Bolted viz run away and I have been 4 hours in the Saddle looking for them. They gave me a hard chase but we finally got them minus some harness. I feel very tired but must close this for mail tomorrow.

WALTER RICHARDSON

The courtship letters of Walter Lindesay Richardson (1825–79) and Mary Bailey (1835–96) are interesting not only for the two writers' use of the letter form to explore their growing confidence in one another as their marriage date approached; they also have a place in Australian literary history. Their daughter Ethel Florence Lindesay Richardson (1870–1946) (see Letter 94) adapted these letters in her novel The Fortunes of Richard Mahony *published under her pseudonym Henry Handel Richardson. Walter Richardson, like Richard Mahony, was born in Dublin, qualified in medicine in Edinburgh and migrated to Australia in 1852, during the gold rush period. After working as a store-keeper he resumed medical practice before his marriage in 1855.*

30. To Mary Bailey, 11 June 1855

Dear Love,

I wrote to you and Mrs Bradshaw yesterday, and I hope you received *all* safely We have had very severe weather last night and today hail, rain, wind and snow, the last remaining on the ground some time, giving us the rare opportunity of a game of that hearty English pastime snow-balling! I hope you are all well I am making *your room comfortable* been at it all day, sewing, nailing &c My poor friend that I left doing so nicely has had a relapse and is I am grieved to say gone to that bourne whence no traveller returns, I called in another medical man to give me the benefit of his advice but medicine is of little avail in that disease; Think my darling how short and uncertain life is and come and give me the benefit and the pleasure of your company thro' life—Good night dearest kiss me. I dreamt of you all last night and did not like to let the day pass without penning a line or two.

Wednesday—I went to the Post Office today no letters from you no lock of hair as you promised; I was at the Police Court all day as witness in the case of a dog that had been once mine, and was claimed by somebody that wished to appropriate her Have not yet been able to go to the White Horse Gully but hope to do so tomorrow Am very cold so you must excuse my wretched scribble tonight, Good night, dearest love!

Friday

I went yesterday to the White Horse Hotel, White Horse Gully M^r. Ed. Bradshaw was not at home, but tho' disappointed in not seeing him I had a very pleasant walk, thro' beautiful scenery wh I long to shew you—it—resembles a gentlemans park in England more than any-thing else. I have caught a cold or rather a cold caught me while standing in the Police Court all day on Thursday but colds and Influenza are now quite "a la mode." How is William? Give him my compliments and ask him if he will be able to attend at our interesting ceremony? I suppose you have perused the service by this time! Ha! Ha! I cant write for laughing!

But joking apart, seriously, it is an impressive service—"Wilt thou *love her, comfort her, honour,* and *keep her in sickness,* and *in health,* and forsaking all other keep thee only unto her *as long as ye both shall live*—Beautiful

And equally as follows "Then shall the priest say unto the woman."

I gathered some lovely heaths yesterday but tho' exquisite in appearance they want the perfume of English heaths, a great loss to the flowers of the Antipodes!—Goodbye Sweet one

Sunday

Good morning dearest Mary many thanks for your kind letter and its enclosures which I received safely yesterday. I am confident your pleasure on receiving my letter was not equal to *my joy* as I had yours handed me and knowing by a squeeze what it contained hurried off to devour its contents in private. I suppose M^{rs}. B. dosent see my letters to you dearest love for altho' there is no harm in love, still one hardly likes to write sweet nonsense for other eyes than the one next the heart Well I was going to say that I hurried off to devour it in private I don't like "My dearest D^r. Richardson", its not kind of you to be afraid to say "*Walter*", is the name ugly?

And so you all went to the cave did you, pretty place that cave Eh? I prefer the scenery a little further on, the wooded water course with the gentle slopes and deep precipices, with the track along the face of the hill, where you gently murmured "*Yes*"! Of course had the ground been a little less rough and the season a little milder I should have thrown myself on my left knee and with one hand on my heart become pathetic but dearest I think we managed it very well, my feelings prevented me from saying all that I should have done ~~but~~ and I fancied I felt you tremble on my arm; I had told Brooke the day before in Melbourne that I had a serious *duty to perform* and I certainly never expected to see him on the Sunday With his usual exuberance of spirits he told me that altho' it undoubtedly was a serious matter he could not look upon any "popping the question" otherwise than a most ludicrous affair & we both laughed heartily.

You ask my opinion of his conduct to "dear little Polly." Now darling I do not see any thing so very unkind, considering dear that he has a great deal to do, always knocking about, doubtless he has written before this, and besides 12 months is a long time and I think he felt rather hurt himself (*as I do*) at being treated somewhat cavalierly! put off for so long. Besides he knows he is safe in the heart of his little betrothed and surely a ride with the hounds was too tempting and perhaps he expected to be home in time for the post. I know he loves her dearly and she is his first and only love, and I would as soon doubt my *own constancy to you,* as his to his second self. Give the little dear my kind love and sympathise between you, sighing after two fond hearts that look upon each of you as part of their existence.

I think Brooke has very much improved and rejoice that he encountered the family for I think the mutual affection has been productive of much benefit to him—When we love, *and feel sure that we are beloved in return*, it does and must have *a beneficial influence* on *our conduct*—for as I would not like to have my body disfigured say by the loss of my fingers or eyes, so I consider now that *my mind should be* purer and the moral standard of my actions higher, is it not so? And is not this one of the good effects of love? is not the state of love one designed for man by an al—creator for his good! undoubtedly dearest! and altho' some are not so happy as to encounter a heart that can beat in unison with theirs every creature on earth loves something. I am not *poetical* on the contrary (you think rather *prosy*) plain matter of sense, I do not like poetry except perhaps on a quiet Sunday morning, or late of a Saturday night; and I'll tell you why *because I love it too much*, can you understand this apparent paradox, at one time of my life I was dosy living in a land of dreams, of spirits, letting the realities of life glide past almost unheeded, that was when at college (when all young men go thro' a little studying and a great deal of what they fancy is fun) Late hours &c impaired my health and it was not until I gave up poetry and nonsense and took to hard work that I found myself able to cope with the combination of angel and devil in my fellow mens composition I cannot read true poetry without feeling my heart beat stronger, I think you have poetry in your soul I do not mean love that you can scribble verses any ass can do that, but I think *like myself* you look beyond *the hour, the day*, don't you,? the *faculty* of *looking up* as it were, *looking to the source of things I mean*! Yes I think we shall be happy, Of course dearest, every man and woman have faults, *blemishes, imperfections* of body and mind, but we must remember that there is *no perfect one*, and remembering this we must *forgive*. Are not the following verses pretty?

The first dear thing that ever I loved
Was a mother's beaming eye
That smiled as I woke on my dreamy couch,
That cradled my infancy.

I never forget the joyous thrill
That smile in my spirit stirred,
Nor, how it could charm me against my will
Till I laughed like a joyous bird.

And the next dear Thing that ever I loved
Was a bunch of summer flowers,
With odours and hues, & loveliness
Fresh as from Eden's bowers.

I never can find such hues again
Nor smell such sweet perfume,
And if there be odours as sweet as them,
Tis I that have lost my bloom.

And so it goes on until it comes to

And the next dear Thing that ever I loved
Is tenderer far to tell,

Twas a voice, and a hand, and a gentle eye
That dazzled me with its spell.

And the loveliest things I had loved before
Were but as the landscape now
On the canvass bright where I pictured her
In the glow of my early Vow.

And so on finishing with old age—*like me* as M^{rs}. B. said! Ha Ha

Well this is a curious letter, but it is amusing and delightful to me to talk to you and this sheet has occupied me as you see many days proving to you that my morning thoughts and my evening sigh has been dear Mary. I have got a little scheme *when you come to me*; you shall write to *my mother* and *I to yours*. I have a dear old mother, that I love dearly, if I were to say that she has been the *finest* & the *cleverest* woman of her day I might offend you, sweet one, but she sang as I never heard *woman* sing, played the piano, harp, flageolet, accordeon, danced in her day played whist and now poor old soul having become old is anxious for me to return home, *oh! a letter from you will comfort her old age* and shew her that her dear son is happy & does not forget the arms that nursed him.

I am delighted that your happiness is *as you say* coming fast, I send you what you ask my darling but I am not accustomed to make bows with ribbon so you must take it as it is a token of my love. You say *"about three months"*, now love let it be the *beginning of August* do there's a dear, I think it wrong, very wrong, to postpone it as if you were afraid of me and as if M^{r}. B. was doubtful of my character. You will find a *humble home* and will have a poor man for your husband, but there's no queen will be more welcome if you can do without society *for a year or two* we will go to England & spend many a happy hour in the society of old friends. Kind love to Mrs. B. Tilly & dear Polly and a thousand kisses from your dear and attached

WALTER.

Mrs Bradshaw] On arrival in Victoria Mary Bailey lived at Bradshaw's Family Hotel, near Geelong, where she was nominally a governess, but in fact engaged in all kinds of domestic duties   William] Mary's brother   Brooke] Alexander Brooke Smith, a friend of Richardson's, worked intermittently as a policeman and tried his luck at the diggings   Polly] daughter of the Bradshaws, unofficially engaged to Brooke, against her mother's wishes. The engagement lapsed.   Tilly] Tilly Bradshaw, sister of Polly

Mary Bailey

31. To Walter Richardson, 24 June 1855

My dearest Walter

I have only a little time before retiring for the Night to write to you dearest for we have been so busy all day a house full of company that I have not had time to begin to write to you before. I received your dearly prized letter on Wednesday but was sorry to hear that you had caught a cold You must take great care of yourself or you will be ill I think it is my turn to talk to you now. I was thinking of yesterday when we did our walk to the Cave we had a very pleasant one indeed & we all climbed up those high rocks & stood & admired the scenery just where you & I stood but I think I looked more at the scenery to day than when *you* [were] with me I could not see that day but I blame you for it I was sorry you did not see Ted when you went to White Horse Gully but am glad you enjoyed your walk I am sure when you have time (when I come to Ballaraat) I shall only be to delighted to take the same walk with you & then *we* shall both be able to enjoy it together Harry Bannister is down he is staying here. William will be up at the latter end of next week I will send a short letter by him I have not asked him what you told me at present about being down in August perhaps I may but I dont much like saying it to him do you not think it would be better for you to do it but I will if you wish me particulary You ask me if I have read the ceremony over indeed dear Walter I have not neither shall I perhaps you will think me superstitious (well I think I am a little though I try to break myself of it) but they say you have 3 years bad luck so I *will* not read it for fear so please do not ask me. I like those verses very much indeed they are very pretty. I am indeed very fond of poetry though as you say I cannot write them. I will indeed dearest Walter write to your dear Mother if you wish I am sure nothing would give me greater pleasure if you think it would please her I wish I could see her but I can fancy & I am sure I should love her I would do any thing to make her happy if she will but let me & *I will* do all I can to make you happy dear Walter but as you say we all have our faults & I am afraid mine are very numerous but I will do all I can to become better & *you* dear Walter must help me I am afraid you will find me rather awkward at first but you must bear with me. You say that if I can do without society &c—indeed & I can I am one that cares very little about & besides what shall I want when I am married but you dear I am sure you will be enough I know no one scarcely but Mrs Bradshaw's family for I have been here so long that I am known as Miss Bradshaw so there will only be my Brothers & sister Rebecca up at Ballaraat. We all feel very fatigued after our long walk this afternoon so you will excuse me writing this so badly & my headaches dreadful I have not been well all the week I have had an attack of Influenza so I do not feel very well just yet I think it will go round the house I think Mrs B. has it she seems very poorley. You made a very good excuse for Brooke but I do not know what you will say when I tell you that he has not written yet

"Now what excuse can you make for him? If you should see or hear from him Just you ask him how he would like to see poor Polly wasted sulky & pale fretting about but he must expect it & to see the looks when any one comes from town the anxious have you any letters "No Miss" how would he like it I wonder? I am glad to say that Mrs Jeffs have returned Ellen has written & ask's whether Mary has had any more letters from D^{r}. R. & if she answers them if so to give her kind remembrance to him so I send it I have not answered it yet but must to morrow Dear Polly & Tilly send their kind love also Mother & hoping dearest that you will excuse this scrawl I must think of saying Good Bye but not before I return you many thanks for what I asked you for the lock of hair I prize it very much I hope I shall hear from you on Wednesday & with very best love & kisses Mary

Believe me dear dear Walter to remain/Your sincere & loving/Mary

Menie Parkes

Clarinda Sarah Parkes (1839–1915), known as Menie, was the eldest surviving child of political leader Henry Parkes and his wife Clarinda (see Letter 17). Born at sea just before landing in Sydney, Menie grew up revering her father. In turn Parkes idealized his daughter and fostered her intellectual gifts. Nevertheless his view of a woman's place was that of a traditional Victorian father.

32. To Henry Parkes, 26 September 1856[?]

My dear father,

I cannot go to the University on Sunday. You must have noticed that I evaded giving a direct answer to Dr Woolley's invitation; simply because I determined that I would not go if I could avoid doing so. My reasons are that tho' I know that "the sabbath was made for man and not man for the sabbath" yet I also know that it is "the Lord's day on which we may not think our own thoughts or speak our own words" and from this I gather that I am not excused in doing any work but the real acts of necessity and the labour of worship (if it is such) on that day, and I am quite sure that my going to the University would be neither one nor other. Besides it is communion Sunday and could I overcome the first objection I could not the second—that it would interfere with my receiving the Sacrament. Imperfectly as I may, and do, perform the perfect will of God, I do not deliberately and determinately disobey Him—and so I wish to refuse this invitation.

And now, my dear father, will you be angry with me for this? Shall I tell you how my own wishes are all panting to go, how I long to tread the halls which will be trod by great men here-after? Shall I tell you how I fear your anger, and how I paced backwards and forwards for hours hesitating before I boldly determined to take this course and refuse to go?

You must not be angry with me for I still read in the Bible which I strive to make my Guide the command 'Obey thy parents' and so if you still wish it I *will* go and cheerfully tho' not willingly.

I remain,/Your's affectionately/Menie Parkes

Dr Woolley] John Woolley (1816–66) Professor of Classics at the University of Sydney

33. To Henry Parkes, 24 April 1858

My dear Father,

I have for some time felt that I should prefer earning my own living, to being dependant on you, as I now am, and have formed a project which I think must meet with your approbation.

I will study pretty closely, during the next twelve months the common course of an English education, the rudiments of the French language and Theory of music; I would then, open an infant School under 12 years of age undertaking to prepare them thoroughly for a higher school, and to teach the elder children the stepping stones to Music, French, and Drawing (things which I know are very little attended to in other schools, because the pupils must practice and so no time is left for theory, but which is nevertheless very important).

I would charge for each pupil, 2 Guineas per quarter and supposing I only had 4 pupils; this would amount to 32 Guineas the year, (sufficient to clothe myself and one of the children but, it is not improbable that I should have 12 or 15.

If my plan succeeded, in a short time I might engage teachers for accomplishments, which would further add to my own gains.

The school hours would commence at ½ past 9 and close at 4, as others do, allowing me plenty of time to rest, beside the periodical holidays, so that, you see, I should not be overworked, but find a pleasant occupation profitable.

If I gained enough I might be able to pay for Music Lessons for myself and Mary and of course I should continue to teach her as before.

Do not throw this aside as a foolish, girlish idea for really I am in earnest and should feel very, very much happier if I saw any prospect of rendering myself independant, and do not think it would be any sacrifice on my part for I shall feel much gratified if you consent to my plan.

I should be in my 20th year at the time I mention

I remain/My dear father/Your affectionate daughter/Menie

Mary] Menie's younger sister

WILLIAM STANLEY JEVONS

Something of the intellectual formation of W.S. Jevons (1835–82), author of the ground-breaking treatise The Theory of Political Economy *(1871) can be traced to his time in Australia, 1854–59. Appointed an assayer at the Royal Mint in Sydney, Jevons arrived in time to observe the social disruptions of the goldfields decade as well as Sydney's rapid urban growth. Isolated in Sydney, he depended on letters to his family for intellectual companionship.*

34. To Henrietta Jevons, 24 January 1858

My dearest Henny

Nothing calls me to write this evening but the simple desire to communicate a few thoughts & feelings to one who will so fully understand them. It may indeed seem strange of me to *complain* of anything. I have here a free cheerful home, the pleasantest little study in the world in a sea-side spot that would delight English eyes; I have a good situation, plenty of money, a little laboratory in town at my own disposal, light congenial work, plenty of pursuits to follow up both at home & at the Mint, & plenty of time to follow them. What can I have to complain of then, or what more to desire? It is that I have not here anyone that can be to me a real friend. You perhaps know what a real friend should be; most people do not. Or rather I should say that the friends which most people require are found on everyside; I cannot find one here at all.

From one week's end to another, I am full of thoughts reflections, hopes, shames, but as they come up to the surface one by one, I have nothing to do but to shove them down again. I have not time to write them out and I have no one to tell them to. Where is the use of expressing serious thoughts to persons who cannot respond to them, or hopes, fears, or intentions to those who will think them absurd. This is my condition; I have everything I can want for a happy life except a *mind* to answer mine.

I have been stirred into a state of unusual agitation, almost boiling over sometimes, by reading two novels by Charlotte Bronte (Currer Bell). They are "Jane Eyre", and "Shirley". I scarcely know what there is about them so much to attract one, but perhaps it is that she was herself a quiet retired *thinker*, to whose original & truthful thoughts few I dare say would respond in common life and society, but who possessed the power of writing them so that all might & would read them and some might understand them. I would give anything to know such a person as Charlotte Bronte. From what I can see in her books I think her religion and mine are all of one kind and differ only that from habit or necessity she retains the use of a few fixed phrases with which I dispense. The sentence which I copied into my last letter to Lucy shows that she perfectly understood the force of what I found all my Faith upon. It is a faith in Humanity; in the fact that man was created for happiness. In nature we find an inexplicable mixture of evil. Pain and death may always come to our bodies, and, say what they will, nature cannot therefore be perfect. It is in the mind and nature of man that we find a provision against this. By a thought, a hope, a wish, an intention, or even the remembrance of a thought, or hope, he can rise superior to evils.

But I must not lose myself in depths which to me are yet dark and doubtful. But when instead of enquiring the foundation of my Faith, I enquire whether I have any and what it is, I find such a solid definite object, extending through every part of my mind, & forming apparently its whole framework that I scarcely care whether it be well founded or not. It is a solid fact. Now such a sort of faith appears to me to be indicated in Miss Bronte's books. In her there is no trace of *conventional religion*. Jane Eyre displays through her life a high degree of morality, and in many cases resists the most tempting pleasures and involves herself in toil & trouble in obedience to indefinite but unmistake-able *principles*. Such *principle* is not what is usually acquired by reading chapters in the Bible or by going to Church. It is of the nature of my internal, unmistakeable but appar-ently baseless Faith. My principles indeed have never been severely tested but I believe they would lead me to reject the most present & tangible pleasures for the most distant and abstract good.

But to pass to less heavy subjects, Miss Bronte describes in Jane Eyre, the inmost construction & motives of a mind as I have never seen them described in any other case. The same is true of Mr Rochester and in a greater or less degree of all the other charac-ters. One thing, too, which distinguishes her most virtuous heroes and heroines, is that there is nothing angelic about them. she displays firm moral principles & good original minds as few others have done, but she always adds the imperfections of spirit or temper which go to make up the human character.

I said that I was greatly in need of a *friend*. There is another want I also experience and of which these books of Miss Bronte have reminded me. I would give anything to find a person *better than myself*. Whom I could respect, admire, and look up to. I really cannot say (what a shocking absence of all conventional humility) that I meet such here. At home I must do; when near such a person I should feel as if I were sailing with the tide. With him (or her) what I think well of in myself would go for nothing. My faults only would stand out.

As I make no question that you wish me home, I daresay you will not be displeased to find that I am not absolutely contented with this place. The result of the most earnest & impartial reflection on the subject comes out more & more plainly to the effect that I must not linger here. When I leave here all of a sudden, & still more when I unexpectedly turn up in England, everybody will ask why I leave a good position & comfortable circumstances here and cast myself adrift again. But no matter; it is sufficient that I have reasons within myself, or that I am not contented to be an assayer of gold all my days, or to rust in a distant colony & different climate till my mind & body are equally unfitted for the society & air of England. *We* know reasons why it should not be. While taking such a step I am not thoughtless as to the consequences; it may be long before I am so comfortably circumstanced again, or it may be never. Still I feel, so to speak, that a hard struggle through the bush toward the right point will be better than miles of smooth walking along good roads away from it. God grant however that I may meet smooth roads instead of bush in England, figuratively as well as literally. But you would scarcely believe what a change in my thoughts the turn of the year has made. Before I thought of myself as a naturalised Australian. Now I am an English Exile waiting for the approaching opportunity to return. Already I look upon my study & my laboratory with the fond eye of one about to leave them, and already I have ceased to undertake any extensive alterations. This is all because what was before counted in years is now counted in months. Within twelve months I hope to make a start; within about two years (D.V.) to see you again. My remaining time here seems so short that I am already putting on a greater pressure of steam to get through the necessary work. But it does not do to dwell too much on the future, which is always uncertain, though we ought undoubtedly to plan it out beforehand and attempt to conform to that plan; now to more immediate subjects.

Music is ever to me the same; a part of my soul; but I have not played so much lately, because it robs me of time, and when I am buried in Mendelsohn Mozart or Haydn the clock fingers go round so fast, that the evening seems half to vanish and my work consequently remains tangibly undone. I find myself a little capricious in music, and poor old Handel might well be in the dumps at present if he looked only to my favour. Mendelsohn is all the go, and I play little except his "St Paul" and "Elijah". These oratorios I regard as quite equal to any of Handels excepting the Messiah & Israel in Egypt *in some respects*. Considering too that Mendelsohn wrote music of all kinds, & all of the most beautiful kind while Handel wrote oratorios only, one cannot but think Mendelsohn the greater musician. I have an uncomfortable conviction that Handel is rather overestimated in England at present. Mozart as I said in my lectures to you, is the musician *par excellence*; he stands alone as the writer of *pure music* of universal style & universal character. Handel is the writer *par excellence*, of *oratorios*. Mendelsohn is equal to the last, & next below the former. Surely he must hold the second place. Then come a crowd of others; Beethoven Haydn, Weber, Rossini, Spohr etc etc in a very slowly descending line; it is unnecessary to judge between them because they are all different in style & subject.

Does it surprise you to consider that a great part of the finest music is a thing of the present day. Mendelsohn is only a few years dead; I remember reading of his death in the paper. Rossini & Spohr are still alive. In some moods there is nothing I like better than the gloomiest strains from the "Last Judgement" of the one, or the "Stabat Mater" of the other.

But to return, the "St Paul" of Mendelsohn is a fine thing when you get fairly into it. It is perhaps rather slow and heavy, but grand & massive in some parts and extremely pathetic in others. There are also some surprising oratorial parts. Such as "Now we are Ambassadors". The air "But the Lord" is only to be compared with "O Rest in the Lord" in Elijah.

Mint. Febr. 10th. I hope you will like the enclosed photographs which I have been working at very hard lately. I send also my last paper on clouds, though I dare say it will not much interest you.

I REMAIN, WITH BEST LOVE/YOUR EVER AFFEC. BROTHER./W S JEVONS.

It strikes me that it is some time since you last wrote.

Bronte] Charlotte Brontë published *Jane Eyre* (1847) and *Shirley* (1849) under the pseudonym of 'Currer Bell'

GEORGE DUNMORE LANG

George Dunmore Lang (1832–74) was the son of the prominent colonial clergyman and politician John Dunmore Lang (1799–1878) (see Letter 38). As a bank manager, the junior Lang had been charged in 1854 with embezzlement and sentenced to five years hard labour. His father passionately defended his son, eventually securing his release in 1857. This thoughtful letter is a voice of colonial conscience on the vexed topic of Aboriginal crime and punishment. It was written not long after Lang's release and is addressed to his uncle, the pastoralist Andrew Lang.

35. TO ANDREW LANG, 31 MARCH 1858

MY DEAR UNCLE,

Allow me to congratulate you on your newly acquired senatorial honors and to hope that, now the Upper House has received so strong a body of liberal numbers into its late exclusive and impracticable ranks, it may be rendered more effective in advancing the interests of the state. I write to you at the present moment more particularly to make you acquainted with the proceedings of the Native Police Force in this district and of the inhabitants generally, in reference to the Blacks; and I am sure you will not only be astounded but indignant and disgusted with the details that I have to communicate to you.

When I first arrived in this district the topic of general conversation was the murder of the Frazer family on the Dawson by the Blacks of that district and the hope was universally expressed that the atrocious actors in that tragedy would meet with condign punishment. I joined in this hope believing in good faith that no illegal nor dishonourable not to say barbarous nor inhuman means should be resorted to for that purpose. On my way to the interior, however, I was undeceived as to the proposed method of punishing the Blacks and I now know that nothing could have been more unworthy of human beings that the procedure both of the members of the Police Force and the white population than their horrid indiscriminate murders of the Blacks.

I learned from various sources that a party of twelve—squatters and confidential overseers—went out mounted and armed to the teeth and scoured the country for blacks, away from the scene of the murder of the Frazers altogether, and shot upwards of eighty men women & children. Not content with scouring the scrubs & forest country they were bold enough to ride up to the Head Stations and shoot down the tame blacks whom they found camping there. Ten men were shot in this way at Ross's head station on the Upper Burnett, several at Prior's Station and at Hays and Lambs several more. The party in scouring the bush perceived an old blind blackfellow upon whom they immediately fired sending a ball through his back, another through his arm which shivered the bone to pieces and a third grazed his scalp. This old man had been for a long time a harmless hanger on at the different head stations and of course could have been in no way identified with the Frazer murderers. A black boy belonging to Mr Cameron of Conambula long employed by that gentleman in carrying messages & rations to his out stations and in going with drays to Gayndah & Maryborough, went to Mr Prior's station on the Burnett and was shot there. A blackfellow was captured in the bush by an armed blackfellow in the employ of Mr Hay who supplied him with a carbine for the purpose. The black brought his prisoner to the Head Station, tied him to a sapling in the presence of all the white residents and having addressed him in the broken English in the most cruel & disgusting manner, placed the muzzle of his carbine to the helpless man's arm and broke it with the first shot he then addressed him again in the same strain as before & shot him through the head.

The Native Police say they have shot over 70 blacks. One of their acts deserves especial notice. They arrived at Humphrey's Station, went to the Blacks encamped near the house, bound two of the old men and led them into the scrub and deliberately shot them; the cries of the two poor wretches were heard by the superintendent's family at his house. I had supposed that these things although acted with seeming openness in the far interior and with evident impunity would not be tolerated in more civilized society and that the neighbourhood of Maryborough the Chief town in the District could not be disgraced by any such barbarities. I was mistaken however. On the evening of Friday & Saturday last the white police accompanied by some white volunteers proceeded to the Blacks Camp near Mr Cleery's homestead between the old & new townships of Maryborough and drove every man woman & child out of it, then set it on fire destroying all the clothing, bark tomahawks & weapons of the blacks and burning wilfully the Blankets which at no inconsiderable expense are sent out to the blacks yearly by the Government. The party of whites then followed and shot a boy of twelve years of age dead—a lad well known in town as a harmless, helpless lunatic and wounded a man with a ball in the thigh, besides. Yesterday the Native Police force under the orders of their white officers performed the same meritorious action for the Blacks in Maryborough setting fire to their Camp, destroying their clothing & blankets and driving numbers of them into the river in sight of the whole town population. Not content with this the Native Police proceeded to the boiling down station about a mile from town and deliberately shot dead two old black men and a young one. I have witnessed no actual murder but I have witnessed scenes that I considered, occurring where they did, in the heart of town, libels on the very humanity of the people, a disgrace to its magistrates its storekeepers its fathers & sons & everything British in the place. For instance the spectacle of a blackfellow endeavouring at the public wharf at eight o'clock last Sunday night, to construct a frail raft of sheets of bark to carry over a river as broad as the Hunter at Raymond Terrace and twice as rapid, a child twelve months old and another but ten days old and all this because he had been chased from his fire and threatened with a ball from a carbine by a ruthless wretch wearing the queen's livery. I may say that the current was so strong and the mother of the infant so alarmed for it that the black in mercy returned when half over the river and gave her her child. I thought that single act more eloquent of the wrongs of the blacks than a hundred lectures and I almost regretted I belonged to the same race as those who caused it. The Blacks must be protected. They suffer a hundred times more at the hands of the whites than the whites do from them. When it is found necessary to punish the blacks a rigid search must be instituted for the cause of the necessity and no indiscriminate selections allowed.

The whites punish & persecute without discrimination: is it to be wondered at then, that the blacks, following the example set them, revenge their wrongs without discrimination too. Blood for blood is the only remedy I can see; if the Government will not institute a proper search, protect the blacks and punish the whites; seeing moreover that the blacks conduct themselves properly and be made thoroughly acquainted with the laws of property & the consequences of infringing them, the result of it all will be that some person will furnish the blacks with firearms and set them in the way of revenging themselves upon their oppressors.

Such interference on the part of the Government is necessary not only for the safety of the Blacks but for the security of all such persons as the members of the Frazer family, who were made to suffer for the misdeeds of others. I suppose you have said long ago where are your magistrates. What are they all about. I reply our magistrates are all here and they might as well be at Jericho. They do not care a fig for either law or justice and in short knowing how matters stand they are as guilty of every act of cruelty as the actual perpetrators of them. They are traitors every man of them and unworthy the confidence of the people.

I do not mean to apologize for troubling you for you are public property now and you see I know it; but the fact is I feel so strongly on the matter that I deemed it necessary to write to save me from taking actual proceedings at once.

Hoping you are well & desiring to be remembered kindly to my aunt & Caroline when you see them and to my aunt Ellen. I remain your affectionate nephew

GEORGE D. LANG

Peter Smith

Glorious failure that it was, the Burke and Wills expedition of 1860–61 has passed into Australian legend. Historian Tim Bonyhady has noted that Burke had 'no experience as a surveyor or bushman, was ignorant of navigation and his only interest in exploration had been to subscribe two shillings and sixpence to the Exploration Fund in 1858 ...' In a testimonial letter to the Secretary of the Exploration Committee, Peter Henry Smith placed a premium on some very different qualities.

36. To John Macadam, 7 February 1860

My dear Dr

My friend and brother officer Mr Robert O'Hara Burke Supt of Police in charge of this district is most anxious to obtain Command of the Expln. Party—Sir Wm. Stawell is acquainted with Mr Burke, and I believe will give him his vote and Interest—Mr Burke is an honorable man, was for many years Captn in a dragoon Regt in Austria where he distinguished himself—subsequently held a Commission in the Irish Constabulary and is now a Supt. in Our Police. Mr Burke speaks and writes French, German & Italian. He is a most active man & very strong—most temperate in his habits—and is kind & gentle in his manners, but possessing a strong will, Ambitious—and has been accustomed to command from Boyhood—Mr Burke is prepared to give up his present Appointment to succeed to that of yours.

In conclusion I am Confident from my knowledge of Mr Burke that there is not another Gentleman in this Colony possessing so many of the qualifications necessary to the success of the undertaking in question as my friend Burke.

I am my dear Dr/Yours truly/P Smith

Charles Nicholson

Statesman, landowner, businessman, connoisseur and physician, the English-born Sir Charles Nicholson (1808–1903) exercised a civilising urbanity in colonial Australia. Among his varied achievements in Victoria, New South Wales and Queensland, he was one of the founders of the University of Sydney and a generous patron of the arts and sciences.

37. To Adelaide Ironside, 20 July 1860

My Dear Miss Ironside

I have just received your letter of April 10th and rejoice to hear of your progress. I know not whether you ever see Colonial papers; or have an opportunity of knowing how your claims upon Australia were brought forward by your friend Dr Lang. If you have I think you will give me credit at all events for not being the *least* discreet of your friends in Australia. I can assure that I regretted very much the mode, [of Dr Lang's approach] which although kindly intended, was I think most injudiciously set about.

I still sigh to see old Rome once more. Having tasted the inspiration of Italy I cannot reconcile myself to the Gum trees and Kangaroos, the objects and aims of Colonial life. I have come to the conclusion, that a people *cannot* be *truly civilized*, or possess a high *moral organization* that is without 'Art', or any of its manifestations. Australia may be like America, rich and prosperous. The people will have plenty to eat and wear—they will live in handsomely furnished houses,—but they will be destitute of all those elevating and refining influences which spring from a familiarity with the *past*—from the contemplation of high works in Architecture, sculpture, painting. Fortunately for those who have never left the Colony, they know not what they miss, whilst they make up by self sufficiency, and conceit for the lack of much that humanizes and ennobles mankind. The members of our legislature look upon any sixpence expended upon *other* than the most practical objects, as *absolute profligate waste*. If they could buy the whole Vatican *for 500 pounds* they would think *the bargain dear* whilst 99 out of every 100 would look upon the Transfiguration of Raphael, with the same devotion as upon a sixpenny print.

I have been residing at Queensland for a short interval filling the office of 'President of the Council', which I was pressed by my friend Sir George Bowen, to assume with the view of helping to inaugurate the new Government. The task having been accomplished (upon the whole I may say very successfully) and the new Colony promising to go on much more creditably than her older sisters, I return to Sydney in about a month, and seriously contemplate returning to Europe at the end of the year.

I sent you a copy of Shakespeare by a gentleman I met in France on my way out here. I think I parted with him at Marseilles. Did you ever receive it? An English Painter might I think find many suitable subjects for his pencil in our great poet. The difficulty would be for an artist to avoid treating any of the subjects traditionally. This I think you might avoid as most probably familiar with Shakespeare *as acted*.

Pray remember me to your mother, Mr Gibson, Mr McBean, and any one else who recollects or cares for yours very sincerely

C NICHOLSON

Dr Lang] John Dunmore Lang (1799–1878), Presbyterian clergyman, colonial politician and ardent republican   Sir George Bowen] George Ferguson Bowen (1821–99), first Governor of Queensland Mr Gibson] John Gibson (1790–1866), English sculptor and a leading member of the English expatriate artistic community in Rome

ADELAIDE IRONSIDE

Adelaide Eliza Ironside (1831–67) was the first native-born Australian artist to study abroad. She left Sydney for Europe in 1855 but Rome, where she settled in 1856, was her real destination both for artistic reasons and for its rich cultural traditions. She was also committed to the cause of the Italian patriots and the ideals of the 1848 revolution. As an artist, Ironside was determined to succeed on her own merits and by her own endeavours, but her death from tuberculosis cut short a promising career.

38. TO JOHN DUNMORE LANG, 3 NOVEMBER 1860

MY DEAR DR LANG

I received your letter dated August, and I must say that I was exceedingly sorry to hear that you had brought my name before the Council as a claim upon Australia.

I wish very much that you had consulted me before doing so, I am sure you did it with the kindest intentions but had you asked my opinion upon the subject I should have immediately said, No. It is quite impossible to the uneducated in Art even to impress upon them Art's own intrinsic value either to a Country or the improvement of the mind of the People—Art requires a life education and constant intercourse with its refining and beautiful creations to be able to fully appreciate its wants—therefore how could the Legislature of a young country like Australia nurtured in the struggles of contrary factions be supposed to conceive that the Fine Arts would raise her in the eyes of the whole world as they would, and will in time I trust most certainly do. My Country has every thing gifted of Nature, wealth unbounded, climate, and the glowing warmth of a Southern Sun, she is worthy of being the second Italy, all save Italy's appreciation and call strong from the heart for the Beautiful.

I do not call upon my Country, Australia must in time call for me!—the opinions of the *few*, who do not want [illegible] other than the narrow wealth will not be *eternal*, and I must beg of you my dear Doctor to tell publicly these Gentlemen of the Legislature, that I should never have taken a *fraction* from them even had they granted it and I have wanted *as a claim upon Australia*.

The time is not far off I trust when they will see that I am not dependent upon Australia for my fame. I do not rank any longer with students, I am now engaged upon a Picture which will make me Master of my Art and place me amongst its Professors. *England* knows how to appreciate and to reward the favorites of Nature. I shall never return to Australia until my fame is fully established in the old world, and that will not be D.V. long in coming—I see my way clearly before me. I suppose they would laugh at the idea of a little picture of mine a foot in width and 7 inches long being considered at a *moderate* price of 100 guineas!—In England pictures are valued at thousands of pounds and any price may be demanded and received when once an Artist has established his name. I must now beg of you dear Doctor, to make this letter public, acknowledging my utter ignorance of your kind intentions and of my *stern disapproval* of any such demand upon the Public Treasury of my Country.

I shall write you a long letter about many things when I hear from you again—as to the news of Italy you know more than we do, at Rome everything is shut up; even the telegraphs are all taken down from communicating with other parts. We can get no news of any direct movement of V. Emmanuel or of Garibaldi—they say that Garibaldi is within 20 miles of Rome or at the Ponte Mollo. I suppose we shall be bombarded soon. Come what may I shall go on with my Art, and cry "Viva Garibaldi", with the Republicans! P. Gavvazzi is at Naples crying down with the Madonna & the Saints for worship—Christ only is to [be] exalted—only to be worshiped! Mamma unites with me in the kindest regards to Miss Lucy and family & yourself and believe me yours very sincerely

A.E. IRONSIDE/AEI. DE AUSTRALIA

The Bible is sold publicly in the shops and caffes at Florence—everything is being fulfilled of which the [illegible] speaks.

> a claim upon Australia] John Dunmore Lang had tried unsuccessfully in the New South Wales Legislative Council to secure a government subvention of £200 p.a. for three years to finance Ironside's studies in Europe   V. Emmanuel] Victor Emmanuel II (1820–78), the first king of united Italy   Garibaldi] Italian patriot Guiseppe Garibaldi (1807–82), committed to overthrowing the hated papal government in Rome and the achievement of Italian unification   P. Gavvazzi] Alessandro Gavazzi (1809–89), Italian patriot and renegade priest much admired by Ironside who had met him in London. She found him 'indeed worthy of being the Ideall of Italy'

WILLIAM JOHN WILLS

One of the most poignant testimonies to the failure of the extravagantly equipped but disastrously executed Burke and Wills expedition is contained in the final letter which the explorer William John Wills (1834–61), not long before his lonely death at Cooper's Creek in South Australia, addressed to his father, Dr William Wills. In mid 1862 Dr Wills published an emotive account of the Burke and Wills story, A Narrative of a Successful Exploration through the Interior of Australia, *which drew on the letters and journals of his son.*

39. TO WILLIAM WILLS, 27 JUNE 1861

MY DEAR FATHER

These are probably the last lines you will ever get from me. We are on the point of starvation not so much from absolute want of food but from the want of nutriment in what we can get.

Our position although more provoking is probably not near so disagreeable as that of poor Harry & his companions; We have had every good luck and made a most successful trip to Carpentaria and back to where we had every right to consider ourselves safe. having left a Depot here consisting of four men twelve horses and six camels, they had sufficient provisions to have lasted them for twelve months with proper economy. We had also every right to expect that we should have been immediately followed up from [Miniminka?] by another party with additional provisions and every thing necessary for forming a permanent Depot at Coopers Creek. The party we left here had special instructions not to leave until our return, unless from absolute necessity. We left the Creek with, nominally, three months supply, but they were reckoned at little over the rate of half rations & we calculated on having to eat some of the Camels. By the greatest good luck at every turn we crossed to the Gulf through a good deal of fine country almost in a straight line from here. On the other side the camels suffered considerably from wet & we had to kill & jerk one soon after starting back. We had now been out a little more than two months and found it necessary to reduce the rations considerably, and this began to tell on all hands, but I felt it by far less than either of the others. The great scarcity & shyness of game & our forced marches prevented our supplying the deficiency from external sources to any great extent but we never could have held out but for the Crows & Hawks & the Portulac The latter is an excellent vegetable and I believe secured our return to this place. We got back here in four months & four days and found that the party had left the creek the same day & we were not in a fit state to follow them.

I find I must close this that it may be planted but I will write some more although it has not so good a chance of reaching you [then follow two words which are extremely faint and close to illegibility in the pencil-written original].

You have great claim on the Committee for their neglect. I leave you the sole charge of what is coming to me the whole of my money I desire to leave to my sisters. other matters I will leave for the present

ADIEU MY DEAREST FATHER/W.J WILLS

I think to live about four or five days. My religious views are not the least changed and I have not the least fear of their being so. My spirits are excellent.

poor Harry & his companions] a reference to Lieutenant Harry Le Vescomte, a cousin of Wills, who had perished on exploration in the Arctic   that it may be planted] the letter was recovered when a relief expedition found the bodies of the explorers in September 1861

Conrad Martens

As a young man, the artist Conrad Martens (1801–78) joined the scientific survey of Patagonia and Tierra del Fuego on board HMS Beagle. He formed a lasting friendship with the naturalist Charles Darwin (1809–82), which was maintained in later years by an affectionate and amusing correspondence. Martens arrived in Australia in 1835 where he became celebrated for his landscape paintings, especially his interpretations of Sydney Harbour.

40. To Charles Darwin, 20 January 1862

Many thanks old shipmate for your kind message which I have just recd by the padre, I thought you had quite forgotten that I was in existence and certainly ~~when a~~ the man who voluntarily sets himself down in such a place as this has no right to grumble if he finds such to be the case.

As it appears however that you have still two of my sketches hanging up in your room I hope you will not refuse to accept another which I shall have much pleasure in preparing and will send you by the next mail.

Your "book of the season" as the reviewers have it, I must own I have not yet read altho Mr Clarke offered to lend it me. I am afraid of your eloquence and I *don't* want to think that I have an origin in common with toads and tadpoles for if there is anything in ~~natur~~ human nature that I hate it is a toady, but of course I know nothing of the subject and they do make such microscopes now adays.

I suppose yours is one of the best that Ross could make by the by I got him to make two eyepieces for a reflector telescope just before he died ~~which~~ two metals for which I had succeeded in making of 6 & 7 feet focal length and so now I can show the good people here the mountains in the moon turned up side down as of course they ought to be when seen from the antipodes

but I must apologize for I suppose you don't laugh at nonsense now as you used to do in the Beagle or rather I suppose nonsense does not ~~now~~ come in your way.

Well, that was a jolly cruize, and I hope you have been well and happy ever since and that you may continue to be so for long time to come is the sincere wish of your old shipmate

I wonder whether the Admiral what is now, I should like to send my kind regards, if you should see him, but, don't if you don't like, coffee without sugar, you know.

"book of the season"] Charles Darwin's celebrated and controversial *On the Origin of Species by means of Natural Selection* had appeared in London in 1859

ELLEN KEAN

London actress Ellen Kean (1806–80) played opposite her husband Charles on their Australian tour of 1863, under contract to Australian entrepreneur George Coppin. They had only a moderate success with audiences in Sydney, Melbourne, Bendigo and Ballarat, some of whom found their style too subdued. Their status, however, ensured fashionable upper middle class patrons and good box office returns for expensive seats. Ellen's letter to her daughter Mary was written from Ballarat.

41. TO MARY KEAN, 23 FEBRUARY 1864

MY DEAREST MARY

I posted my letter to you this morning at St Kilda. We started by railroad at half past eleven o'clock from Melbourne, and arrived in this most strange place at ½ past three. We have passed through a country (for four blessed hours) about as interesting as Salisbury plains minus Stonehenge. All appears "flat and unprofitable" the whole way, but we reach this place by a gentle rise which brings us 2.000 feet above the level of the sea and the flats are not unprofitable being excellent sheep walks. All is now however so dried up by the sun that it has a very sterile appearance. When you get within a few miles of Ballarat there is a little variety of scene. You see hills in the distance, a patch of primeval gum forest with here an iron hut and there a wooden one or a strange looking long building, the Hotel of the woods.

[sketch here of "Forest Home Hotel"]

The gum tree stems grow all sorts of ways just [as] I have put the three things above. They say a gum forest in perfection is like a Cathedral aisle but I have not seen any such perfection yet. I have grown to think an old gum tree a fine venerable looking thing but I see no beauty yet in a *gum forest*.

We saw innumerable Magpies. They are not so handsome as our Magpies either in plumage or shape and they are black where ours are white, and white where ours are black. I also saw several Rosellas. As we neared Ballarat we began to see the shafts of some small mines, and in the near distance many large ones. The town does not look like anything I ever saw before. It is neither English, continental or Yankee. It is "the diggings". I enclose you the view opposite our Hotel window.

The Hotel is *first rate* with every convenience and excellent cooking. They give us good soup stewed sole (native sole) a [illegible] of veal and wild duck, an excellent light pudding and fresh apple tartlets, good sherry and good soda water. The air is sharp and cold but I think pleasant and invigorating.

This place is only ten years old. It has now much fallen off and the people complain of bad times. When gold was first discovered here it was what they call *surface gold*, that is, it was on the alluvial soil and all the capital a man required was a spade, a tent, some tea and coffee and some biscuits and preserved meat. The luxury of a Parrot Pie was at his command if [he] chose to go "*a birding*". He had nothing to do but to dig in easy ground and the earth teemed with wealth. *They ran mad with luck* and in bravado would eat five pound notes between their bread and butter as money sandwiches. All at once they came to quartz and to grief. The soft soil stopped and the stone proved too hard for the pick-axe. Now they have to blow up the rocks and have steam crushing machines to extract the gold. Companies are formed great expenses incurred and latterly no amount of gold has been found to remunerate them for their great outlay. Now the favorite place is *Gipps Land* but it is in quartz there, and requires capital to work it, it is besides on a mountain and no road by which to convey machinery. We passed part of the land coming from Sydney. Mr Coppin gave a dinner to 50 people in Melbourne yesterday and in his speech told them that Charles Kean that Prince of good and worthy fellows had enabled him to pay his creditors 20 shillings in the pound. It is true, our engagements have lifted him out of debt. We all like Coppin. We find him a very honest minded man, much respected and looked upon as very trustworthy.

I can see nothing and hear nothing in this country to warrant the character he has got in England of being a dangerous person to deal with. He makes excellent terms for us everywhere and sticks up for Papa's interests. He is very fond of Patty, and I think likes me. We all got on very well. Our engagement for California was signed to day, so we really do go and Coppin goes with us.

Patty has managed a beau although she has not been here many hours. A box has arrived from a Mr Marsden filled with roses and carnations. And for the matter of that *so have I*, for Mr Everett has bought me a magnificent bouquet of roses from a digging called *Sebastopol*. Our room is *oderous*.

Wednesday 24th. We have all had a good night in good beds, clean blankets and sweet linen sheets and have enjoyed an excellent breakfast of capital black tea, *fillet de boeuf a la Parisien*, fresh eggs and good bread and butter. Wonderful lodging and fare for a town in the wilderness not yet twelve years old. There is quite a colony of Chinese here and we heard the tum tum and the gong at their theatre until quite late last night. There is a Christian Chinese minister here with his wife and baby all in full costume but we have not yet seen them. We go to the theatre at 12 o'clock and Papa has just read in the morning paper that they are to deliver an address to us on the stage, not right to take him so by surprise, but he is sure to say a few pithy words in reply.

I should like you to see this place, it is so curious. The morning is bright and fresh and is like a clear morning with us early in May.

It is now decided that we go to California. The deed was signed yesterday by Mr Coppin in Melbourne witnessed by the American consul, but our time for starting is not settled. It may be in the month of May and perhaps not until June.

I enclose you the announcement here. The prices are high, ten shillings dress boxes, six shillings stalls, five shillings upper boxes, four shillings pit and three shillings gallery.

Now Goodbye, God bless you darling. Papa is *so* well this morning. The place will agree with him.

YOUR AFFECTIONATE MOTHER/ELLEN KEAN.

Mr Coppin] George Selth Coppin (1819–1906), actor-manager, insolvent in 1851, repaired his fortunes by promoting tours such as that of the Keans   Patty] Patty Chapman, niece of the Keans   Mr Everett] George Everett, an actor in the Keans' company

CHARLES KEAN

A son of the celebrated tragedian Edmund Kean, actor-manager Charles Kean (1811–80) expected to revolutionise colonial taste on his tour of 1863. His letter from Melbourne to his daughter Mary reflects his disappointment with tepid audiences, dislike of the climate and conditions and the illness which had interrupted the tour.

42. TO MARY KEAN, 22 APRIL 1864

MY DARLING MARY,

I am so occupied with one thing and another that I can only write a few lines to tell you how grieved and vexed I am at your accident. It is a great comfort to know that you are under Fergusson. He is now the *first* surgeon of England. Strange that you should have suggested my sending him a present for I had ordered one to be prepared a fortnight since and it started by the sailing ship *Roxburgh Castle* the day before yesterday and may be expected in London Docks about the middle of July. It consists of 2 cases composed of Emeu eggs mounted in silver and are very beautiful. They are directed to George St. Tomorrow at one o'clock I and your mother are summoned to the Town Hall to hear an address read to us by the Mayor of the city and which has been signed by all the important people here.

The signatures are headed by the Ministers followed by the members of both Houses of the Colonial Legislature. Of course the Governor's name is not attached to it for as the representative of Majesty it would be out of place and contrary to custom. Of course I shall have to make a speech in reply, which you well know always makes me nervous.

Tomorrow being the anniversary of Shakespeare's birthday, has been chosen for the presentation and in the evening we perform *four* different acts of his plays, namely in the fourth (trial scene) of *M. of Venice*, Jacques scenes in 2nd act of *As you like it*, then 2 scenes out of *Romeo and Juliet* in which your dear Mother will act the Nurse for the 1st time and Patty Juliet ! To finish with the 3rd act of *King John* so there's a hard night's work.

Cathcart tells me on the authority of his wife's last letter that our Susan and Elizabeth were engaged at the Princess's to dress the children in the Pantomime. Rather a fall from dressing Mr. and Mrs. Kean !

We finish here next Saturday and on the 4th May and three following evenings we act in Sandhurst (the second mining city of the Colony) receiving £100 pr. night for our services. On the 9th and 10th May we give readings at Geelong, ditto here on the 11th and 12th and the same at Ballarat on 13 and 14 May. Monday week we go to a ball at Mrs. Fellows. He, Mr. Fellows is one of the leading barristers here and till lately was in the Ministry. Mrs. F. is one of the leaders of fashion here. Next Sunday we dine with Sir Redmond Barry one of the Judges. The first steamer after the 15 May will convey us all to Sydney and about the middle of June we hope to get a vessel to San Francisco.

If you have any doubt of finding a *home* till our return to England you had better pay Miss Hebert £200 pr. annum and make her house your head quarters.

I do not like your going out begging to be taken in anywhere. You will see how the land lies and act accordingly but remember you must not live in lodgings alone that would never do for my daughter.

I am very fidgety about it altogether. I hope the Youngs will take compassion on you.

I shall be delighted to get away from these Colonies for I neither like the climate or the people.

Patty, strange girl, says she would rather live in St. Kilda than any place she has ever seen after Paris ! Paris first, St. Kilda next ! ! Why the very insects here are enough to disgust one. The swarms of flies are truly a plague, spiders crawl upon your pillow, some poisonous. The mosquitoes are counted by myriads. I have totally lost all appetite through these wretches.

At breakfast I am compelled to place my saucer over my cup making hasty snatches at my tea to prevent the flies falling into it. The weather is cooler now but yet these disgusting creatures do not diminish. This is Town life, but in the country it is truly awful. Snakes and everything horrible you can think of. I stood Godfather and your Mother was Godmother last Wednesday which cost me £10 in a present to the blessed baby whose name is Charles Edward Kean Patmore, Edward being the name of the other Godfather. The child has capital lungs for he squalled magnificently all through the service. The Nurse was so proud of the Sovereign I gave her that she declares she will never part with it.

Patty has grown very thin. I think her family bother her, her brother John through our influence got a job in the Government printing house the other day for a fortnight but was dismissed at the termination of the first week. Patty tells me because there was not sufficient type to supply all the hands. I hope for her sake and for his that may be the true version but I am afraid it is not so. What is to become of him and that fool Maria I do not know, both are out of employment now and nothing seems to offer.

They have one and all, Patty and Nancy excepted, behaved so badly to me that it has destroyed all ties of tenderness and care on my part towards them. Fancy during my illness at Sydney when the daily telegrams intimated I was dying, that girl Maria never wrote one line to her sister inquiring after me, not one word has she written to Uncle and Aunt since our arrival in the Colony. Is it not my dear Child enough to harden the kindest heart.

I wish I were at home again safe and sound taking my farewell round of acting.

America will assist my retiring pension I expect by at least £2,000 to £3,000, perhaps more. The poor little Doctor won't like this Yankee trip.

Did you ever hear of an insect somewhat resembling a grasshopper, called a mantis. Well one of these gentlemen fell on my newspaper the other morning while reading in bed, in the act of devouring his breakfast which consisted of a good fat fly which he tightly held in his long arms. Such are the pleasures of Australian life. The wind is now howling in the most piteous manner although the Sun is shining brightly.

God bless you my beloved girl/Your affec.^{T.} Father

Sandhurst] now Bendigo, a major Victorian provincial city   Sir Redmond Barry (1830–80)], Irish-born Supreme Court judge, was a leader in Melbourne cultural life

RACHEL HENNING

Rachel Henning (1826–1914) came to Australia in 1854 to join her brother; after two years of homesickness she returned to England. In 1861 she came back to Australia and happily accepted the challenges of pioneering on Exmoor, her brother's cattle run, inland from Port Denison (Bowen), Queensland, until her marriage in 1866. A series of letters to her sister and brother-in-law in England, Henrietta (Etta) and Thomas Boyce, charts Rachel's daily life: a selection was published in 1951–52 in the Bulletin *and later in book form.*

43. To Henrietta ('Etta') Boyce, 18 April 1865

My dearest Etta

We received your double letters by the last mail. You will imagine that the contents were very welcome & equally dispiriting. I really believe we owe this legacy of Mrs Taunton to Aunt Henrietta for the old lady could never have even known our names except from her. I think like you that the pleasure of this piece of good fortune is much marred by Amy & Biddulph being left out. I think perhaps she has selected those of the family who wanted it most. I hope now Tregenna will pay his debt to Mr Sloman & very likely he will go home. I think it is far the best thing he can do. I have had so much writing to do & have been so busy with starting Biddulph for the Port that I have hardly yet taken in how much better off I am than I was before. Nearly one third richer. I can hardly fancy it & Uncle William seems to think that we & yourself (the females mentioned in the extract from the will Mr Boyce sent us out) will be able to get our shares sold out & handed over free & unfettered a great thing for those married or going to be. I feel very much obliged both to Aunt & to the unknown friend who has left us the money it has made me well off at once & Annie probably will be able to be married.

And now I must thank you my dearest Etta for your share in the watch parcel altho' I have not yet seen it as it is not yet come from Sydney. I shall be delighted to have Enoch Arden for my own possession. I have seen it as I told you in my last letter & liked it

[82]

greatly but you do not half enjoy a poem in reading it once through. Tennyson's especially the book was only lent us for a short time by our neighbour Mr Paterson. Biddulph has no telescope & it is just what he will like tell Mr Boyce. I can hardly fancy dear little Constance big enough to work a kettle holder. I shall like it so much as her work. It is vexing we were not at Sydney when the parcel arrived. I have written to Emily to send it on here at once to Port Denison that is to be got here by the first opportunity. I want exceedingly to see the [illegible] sketches. I wish they were come up. Biddulph liked the idea of seeing Parr Hennings genealogies though I dont think he is exactly prepared to believe them. I thank you for sending me the stamps. I am afraid you paid for them unless they came out of the [illegible] interest.

I am very sorry to hear of Aunt Vizard's serious illness. I wished I could have been with her to nurse her for my own sake I mean for I have no doubt she was taken every care of. She told me some time ago she had heart complaint. It is very sad to think I may never see her again. She was always so very kind to me & I have spent such pleasant days at that beautiful Dunsley. I do not suppose they will ever come back again.

You will see that I have been troubling Mr Boyce with a commission again & Annie ditto you perhaps you will some day both take a trip to London to execute them for us. If you do accompany Mr Boyce as I hope you will do not "hold his hand". We want almost the best plain watch that he can get & are prepared to pay accordingly. I forgot to mention about sending it out when I was writing to him. I suppose it would be best sent by a parcel & insured. Not to the Tuckers they really must not be bothered any longer but directed to *Biddulph* care of Mess*rs* Danpar Gilchrist & Co. Sydney. As you know the watch is a present to B from A & I.

Biddulph left us yesterday for Port Denison whither he has gone to load his drays and start them for the Flinders river Station they are to take supplies for a year for the Colony out there. I do not think we shall ever go out there to live. I hope Biddulph will sell it & keep Exmoor. he talks of doing so & I should be so sorry to leave this place. He set off quite in style yesterday driving the buggy & pair & with his big hairy dog "Tiger" running after him & Jimmy one of the black-boys riding on horseback behind the said Jimmy being gorgeous in new white trousers slightly too large for him a scarlet crimean shirt & scarlet cap. Biddulph bought scarlets for both the black-boys when he was last in Sydney they are so fond of bright colours & look best in them. Nearly all the squatters take a black-boy with them when they are going a journey as a sort of groom they are very useful to get up the horses of a morning &c. Biddulph has a great many things to bring up from the Port & this is the reason he drove down instead of riding among other things we have bothered him with commissions to get us boots & winter petticoats as we are sure to be here through the winter—I think B will be away about ten days I hope he will not be more.

Old Mrs Lack is staying with us now. She is the mother of the Mr Lack who owns Blenheim the next station to this she was here for two or three days last year now she has been here about a fortnight & will stay a week longer. She is rather a nice old lady very gentle & lady-like though slightly meandering but when you have lived a long time in the bush you get lazy & do not like the trouble of entertaining anybody. Gentlemen visitors are different as they entertain themselves or you. Mrs Lack rode on horse-back the first 5 miles of the way & we drove over with Buddulph in the buggy & met her about 8 miles from here & I rode the horse home as we thought she would be tired. She goes home next Friday I believe. Mr Lack is coming over on Thursday evening to slay beef for us & takes his mother back next day.

I told you when I last wrote that after all Biddulph had not to go to Rockhampton in March as the cause was put off till September. He is sure to go then & Annie & I shall probably go so far with him & then go on to Sydney he certainly will not be able to accompany us at that time of year as it will be just before lambing & shearing but I suppose we shall go as we shall then have been up here three years & it will be getting time to see Amy again besides w$^{\underline{h}}$ there will be many purchases to make by that time. I do not know whether Annie means to be married then or not. Mr Hedgeland is not come back from the Flinders yet. There is nobody on this station except ourselves till Mrs Lack goes & B comes back.

We are having a new fire-place built against the cold weather comes tho' at present there seems no chance of any cold the hot weather has lasted longer than usual this year & it is still hotter than any English summer in the middle of the day but the mornings & evenings are cool and pleasant. The old fire-place which was a great farm-house "ingle" the whole width of the room was taken into the room when it was papered the new one is smaller & is built outside again & is to be lined with stone & have iron dogs for burning the wood. The side-board will have to be moved to make room for it.

I have been telling Aunt that the first grave has been made at Exmoor an event in the history of the station a family travelling with two drays & horse teams passed the house & camped over the creek one evening a few weeks ago & a man came up after dark to ask for some medicine &c for his little girl who had been ill a fortnight of diptheria I should think from his description. We gave him some milk & promised to come & see the child next day but at daylight next morning he came over & told Biddulph the child had died in the night & asked for some old cases to make a coffin. B offered to have one made & send it over but he preferred doing it himself. We asked if his wife would like us to come & see her but he said she would rather not which I did not wonder at. B also offered to come over & read the service when they buried the child but he said he did not care about it so we could do nothing for them. He had 3 children this was the eldest a little girl of 5. There were several men with the drays & they buried her in the morning & then harnessed their horses & went on their way. I went across the creek in the evening to where they had camped it was very sorrowful to stand by the little lonely nameless grave among the gum-trees and think what it must have been to the poor mother to drive away that morning & leave her little child among strangers. We did not even know their names. The grave is in a beautiful spot on a high bank shaded by trees & the creek flowing beneath. It is fenced in most securely with whole trunks of trees so that it can never be disturbed. That is the first grave. I thought who can tell whose the next will be?

The mailman is just come in so I must not write any more now. My kindest love to yourself and the children. I wonder do they rejoice as we used to do at the coming on of spring & the buttercups & daisies coming out & the hawthorn in blossom on the downs. I think it w<u>d</u> be pleasant to be a child again.

GOODBYE ONCE MORE MY DEAREST ETTA./BELIEVE ME YOUR EVER AFFEC*te* SISTER/ RACHEL HENNING

Amy and Annie] Rachel's sisters   Biddulph] Rachel's brother

ANTHONY TROLLOPE

The novelist Anthony Trollope (1815–82) made two visits to Australia to see his son who lived on a country property near Grenfell, New South Wales. His first visit, in 1871–72, resulted in the publication of Australia and New Zealand *(1873). In an amusing, if world-weary, letter written from Melbourne to George Eliot (1819–80) and the writer George Henry Lewes (1817–78), Trollope contrives to give an account of colonial deficiencies. Eliot was then at the height of her fame as the greatest living English novelist.*

44. TO GEORGE ELIOT AND G.H. LEWES, 27 FEBRUARY 1872

DEAR FRIENDS,

I was so glad to get a letter from Priory! I ought to have written sooner myself;—but I am hurried from place to place, and have no rest for my foot, and do not do the things I ought to do. I am beginning to find myself too old to be 18 months away from home. Not that I am fatigued bodily;—but mentally I cannot be at ease with all the new people and new things. And I find myself asking myself that terrible question of cui bono every morning. I am struggling to make a good book, but I feel that it will not be good. It will be desultory and inaccurate;—perhaps dull, & where shall I be then?

Forsters first volume is distasteful to me,—as I was sure it would be. Dickens was no hero; he was a powerful, clever, humorous, and, in many respects, wise man;—very ignorant, and thick-skinned, who had taught himself to be his own God, and to believe himself to be a sufficient God for all who came near him;—not a hero at all. Forster tells of him things which should disgrace him,—as the picture he drew of his own father, & the hard words he intended to have published of his own mother; but Forster himself is too coarse-grained, (though also a very powerful man) to know what is and what is not disgraceful; what is or is not heroic.

Cigars! Yes, indeed, you in your comfort smoke cigars I dont doubt, and drink coffee, and look on the pleasant faces of books, and write with good ink at a comfortable

table,—and are civilized. I am reduced to the vilest tobacco out of the vilest pipe, and drink the vilest brandy and water,—very often in very vile company. But perhaps I shall live to get home when,—not the noctes cenae [que] deum—but the pleasant morning table may be spread for me again with just that sufficiency of the divine aura which rescues an hour of sensual enjoyment from any touch of reproach.

MY BEST & KINDEST LOVE TO BOTH—/YOURS ALWAYS/A. T.

Priory] the London house at 21 North Bank, Regent's Park, occupied by Eliot and Lewes from 1863 Forster] John Forster (1812–76), whose biography of Charles Dickens was published in three volumes 1872–74   noctes cenae [que] deum] nights and feasts of the gods, Horace, *Satires* 2.6.65

JOHN CROSS

John Walter Cross (1840–1924) was a merchant banker with a fine sense of British superiority. He visited Melbourne in 1872 to negotiate business matters on behalf of his family who had property investments in Victoria. In 1880 he married the great English novelist George Eliot. Widowed only seven months later, he published (1885) an account of Eliot's life based on her letters and journals. Writing to his mother from the Melbourne Club, Cross rather bit the hands of his various Australian hosts.

45. TO ANNA CROSS, 13 APRIL 1872

MY DEAREST MOTHER,

I wrote you a line last Monday by the California Steamer telling you of my arrival, and I will go on day by day since then. Not that there is much to say; but they are my impressions, such as they are.

I have been busy most mornings looking after business matters, which are more hopeful than I had anticipated. On Tuesday afternoon Robert Sellar took me over the Parliament Houses, the handsomest public building here. Only one front is yet finished, faced with a yellowish sandstone, and that is good enough; but the other front is in a most ghastly unfinished state—and it is the most important as it faces one of the principal streets, and the other looks more or less into space. They have a House of Commons & an Upper House, got up as much as possible after the English pattern, and a first rate Library. Altogether it is done in very good style—The House of Lords being a trifle gaudy and somewhat in a Gin Palace style of florid decoration. I daresay however in time when it is all finished that it will be a himposing hedifice.

The general impression left on one's mind by everything here is that their ideas are a good deal ahead of the capabilities of the place. In fact, it has to grow up to its institutions.

There is the same incongruity in the architecture as is noticed to exist in New York in a most entertaining article in a late 'Macmillan'—only more so : there are fewer palaces & more shanties. Very few of the shops or Houses in the principal streets are over two stories high, and very many only one storied wooden cottages. Still, the Town Hall, Post Office, and many of the Bank Buildings are really handsome, if a little ambitious.

The streets are extremely broad, but have no trees like New York. All the drainage is done by open gutters some four or five feet broad, running down the sides of the streets, which remind me very much of New Orleans. In fact the whole place is a sort of cross between New Orleans, Chicago, & San Francisco. The street this Club is in is Collins Street, which about answers to Broadway in New York : capital shops at the lower end— near the bay—and at the Upper end it is faced by the Treasury buildings, which are close to the Parliament Houses, which latter again are at the head of Bourke S^t to the South. The town is laid out rectangularly, with a very broad street such as this Collins Street, then a narrow street called Little Collins Street, & then a broad street again such as Bourke Street—and so on, alternating broad & narrow. The town covers a tremendous space of ground, and the good buildings are consequently very much detached from one another.

As far as I can make out no one lives in Melbourne, but as in Liverpool all the world goes to the suburbs. Doctors seem to me the only inhabitants for instance of the Upper part of Collins Street, which is I suppose the most desirable location in the town. And indeed one can't wonder at it, for the suburbs are very pretty and very comeatable. St Kilda for instance, which is within less than quarter of an hour of Collins Street by rail, is very much such a place as Bognor or any other small coast place—villas & the sea. Looking out from my window here in the Club, which is on the third story, I have a very pretty view of the surrounding country, for there is nothing between me & it but the houses on the opposite side of the street, and then the ground takes a dip; there is one further narrow street beyond and then one broad one, which latter is really a road with nothing on the other side but the country—so that as the dip is sufficient to let one see easily over the tops of the Houses, I have a really fine view when it is clear as far as the 'Dandenong Ranges', the name of some high hills 30 or 40 miles distant. It is rather a pretty rolling country, fairly wooded. Melbourne itself too is very rolling—Up & down hill, a good deal like Glasgow in that respect.

On Tuesday afternoon I went & presented my letter to Professor Irving (from Mr Jowett). He is a tall fine looking man with very deep set eyes which he looks down on the ground with in a shy sort of way; a very pleasant voice & manner; and knows a lot of William Sellar's friends. He has given up his chair at the University, and is now head Master of the Wesleyan School here & is very busy, so I only staid some ten or fifteen minutes with him, and have not seen him since. Next day I called on Professor Wilson, to whom Macmillan gave me a letter. He seems a clever little fellow, but he could not get through 'Romola', and his idea of a good novel is 'the Bramleighs of Bishop's Folly', so that we have not a bond of union in leeterature. He asked me to dine with him yesterday, but I was engaged to Mr Philip Russell, a cousin of George Russell & of course connected with the Elie.

Yesterday I called on Mr Yencken, and he asked me to dine also that evening, which I could not do; and I am going out to see Mrs Yencken on Monday. Tomorrow I am going to take an early dinner—it being the Sawbath—with a Mr Robert Simson, who is some connection of the Russells & had met Papa & Zibby at Elie years ago. He is a vulgar sort of fellow, but goodnatured & friendly, & I believe has a very pretty place in the suburbs. On Thursday night I dined with one of the young Hentys, who have done our business since McCulloch, Sellar & Co. ceased to act as our agents. They are decent respectable people, but slow to a degree. They had a very selfcomplacent Clergyman & his wife—a M^r & Mrs Vance, the former of whom told with a shudder how Jowett had examined him in Divinity at Oxford & seemed to consider the examination a joke—'in fact, his very eyes twinkled'. I can easily believe it!

The party at Philip Russell's last night was entirely of men—Simson, Robert Sellar, two or three other members of this club, and a Mr Officer who I think is some relation of D. Wood's, in whose marriage all the Fife people here seem to be interested! It was a capital good dinner—excellent wines, some very fair whist after dinner, and altogether very first chop colonial I have no doubt. Lots of 'capital jokes' on local subjects; but not what you would call feverishly gay to an outsider—though one's reception was most cordial and kindly. I should think the sort of thing very much like a Glasgow dinner. It was better than the Hentys, for though Madame H. is quite a pretty woman she was werry colonial, and he though a good fellow is a considerable prig with an absolute want of humor but apt to let off small jokes & feeble puns.

The Hentys live at a suburb called Kew some five miles from town, and Russell beyond Robert Sellar at St Kilda, so you may imagine from the distances that Melbourne is not a very sociable place. They seem to be divided up into small local cliques, and are all apparently very churchy. I don't think, my lambs, that the society as far as I have seen of it would be attractive.

There is a clear distinct difference between a colony & a new country like America. It is evident in Canada : it is equally—perhaps more—evident here. All you can say about Americans & American society is that they are different from English—here inferior, there superior; but this & all Colonial places I have seen are simply inferior English or Scotch. There is a distinct want of individuality about them. It is very curious : I wonder whether they would improve by being left to themselves. Certainly as far as I have seen the Americans are infinitely ahead of the others. There is a go & an independence about them that one doesn't find here. If I were an emigrating laborer I should not have one second's doubt about choosing the United States for my future. As far as one can see, however, that class are pretty well off here. There are no painfully visible paupers. No doubt there is some distress, but it is of a mild character—in fact, a man has only to go up country to get all the beef & mutton he wants every day of his life. I have not yet seen a beggar.

Then they have a most excellent Free Library here. I saw no end of working men reading there—and the education is lying there for them. The University too is very cheap; and with Irving as master of the Wesleyan School, a first class education is within the reach of large numbers. Wilson took me all over the University. He lives there in very nice rooms. None of the undergraduates reside. It is like a Scotch University in that respect. A fine stone building with a quadrangle, which will be handsome enough when finished, but like the parliament Houses with a great deal still to be done to make it look sightly.

In walking out to Russell's House yesterday R. Sellar & I went through the Botanical Gardens, which promise to be really very pretty. They are building a House for the Governor overlooking them, which is to cost £50,000. It's a pity they don't finish one thing before beginning another. The Yarra river runs through the gardens—a narrower stream than the Thames at Maidenhead, with plenty of skiffs & four oared wherries, not unlike dear Father Thames. The banks are well wooded, but not with pretty trees. The great tree here is the gum tree, which is an evergreen with pendulous leaves, but rather dreary.

19 April 1872

I dined with the Simsons on Sunday & again on Monday, when they had a little party with some young ladies. Style bad English—not interesting. On Tuesday I dined with the Yenckens, who live at Windsor, some 4 miles from the city. They have a very nice house which Fred. Druce built for them when he was out here. They have six nice children—two young ladies, the boy who was at home last year and two smaller boys, & a young one of 3 years. The eldest of the girls has been ill and looks delicate; but they seem a very happy & united family. After dinner Mr Yencken & his eldest daughter played charmingly together on the piano. The girls seem to go out a good deal, & altogether look very happy. Mrs Yencken, whom I had not seen before, is very nice and asked most affectionately after Anna & Albert.

On Wednesday I went to a large public ball at the Town Hall, principally to see the room, which is really very handsome; the company very common. Last night I dined with the R. Sellars who had a little party—not very lively; & tonight I am going to a large ball at a Mr Francis', a political gentleman. So you see I am having 'quite a gay time'.

Tomorrow I start up country to visit our Stations. I shall be back before the mail comes in from England—& oh! how glad I shall be to get your blessed letters & to hear how all the honorable famille are getting on, & what new flights of genius Alky Palky is exhibiting. I am wearying now for the 22 May, when I hope to get on board the good steamer 'Baroda'. I long to be back with you all. I daresay the Spring will be very lovely with you now, & before you get this it will be well on to summer & the woods will be leafy again. God grant that you may all have kept well through it all, & that this will find you strong & well, without trouble or grief. My soul longs to be with you.

Ever, with dearest love to one & all, Thine,/J.W.C.

Robert Sellar] (1828–1900), businessman who established the Melbourne firm of McCulloch, Sellar & Co in 1861   Macmillan] Magazine   Professor Irving] Martin Howy Irving (1831–1912), Professor of Classical and Comparative Philology at the University of Melbourne and, from 1871, headmaster of Wesley Grammar School. He was later vice-chancellor of the University of Melbourne   Jowett] Benjamin Jowett (1817–93), master of Balliol College and Regius Professor of Greek, Oxford University   Professor Wilson] William Parkinson Wilson (1826?–74), Professor of Mathematics and one of the four foundation professors of the University of Melbourne   'Romola'] George Eliot's novel published 1862–63   Philip Russell] pastoralist (1822?–92)   George Russell] pastoralist (1812–88)   the

Elie] Scottish coastal village which was home to members of the Cross and Russell families
Mr Yencken] Edward F. Yencken, accountant   Robert Simson] (1819–96), pastoralist and a member
of the Victorian Legislative Council 1868–78, a cousin of the Russells   Hentys] members of the
notable Victorian pioneering family. Cross probably dined with Herbert James Henty (1836–87), who
lived in the Melbourne suburb of Kew where he served as mayor 1868–69   Mr & Mrs Vance]
George Oakley Vance (1828–1910) and his wife Harriett. Vance was the first headmaster of Geelong
Grammar School. In 1870 he was appointed vicar of Holy Trinity Anglican Church, Kew, and was later
Dean of Melbourne   Mr Officer] Charles Myles Officer (1827–1904), pastoralist   Mr Francis]
James Goodall Francis (1819–84) represented Richmond in the Victorian Legislative Assembly 1859–74

John White

*Aboriginal dislocation has taken many forms in Australia but none more powerful than the
separation of Aboriginal people from their own land or 'country', precise areas to which clans
were attached. In this poignant letter, direct expression is given to the meaning of separation
as John White exhorts his former employer Samuel Pratt Winter (1816–78) to assist him to
return to 'my country'. White was resident at the Lake Condah Aboriginal Station in western Victoria, only a few miles away from the Wannon district where he was born.*

46. To Samuel Pratt Winter, 7 January 1877

Dear Sir

I want to come back to Wannon, I knew you ever since I was a boy you used to keep
us live, I recollect about thirteen or fourteen years ago when you used to travel about five
or six miles to bring us to your place, so will you be obliged to write to the government
to get us off this place, so if you will write to the government for us, and get us off here,
I will do work for you and will never leave you so I wish you to get us off this place, I
always wish to be in my country, and to be in my country where I was born, I'm in a
mission Station and I dont like to be here, they always grumble and all my friends are all
dead, I lost my friend Doctor Russel. I recollect him living at Hillgay when Mr and Mrs
Russel were young, and now we are old, and I am now miserable, all the Wannon black-
fellows are all dead and I am left, my poor uncle Yellertperne is dead he was quiet young
where he came here when I see his grave I always feel sorry, I cant get away without leaf
from the government. This country dont suit me, I'm a stranger in this county I like to
be in my county. When I used to places where I ought not to be Mr Russel used to get
me out, whenever I used to be on a Station I used to work.

Mr Jackson wanted to give us ground and we did not take it so I am very sorry that
we did not take it. This is all I have to say,

I remain/Your affectionate friend/John White

I knew you ever since I was a boy] Winter took a special interest in the Aboriginal people. At the end of
his life he had instructed his brother to bury him on the family property where the Aborigines lay, the
grave to be marked only by a large stone cairn.   Doctor Russell] Francis Thomas Cusack Russell
(1823–76), Anglican clergyman known as the 'Apostle of the Western district'

JAMES A. WATTS

During the last six months of 1880 thousands of visitors poured into Melbourne to attend the International Exhibition. James Watts (1845–1929), a saddler from Coleraine in the Western District of Victoria, was one of them. In a week of high excitement in the city, coloured by the dramas associated with the imminent execution of a notorious—and soon to be legendary—bushranger, Watts wrote a brief report to his wife.

47. TO ROSANNA WATTS, 7 NOVEMBER 1880

MY DEAR ROSE

I hope yourself and little ones are well, you must not feel disappointed that I did not get home at the time promised viz Sunday or Monday, the fact is I have not finished my Business with the wholesale Horses yet, but hope to do so tomorrow or Tuesday at furthest. I spent the best part of Two days at the "Exhibition" and really I could not convey a discription, as it would baffle a more graffic pen than mine. Exhibits representative of the different countries are beautifully displayed and so exaustive in variety that it would take three months to go carefully through them—but I shall be contented with three days. Louis was very foolish that he did not come as a visit to the Exhibition would well repay any Mechanic. I spent my Sunday between attending St Francis in the morning, visiting two large Troop Ships in the bay viz the "Wolverine" and "Emerald" which are two splendid boats, the officers and crew were most courteous to visitors and every thing was explained to us from "stem to stern". There is to be a grand review on next Tuesday and the Red and Blues are expected to turn out in large numbers, I would like to see it but I cannot give the time. Exhibition for choice—.

You will have noticed by the Press that a great number of the Melbourne people are signing Petitions for Ned Kelly's reprieve—and parties to my astonishment were posted with Pen and Paper at the entrance of St Francis. Scores of People, men, women & children could be seen signing their names before going in, and coming out of chapel. I gratified my curiosity by going to the Hotel where the crimnels friends are staying to have a look at them. Mrs Skillion is a fine looking woman but Kate Kelly looks very miserable and careworn and looks as if Trouble was eating her life away. "The unfortunates" appear to inlist a great deal of Public simpathy but it is, I hear, to no avail and the execution will take place as sure as there is a head upon his Shoulders—.

I saw John Robertson to day he called in at Smiths, he looks disgustingly bloated, and appears to be drinking as bad as ever, he still sports a pair of ponies about Melbourne but I hear his allowance is very small. I suppose Business still continues dull, I will be glad as soon as I can get my things shipped and start for Home.

I received a Telegram from Cunningham to get some Poney [harnesses?] for him— I saw him at the races but he did not mention anything about it—I will be glad if you can give the Shop as much of the time as you can spare, as I am passed the time I allowed to reach home.

I called at the Post Office twice expecting to hear from you, possibly you may write before I leave when I will glad to receive a letter—I hope yourself and the dear children are well as I am beginning to feel anxious and wish I was at home again with best love to yourself and little ones

I REMAIN YOURS FAITHFULLY/JAMES A. WATTS

St Francis] St Francis Roman Catholic Church, Lonsdale Street, Melbourne, erected 1841–45 "Wolverine" and "Emerald"] HMS *Wolverine* and HMS *Emerald* were part of a gathering of international naval vessels present for festivities associated with the Exhibition and the city's Spring Racing Carnival a grand review] Tuesday 9 November saw celebrations to mark the birthday of the Prince of Wales Ned Kelly] the bushranger, Edward Kelly (1855–80) who had just been found guilty of the murder of a police constable Mrs Skillion and Kate Kelly] Margaret Skilling (1857–96) and Kate Kelly (1863–98), sisters of Ned Kelly the execution] Kelly was hanged at the Melbourne gaol on the morning of 11 November after the Victorian Government rejected public petitions for a reprieve

MARGARET NIHILL

Written from Adelaide, this letter from Margaret Nihill (c. 1815– ?) to her ten-year-old great-nephew Henry Cudmore at Avoca Station, South Australia, reflects the early settlers' nightmare of the lost child and the wish to instruct through cautionary tales.

48. TO HENRY CUDMORE, 4 MAY 1882

MY DEAR HENRY

I would have sent you a letter long before this but the heat made me very weak, and Aunt Rebekah & myself were hoping Papa would be in town and that you might send us a letter by him, telling us how dear little Mary Avoca and yourself are, also our dear little Mowland and all about your own little garden, the birds, little lambs, and pretty playthings papa and uncles brought home from the exhibition—Ask Miss McIntosh if she will help you to write a little letter to me.

Your cousins James, and Arthur, are growing big boys. Arthur is very clever, and got a beautiful prize last Christmas for being good at his lessons.

Grandmamma was here today and brought us a present of some nice fish, a bottle of milk and some nice fresh butter.—Now I must tell you what happened a short time ago—two little boys went out for a walk by themselves, and lost their way in the wild bush. They were out all night in the cold and wet they lost their hats and boots, their poor little feet and hands were cut and bleeding from the prickly bushes, and walking on the hard ground, a great many people and the police were out on horse-back looking for them, at last they were found sitting under a tree in the scrub; in a sad plight so tired and hungry, they told their papa they would never again go out of sight of the house without someone to take care of them.

—And a week or two ago, another little boy went too near the river at Port Adelaide, where he was told not, he has not been seen since, it is feared he fell in and was drowned, and that the big fish have eaten him up!

So you see how naughty it is for children to go near the banks of a river when they are told not—

When you write tell me if you got the Christmas cards I sent you and little Mary, and if you like them, and be sure to say if Miss McIntosh thinks you are good children, and always very obedient—

Now dear I must say good bye, give our love to Papa, Aunt Netty and your uncles— you are to kiss Mary, little Mowland for aunt Rebekah and myself—

I am always your affectionate grand-aunt./Margaret Nihill

Avoca] name of pastoral property

Lucy Jones

This letter-diary written by the unknown Lucy Jones is one of many treasures discovered by Lucy Frost in manuscript collections and published in No Place for a Nervous Lady: Voices from the Australian Bush *(1984).*

49. To her family, 18 May 1883

My dear Aunts, Uncles, Grandma, Cousins, Nellie Tucker, and Birdie Price This must be passed round to you all.
My Diary

1st Day   Started from near Goolwa on a Monday   going up a hill dray pin slipped out, dray tipped up with furniture, fowls &c. Took Pa and boys over an hour to prop it up fasten pin and secure with chains, I drove spring cart, two horses. Scenery, trees and sand.

Camped in an old deserted house. Pa and Will got in broken window. Unscrewed door lock. Fine paddock, good well water. Ma and I slept in cart, boys and pa under dray. Too many fleas in old house. Slept in clothes and boots.

2nd Day   Rose at moonlight, started at sunrise. Cat got out box   rode rest of way on bedding in cart   sometimes on cart seat   Very rough road, horses took bad drinking muddy water, one fell down in dray shafts. Pa took him out, physiced him and whipped him along to keep him warm. Another horse fell down. Camped near fence, physiced all horses. Scenery, gum trees. Bad road. Camped at Mulgundawa opposite hotel. Passed lots of wild turkeys and native companions. Slept as before.

3rd Day   Started 6 o'clock a.m. Very cold, ice on water. Coorong on one side. Good road till reached Wellington, then hill of sand above axles, horses on *noses* pulling. Unloaded dray at Jetty, crossed in punt to pretty landing place, willows and tall grass on either side. A long drive. Wellington properly styled 'The Sand Hole' is a small place houses half buried in sand. Stores some yards from road. My gloves fell off, worn out with driving. Hot day, faces and lips nearly blistered. Wrote the above on stockyard rail Wellington while men reloaded dray. Picked up a tramp, gave him 4 miles ride. Camped at fenced paddock, good feed for horses, boys had to take them 3 miles to water. Slept as before.

4TH DAY   No water to wash faces, enough for tea. Road puzzling, perfect circle round dry salt lake, could pick up handsfull of salt. Missed top of lantern   Will rode back three miles   Chinaman coming same way picked it up gave it to Will. Pa went up a steep sandy hill, sand up to axles, to a cottage. Asked an Irish woman if we were on right road, she replied, 'You great big silly, why didn't yer go to yer left instead of comin' up this 'ere 'ill.' Good road for some time, then a steep sandy hill with stones half a yard above ground. Again good road along Coorong. Fine scenery, green grass, birds of all species swarming on water. Passed flocks of dead and living cattle and sheep. Reached Meningie at sunset, mail steamer arrives at night there. Camped in hotel yard. Ma and I slept in hotel, men in cart. Landlady asked me to play, her husband with the station master and two other young gentlemen spent the evening with us singing and playing, the lady was very fond of my waltz   asked me to play it three times over, did so. I played all accompaniments.

5TH DAY   Started at sunrise, made another circle round dry salt lake came to banks of Coorong midday. Turkeys, pelicans, swan, fine great geese and other birds on water. Sheoaks, Gums and pretty trees on side of road. Kangaroo dog chased a sheep down, tied him behind cart. Camped under Sheoak tree   poured with rain. Will cooked chops. Slept as usual, but pa watching horses all night. Ma fretted, could not find kerosine or matches for some time.

6TH DAY   Caught enough water on top of canvas over cart to wash faces in. Started at sunrise. Jack's birthday. Continued by Coorong, scenery the same as before. Dogs chased kangaroo 'no catch him'. Several hares sprang over road. Stopped at Wood's Wells, bought milk. White girl buried there who was murdered by Mileky Martin 20 years ago. Bad road, lots of Teatrees. Passed several dead and living cattle, pigs and sheep. Camped at Salt Creek where Mileky Martin murderer of the white girl lived. Water salt in Creek. Slept as before.

7TH DAY   Sunday   Woke at 3 o'clock a.m. Poured with rain all bedding &c. soaking through, flood all round cart, horses strayed away. Took me till 10 o'clock a.m. to bail water out of cart, found horses 3/4 mile away. Stopped all day in cart. Will cooked chops, pa waited on us in cart. Rained all day, wind blowing, rocking cart like a cradle. Blacks camped near us their dog ran away with our boiled beef out of boiler on fire. Jack's straw hat smashed, table broken with wind. Kept awake all night by wind and rain. 'Cart too muchy rocky'.

8TH DAY   Started 8 o'clock a.m. Poured with rain, miles of deep sand, miles of road covered with 4 feet of water. Plenty Kangaroos on side of road. Pa told me to drive on to Kingston 32 miles ahead for food, he took one of my horses to ride back and help the boys through the sand. Ma and I in a fever, sand up to axles my horse done up   went some miles came to Coolatoo hotel. Camped, horse's back all raw, Pa came galloping after us for fear we could not get on, glad to see us camping, galloped back for boys who had camped, Tackled up again came 8 miles through heavy sand and water   pitch dark   raining. Ma and I waiting with clenched hands, reached hotel, had tea, slept there, bedding cart too wet, dried some blankets in hotel. Will's accordeon box smashed, tied it up in one of my dresses.

9TH DAY   Started at sunrise, rained all day. High wind blowing. Road fearful 9 and 10 miles through deep sand and water, in one place above the axles of the dray in sea sand and stones, to avoid newly metalled road. Dray horses done up, left them in paddock, dray on side of road with all in it, 8 miles from Kingston. All went on in spring cart through a river of rain on road, could not find road but for water shining, pitch dark. Reached Kingston 8 p.m. had tea at Mrs Tuff's hotel   wife of Mr Tuff's brother of Currency Creek. I was playing at Mrs Tuff's request my pieces, when three gentlemen, musical gentlemen, asked her to allow them to come and hear me. She introduced them, one a doctor, a very musical widower, he had one of his thumbs shot off some time ago, he was delighted with my pieces, said 'My dear, keep up your music, the Almighty has endowed you with a wonderful gift, if you only keep it up your fortune is made, I only wish I were younger &c, &c, &c.' Flattery, flattery, Oh the gentlemen! One of the young gentlemen played some quadrilles, the other sang a nice song. Slept in hotel, men in cart.

10TH DAY   Pa went back for dray. When starting from hotel the Dr gave me a book. Started midday, boggy stony rough road, Sheoaks on either side camped under tree.

11TH DAY   Started at sunrise   road boggy   sand hills and rough stones, beautiful trees on one side   Lost one of pa's hats. Camped on roadside splendid feed for horses, had to go over a wide deep ditch for wood. Passed several flocks of living and dead animals during day, went through river up to axles. Slept as before.

12TH DAY   Started after sunrise, lovely day. Road stony and stumps half a yard above the ground. Reached Lucindale 12 o'clock a.m. Pretty little place, nice stone buildings. Road continued boggy sandy and stony. Kangaroos in great numbers, too fleet for dogs to catch. Beautiful trees. Malee, Tasmanian Blue Gum, Red Gum, Honey Suckle Teatree, Sheoak, Stringy Bark and others, Rosellas and other birds. Lost stirrup off saddle coming through thick scrub. Some of the limbs had to be chopped down to allow us to pass. Camped under tree. One horse bad, physiced her.

13TH DAY   Started after sunrise. Bad stony road through thick scrub then good road. Lake on either side, good grass, native companions feasting in grassy paddocks. Reached Naracoorte about 4 o'clock p.m. Pretty place   fine buildings good gardens, fine government buildings with livery stables. Found a horse's bit in thick scrub. Camped at a native well. Little cat rode on my horse's back for a little distance. Poor fowls *bumped* about, glad to have some fresh grass put in cage.

14TH DAY   Sunday   Started early, went 10 miles on metal road. Met some young gentlemen *out shooting*. They told Pa we were 8 miles on wrong road, turned back to proper crossing and bad road, one of my horses lame. Pretty trees, several fine stations with fine fruit gardens. Camped under gum tree.

15TH DAY   Started about 10 o'clock a.m. Horses gave us a hunt of five miles for them first. Fearfully rough road rest of way. Reached Binnum, a wretched place with 3 hovels and a station in it about midday. Found our things which had gone by sea all exposed to weathers, the piano case *bottom upwards* and partly prized open and ma's large sea chest ditto. Camped in paddock, pa went 17 miles for Mr Beard and his bullock waggon to cart our house, could only carry half. Then had to go several miles in dark for chaff for horses. Slept as before.

16TH DAY   Old dumb tramp came along gave pa a paper begging. Pa gave him a shilling, he picked up his swag with the arm the paper *said* was useless, and trudged on. Took Pa and boys till 2 o'clock p.m. to turn piano case right way up and unload trucks, which had our belongings on. Bad road   heavy sand stones, &c. Reached Mr Beard's at dusk. Mrs Beard kindly sold us bread and pork.

17TH DAY   Started with Mr Beard's two sons for guides with bullock waggon, about 8 o'clock a.m. Heavy sandy road, thick timber, had to cut some down. Camped near 'Bring Albert' station, a fine place situated on the bank of a fine lake, beautiful fruit garden. Pa rode on to find road. Slept as usual.

18TH DAY   Started sunrise, bad road, pretty trees, lots of birds. Pa went before with axe to cut a road through thick Stringy Bark scrub. Reached our land about noon. Scenery like Currency Creek. Fine dam on Clara's block. Plenty tadpoley water for use. Plenty wood. Spent rest of day rigging up galvanized roofing for hut to put luggage under. Lots of wild birds.

19TH DAY   Will shot wild duck and rosella. Cooked bread outside. I made a mud fireplace and washed socks in Tadpoley water. Several parties of surveyors and station hands passed here, boiled their tea on the land.

~ ~ ~ ~ ~ ~

Ma and I still sleep in cart, men under iron huts. Pa went 7 miles to post yesterday received letters from Uncle Will and Ethel   Uncle's advice came too late, but his letter was welcome. It was the anniversary of Pa and ma's wedding day yesterday. I am kneeling on the men's bedding by a box writing this, ma is cooking outside. The boys gone chopping trees, & pa gone for a sheep for 'muttony'.

We are like a lot of bears let loose in a desert, and will have to go 30 and more miles over fearful roads for provisions. We have kept pretty well excepting colds which Jack and I have. Please tell Burnet the Australian stamps are no use to *Victorians* so I have returned them, excepting two which pa wanted. Now with much love to all I must say farewell.

It is cold, and I must go to sewing, fancy we have had to go for days without washing our faces or hands. Plenty of water now. Hoping you are all well now and happy, as we are not *yet* and with love from all to all,

I REMAIN/YOUR LOVING RELATIVE AND FRIEND/LUCY JONES

27 May 1883

My dear relatives and friends

You will see this epistle was written on the 18th, Pa took it to Booroopki Post Office then to post it. When turning out his coat pocket yesterday 'Lo and behold!' There was this letter, so I opened it to add this.

Will went out shooting a day or two ago, shot at an *old man kangaroo*, wounded him, he turned to *scoff* Will but he hit at him with the *butt* of his gun splintering it in the act, but killing *Mr Kangaroo* with such *vigor* that a piece of that *brave* creature's head bone entered the woodwork of Will's gun, and remains there. Will mended his gun though it was badly splintered.

Ma manages to cook a damper, pancakes, and meat outside. The piano which pa and Jack brought the other week from Binnum is out in *hail rain &c* only a tarpaulin over it. No room under iron for it. Pa and boys commenced building chimney today. No stone here. The chimney is to be made with Bulloaks and filled with pugg (mud). The Squatter's sons came here yesterday, they seem very nice. We see station folks pass every day, nearly all come up to have a *chat*.

I have been washing today. The clothes are completely *spoilt* [with] *iron-mould* and mildew and some rubbed in holes.

I helped dig a small waterhole yesterday, chopped down several trees and wood, so you can imagine what nice hands I shall have for piano (If it be any good after the *exposure*!) We had a letter from Walt on Thursday, he was well and busy. It seems so *unpleasant*, here we are with our things all tossed together sleeping in [the] cart with rain sometimes soaking our pillows, or ice on water, and piano &c exposed to rain, our clothes all mouldy. We cannot change those we have on either for the water is full of *toads*, and our clean clothes are mouldy in boxes.

I believe the journey through rain has ruined £20 worth of bedding and clothes. When uncle Will comes over he will come by mail and not see the horrid roads. A good thing too! He would be too disgusted to get here. Of course, we came a different way.

Please Nellie tell Fred the boys will write when their busy time is over, they are always saying 'My word, *wont* we have fun when Fred comes over to stay with us by and bye.' Nellie you should see the poor puny looking folks here. Of course I have not seen many. There are two Squatters living not far from here. Mr Hamilton and Mr Broughton. The former has a daughter who plays the piano, *so we heard*. Her two brothers called here yesterday, one is 22. There were 7 young gentlemen here one day.

Must close this with love to all relatives,/I remain,/A conglomeration of *wonder* and *hope*!/Also your wellwisher/'Luce'

near Goolwa] the Jones family set out from the South Australian coastal township of Goolwa to take up new land in the Wimmera region of Victoria   native companions] brolgas, large silvery-grey cranes the Coorong] a salt-water lagoon in south-eastern South Australia which extends for 145 km south-east from the mouth of the Murray River

MARGARET HARRISON

In 1884 Margaret Harrison, an Aboriginal woman resident on the Ebenezer Mission Station near Dimboola in Victoria, heard of the death of one of her daughters, Edith Taylor, at the Lake Condah Aboriginal Reserve near Hamilton in the Victorian Western District. At the time Harrison was separated also from her other daughters. Her plea to Captain Page, Inspector to the Central Board for the Protection of Aborigines, to be reunited with her daughters was not opposed.

50. TO CAPTAIN A.M.A. PAGE, 9 APRIL 1884

DEAR SIR

Please would you kindly allow me to have my two girls with me here as one of them died & I have not see her before she died and I should like the other two to be with me to comfort me.

Please do not disapoint me for my heart is breaking to have them with me. Please to send them up here as I shall not leave this Station.

Please to ask Mr Stahle to let them come.

I AM YOUR OBDIENT SERVANT/MARGARET HARRISON/P.S. LET ME KNOW

BARCROFT BOAKE

Barcroft Henry Thomas Boake (1866–92), poet, born in Sydney of Irish immigrant parents, worked as a drover and boundary rider in the Snowy River country of New South Wales. This letter reflects the depressive temperament and the recurring financial troubles which led to Boake's hanging himself with his own stockwhip in 1892.

51. TO BARCROFT CAPEL BOAKE, 20 NOVEMBER 1889

DEAR DAD

In my last letter I omitted to mention one or two things, so as I have lots of time now worse luck I may as well write you a few lines.

Besides I feel very lonely here a stranger in a far land and the time hangs very heavy. I am waiting till Leeds comes back to start a mob of cattle away we finished the last trip much sooner than was expected I don't expect he will be back till the end of the month—

In regard to that affair of Reece's if you will procure me his address I will write. As you say, it is a matter that wants looking after, perhaps Higinbotham knows his where-abouts, but I am much mistaken in my knowledge of Reece if a letter will make him ante up—and most unfortunately I don't see that I have any claim in a legal point of view—of course if he were a man of honor there would be no difficulty but I am afraid Reece &

honesty quarrelled long ago. It is not a bit of use though crying over spilt milk—When I think of that miserable episode I feel as contemptible in my own eyes as you must have found me then—Only for that I would in all probability be in Sydney now it is strange how easily the current of our life is turned.

I don't think in Sydney I could have found the pleasure in life that exists for me here that is at times, oftener I feel sick of the whole thing and long for some other country and a more stirring life—There is a pleasure in a mad gallop, or in watching the dawn of day on a cattle camp—to see the beasts take shape and change from an indistinguishable mass of white & black into their natural colours—Or in the dead of night to find yourself alone with the cattle all the camp asleep perhaps only a red spark betokening the camp—I always (when I think of it) find something unearthly in this assemblage of huge animals ready at any moment to burst forth like a pent up torrent and equally irresistable in their force—when every beast is down, asleep or resting just pull up & listen, you will hear a low moaning sound rising to a roar then subsiding to a murmur like distant surf or as I fancy the cry of the damned in Dante's Inferno—when the cattle are like that it is a good sign—But in the moonlight this strange noise the dark mass of cattle with the occasional flash of an eye or a polished horn catching the light—it always conjures up strange fancies in me I seem to be in some other world—If I could only write it, there is a poem to be made out of the back country, some man will come yet who will be able to grasp the romance of Western Queensland and all that equally mysterious country in Central & Northern Australia, for there is a romance though a grim one a story of drought & flood, fever & famine murder & suicide; courage & endurance, and who reaps the benefit not the poor bushman, but Messrs. So & So merchants of Sydney or Melbourne, or the mutual consolidated cut-down-the drovers wages Co. Litd or some other capitalist, if you showed them the map half of them could not point out the position of their runs, all they know is that their cheques come in regularly from the buyers and if the expenses pass the limit *they* in their ignorance place, they sack the manager and get another easy enough

Yes—I wonder if a day will come when these men will rise up, when the wealthy man perhaps renowned inside for his benevolence, shall see pass before him a band of men, all of whom died in his service & whose unhallowed graves dot his run—The greater portion hollow, shrunken, burning with the pangs of thirst others covered with the evil slime of the Diamantina Cooper and those far Western rivers—burnt unrecognisably in bush fires, struck down by sunstroke, ripped up by cattle, dashed against some tree by their horse—killed in a dozen different ways and what for? a few shillings a week and these are begrudged them; while their employer travels the continent and lives in all the luxury his wealth can command, they are sweating out their lives under a tragic sun on damper & beef—this is no exaggerated picture I can assure you—Marcus Clarke has grasped the meaning of Australia's Mountains & forests in his eloquent preface to Gordon's Poems but neither he nor Gordon have written about the plains & sandhills of the far west it remains for some future poet to do that

I got a volume of Gordon here the other day and at length had an opportunity of studying his writings in their entirety I have long been familiar with his most well known poems, there is no man within the last century who has achieved such lasting fame as he has, his poems appeal not only to one class of cultured minds as Tennyson or Browning and that lot, but there is not a bushman who does not know a verse or two of ... 'how we beat the favorite' or 'the sick stockrider' I call this fame—Gordon is the favorite I may say only poet of the back blocker and I am sorry to say Emile Zola is his favorite prose writer, his books are published now in very cheap form and have a tremendous circulation a strange partnership indeed for these two men so different in their tone, to share popularity. I am afraid after all the bushman is not a very fine animal but at any rate even in his most vicious moments he is far above many of the so-called respectable dwellers in towns—well I must write a letter to Addie now so will say goodbye—give my love to Addie and Grannie

YOURS AFFECTIONATELY/BARTIE

Addie] probably Boake's sister

ALFRED DEAKIN

In 1890 Deakin (1856–1919) (later to become Australia's second prime minister) was travelling in India where he had been commissioned to write a series of newspaper articles. From Lahore he wrote to his wife Pattie, reflecting on their marriage.

52. TO PATTIE DEAKIN, 28 DECEMBER 1890

Dearest of sweethearts & sweetest of wives—no news from you or of you—& I am still dreaming of you day & night. Do you remember the night we were all at the Opera House before we were engaged when I leaned on you & they played "Soft as the stars that are shining"—Do you remember at Park House when I held your hand in the circles & sometimes passed my palms over your head—Do you remember our evenings alone in the drawing room or that day—that never forgotten day when you came to me on the landing to try on the ring before we went to be married—The evenings in the gardens or on horseback—The happy times in the little front room at Adams St & that other where I found you lying faint & tiny little Ivy in the corner—Mailton when we walked out together—Walsh St when I said goodbye—Llanarth when I rushed upstairs & found you dressing on my return—Our last goodbye at the dining room door; & the other upstairs I remember them all—recall them & dwell upon them—for they are you & alas all I have of you now—I have done with travelling—It costs too much—Too much heart ache—too much anxiety—too much longing—Last night I was whistling & singing "Waiting" thinking of you singing it at Park House often & especially the night before I went to Fiji—I never thought Park House was so dear to me as I now find it to be—I wonder if any man is as contented with his choice as I am—I have never yet regretted it—never wished it undone—never seen anyone whom I thought I could have married except you & this after nearly nine years of wedded life with so capricious & captious a being as I am—is it not wonderful! Because it is not as if I am contented that you should be only as you have been as I am always wishing you to grow & be better sweeter & stronger—that is for your own sake & in yourself—for my sake & as regards me I am absolutely satisfied even if you had never developed—I wish you to be a nobler wife & a grander mother & a holier woman but it is not for my comfort & happiness as your husband—I am as happy as I can be loving you & having you while you are happy & well—I am your lover still & as such have no fault to find with you—as your spiritual companion I am critical & often try to open you out—perhaps unwisely—But if you knew how I loved you this would only make you more bright & glad because of the sincerity of the love that is satisfied for itself but never satisfied for you either with itself that is my love or with your soul unless it glows brighter & purer every day—Nothing have I to send or say but love unending & inexhaustible for you & for my darling children—love them for me & from me & tell them how I cherish them & pray for them & you to God morning & night my dearest my angel

Please keep papers with my articles in—a clean copy of all

KISSES AGAIN &/AGAIN & ALWAYS —/ALFRED

Park House] the home of Pattie Deakin's parents, Hugh and Elizabeth Browne, in East Melbourne held your hand in the circles] a reference to the spiritualist meetings at the Brownes', in which Pattie was the medium   Adams Street] Deakin's parents' house in South Yarra   Ivy] daughter of Alfred and Pattie Deakin   Llanarth] Alfred and Pattie Deakin's house in Walsh Street, South Yarra

HERBERT CURLEWIS

When he first proposed marriage to Ethel Turner, Herbert Curlewis (1869–1942), later a judge of the Industrial Arbitration Court, was a Sydney law student, and Ethel Turner (1870–1958) was just beginning her writing career. As promised in this letter, Curlewis returned Turner's letters, dance programmes with her name in them and two withered roses. Within a month they were seeing one another again, and in May 1891 they were unofficially engaged. By the time they were married in April 1896 Turner was the much celebrated author of Seven Little Australians *(1894). (See Letters 74 and 143)*

53. TO ETHEL TURNER, 5 MARCH 1891

DEAR MISS TURNER

In answer to your note I have nothing whatever to say except to thank you for the gentleness you showed in doing what you felt to be your duty.

You must not ask me ever to see you again—my pain is now greater than I can bear and I could not trust myself to increase it.

I have various letters and tokens of you that I have not the courage to destroy and so shall ask you to do so for me. I shall ask Creed to give them to you—he knows I never go to your house though he does not know why.

So ends the last letter I shall write you—God bless you and keep you my darling— you will I know always think kindly of me.

I REMAIN/YOURS SINCERELY/H.R. CURLEWIS

Creed] J.P. Creed married Ethel Turner's school friend Louise Mack, author of *Teens* (1897)

WILLIAM SCHRODER

The historian Victoria Emery has noted the characteristics of the testimonial letter: it is both a story and a political transaction; it defines a relationship between subject and writer; it draws on the relationship of the writer to some form of authority. Testimonials prepared for William Schroder following his 'breach of Faith & Honesty' did not save him from the personal catastrophe of dismissal.

54. TO CHAIRMAN, FINANCE COMMITTEE, 23 MARCH 1891

To the Chairman and Gentlemen of the Finance Committee

Being suspended I beg to ask you to give me a chance to retrieve my good character, I have served you well the 4 years I have been with Mr Matthias.

I was induced by Mr Britton to let him have the Dog, it was kept for a week to see if it would get better under my treatment. But in an evil moment I sold it notwithstanding Mr Matthias always impressed on me no Dogs could be sold (or given away) but by Public Auction.

I have sent the money 15/- to the City Treasurer.

It is the first time I have committed mysilf, should you be merciful to me this time, I will solemnly vow not to transgress again.

You can refer to the City Treasurer & Mr Matthias as to the manner I have conducted myself during the time, hoping Gentlemen you will act mercifully

FROM YOUR HUMBLE & PENITENT SERVANT/WM SCHRODER

55. TO CHAIRMAN, FINANCE COMMITTEE, 24 MARCH 1891

To the Chairman & Gentlemen of the Finance Committee

SIR

I am sorry to have to report to you that Mr Schroder the man who has been with me for 4 years taking stray dogs & also having the care of the Dog house has committed a breach of Faith & Honesty. The facts are as follows. Some time since Sir Benjamin

Benjamin required a Dog taken away. it was duly fetched by Schroder and after a few Days Sold to Mr Britton of Swan & Richmond for 15/-. Mr Brown the former owner of the Dog saw it in the Eastern Market placed there for sale by Mr Britton & reported it to young Mr Benjamin. The City Treasurer was kind enough to see Mr Britton with me when he stated that he bought the Dog at the Dog house & paid Schroder 15/- for it but he was obliged to have it poisoned by Mr Richards Druggist being near him it being so bad.

Schroder has paid to the City Treasurer the 15/- & the Mayor has suspended him for the Matter to be dealt with by You.

I may say I am sorry for him as he has done his work well for the last 4 years never getting into undue friction with the Citizens or Larrikins—Some 2 years back a large Quantity of Tweed cloth & winter Coats were found by him in the yard of the dog house at 8 o'clock in the morning it was reported to me before 8.30. I reported it to the police & the owner told me there was nothing missed and its a wonder sombody did not take a suit of clothes out of it he has been most Careful in his Duties & he has a 12 years Good caracter from his last place—

Sir Benjamin Benjamin] (1834–1905), a Melbourne merchant, philanthropist and Jewish community leader

56. To Chairman, Finance Committee, March 1891

Sir & Gentlemen

I would suggest the next Man may do the same—& Mr Cs Bowen thought the Case may be met by a fine of a sum of money as he has Known him for 30 years & he Schroder has 2 daughters & 2 Sons Grown up

I have the honor to be Sir & Gentlemen/Your humble Servant/
W Matthias

57. To Chairman, Finance Committee, 24 March 1891

As I understand this matter the man has deliberately put in his pocket the proceeds of the sale of a dog which his duty was to kill and not to sell, and I recommend that no excuses be accepted from him but that he be discharged for such misconduct

E G FitzGibbon/Town Clerk

E.G. FitzGibbon] Edmund Gerald FitzGibbon (1825–1905) was appointed town clerk of Melbourne in 1856. In 1891 he became the first chairman of the newly established Melbourne and Metropolitan Board of Works

Arthur Streeton

In the 1880s in Melbourne, Arthur Streeton (1867–1943) joined a group of artists which included Tom Roberts, Frederick McCubbin and Charles Conder. Their outdoor paintings 'full of light and air' set a new direction for Australian art. If art historians have sometimes expressed disappointment that in his letters Streeton did not engage in any technical discussion of painting, they have perhaps also failed to observe that he is one of the great Australian letter writers. In 1891, Streeton left Melbourne for a time to work in Sydney and in the New South Wales countryside. From those years we have in letters his descriptions of the harbour and its foreshores and his vivid pen pictures of daily life.

58. To Theodore Fink, September 1891

Dear Fink,

Here do I sit under a banana tree, all in a garden fair—with orange & scarlet nasturtiums, violets, aloes peach blossom, bright geranium, marguerite, Roses & Everlastings & all these are sleeping, & dreaming with me in the hot noon.

Tuesday morning found my mother Roberts & I on the 'Massilia'—we leave the pier, hand-shakes, kisses, tears, & tender adieu our vessel moves off, Melbourne growing fainter & fonder like a thin line on the horizon with its spires (& tripy Government House very much on the line).

—Long gazing at the receding line of civilization as the good old sun drops low— then again looking east, one sees the brilliant 'Mercury' proudly riding high over the long impressive line of the Dandenong Ranges (the latter like a great pale blue dragon dreaming in the twilight)—and one doesn't feel Smike any more, but Byron instead &

'Yon sun that sets upon the sea
We follow in his flight,
Farewell a while to him and thee
My native land, … Good night …'

On deck again after tea. Wilson's Promontory & the general coast dim. The throb of the giant machinery & the pulse of the mighty ocean gently lifting the good ship a little. 'Smike' lies smoking an Indian (6 a bob,) on a deck chair, blinking at the new moon, which plays hide-and-seek behind the great black funnel, bravely breathing across the 'Milky Way', & with a slight pulsation the firm masts knock across the bright 'Southern Cross'.

9.pm—I'm writing in a room where they're all singing hymns & find it darn hard write at all—'Oh Yes singing 'Those in peril on the sea' therefore do not so critical.

Let's see where was I in the sun this morning—Oh Yes Thursday morning we enter the heads, slow winding up the harbor, past men-of-war who salute & dip their flags in honor of ourselves & R M 'Massilia' & one feels beastly proud

'And the chest expands with its madd'ning might—
Gods glorious oxygen'   Gordon

Then Circular quay with many steamers busy & bright—towering behind em Metropole Customs & Morts, & beautiful Sydney all glowing & oriental—Little steamers puffing hard and skipping over the blue water clouds of smoke, next the steamers whistle & flute in different keys & over all the bright harmony the warm palpitating sky of the Sunny South—

Sydney is an artists' city—glorious—Roberts & I go to Mossman's Bay & pull through the lazy green water, & then lunch under the shade in the open air, eggs, meat, cheese, & 2 big bottles of claret grown in Australia—The little Bay seemed all asleep & so very peaceful—Oh Such a rest—Warm balmy air blue orchids & the purple glory of sarsaparilla—

A Land of passion-fruit & poetry—

In the afternoon down to Coogee—where the great green rollers tumble in like huge heavy cylinders of liquid glass, spreading glory everywhere, & playing a great symphony of thunder on the golden shore, where the lovers sit in safety & watch & murmur, & kiss in the twilight, before they cross the heavy silver sand towards the tram, when the flowing tide comes in.

I'm reading my 'Joaquin Miller' & also a fine book given me by Telemachus 'The Golden Treasury'.

YOURS TRULY/SMIKE

Fink] Theodore Fink (1855–1942), solicitor, newspaper proprietor, educationist and longtime friend of Streeton   Smike] Streeton's nickname from the character in Charles Dickens' *Nicholas Nickleby*   an Indian (6 a bob)] cheap cigarette, six for a shilling   Metropole] Hotel Metropole, opened in 1890 in Phillip Street above Circular Quay   Customs] Customs House at Circular Quay, built between 1885 and 1887   Morts] Mort & Co's wool store, built at Circular Quay in the 1860s, and demolished in 1960 for the first AMP Tower   Gordon] the poet Adam Lindsay Gordon (1833–70)   'Joaquin Miller'] Californian poet, novelist and playwright   Telemachus] nickname for Francis Myers, journalist of the Melbourne *Argus*   'The Golden Treasury'] Francis Turner Palgrave's *The Golden Treasury of the Best Songs and Lyrical Poems in the English Language*

In late 1891 Streeton made the first of a number of painting excursions to inland New South Wales. Three or four months were spent at Glenbrook in the Blue Mountains where he painted one of his greatest works 'Fire's On', Lapstone Tunnel, now in the Art Gallery of New South Wales. The painting tells the story of the construction of the rail-link to Sydney. Matching the drama of Streeton's painting is his vivid account, in a letter to fellow painter, Tom Roberts (1856–1931), of the death of one of the construction workers.

59. TO TOM ROBERTS, DECEMBER 1891

DEAR 'BDG'

This morning hot, windy & warm as I travel down the line & the mirage sizzling & jiggering over the railway track. I arrive at my cutting 'The fatal cutting' & inwardly rejoice at the prosperous warmth all glowing before me as I descend & reascend the opposite side up to my shading, shelving, sandstone rock, perched right up. I wipe the wholesome moisture from my pale brow—& having partaken of a pull at my billy (like a somewhat lengthy & affectionate kiss) I look up & down at my subject—is it worth painting? Why of course damn it all!—that is providing I'm capable of translating my impression to the canvas.—all is serene as I work & peg away: retiring under the rock a bit when the light any shots—then 'Up with that Bl— F—g waggon Bill'. x —

11.20. the 'Fish' struggles over the hill & round to Glenbrook.

12 OCLOCK The next shift comes toddling down the hot track with their billies, & I commence to discuss my lunch & tea (of which I consume over a qt of every lunch)—& now I hear 'Fire! Fire's On!' in [illegible] the gang close by rest my billy on the rock take out my pipe & listen for the shots with my eye watching the bright red gum yonder—BOOM & then rumbling of rock, the navvy under the rock with me & watching says, Man killed—He runs down the sheltered side & cries 'man killed!'; another takes it up & now it has run through the camp. more shots & crashing rock we peep over & he lies all hidden bar his legs—& now men, nippers & 2 women hurry down a woman with a bottle & rags—all the shots are gone but one & all wait & dare not go near—then someone says the last hole was not lit—& they raise the rock & lift him on to the stretcher, fold his arms over his chest & slowly 6 of 'em carry him past me—Oh how full of dread is the grey mysterious expression of death—'tis like a whirlpool for the eyes —

Blown to death 20 yds from me—& as a navvy said 'twas 'Anorrible sight'—By jove—a passing corpse does chain your eyes & indeed all your senses just as strongly as love—all the men followed slowly up the hill & now all are gone but me & the fatal rocks & I dont feel up to my lunch—so have a smoke & peg away at my gem: but the poor chap, who I was speaking to only yesterday haunted me so that I put my gem away & came away too—& had a shower & smoke & read & thought of him all the while—I asked a navvy if the chap was married—'No Sir. But one of the Shannon girls is a good bit cut up'—it seems he was engaged to be married—

THURSDAY

The men didn't go back to work—this sort of thing skeers em a bit. go tomorrow all right I suppose.

GOOD NIGHT &/HOW ARE YOU GETTING ON/SMIKE

'Bdg'] abbreviation of Bulldog, Tom Roberts' nickname   'Fish'] name given to the train which ran between the Blue Mountains and Sydney, called after an early driver, Jock Heron. The surname was corrupted to Herring and subsequently to 'Fish'

OVEREND DREWRY

The West Australian Police Department Records hold this letter from the unknown Overend Drewry, in which he reports to Sheriff J.B. Roe on the 'success' of a hanging of three Aborigines at Halls Creek on 18 February 1892, about eight miles from the scene of the murder for which the men were convicted. A second letter to Roe refers to an inquest, at which the coroner questioned whether the process of the law had been carried out, since the Sheriff had not explicitly ordered execution. Drewry's comment to Roe: 'I hanged them first and faced the music afterwards'. His confidence was supported when the jury held that 'the natives were lawfully hanged', but he advised Roe in any future cases to send a copy of the warrant of execution.

60. To J.B. Roe, February 1892

Sir,

I daresay you will be pleased to have a private and fuller account of the hanging at daybreak on Feb 18th. I got horses for dray and mounted men as soon as horse was in the shafts I handcuffed hands behind and pinioned two prisoners to Annetts one, had hole dug under branch to act for drop and afterwards grave, which the dray was backed up to whilst Annett placed ropes round necks. I was up tree allowing drop and making all secure, came down, asked if all was correct, Annett jumped out of the dray I shot the bolt and dray tilted and was drawn forward at same time; from time of handcuffing to drop 20 minutes the whole affair was a success from start sixty seven natives witnessed it. Annett is too old for bush hangings on any other occasion when blacks are to be hanged I dont think it will be necessary to send anyone thro expressly for that part of the business. I enclose you my account with Annett he has also got money from the Magistrate here contrary to my ideas, so I think any moneys due to him should be held by you until they have time to come in. I shall be obliged if my remuneration for this business is paid in to my account at Union Bank Perth.

Thanking you for your consideration in selecting me as your representative pro tem
I have the honour to be,
Sir/Your obedient servant/Overend Drewry

HENRY LAWSON

In the drought year of 1893, unable to support himself as a writer in Sydney, Lawson (1867–1922) tramped with his swag between Bourke and Hungerford. This trip, funded by Bulletin *editor J.F. Archibald (1856–1919), provided material for short stories and poems and confirmed Lawson's sense of the bush as a place of torment.*

61. To his aunt, 16 January 1893

Dear Aunt,

I found your letter in the Post Office of this God-Forgotten town. I carried my swag nearly two hundred miles since I last wrote to you, and I am now camped on the Queensland side of the border—a beaten man. I start back tomorrow—140 miles by the direct road—and expect to reach Bourke in nine days. My mate goes on to Thargomindah. No work and very little to eat; we lived mostly on Johnny cakes and cadged a bit of meat here and there at the miserable stations. Have been three days without sugar. Once in Bourke I'll find the means of getting back to Sydney—never to face the bush again. I got an offer to go over and edit a New Zealand paper and wrote to say that I doubted my ability to edit but would take a place on the staff. They seemed anxious to get me, and asked me to state my own terms. Simpson is negotiating with 'em. You can have no idea of the horrors of the country out here. Men tramp and beg and live like dogs. It is two months since I slept in what you can call a bed. We walk as far as we can—according to the water—and then lie down and roll ourselves in our blankets. The flies start at daylight and we fight them all day till dark—then mosquitoes start. We carry water in bags. Got bushed on a lignum plain Sunday before last and found the track at four o'clock in the afternoon—then tramped for four hours without water and reached a government dam. My mate drank nearly all night. But it would take a year to tell you all about my wanderings in the wilderness.

It would not be so bad if it was shearing season—then, at least we'd be sure of tucker. But the experience will help me to live in the city for the next year or so. So much for myself.

I'm real glad to hear that you are still at North Shore (you may expect me there within the next six months—as soon as I get a few decent clothes). Sorry Don is dead.

I'm writing on an old tin and my legs ache too much to let me sit any longer. I've always tried to write cheerful letters so you'll excuse this one. Will tell you all about it when I get down.

And now for a lonely walk of 140 miles. Will write from Bourke.

Your affectionate nephew,/Henry Lawson

P.S. I'm going off the track to try and get a few weeks' work on a Warrego station. Will write from there if successful.

Johnny cakes] small flat damper of wheatmeal or flour, cooked in the embers of a campfire or in a camp oven

The last 20 years of Henry Lawson's life were marked by alcoholism, debt and depression. He spent short periods in prison in Sydney for drunkenness and failure to pay maintenance to his wife and children; he was also treated in mental hospitals. This letter to his publisher was written from Darlinghurst Gaol.

62. To George Robertson, 27 August 1908

Dear Robertson,

I want you to read this letter. I did not waste a shilling of that £5, but paid it where it was long due and sorely needed (a grocer in North Sydney, crippled with rheumatism and his wife about to be confined). Mrs Byers can tell you this. I thought I would be all right. I thought I would be able to finish a story and some verses I had on hand, but I was hunted too much. I was sober when brought here, and sober the day before. I gave myself up, when things seemed hopeless, to get a sleep. I am sending Mrs Byers to see you this morning. She will tell you what she has done, and what money she has got.

I have been here three weeks and it is more than enough. I was three days under separate treatment, and then on the works, but broke down and was brought from the cell into the hospital out of my mind. If I am not released I shall have to go back to the cells again, and that will spell *finis* as far as my brain is concerned. I sent some work to Bland Holt before I came in, but we have not been able to get in touch with him yet (he is travelling) unless Mrs Byers has.

We are not allowed to write here and will not be allowed to smoke for six months (except when ordered by the doctor in the hospital). It is the waste of time that is killing me now. It is refined torture to have a brain teeming with ideas and not be able to write them down. I dare not even compose to any great extent, and try to keep my mind off it, lest I forget lines and may not be able to take the thread up again when I come out. I could not live on prison fare, and without smoke, and remain sane, and the horror of the place is on me this time, and was before I came in. I never experienced cells before. Think and imagine the effect of such confinement on a temperament like mine—and think of the associations. I can get no new material out of them—I have got all the material I want for a lifetime. I could do brilliant work now, if I had my liberty, and right on up to Christmas—I could wipe off the amount under a fortnight. There is one story, drafted, in Shenstone's office, "Their Mates' Honour", which would bring me £15 or £20. I could finish it in a few days. And there is a lot of good, strong unfinished verse. I would be sure of a month's rest, or time from the maintenance order.

And, I understand, the maintenance order will go on, or be in operation all the time I am rotting in idleness here. Think of it. Mr Hugh Langwell (Western Lands Board, Bridge Street) would, I believe, help in part. You could ring him. I have tried others, and so has Mrs Byers, but I don't know yet with what result, as all the letters and business is being done through her and I only get letters once a fortnight, and she can only see me once a month. I am not writing this because I am on the wrong side of the bars, but I'm done with the drink for twelve months at the very least after I get out. I made up my mind to that three weeks ago. I kept it for two years, last, you know, through seas of trouble.— But now to the business side; and a lot of splendid material. I get £2 2s. per page from *Lone Hand* and £2 10s. from *Bulletin*, and could give an order for, say, half my earnings, to pay back you, or any one you know who might advance money to get me out of this.

And the Bulletin is settled with in full for advances. They saw to that recently, as I told you. I don't owe the firm much. There's £100 sunk in the autobiography, the first part finished and paid for; but the second part, for which we suggested another £100, if real good, will be finished early next year. *And it will contain stronger work* than we ever dreamed of. I will tell the truth in it as far as you dare publish it. It is the thing all my readers are waiting for. Remember I always paid up advances from the firm as far as possible whenever I got a windfall. Half for the *Lone Hand's* selection from auto, and out of that £50 from Lothian. And you must have had a real good sale of cheap editions during the holidays. I know you have done a great deal more than the others would, but I am not asking for anything I cannot or will not pay back. You *must* know many who would help me if they thought I would keep straight. And, remember those verses of mine

> "When a man's in a hole you must send round the hat
>   Were he gaol-bird or gentleman once."

Read, or re-read the skeleton autobiography in the *Lone Hand*, think of what you know, or of what I have hinted to you of my past life, both at home, homeless, and married, think of the struggle to keep right and the success and ruin (not through my fault) in England and afterwards, and say if I haven't suffered enough without this. (My very composition is getting the gaol atmosphere.) With all my faults, and it was drink only—and I was fairly hunted to that, if ever a man was—this is but a very poor end to twenty-five years' good and faithful work for Australia. Work that shall be looked upon as grand, unique, and historical yet. And think of the amount of work I did last year— "Joseph's Dreams", etc., etc.—and not placed yet. Nor will it be till I get my own magazine.

Do your best to get me out of this and into the sunlight without delay and you will never regret it.

Yours truly,/Henry Lawson

George Robertson] Lawson's friend and publisher (1860–1933), was a founding partner of Angus & Robertson   Mrs Byers] Isabel Byers sheltered and cared for Lawson from 1904 onwards   Shenstone's office] Fred Shenstone was secretary and also official manager of the publishing department of Angus & Robertson   Bland Holt] actor-manager (1851–1942)

F. J. GILLEN

F. J. Gillen's (1855–1912) 1894 letter from Alice Springs to Sir Walter Baldwin Spencer (1860–1929) in Melbourne marks the beginning of a long and fruitful partnership in recording the culture and beliefs of Aboriginal people. Although Gillen was a self-educated postal employee and Spencer was foundation professor of biology at the University of Melbourne, their fieldwork and writings were cooperative, with Gillen by no means the junior partner. Key figures in anthropological research and co-authors of The Native Tribes of Central Australia *(1899), Gillen and Spencer were unusual in their time in their concern for Aborigines' welfare and respect for their culture. Although the usage of 'Nigger' and 'Nig' in Gillen's letter will affront modern readers it did not for him carry the overtone of contempt which it has today.*

63. TO BALDWIN SPENCER, 8 SEPTEMBER 1894

MY DEAR SPENCER

How is the world using you? As I sit here in the old ochre smelling den, which you know so well, I can imagine I see you demonstrating the anatomy of a Cockroach to a lot of Callow Youth of both sexes, do you, I wonder, ever wish *that* you could transport yourself to the wilds of the McDonnells. I often wish that you could, I missed you very much indeed, you were here just long enough to make yourself a part of our home life and in such a small Community it. I got thus far when the hope of the House of Gillen appeared upon the scene with a long time dead and much mutilated lizard which he insisted upon me examining. He then deposited it in my Photographic Material box observing, 'Fessa papa, Fessa, Blib Baloo give Fessa.' Whenever the young imp sees a lizard or any crawling creature he recollects you and your surroundings in this room, which you would hardly know now it is so beastly band boxafied. I am sending you a few Prints this mail, most of which you and I developed. I am forced to admit that with less exposure than of old I am getting much clearer and better pictures, as far as possible I have sent you unmounted copies. The developing and printing material arrived a few days ago and I tried my hand at printing on Bromide paper with awful results, sample of which I enclose. Have not yet had time to try silver printing but hope to have some good results to send you next mail. Have taken a number of Corroboree pictures since you left and shall get some more in a few days. If I am successful in printing you shall have a copy of anything I consider sufficiently interesting. If there is any picture that you would specially like to have you can let me know. Have got a splendid lot of stone Chooringa together since you left, including some from the Kytiche tribe, Barrow Creek. I have taken impressions of some of them in ink, and am sending on to Stirling this mail. Some Glen Helen natives are now En route with a selection from the tribe inhabiting that locality of which I think you have some personal Knowledge, since you left I have learnt that a number of Chooringa belonging to the Chichika tribe are deposited in a cave known to one of my Niggers *and situated* about 105 miles North West of here and I am about to organize a little expedition to annex the whole collection. No rats since you left though Nigs have been on the look out, but we have just had some nice rain, the weather is becoming warm and we hope to have some before next mail. Byrne tells me they are plentiful at the Charlotte after rain, he is sending French a couple by this mail. I was glad to hear that he gave you those moles, he sent me a very fine one this mail and is to send me another later on. Stirling has been interesting himself in Souths affair, the upshot is that South is not to be removed until the beginning of the year and if he plays his Cards well he may be allowed to remain altogether. We had one rather amusing Case on Court day this week and I thought of you during the proceedings which would, I am sure, have interested you and disturbed your risible faculties pleasantly. It was a typical bush case of which only a Mark Twain could do justice to—Here's the Wife announcing *tea* Bacon and Eggs. She joins with me in kindest regards and all the members of the staff, including Hanley, send kind remembrances.

Slianthe./Yours faithfully/F.J. Gillen

PS Would Mrs Spencer like an Alexandra parrot? I hope to have some shortly. FJG

our home life] Spencer had stayed on with the Gillens at Alice Springs after the Horn Scientific Expedition ended in July 1894   hope of the house of Gillen] Brian, eldest son of F.J. Gillen   Baloo give Fessa] Brian's name for himself was Baloo, and Professor Spencer was Fessa   Barrow Creek] an Overland Telegraph Station   Stirling] Professor Sir Edward Stirling (1849–1919), physiologist at the University of Adelaide and Director of the South Australian Museum   Chooringa/churinga] usually stone or wooden objects with carved designs of ancestral significance   Byrne] P.M. Byrne (1856–1932), brother-in-law of Gillen and telegraph operator at Charlotte Waters   French] Charles French (1868–1950), naturalist   moles] the marsupial mole was of interest in evolutionary theory South's affair] South was the arresting officer in the case of Mounted Constable Willshire, whom Gillen, in his capacity as Justice of the Peace and Sub-Protector of Aborigines, had charged with the murder of Aborigines. The case was dismissed and Gillen ridiculed for his part in it   Court day] the Magistrate's Court at Alice Springs   Hanley] Tom Hanley, a maintenance worker on the Overland Telegraph line Slianthe] good health (Irish)

Nellie Melba (Helen Porter Armstrong)

Melba (1861–1931) owed much of her success as a singer to her remarkable teacher Mathilde Marchesi, with whom she worked in Paris before her debut in Rigoletto *in Brussels in 1886. As well as appearances in opera in Europe, the USA and Australia, Melba made many profitable concert tours.*

64. To Mathilde Marchesi, 11 April [1895]

My Dearest Madame—

How far away from all my dear friends—We are travelling night & day & singing 3 times a week to enormous houses—We arrive in San Francisco in a week, where we stay 10 days then we begin our journey homeward thank goodness. Of course I am travelling very luxuriously I have my own car which is fitted up like a house—I have a piano & organ three men servants & two maids.

Toronta & her mother are my guests & they seem very happy—Did you know […] Bennett is with me now, as Dora had to go back to England—My voice is wonderfully fresh & I feel very well—I will write you again from San Francisco—And now Goodbye with much love to you both

Believe me/Your very loving/Nellie Melba

This little article will amuse you!

little article] Pasted at the head of this letter is a clipping from an unidentified newspaper which describes Melba's private rail car as 'worthy of any realm of the old world … for she is the reigning queen of the song world'

65. To Mathilde Marchesi, 23 November 1895

My darling Madame

I wonder if you realise how far I am away from you—out in the far west of America, I never felt so lonely in all my life, so I shall have a nice little chat with my dear little Mother.

To begin with my concert tour is *extraordinarily successful*; if it continues like this till the 21st of December I shall have cleared nearly 400,000 francs in 3 months, no one has done this except Patti. Are you not glad! In spite of all the hard [work?] & travelling my voice is still in beautiful order, all the critics saying they have never heard me to better advantage — I am afraid I am blowing my own trumpet which is a thing I particularly *object* to : but I know all this interests you. I join the Abbey troupe on Dec 27th when I hope my sister & brother will have arrived. I shall be glad to see them—I hope you are quite better & that Blanche & the twins are quite well—I am to sing Zerlina do you approve of this? I think the part will suit me Patti always sings it I telegraphed you to send me your score—I hope you did not think me very cheeky.

Much love to all/from your loving/Nellie

Mr Adamowski whom I saw in Boston sent you all sorts of messages.

Patti] Adelina Patti (1843–1919), Italian soprano   Adamowski] probably Timothee Adamowski (1857–1943), Polish-born violinist who was living in Boston at the time of Melba's tour

George Morrison

George Ernest ('Chinese') Morrison (1862–1920) was born and educated in Geelong, Victoria, eventually graduating in medicine from Edinburgh. An intrepid traveller and adventurer, he became in 1897 the first permanent correspondent of The Times *in Peking where he remained for over twenty years, earning an international reputation. In his letters to Charles Frederic Moberly Bell (1847–1911), the influential manager of* The Times, *Morrison demonstrated the resourcefulness which contributed to his standing as a great newspaper correspondent.*

66. To C.F. Moberly Bell, 12 June 1896

My dear Mr Moberly Bell,

I regret that I have been delayed nearly a week by the action of the authorities. My request for a passport has to be referred to India from whence came back the unsatisfactory reply that British officials cannot issue passports to China; such documents can only be attained on application to Peking or to the Chinese Authorities on the frontier. 'Dr. Morrison,' it said, 'should not be permitted to enter China without one.' Then I induced Mr. Stirling—who has sent endless telegrams urging speed—to telegraph asking permission to make this application for me. After two days permission was given him. Accordingly I am leaving today for the frontier, armed with an application form in English, Shan and Chinese addressed to the Chinese authorities on this frontier.

We *will* persist in treating the Chinese as a European people and because 'Frontier authorities' are spoken of in the article XIV of the Convention of March 1st 1894 we infer that the Chinese have frontier authority. This, I am sure, is not the case, so when I get to the frontier I will go on and look for the authorities. I am very anxious to go to Ssumao.

Unfortunately while delayed here I caught fever and was on my back a day or two. This has pulled me down a little. I have bought two ponies and engaged men to go with me to Keng Tung. The Chief Secretary of the Chief Commissioner in Burma has telegraphed to me: 'Is it not rather risky travelling at this unhealthy season.' And the Burmese frontier agent here informs me in writing that the road is 'infested with Chinese brigands'. This is an unhealthy place at present. Of the 600 men in the regiment, 127 are down with fever.

If a Chinaman were able to read English he would be struck with the very free translation of the English application for my passport. My English reads like this: 'Dr. Morrison wishes to travel and I therefore beg of you to kindly grant him the necessary passport.' This I have reduced in translation to convert into: 'The Prince Doctor, the learned man friend of his Excellency The Viceroy of Yunnan intends to travel into China. I therefore require that in accordance with treaty he shall be given the necessary passport that he may travel in safety with the protection of His Majesty the Emperor … etc.' It has two seals, and every line is underlined with red. The envelope is the largest in the Station and I have stamped it on the outside with a magnificent official looking seal, but as I had no seal I have used instead what does equally well—the lid of a Van Houten's Cocoa tin …

If this passport does not ensure me respect, then I don't know the Chinese.
EVER YOURS FAITHFULLY/G. E. MORRISON

P.S. I am sure you would be pleased to hear the warm-hearted way in which the men in this outlying frontier of the Empire praise the splendid action of your paper all through that crisis when all the world seemed to be leagued against England. They say that your patriotism, your courage and your enthusiasm stirred the hearts of Englishmen in Asia, and made even the timid brave. The chief Indian paper that comes here is the *Rangoon Weekly Gazette*. This paper publishes every week two or three columns lifted from *The Times*.

Mr Stirling] George Claudius Beresford Stirling (1861–1929) at that time Assistant Commissioner and Political Officer in the Burma Political Department   Article XIV] reference to the authority under which passports were to be issued by Chinese officials to British merchants and others wishing to proceed to China from Burma

In England on 26 August 1912 Morrison married Jennie Wark Robin, his New Zealand-born secretary twenty-seven years his junior. The marriage brought Morrison 'new happiness and emotional security'. He attended the Versailles Peace Conference in 1919 as an adviser to the Chinese delegation but illness intervened. He died at Sidmouth in Devon the following year, his devotion to Jennie undimmed.

67. To JENNIE MORRISON, UNDATED

MY DEAREST JENNIE,

I was lying in the easy chair in the court yard thinking of you always thinking of you when your kind note came. It is impossible that sometimes I shall not feel dispirited when I think how unworthy I am of you and when I contrast your bright young life with what I see of myself. Oh God how I love you. I never knew before what it was to love and worship as I love and worship you my dear. What can I do to make you happy, that is all I think about, and make you contented and show you my devotion.

May God Bless you always my dear and shield you and guard you from all harm and give you all the happiness possible in the world.
EVER YOUR LOVING/ERNEST

Mary Broome

Mary Anne Broome (1831–1911) was the wife of Frederick Napier Broome (1842–96), Governor of Western Australia 1882–89. Shrewd and capable, she was credited with being the power behind her irascible husband and beguiling his opponents with her charm. Each of these qualities was called upon when, after Broome's death, she wrote to John Forrest, Premier of Western Australia, seeking a pension. Mary Broome had been married previously to Sir George Barker (d. 1861). Using the name Lady Barker, she wrote novels as well as books on travel, colonial life and cookery.

68. To John Forrest, 3 December 1896

My dear Sir John

I cannot let this first mail go without trying to express to you my deep, deep gratitude for the message Sir Malcolm Fraser conveyed to me from you and your Government and the Colonists on the 28th Nov.

It is just the one, only comfort I have under this frightful and crushing calamity, to know that my lost darling is so warmly and generously appreciated & so tenderly regretted in the Colony we both loved so well, and where by far the happiest part of our lives was spent. To the very last he took the keenest interest in every thing concerning Western Australia—we had each received your pamphlet just before sailing containing the splendid speech you made on the subject of the Coolgardie Water supply, & we read it on board ship, and talked it all over with such pleasant reminiscences, and admiration of your own ground work for the place. I am so shattered that I cannot write a more formal letter of thanks to you, as Premier. This is only a private word from my heart to your kind & feeling one. Your letters were always a great pleasure to him—and we were both, in our new home, surrounded by mementoes of dear West Australia. The Addresses were nearly all framed, & hung round his large office & the Corridor which led to it. Photographs of the House & everything connected with our happy life were always before our eyes.

The magnificent wreath which Sir Malcolm laid on his grave by your orders, is still there (for I go every day to where my poor darling is). I took, last time, a little sprig of myrtle from it, which I am trying to make grow, & the piece of paper conveying the love & regret of the people of W.A. will always be my most precious possession, & I have already asked that it may be placed in my hands when the welcome hour of my own release from "this troublesome world" comes.

He suffered so cruelly at the last, that his one cry was "I want my rest". That is mine also, for I am like a wounded animal who only wants to creep into a hole & die. It is a great comfort that I am so old & that it cannot therefore be very long before I can go to him. I am sure, wherever he is, he wants me. We have been such friends & companions as well as lovers all our lives, that I cannot take up what remains to me of life without him. The fact of my being so much older prevented the idea ever occurring to him or any one else, that I should survive him & need to be provided for, so the only thing he was able to do was to insure his life about 12 years ago for 5000 pounds (which will give exactly 200 pounds a year) and that was intended to continue our eldest son's very modest allowance of 157 pounds a year as a Lt. in the R.A. Without that he cannot remain in the Regt. and at 26 it is too late to start in another career. So in order to prevent his young life from being ruined at its outset, from no fault of his own, poor boy, I am going at 65 years old to start as a practical worker again, & am begging all my friends to find me a place as house keeper, or to take care of Motherless children. This is all I can do, but if by any personal exertion, I can earn a crust & a roof for myself that would enable me to help Guy. Louis is happily independent. What I fear is, that no one will have any thing to do with so broken & shattered an old woman.

My darling was ill 3 months & all that time strength was given to me never to leave him night or day for a moment. I never saw my bed all that time. Every one is so good & kind to me. Mr Chamberlain writes both publicly & privately such beautiful praise of him Ah, it is all too sad & tragic. Such a "bolt out of the blue".

Forgive my being so egotistical. Grief seems to make me so. With my love to your dear wife & kindest regards to you, I am

Yrs faithfully/M.A. Broome

Sir Malcolm Fraser] (1834–1900) Western Australia's first Agent-General in England 1890–98. As colonial secretary in Western Australia 1883–90, he was one of the few senior political figures of the colony to have worked in harmony with Napier Broome   Coolgardie Water supply] the Coolgardie Water Scheme inaugurated in 1895 and completed in 1903, one of the great public works conceived under the premiership of John Forrest   R.A.] Royal Artillery   Guy/Louis] the sons of her second marriage   Mr Chamberlain] Joseph Chamberlain (1836–1914), British Colonial Secretary 1895–1903

Joseph Furphy

Furphy (1843–1912), self-described as 'half bushman and half bookworm', had been contributing short sketches of rural life to the Bulletin *while working in his brother's foundry in Shepparton, Victoria. His novel was published, after extensive revisions, in 1903 as* Such is Life: Being Certain Extracts from the Diary of Tom Collins.

69. To J.F. Archibald, 4 April 1897

Dear Sir,

Circumstances compel me to solicit a private reply of two or three words only.

I have just finished writing a full-sized novel: title "Such is Life"; scene Riverina and northern Vic; temper, democratic; bias, offensively Australian.

Now what publishing firm should I communicate with—Melbourne preferably, but not necessarily? I am absolutely in the dark here, and have no other referee. I am, Sir, Yours very truly,/Joseph Furphy./(Tom Collins.)

The friendship between (Stella Maria(n) Sarah) Miles Franklin (1879-1954) and Joseph Furphy began soon after she published her autobiographical novel My Brilliant Career *in 1901. In spite of Furphy's urging her to stay and write in Australia, Franklin left for the USA in 1906.*

70. To Miles Franklin, 17 July 1904

Dear Miles,

(Which, in view of your unsubstantial, Mahatma-like nature, must be taken as an apostrophe or invocation, rather than as a conventional address)—

It is superfluous to say that I hope you are well, and that you are indenting further boot-marks on the quartz-tailings of Time. And though it must always be a pleasure to render epistolary homage to an intangible Vision (a sort of Sweet Hour of Prayer), I have a special, though small, excuse for the present oblation. Perpend.

Miss Drewitt (you remember her?) in a recent letter referred to Miles Franklin's "bright discourse, and brighter grey eyes—pure grey for intellect." Replying to this, I hinted that, though by no means a gambling man, I had a loose –/6 which said that the colour of Miles's eyes was a pure, soft, treacle-brown. Wasn't I right?

And what are you doing all this time—if it's a fair question? Scorching along the Inky Way?—or collecting more Experience?—or merely sitting on the river's brink, with Old Khayyam? Are you in touch with many, or any, of the lyre-bangers and raconteurs now cumbering this dry continent?

Don't go to America or Europe, Miles. There is variety enough here; between the seething Pandemonium of the cities and the hallowed solitudes of the Out-back; between the serrated profile of the Great Divide and the long, long levels of Riverina. And Literature has hardly yet touched the fringe of Australian life-conditions. Practically nothing has been exploited but the amenities of the Home-station, the hardships of the Selection, and the most unlikely nugget found by the reduced gentleman. Stay among the eucalypti, Miles, and earn the adoration of your countrymen by translating the hosannas and elegies of the Bush into vernacular phrase.

For myself, I am doing a little revision on "Rigby's Romance" in a semi-despondent frame of mind, whilst waiting on that immoral red-covered journal for ungracious acceptance or gleeful rejection. A.G.S. still waves me off, with characteristic dignity: "Take that, ye divvle!" was the postscript to his last letter.

I have been reviling myself for not getting your photo copied, ever since posting it away to Sylvia. Indeed, I am half-resolved never to keep faith again, but in future to follow the devices and desires of my own heart, and let integrity slide. Meantime it rests with you to renew me spiritually, so to speak; and the capacity to do so—if you understand me—seems to embody a certain responsibility.

Yours most sincerely,/Joe Furphy.

that immoral red-covered journal] the *Bulletin*, which published Furphy's work   A.G.S.] Alfred George Stephens (1865–1933) edited the *Bulletin*'s literary section, the Red Page, and was responsible for the *Bulletin*'s book publishing division 1897–1906

71. To Miles Franklin, 28 January 1907

My Matchless Miles,

I approach you to-night in the unaccustomed attitude of a suppliant; spare thou therefore the bloke who confesses his faults; restore thou the cove who is penitent; and it shall be well with thee both here and hereafter.

In the delight of receiving your p.c. I, of course, resolved to reply on that very evening; but something came in the way. And (without a word of a lie) every day since then I thought of you in a strange land, and determined to devote that evening to you—not as a duty, mind, but as a privilege. But the resolve to write a mighty letter when I *did* start has kept me from writing even a modest reply. Profit by my experience, Miles; but use me as a shocking example rather than a copy.

I am almost out of touch with the word-painters and lyre-smiters of our sunshiny land. In fact, my correspondence has dwindled to almost nothing, though my heart is still in the same old spot. I have had nothing in the "B." for 12 months, and only one yarn refused; whilst "S.R." has published about three within the same period, and has now under consideration a short serial. "R's R." is in the hands of Geo. Robertson, to be judged on its demerits, and probably fired-out.

I am very glad to hear that the aroma of the gum-leaf and the perfume of the wattle-blossom haunt you still. But ah me! Miles, wait till Col. Themistocles Z. Corncob tells you through his nose that you are his stately white gum, and his pensive she-oak, and his matchless river wattle. Mind you, I love the American—as was incidentally demonstrated some time ago, in the choice of Rigby's nationality. But Australia cannot spare you, Miles. We want to make our land a classic land; we want to be the Ionians of modern time (the term "Greeks" is too wide). And of all Australian women we can least spare Miles. There is a false note in Australian literature, a note which your own mental temperament, without any forcing, may largely correct. I mean the note of cynicism, or contemptuous pessimism, arising simply from lack of faith in the potencies of human nature. And this is most shallow. Young as you are, Miles, you can see the world much better—more intelligent, humane and refined—than in the days when little Syb burnt her fingers with Popper's pipe. And your business is to make a record; that's what you are here for, and that's what your broad forehead was given to you for. The question is not whether you'll transform the world—grasp this sorry Scheme of Things entire—but whether you'll apply your little pick and shovel to the vast alp of Ignorance which still obstructs our view of the Promised Land … To be sure, I myself am doing nothing in the shape of mental navvy-work just now, but that is because I am working about 12 hours per diem at a new home for one of my boys—clearing scrub, fencing, well-sinking &c. But when the long winter evenings come! by the powers, Miles, I'll make up for it all.

Now dear girl let us keep in touch for the future. A p.c. from you will content me, if it must be so; and this delay won't be repeated … It is moonlight, and I'll go down the hill 100 yards to get a leaf of jarrah for you to weep over.

Your sincere friend, /Joe Furphy.

'The B'] the *Bulletin*   S.R.] refers to the journal, *Steele Rudd's Magazine*. Steele Rudd was the pseudonym of Arthur Hoey Davis (1868–1935), author of *On Our Selection* and other stories of bush life   R's R] *Rigby's Romance* was not published in full until 1946   Geo. Robertson] George Robertson (1860–1933) was co-founder of the Australian publishing firm Angus & Robertson   'little Syb'] the heroine of Franklin's *My Brilliant Career*

Patrick McMahon Glynn

This proposal of marriage was written in Sydney during a session of the Federal Convention at which the Australian Constitution was being debated. Irish-born politician, lawyer and journalist, Glynn (1855–1931) was one of the Convention delegates from South Australia. His proposal to Abigail Dynon (1864–1929) was accepted and he was married at St Francis' Church, Melbourne, within the week.

72. To Abigail Dynon, 7 September 1897

Dear Miss Dynon

I suppose it would do poor justice to the reputation my countrymen bear for courage—though in this case it may be called audacity—if I did not risk, as so many others in other cases have, with better or worse fortune done, the inevitable question. The world is made up of incompatibles, or rather contradictions; without the Union of opposites there would be no possibility of the average that makes progress. I am, in most of the qualities that build a character, at one pole, you at the other; but your sex is born to redeem, and Goodness Knows there is a big field for redemption in my case. Well, you can well think that I am, for once at all events in my life, in a bit of a muddle. I have written pamphlets, leading articles, essays etc., by the mile, but never before put in writing the impertinence of a proposal of marriage. And this has to be done, at the table of the Legislative Assembly of New South Wales, with the Federal Convention sitting, and Mr. Lyne, within a yard of me, pouring on the too-thinly-protected top of my head, a niagra of figures. However, I must attempt it.

Well, Dear Miss Dynon, to be candid, which indeed is my dearest desire. I heard of you six or seven years ago, and from what a lady who knew you well said of you then, I know, if on meeting you I did not feel it instinctively, that you are as deserving of the reputation you bear as I am under the Estimate many, or rather some of my generous friends in Kindness form of me. I say this, because it will tell you at once, that I cannot possibly misunderstand you. You unfortunately—or rather, perhaps, fortunately for myself,—know little of me; that is, outside my reputation as a public man. But as far as *I* can say it, I feel I am a Bohemian in temperament, fond of the softer—I don't like to say poetic—side of life; liable, like many of my too romantic country men to extremes of spirit, by no means correct as the world goes, but at all events capable of discerning, if not following, the Right. The girl that takes me will deserve an indulgence—a dispensation from purgatory, so that I may have at least a negative recommendation.

But I find, with my usual want of pluck in matters outside my line, I am becoming all preface. The Sum of it all is this, if you consent to marry me, Miss Dynon, you will, for the sacrifice, deserve Heaven, and probably save me from somewhere else. May I ask you to do so. I am by no means well off—but why should I say that to you—but I can and do work, and though, if I may use the term for the Sake of its expressiveness, devil-may-care in most matters, will try under the great responsibility, to become financially orthodox, I don't care the proverbial rap for the Ceremonial side of life.

If you consent to become my wife—a great word—why should we not be married at once. It will have the advantage for me that the matter will be inevitably settled before you know too much of me. It is a great occasion here. I have plenty of friends here now, and, though a bit of a reprobate in Religion, an aunt, Superioress of the Sisters of St Joseph, who would back me up if necessary. And she reminds me of one, who gives a relative merit to her son. I have a Mother that, apart from prejudice, I can from the bottom of my heart say, is, as my aunt said on Sunday, a saint, if ever a woman, who is no narrow puritan, can be one. I never yet met a man or woman that did not respect her disposition; an able, self-sacrificing, as well as thoroughly human and feminine woman.

If you have me, I can honestly promise you to give you no divided heart, and to live no double life. You will know me, for good or bad, as I am.

Well, if you will bless me, I will with your consent, go for you on Friday, marry on Saturday, and return same day. If you will come—anyhow I wish you would—over at once, so much the better. We can be married on the arrival of the train. My friend Mr. O'Malley will give me away; I hope he has not done so already. This is a lot to ask, but the occasion is my great excuse. I am not my own master now—we are the servants of the Nation and its destinies. Besides as I said, I know you thoroughly—and after we can call one another wife and husband; well what does the unorthodox way of settling the bond matter.

In Hopes of a reply that will enable me to really begin to live, I am, Dear Miss Dynon,

YOUR ADMIRER AND FRIEND UNDER ANY CIRCUMSTANCES/P. McM. GLYNN

Mr. Lyne] William John Lyne (1844–1913) became Premier of New South Wales in 1899. As a delegate to the 1897–98 Australasian Federal Convention, Lyne argued that sections of the draft Federal Constitution bill disadvantaged New South Wales   my friend Mr O'Malley] King O'Malley (1858?–1953), later Minister for Home Affairs in the Federal government, was best man at Glynn's wedding

73. TO ELLEN GLYNN, 4 JANUARY 1901

MY DEAR MOTHER

I am, as you may suppose, here for the celebrations connected with the Inauguration of the Commonwealth. The New South Wales Government are the entertainers, and their hospitality is lavish. My residence is at the *Grosser Kurfurst*, a German vessel of 13,000 odd tons, at which the distinguished visitors who are the guests of the Government—or rather some of them—put up. We have Ministers, Knights, leading Politicians, Judges, Bishops, and other celebrities there. The wonderful Sydney Harbor is alive with Steamers & crafts of all sizes, ablaze with festoons of Electric Light and other illuminations at night. As a Harbor, with its 11 or 12 hundred miles of bays & inlets, its depth at all places up to the greatest tonnages, and its bustle of boats, it is beyond one's dreams. The city is lit at night with marvellous devices of electricity & gas; the Electric trams bright with light & people; bands playing at intervals; the Streets Packed with the best mannered, best humored, and most sociable, People I ever met. Their bearing is a lesson in the refining influence of the pervading sense of democratic institutions and corporate ownership & control.

The City is given over to eight days Rejoicing. This morning I went round Part of the Harbor in a Government Steam Launch, and tonight, the night of Special Harbor illuminations, view the Pyrotechnic Display from one of their vessels. But the Papers I send you will give the details of Present Sydney Life.

The First Federal Government is formed, but though of on the whole able men, of men mostly for a time ambitious of the Position and who Played their cards accordingly. I was to leave tonight—but G. H. Reid, who but for Political accidents would have been first Premier, asked me to spend Saturday and Sunday with him and on Monday leave with him for Melbourne. He is perhaps the Best Platform Speaker in the Empire, and will, I think, be the Second Federal Premier. We crossed swords on the convention, but our lines—a free trade tariff—are now convergent, and when others, looking for Federal office, hesitated and trimmed, I took up his work of educating the People against Protection.

WITH BEST WISHES FOR THE NEW CENTURY TO YOU ALL,/YOUR AFFECTIONATE SON/P. MCM. GLYNN

G.H. Reid] George Houston Reid (1845–1918) Premier of New South Wales 1894–99, Prime Minister of Australia 1904–05

ETHEL TURNER

Ethel Sibyl Turner (Mrs Curlewis) (1870–1958), author of Seven Little Australians *(1894), began her literary career at Sydney Girls' High School, where she and her sister Lilian edited a school magazine. Later the Turners founded the* Parthenon, *a sixpenny monthly for which the sisters wrote romantic fiction of the kind described in the letter with which Ethel dedicated* The Camp at Wandinong *to Lilian.*

74. TO LILIAN TURNER, 1898

TO MY SISTER LILIAN

It seems but yesterday when you were fifteen, I not far behind, and one of us was suddenly seized with a desire to write something.

And immediately the other was seized with the same overwhelming desire,—had we not all our little lives done everything together, and cared for nothing the other could not share?

We used to lock the bedroom door and write at the old marble washstand that was so generously roomy; no housewifery has ever been able since to take those ink-stains from its surface. Do you remember the characters we conjured up? Our heroes with their proud black eyes, and their invariable habit of grinding their heels into the gravel in moments of annoyance? My heroines, who had brown starry, heavily lashed eyes, and were always attired in clinging cream dresses, with one crimson rosebud nestling in their regal coronets of hair? Yours, who had dreamy violet orbs, wore robes of dead white silk on every possible and impossible occasion, and were always drawing their slim, willowy figures up to their full height and gazing at their persecutors in noble indignation?

Oh, the paper we wasted, and the lessons we left undone that we ought to have done! Oh, the candles that burnt to their last breath, and used to flicker and go out near midnight, just when the whispered reading of closely written pages reached the most thrilling point!

You were never satisfied with your stories unless you could work in a murder, and your most harmless people used to kill each other for entirely insufficient reasons. I was never happy unless my favourite character or characters had died on beautiful death-beds to slow music. Do you remember that story I wrote where, when I scribbled "Finis" (we scorned the word "End"), there was no one left alive but the old, faithful servant—I mean retainer?

Our faith in each other in those days made our mutual criticisms gentle and our admiration boundless.

This plain little tale bears your name, and gleans its grace in bearing it. So the gift must make you as a child again, blind to all faults and pleased to offer praise.

E.S.C./MOSSMAN'S BAY/SYDNEY

SIDNEY WEBB

*The Fabian socialists Sidney (1859–1947) and Beatrice Webb visited Australia in 1898
at the end of a tour to investigate municipal affairs in the United States, New Zealand
and Australia. In 1895 the Webbs had founded the London School of Economics and
Political Science. Graham Wallas (1858–1932) was one of the first staff appointments to
the new institution. He was appointed Professor of Political Science in 1914.*

75. TO GRAHAM WALLAS, 26 OCTOBER 1898

DEAR WALLAS

I just snatch a few minutes before the mail to write a much delayed letter. We are
flying around among Premiers and Civil Servants, Mayors and Socialists, picking up
many hints. I am afraid we shall not be able to bring you back any new or complete
theory of Democracy—things here are cut in much the same mould as in England, and
why, after all, should there *be* any completely rounded and systematically perfect theory
of anything whatsoever?

One practical observation is interesting. Australia is utterly and completely unlike
America in every respect. From top to bottom there is absolutely no likeness or analogy.
So whatever discouragement you derived from America—in the quite unfounded belief
that the U.S. is a Democratic country—this place would restore your spirits, and
persuade you that what is wrong in the U.S. is the peculiar copy of 18th century Toryism
that Hamilton fastened on America 120 years ago. Not that this place is 'advanced'—it is
very much what England was in 1870. But owing to their having copied the real English
Constitution of 1850–60, instead of the nominal English Constitution of 1789, you
have here a genuine Democracy, the people really getting what it wishes to get. The
politicians and the newspapers are in fact, the *best* product of Australia; and they are very
good indeed. The trouble is that the people are an exceptionally Individualist graft from
our Individualist epoch (1840–70); and they are all of them gambling profitmakers keen
on realising the Individualist ideals of the lower middle class of 1840–70.

We shall bring you back a new crop of reasons why you should be satisfied with our
Voluntary School compromise—refusal of aid to the Denominations, exclusion of Religion *and History* from the State Schools, consequent isolation of 1/5th of the children in
uninspected R.C. schools, and terror of every Education Minister at 're-opening' the
question preventing any improvement in the State School system.

Our experience of Payment of Members leads us to attach *less and less* importance to
all the objections yet urged against it. (We have discovered however a new drawback of
some force—yet on the whole not outweighing its advantages, or their practical necessity.)

We have just seen the new School prospectus and in it the paragraph as to your
lectures, which will be very interesting. But I don't find that the Australian Democracy
was or is based on any abstract ideas, or arbitrary psychology. We are interested to find it

really an admirable success in all essentials—purity, public spirit and results—what it lacks is intellectual leadership, but this is lacking in the Colony as a whole. What there is goes into politics, and certainly no conceivable other system or government would have produced anything like such good results.

WITH LOVE/SIDNEY WEBB

BEATRICE WEBB

It has been said that while the Webbs were one of the best-known couples to have visited colonial Australia, they were little understood or appreciated. In the case of Beatrice Webb (1858–1943), this was due to a snobbishness and arrogance which placed her at odds with the Australian temperament. In this letter to her sister Mary Elizabeth Playne (1848–1923), Beatrice Webb gave a lively but opinionated account of a visit to the Melbourne Cup. The Bulletin *commented later that the Webbs had investigated 'the working of the crack racecourse much as though it had been a factory'.*

76. TO MARY PLAYNE, 7 NOVEMBER 1898

MY DEAR MARY

This will be the last time of writing before we leave for England, and I feel that I owe you the letter.

We finished up at Melbourne with the great racing carnival—the Melbourne Cup—the meeting place of all the rich folk of the Australian colonies. There must have been over 200,000 present, but the arrangements were so perfect that there was no sense of hurry or crowding; the three sections of the community—the working-folk who go without payment on the 'Flat', the middle-class who pay 2/6 and go on the 'Hill', and the well-to-do who pay 10/6 for the 'grand stand', being kept *absolutely separate*, with separate trains and separate stations and separate entrances—a most undemocratic arrangement! (but then Australia is the most *un*democratic as it is the most *un*aristocratic nation in the world—unadulterated bourgeois!) Sidney and I went off tolerably early and wandered about the Flat and the Hill, watching the bookmakers, the pedlars and the 'Comic men' before we joined our friends in the grandstand. We had been provided with four tickets as honorary members of the Victorian Racing Club—(the organisation which runs the whole of the colonies' racing)—and the secretary had been deputed to show us round the saddling paddock, the jockey's quarters and the Ring. All the rich women of Australia put on their best dresses for the Cup: I never saw an uglier crowd—a predominance of cheap silks and satins (Sidney says the result of our ad valorem duties!) elaborately made: figures like those of town-bred servants and no notion of how to walk or hold themselves. We lunched with the leading members of the club: a nondescript body including past Conservative premiers, judges and dignitaries. The present radical government was conspicuous by its absence. We were placed in the 'Governor's stand' for the race—the vice-regal party including four of the Australian Governors, their wives, daughters, and A.D.C.'s—the latter small-headed youths of aristocratic family and tame-cat manner. (The A.D.C.'s are the weak point at the 'Government Houses' and are productive of much evil—passive and active.) Altogether the whole business interested us; but the crowd of over-dressed ugly people who were betting heavily because they thought betting the 'right thing' was somewhat depressing and we were glad to get away and spend the evening with one of the university professors and talk 'shop' with Judge Chomley who is now engaged in reorganising the Victorian Civil Service.

From Melbourne we payed a flying visit to the two goldmining towns—Bendigo and Ballarat and thence to Adelaide—the last stage on our journey. Here we found your old friend Edward Wallington in command of Government House, (the Governor, Sir Fowell Buxton, having gone to England.) Curiously enough we had heard of him throughout Australia as the ideal *aide de camp*—always instanced to us, by thoughtful observers, as a proof that a permanent professional official would be far better than the flighty young aristocrats brought over by governors; but I had never connected him with the Wallington we used to know. He, on his side, had been instructed by the Governor before he left to look after us without in the least knowing who we were except that we were 'literary people'. So you can imagine how pleased we both were to find that we were old friends! He came to dine with us yesterday and talked to us very freely of the three or four 'Government Houses' he had served in, and the different excellencies or defects of the various governors.

He is just the same pleasant discreet man as of old, quick at understanding a suggestion and with a wily shrewd judgement of whether it is practicable. He is vastly superior to any of the '*aides*' or governor's secretaries we have met and ought to be taken on as the permanent 'Society' official when a 'Governor-General' is appointed for 'Federated Australia'. He has grown distinctly 'old-maidish' and his mental attitude towards all creeds and political views has been emphasised by his 15 years service at the Government Houses of various colonies. He enquired after you and Arthur, Bill and Mary Pollock most affectionately.

The Acting-Governor—Chief Justice Way—is a fussy little Methodist who is violently hostile to the present Premier—Kingston—a burly ruffian who works tremendously hard and is an unsavoury combination of the demagogue and a London vestryman of the old type—he is also somewhat disreputable in his private life. The Bishop and his wife are said to be charming people and we dine with them tomorrow. Otherwise I don't think we shall find such interesting folk here as at Sydney and Melbourne.

We arrive Naples December 16th. *Rome* December 20th and remain there over Xmas. Do write Poste Restante.

EVER YOURS/BW

Judge Chomley] Arthur Wolfe Chomley (1837–1914), a County Court judge in Melbourne
Edward Wallington] Edward William Wallington (1854–1933) served as private secretary to several

Australian colonial governors and, after federation, to Lord Hopetoun as Governor-General of Australia
Kingston] Charles Cameron Kingston (1850–1908), Premier of South Australia 1893–99, a supporter
of federation and a member of the first Commonwealth Parliament.

Herbert Brookes

*In 1897 Herbert Robinson Brookes (1867–1963), mining engineer, later businessman,
pastoralist and philanthropist, married Jessie (Jennie) Strong, daughter of the Reverend
Charles Strong of the Australian Church. Jennie died suddenly in April 1899; this letter
is addressed to her memory. Befriended in his depression by Alfred Deakin, Brookes
married Deakin's 21-year-old daughter Ivy in 1905.*

77. To Jessie (Jennie) Brookes, 11 May 1899

Amavimus, Amamus, Amabimus
Dear Angel Lover

It is May 11 1899 at the mine. I am here without you. How I am going to bear up
throughout the future however long however short God & your own dear spirit knows
not I. Whatever happens dear I want to feel your continual presence up-lifting me &
prompting me to pure good deeds in thy dear name. I want to be a living witness of the
truth that 'No lapse of years can conquer love' 'nor canker love.'

To the nurse on that awful Tuesday afternoon when your fatal agony commenced so
suddenly & so unexpectedly & whilst the train was bearing me back from the mine in
calm sweet happiness to your loving arms (as I thought & you promised)—To the Nurse
you said 'I know I am going to die dear Nursey & it is not half bad tell Bert that *I am
always His*'

You lived to meet me lover on the Tuesday evening & till Thursday night at 12
o'clock & told me many things & wished to tell me more but strength failed you. But I
knew everything you could have said dear love—we could read each other's thoughts &
how often we did

'And in sweet Auburn's Fatal Grove
God's finger touched you & you slept'

'Tell him I am always his' this loving message set to wizard music in my soul will
carry me down the corridors of life till I rest beside you in 'our' modest little grave. Oh
lover! Would that I was with you now. But I'll bear up & 'mingle all the world with thee'
Amavimus, Amamus, Amabimus.

These were the three words inscribed on your hero Kingsley's grave, & which you
said we should have on ours. They are going on dear lover. What have you not done for
me darling precious both during your brief sweet sunny life & now that you have passed
to rest or to heaven the home of our loved ones

You have made me forget myself & to count the body as naught—though not to abuse it.

You have conquered my fear of death—& my hatred of the grave & the cemetery

You have taught me to pray again as my mother did as a little child

You have made me realise God's presence

Hold him very near

You have proved to me dear angel lover that Love conquers all things, that love is stronger than Death nay that love is actually broadened, deepened, chastened & purified with death.

Lover—you Loved me & I saw God through your dear eyes.

How I have borne up under the awful strain of our parting God & your own sweet self know only—this I know—it has not been through any virtue or reserve strength in myself but through you & your complete & perfect love for me which made me feel that I must weed myself & my comfort out, bear up & move onward to heigher heights, making my soul worthier thine with the prime conviction that we too some time some where will meet again. God comfort me & send you to guide & guard & watch my stumbling feet.

I am writing this letter to you dear lover & am going to have it sealed up in the tin box in which you placed a piece of our wedding cake & which was to have been sealed up & kept for our silver wedding.

My God! Our Silver Wedding. May we keep it in heaven dear lover! If I am ordered by God to live to celebrate it on earth in the flesh alone—then dear lover you must come in the spirit & be with me then & always but more than ever on the 27 October 1922

Good Lord! 1922! Can I face it, I doubt it. God help me to keep your memory clear pure unsullied unspotted. God help me to keep down my sensuous frame in complete subjection—that frame dear lover which was dedicated to you & which is now Sacred to your Memory.

Oh God! the heart of life is taken clean away from me & my interest is in the other world where my angel lover shines like a star. Dear God! Whilst I am here put a little heart into life, send my little angel lover to me to help me to do some little silent deeds in memory of her & in your dear service. My soul responds. God & my dear lover helping me I will. God comfort me!

Lover mine come to me & keep me pure in heart till I fade away from this life & dawn into the other where you will be awaiting me with loving outstretched arms.

God & my Lover princess [?] be with me during the long dark years & make them bright.

My own dear Lover I feel as though your coffin is being sealed up again. I am just about to put this hurried letter to you in the little box you prepared for our wedding cake & with it I am going to put some little Kodak prints of our home at the Berry West— and then get the pipeman at the mine to solder it up to preserve it as best we can against the decay of time.

Lover my heart is broken
Goodbye!
And though my lips say Adieu they cannot think the thought Farewell.
Mine Mine for ever ever Mine!
'Tell him I am always his'
Yes dear God & tell her that I am always hers.
Soul of my Soul heart of my heart/Princess [?] Lover Goodbye/Yours for
Ever Bert.

Amavimus, Amamus, Amabimus] We have loved, we love, we shall love

ALEXANDER MORRISON

In 1857 Alexander Morrison (1829–1903), sixth son of a Morayshire farmer, who was then headmaster of a Lanarkshire grammar school, was invited by the Free Church Presbytery of Victoria to be headmaster of Scotch College in Melbourne. The school flourished under Morrison, and he became an influential figure in Melbourne's cultural life. His part in organising a Public Schools Demonstration of loyalty during the royal visit of 1901 (see Letter 79) is described in this letter to his sister in Scotland.

78. To Kate Morrison, 25 May 1901

My dearest Kate,

It is a long time since I have written to you or heard from you. I daresay the blame lies with me. I intend now to shift the blame on to you and to give you a chance of answering a letter. And during the last month there has been no lack of matter to write about. I daresay you will see in the papers all the movements of the Duke and Duchess of York and Cornwall. I never expected to be brought so much directly in contact with royalty and to get very gracious words from our future King and Queen. The Colony (not now a Colony but a State) gave them a right royal reception, and they have won, especially she, golden opinions from all. The arches, illuminations etc. were really splendid, and the enthusiasm of the people was boundless. For ten days, all business was virtually suspended, and there was nothing but receptions, processions etc. The great function was the opening of the Commonwealth Parliament held in the Exhibition Building, capable of seating comfortably twelve or thirteen thousand people. It was a great historic occasion and well worthy of the honour conferred on us by the King sending his son to open it. The second large function was the Public Schools Demonstration again in the great Exhibition. I had the honour and the work of initiating and carrying out this great function, and I have been praying that in my lifetime no Royal Duke will visit Australia. I have never in all my life had such a task imposed on me. I had the principal share in getting up a similar function thirty six years ago on the occasion of the visit of the Duke of Edinburgh, but all the then Headmasters of the other Public Schools are dead long ago—some since then have had four Headmasters. The present Heads are all good men, but young, and without much knowledge or experience of the community or the world. As soon as it was announced that the Duke and Duchess were coming out I had a meeting of the Headmasters and proposed to follow the example and precedent of 1867. They gave me all throughout cordial assistance. In various ways I had been brought, when he was Governor of Victoria, into close contact with Lord Hopetoun, the Governor-General, and very early opened communications with him, and got at once his consent to include our Prize giving among the functions for the Royal Visitors. Everything had to be submitted to Chamberlain and when his consent was obtained, Lord Hopetoun took charge of it. Everything that was to be done—every visit—all was arranged by him! He is a dear man, a true great man and I'll never forget his kindness to me. We had to be most careful about precedence as we had distinguished men from all quarters of the globe, and to secure that all got places to rank was no easy matter. I had been present at all the other entertainments and Public functions and the Headmasters all took notes and kept our eyes open. We had a great University Commencement—a conferring of degrees. On that occasion on account of being the Senior member of the Council, I had first the honour of leading the Duchess to her seat and then joined the Council and the procession that conducted the Duke to his seat on the dais and I sat next him on his right hand. He, Lord Tennyson, Governor of South Australia, and Barton, premier of the Commonwealth and many others then took their degrees in our University. The Duke talked just like any other young fellow and laughed heartily at some clever points and songs by the students. On shaking hands with them at her leaving the Duchess said to me: 'I hope to have the pleasure of meeting you at your own great demonstration'. On the Saturday night before Tuesday the 14th I happened to come across the programme of our proceedings—printed on satin paper—of our Speech Day in 1867—when the Duke of Edinburgh presided and I sent it over to Lord Hopetoun with a short note. He evidently showed it to the Duke and Duchess for on meeting her afterwards at the head of a very influential number of gentlemen—on shaking hands, the first words she said were: 'I thank you so much for your kindness and consideration in sending the programme and I appreciate it highly'. All aver that our function was splendidly managed. I was in the Chair, the Duke on my right taking in the Countess, the Governor-General on my left taking in the Duchess. The proceedings went on like clockwork. I had promised faithfully to have the first part of our function over in forty minutes. I showed on my watch to Hopetoun that we were over three minutes before time. The second part was to finish by one o'clock (we began at twelve). We were all over and they left the dais five minutes before one o'clock. Both were most gracious and professed themselves delighted with the proceedings. Royalty will stand only an hour at any function so Lord Hopetoun told me and he was much pleased with our proceedings. Four hundred and fifty prizes were presented, my speech and the Duke's reply, which you will see in the papers were all done in about forty or forty two minutes, and there was no hurrying, no confusion. I got a very nice letter from Lady Mary Lygon, lady-in-waiting to the Duchess, expressing by command how greatly she was pleased with my kindness in sending a memento of the Duke of Edinburgh and the Press and Public all allow that it was an historic occasion so many boys seeing and getting their prizes from their King to be, and had I been a younger man I should have been much elated. Of course it is pleasant to feel that you gave thirteen thousand an excellent opportunity of seeing the Royal pair, but after all, my greatest pleasure from the event consisted in the fact that I was able to do my part well on a great occasion when so much was expected of me. I was as cool as at an ordinary Speech Day and I was much helped all along by the text 'In quietness and confidence shall be your strength'. I have sent papers to all the clan—few alas now remaining—which will give a full description. Representatives of all the great British papers were present, and I daresay you will see some accounts in the Home papers. The only unpleasant thing from the whole arose from my inability to give tickets of admission to thousands who applied for them. I was literally besieged by them, morning noon and night I had no rest. And after it was all over I took my luncheon and fell asleep about a quarter past two and slept soundly for two and a half hours and next day was as well as ever.

I am writing very hurriedly, as I came down here to rest not to write letters. The Duke made an excellent speech, read it in a clear distinct voice. Of course in such a high building, no voice could reach all. I am thankful that all passed over well. At the College we are all well. I have the children with me, dearer and more prized than ever. I had them in good places to see the Duke and Duchess and the boys taking their prizes. I am sorry I cannot write to all Home friends. Tell them about the event when you see them. Write to me at length, I get few letters from home now.

My love to each and all and ever my dearest Kate/Believe me, Your very loving brother/Alex. Morrison.

Chamberlain] Joseph Chamberlain (1836–1914) English statesman who held office as Secretary of State for the Colonies 1895–1903

George, Duke of Cornwall and York

The future King George V (1865–1936), accompanied by his wife, visited Australia in 1901 to open the first Federal Parliament in Melbourne. The Duke and Duchess were the guests principally of the recently appointed Governor-General, the Earl of Hopetoun and Lady Hopetoun, though visits were made to other states and to New Zealand. Complex protocol added a dimension of strain to this long and ambitious tour which, however, passed smoothly enough, at least as far as a grateful Royal Duke was concerned. This letter of thanks was written on board HMS Ophir *off the coast of South Australia.*

79. To John Hope, Earl of Hopetoun, 8 July 1901

My dear Hopie

It was more than kind of you & Lady Hopie taking the trouble to come all the way to Tasmania to help the Dodds's to entertain us, without you both, our visit would not have been the success it was, nor anything like as pleasant. It was I assure you my dear Hopie with the greatest regret that I took leave of you on Saturday morning: as with the exception of our visit to New Zealand we have practically been together since the 6th of May, & besides the great pleasure of your companionship, your excellent & kind advice so readily given has been invaluable to me. Neither the Duchess or I will ever forget the kind hospitality of Lady Hopie & yourself, while staying with you, we felt exactly as if we were at home & we cannot exaggerate our appreciation of the manner in which you received & entertained us & our large Staff, during those very happy & memorable weeks. I should like to add how very grateful we were to all members of your Staff, for the great & willing assistance which we received from them at all times; if you will allow me to say so, I think you have got a capital lot.

It is not for me to say that our visit to Australia has been a success, but if that is the general opinion, of one thing I am certain—that success was almost entirely due, to the fact of your being Governor General & that your kind personal attention was given to every arrangement & indeed detail, which could possibly conduce to our comfort & convenience.

Australia is indeed to be congratulated on having you at the head of affairs in these early & anxious days of the Commonwealth, may your work prosper, & when you return home at the end of your labours, no one amongst your many friends, my dear Hopie, will greet you with greater affection than your sincere friend

George

Hopie] John Adrian Louis Hope (1860–1908), 7th Earl of Hopetoun, later 1st Marquess of Linlithgow, first Governor-General of the Commonwealth of Australia, 1 January 1901–9 January 1903 Dodds's] Sir John Stokell Dodds (1848–1914) and Lady Dodds. As Chief Justice of Tasmania, Dodds administered the government of that state from 14 August 1900–8 November 1901

Miles Franklin

(Stella) Miles Franklin (1879–1901) (see Letter 70) grew up in the Tumut region of New South Wales. Her literary career began with the autobiographical novel, My Brilliant Career *(1901), published by Blackwood's of Edinburgh with a foreword by Henry Lawson. Her letter to the* Bulletin *editor J.F. Archibald is a scarcely veiled reproach for his having failed to give her the encouragement she had from Lawson. Her commitment to literary nationalism and her feminist beliefs are seen here, as in her other writings.*

80. To J.F. Archibald, 6 September 1901

My dear Sir

Per same post I send you a copy of a self-written yarn entitled, "My Brilliant Career"; if you would kindly accept same you will afford me much gratification. Don't imagine me so unsophisticatedly green as to think the ignorance and inexperience of a bush [girl of] 18 years. (most unadulterated too) could produce anything that a litterateur of yr. experience would bother reading but spare me a moment's explanation:—

In '99 I sent you an MS. You, or "Alex Montgomery" for you, wrote to me and said you hadn't time to read it but from glances here and there thought the story fairly well written and gave me some good information-advice. It was the first honest letter I received since attempting fledgling gyrations in a pen and ink career and I shall always remember it.

The scribbling submitted to you was rough draft of this yarn. I rewrote and appealed to our Poet Lawson for help. You know him as yr. name is in his book; so you will know he didn't hum & haw but came to my rescue oh! so kindly & sympathetically as only a Henry Lawson could or would. You see the result.

The title should be:-

"My Brilliant (?) Career", also any passages not sufficiently tame for the Sunday school ilk of readers have been omitted reducing the yarn to a correct girly-girlishness. To the discretion or prejudice or something of Blackwood I am indebted but without gratitude for this. In the printing many mistakes have been made in vernacular "corker" being substituted for "cooker", "choke" for "chock" & other errors.

Mr Lawson says the book is true to Australia—this has made me happy. My sex, brain & much etc. preclude me from being great or wise, but the commonest of us can be true & as that has been my careful endeavour I am pleased with the remark.

Thanking you for that letter,

Sir,/Respectfully/Miles Franklin./(A bush-whacker from "the Land O'lots of time".)

PETER HANDCOCK

Peter Joseph Handcock (1868–1902), soldier and blacksmith, was born at Peel in New South Wales. In 1899 he enlisted for the South African War in the 2nd Contingent of the 1st New South Wales Rifles, later transferring to the Bush Veldt Carbineers where he came under the command of fellow Australian Lieutenant Harry Harbord Morant (1864?–1902), known as 'The Breaker'. They and two others were charged with murdering eight Boers. Morant and Handcock faced a court-martial, were found guilty and sentenced to death by firing squad. They were executed in Pretoria on 27 February 1902. The case, with its manifest ambiguities and uncertainties, aroused bitter controversy. Handcock's stoic acceptance of his fate is apparent in this poignant letter of farewell.

81. TO MRS DEMPSEY, 27 FEBRUARY 1902

DEAR SISTER

I have but an hour or so longer to exist and altho my brain has been harrissed for four long weary months I cant refrain from writing you a few last lines, I am going to find out the grand secret, I will face my God, with the firm belief I am innocent of murder. I obeyed my orders and served my King as I thought best. If I oversteped my duty I can only ask my People and country for forgiveness. Tell poor Polly to take care of little Illem for me at all costs. They were my greatist comforts at Home & my greatest trouble now I hope my country will see my children cared for I will die brave for the sake of all, God, forgive any enemys. I give you peace forever I have not heard if our Brother Eugene was killed in this retched war or not But if not tell him & Will I have gone to rest Tell Peter and Willie to be good to their sister, God, be with you in your trouble

FROM YOUR FOND BROTHER/P. J HANDCOCK

Australia for ever

Amen

best love from Koko to all old friends especially P. Benehenan & G. Seaman & Gibbons was one of my best here a Bathurst Boy.

my children] Handcock was survived by his wife Bridget, two sons and a daughter   a Bathurst Boy] as a youth, Handcock had worked in Bathurst; in July 1888 he had been married in the Bathurst Cathedral

J.H. Morrow

A postscript to the tragedy of violent death and the subsequent execution of 'Breaker' Morant and Handcock which had been played out on the Imperial frontier is given in this letter of consolation from the unknown J.H. Morrow, Gaol Warder, to Handcock's sister in South Australia. Through the uncertainties of spelling and composition comes a message of the greatest dignity and sincerity.

82. To Mrs Dempsey, 28 February 1902

Dear Mrs Dempsey

I Hope you will Excuse Me for taking the Liberty of writing to you it is with regret I have to Do so I was the Last warder on Duty over your Brother *an my* friend. A *South Australia* H. H. Morant was out here over 2 years in the South Australian Mt. Rifles an served trough the war he got the *Bar* for 'Cape' Colony an A *Bar* for Johannesburg an A Bar for Pretoria also the *Bar* for *Belfast* Medal also I was his Greatest friend all trough an got the same Honors But the troops went home over 12 months ago an Morant went on as Lieut in the Bush velth. Carboniers an I went on as Guard on the Railway an only got Transfered to Pretoria Prison A few weeks as *warder* an on the 22 your Brother an morant an 2 more *Lieutenants* 1 Victorian an one from Newzeland 4 in all 2 sentensed Penelservitude an the other 2 shot the fased Death without A Murmur an *had* only 48 hours notice of the fact your Brothers trouble Was you an his *children* he faced Death 'as' Brave men could an I was with them until the Last shot 30 odd Boars on Account of the Boars shooting there Captain the say the are not Guilty of the charge the were sentensed to Death for shooting there mates it was as nice a funerl as Ever Left the Gaol there was less than 20 officers on A Number of australians followed the Remains there will Be A Head Stone Erected By australians then we will send you the Poto of the Grav He Died as Brave as Men could saying Good By to each other. Everyone that looked on said it was a Shame to shoot 2 so Brave men I hope you will for his mates sake an your Brothers do your Best for the children his Person Belongings will Reach you Later on when the are Given out from the Prison you will get several Letters from friends here mostly from Cangroo Land. I must Draw to A close this time By saying good By God Bless you all from your *sincire* friend

J. J. Morrow/Warder Pretoria/Gaol/Transvall South africa.

friends ... from Cangroo Land] Australians

MINNIE KORAN

In July 1902 Minnie Koran, a young Queensland Aborigine, was forcibly separated from her Pacific Islander husband Tabby Koran, apparently at the instigation of Archibald Meston, Protector of Aboriginals for southern Queensland. He had proposed that she might marry a young Aboriginal man from the Woodford Mission Station. Meston claimed that he was unaware of Minnie's marital status. Given the circumstances, Minnie's letter is as remarkably self-possessed as it is touching in its remembrance of her circle of friends and neighbours.

83. To Tabby Koran, 9 July 1902

My dear Husband

Just a line to tell you how I am getting on. I have been staying in Brisbane for a week & our little boy is at the Mission Station Woodford. Mr Merton wants me to get Married to a Black boy at Woodford Mission Station; but I wont get Married to nobody as I am Married already to you. Everyone in Brisbane told me not to get married to no one but my own man; I will try to get back to you somehow, if I can. I am going by the Coach this morning to Woodford. With love I am your affectionate wife

Minnie Captain

PS. Please write to me & address my letter to Mr Elder, Woodford.

How is Mrs Brown getting on & the little baby Rachel & Jessie Brown & Eddie how is Mrs Leo & her baby & how is her Husband George & his wife & I would like to know how is Mrs Wakehill & her husband & Lizzie & Bob & Mrs McGee & little Hannah & Mrs Cuna and her Husband.

Goodbye hope we/will soon meet/Minnie Captain

Mr Merton] in fact Archibald Meston (1851–1924); in addition to his work with Aborigines, Meston had been a journalist, civil servant and explorer. It was in this latter capacity that he had come into contact with Aboriginal people whose customs, habits and languages he had studied.

PERCY GRAINGER

George Percy (later Percy Aldridge) Grainger (1882–1961) left Australia in 1894 to pursue an international career in music, principally as a concert pianist and composer. Although he never again lived in Australia, he made a number of successful tours as well as private visits. The Grainger scholar Kay Dreyfus has noted that he 'retained a ferocious nationalism, an intense love of the landscape and a rather quixotic view of the virtues of the Australian character'. These values and his own intensely mercurial character are vividly demonstrated in the letters written to his mother Rosa (Rose) Annie Grainger (1861–1922) during his two Australian concert tours of 1903–04 and 1908–09.

84. To Rose Grainger, 23 October 1903

Had the lovliest of days. From 12 till about 4.15 with J.J. on a sea-side tramp; taking in the rippingest views. Soon out of the wing town sand-dunes began—white, clean stuff, grass-set to hold sand from being wind-swept over town & growing-grounds.

We got wet some, (but that wont hurt flannels any) but discomfort was well made up by the farnesses (endless stretching snowwhite sand beaches & landwards from them hummocks) softened by rain-drifts.

Landwards from the hummocks marshes; [old riverbed, which's outlet into sea stuffed by inblown sand—winds strength raised it to small hills where once the dead flats of river-mouth] & near these the dells 'tween the dune-heights grow shrubs & wildgrowths; of vivid green, flowering the most. I've picked tips of most sorts & will send pressed tomorrow with this. Posting today useless, as no today's train would get Melb in time for over-land mail.

The river's been turned now into a canal, & this (on home path) cutting off our back-coming, I coo-eed a house owning a punt. A Melbourne-born man turned out, ferried us, & later sailed us townwards; a most refined, kindly, pleasant-tho-familiar sort, for whose wife we're getting 2 ticks for tonights' show.

The sights I saw were in keeping with some of my fondest mindings of Australian shore-showings: The broad flat white beaches we love, & lacked in Europe, the rolling dunes, with sage green tufted grass, as such:—

[sketch by Grainger included here]
you know.
A far kin of Denmark:—

'Agnete hun sidde paa det ensomme Strand
[Agnes sits beside the lonesome strand]
Saa sagtelig de Bølger slaar op paa hviden Sand
[So softly break the billows upon the snow-white sand]
As, ja, ja! saa sagtelig' *& soon.*
[Oh, yea, yea! so softly & soon.]

Dates stand as:—

be in	Brisbane	31st till 3rd
	Sydney	5th till 8th
	Melb (on & off)	8th till 10th

(B & Syd address C/o Palings Musicshop
Melb C/o Her Majesties)

Splendid take last night; did real well [added next day]

85. To Rose Grainger, 26 October 1908

MY LITTLE DEAR MOTHER,

Well, I did a nice walking match yesterday, 46 miles, as you'll see by enclosed cutting. I started at 6.45 morn from Yarram & got here about 7.10 evening; taking 30 mins off for lunch at about 1 o'clock, & 2 very short halts in the afternoon. Fancy, my feet arent even blistered, & I'm hardly at all stiff this morn. It's undoubtedly the best walk I've ever done. I did the 1st 26 miles from 6.30 to about 1 oclock (or 1–10?) & finished up in Sale at 5 miles an hour, at which speed I did a big part of the last 10 miles. Most of my former walks took place as antidotes to fit of "bad habit", whereas this trip opened out with no such sickly handicap. My veins gave me no trouble. I did not feel them, & an investigation of them on the road found them wholly unswollen. I girthed & saftypined my holder up at just the right toughness & on unbuckling was firm as apples.

So all that shows that my vein biz does not affect my walking powers, nor does my walking worsen my veins. I was happy as a lark all the way relishing my day from fresh morn to balmy eve. No trace of pain or weariness. What can better cool mornings in warm lands? And the laughing jackasses & magpies & other dear birds. Sweet & wild the songs are of our native birds, queer quaint & ownish as you & I, dearie. Dont lose a chance, if you get one, of rising early one morning out of town & hearing what the "feathered warblin' songsters" (their charmin' notes so sweet did tune) have to tell of the very soul of our climate & land.

The future of Australia may not lightly be dismissed by judgement upon her money earning folk of today. The scenery, the animal life, the air, and so on of the country is wondrously tender, pure, high souled, aloof, delicate, refined. Sooner or later its darling influences *must* tell, & we will get weird lovable ravishing *highly unworldly* human showings.

The teetrees are in blossom. They grow in the shapliest most luscious clusterings & groupings by creeks, some of them (dying trees?) radiant in pale purple coloring; etherial, angelic. Surely the teetree is every bit as precious as the gums! I gloated over a lovely colored parrot, tail & wings of purply blue (*rich*) & body of blood red flame. Also a small bird of peacock bluegreen. But I was most glad of the laughing j.as. [Their] very heads are embodied chuckles (not chuckles of mirth—far from it—but chuckles of unkeep-downable ingrained *queer*ness)

I feel very like them.

I had a dangerous encounter with a turkey.

"Run away, run away"!

This is my 1st long walk in Australia. Its good that it has been at last. The sight of the gums, & the suck of their young leaves upfreshened me chiefestly on my NZ trudges, & here they are in greater generosity & "at home" into the barg.

Dear mother, dont neglect to take a chew at young gum leaves sometimes. They tell to the palate what the birdcalls preach to the ear; they deftly sum up all the influences of the land. Just so pure, queer, angel-fresh ought our art to be when it turns up. What is the prevailing taste in gum? I find no used expressions to fit it. It's not salt, sweet, bitter, sour. Is it acid? Sharp it is, but that's not its overweighing quality.

My walk was full of fond thoughts of you. We are, as you write, trully harmonious. We, as a couple, are so outrageously harmonious in our bedrock that we can afford, like I can as a composer, to be specialists in surface discords.

How lucky I am in having you born in the land I so love certain phases of, so jolly that we can share the pride of birthright claims to it all. If you had come here from else-where I should need to gloat lonelily.

Lovely winepurple (never noticed just that particular shade before) sunset gloamed over the last few miles wherin I passed over father's swingbridge.

The river views about Sale seem jolly pretty. You know them I think.

I am glad you are sorry for Karen being left partially alone over there. I always feel ever so sorry for women being lonely, left without their particular lightbearing loved ones, for for them it is so many times worse to bear than for us. If they had not the particular quality that makes folks absence so heavy for them they could not make their presence so strangely enthralling to men as they jolly well can.

It is always my personal feeling that the joys of intersexual comradeship (be it mother–son, sister–brother, man–woman, young boy–old woman—it is quite the same) well up from out of the female's nature rather than the man's. She is creative in that particular deal, man more merely appreciative & responsive.

Keep on addressing to Her Majesty's Melbourne. As for you & I it wont be long before we're together. I dont know yet for cert, but about a 14 night will do it, I think.

I'm *so* sunburnt, though not painfully so; face, neck, legs. I wore only cap, shirt, white drawers sewn together, belt, 2 thick pairs of socks (one over the other) *well* soaped & my black boots. I picked prances of wild flowers & carried them 15 miles to give to Ada. She & the party only overtook me 2 miles out of Sale, though they started only 4 hours later from Yarram.

I got tons of cheering on the road, & on reaching Sale.

father's swingbridge] bridge designed by Grainger's father, the architect and engineer John Grainger (1855–1917) erected 1880–83 over the La Trobe River, south of the Victorian town of Sale   Karen] Karen Holten (1879–1953) for a number of years Percy Grainger's lover

86. To Rose Grainger, 16 May 1909

I got Dr Russell to fix up that I heard Prof Spencer's phonograph records Friday evening, & we spent an unforgettable time there, (at Spencers.) Spencer is one of those ultrarefined calm just Englishmen who a wife & 2 grownup daughters cannot turn from being a delightful batchelor & who is too niceminded to be properly conscious of the commonness of the Colonies &, appreciating their wide future, soon loves them better than the old country. Such a man is a haven for every tender, or great artistic sprouting. He has long been a friend & keen admirer of Streeton & is now buying in a glorious collection of Gordon Lindsey's pen & inks & washes.

It is of Gordon Lindsey that I want to write you. Streeton a year ago showed me some of his stuff in Lon & I at once woke up to it rather.

It is useless for me to guess at his technical worth as a painter, or worth *to* a painter, als fach mensch. But Streeton said he is *absolutely firstclass*. So I would think also. I am bothering only about his emotional value, his national typicalness, which, to my mind, makes him & me (as far as my knowledge goes) the only 2 lastworthy artistic voices of Australia, so far. Both Victorians.

That G.L. might one day loom like A. Beardsley, in his own O so different way, would not surprize me, though, not being a painter, it would be shallow of me to foresee it.

He is above all an overflowing exultant sexualist. I can recall nothing striking of his that is not very overweighingly sexual & fleshy. He loves nature's victories. His art is one long approving chuckle at nature gaining her sweet terrible way.

It is not the purity of upliftedness of sex that he voices, but rather a healthy rankness; his Scotchness therein coming well to the fore. If the whore & the roué inspired Beardsley it is the fast Australian girl & the larrikin that sends G L to laughing victory.

His men, his rude lovers, are all larrikin faced, & his girl & women folk are leggy, limby, & plump as they're grown here. But he makes them attractive alright.

His art would fit far easier in die Jugend or foreign publications than in English. He revels in urwüchsig themes, stoneage men smashing each other up, Amazons fleeing, & the "old gods" of Greece & Swinbourne are ever playing their wicked wanton lovely tricks over his paper. The "joy of life" lives here as surely at home as in the Rarotongan partsinging. His & my art form surely a convincing warant for Australia's healthiness! Not a hint of weakness, morbidness, lifetiredness in his work anywhere, but exultant, rank, eager, exstatic; common & game & sure & greedy.

But tho his way is rank his steps are exact & nice. He does luxurious leafage (like his humanity, so flourish also his trees & landscapes in luscious overwealth) with tender true technic, & can be delightfully economic & frugal in his methods. He has a face like a street brawler, but Spencer says he is a dear thing, hard working & simple, & 27, (has done spiffing work for 10 years—like me) & healthy & robust as his work.

What lies stand in the Musical Histories re Australian native music, that it moves over a few notes only & is mere repetitions of primitive phrases; not at all! Generally *over* an octave in compass, a tune is often made up of 4 or 5 distinct phrases, & is *no less complex* than many European tunes.

I took down 3 interesting tunes which you will hear.

Spencer's records are *excellently* taken. He says the Inland blacks are wholly harmless to nice sensible whites.

He & they chummed grandly. No wonder. Such a man would find few races hostile.

Dr Russell] Dr Robert Hamilton Russell (1860–1933), physician and Grainger family friend Prof Spencer] Sir Walter Baldwin Spencer (see Letters 63 and 89) Gordon Lindsey] Norman Alfred Williams Lindsay (see Letter 115) als fach mensch] as a professional urwüchsig] primitive

BARBARA BAYNTON

Born in the Hunter Valley region of New South Wales, the daughter of a bush carpenter, Barbara Baynton (1857–1929) is best known for the stories of deprivation and cruelty published in Bush Studies *(1902). Deserted by her first husband, she married a wealthy Sydney doctor, and after his death moved to London. Her letter to Melba dates from her early years as an expatriate making her way into London society. After a third marriage, to the Viscount Headley, from whom she soon separated, Baynton returned to Australia.*

87. TO NELLIE MELBA, 15 NOVEMBER 1907

DEAR MADAME MELBA,

Five years ago I came to London, and as with all Australians, my fear of the unknown evil of this great city was my dominant feeling. Then on my first Saturday night I went to hear you sing, and you stirred some depth in me that made me oblivious to all personal danger—even to the fact that at the close of the performance I had got separated from my two companions; for I was alone in the opera house waiting, hoping for you to come back once more. One of my friends had the latchkey, the other had my purse; yet when I gradually realized the position, I was utterly indifferent. Nothing mattered since I heard you sing. I gave my cabman a ring and told him to call in the morning. Then, as I could not make anyone hear, I went down the area steps. Some thoughts are more refreshing than sleep, and these were mine till the dawn came.

Many times since I have heard you, for now with my daughter I live in London, and to us both the experience of your singing is always the same—an exaltation that soars above life, or even death.

I trust you will soon come back to reign over us aforetime, and bring confusion to those enemies begotten by your greatness.

Some day we may meet. Till then and after, may the God who made you, He of your Scottish forebears, keep you safely. With the love of two you have never seen

FAITHFULLY YOUR ADMIRER/BARBARA BAYNTON

ALGERNON THOMOND

In We of the Never-Never, *first published in 1908, Mrs Aeneas (Jeannie) Gunn (1870–1961) created an Australian classic. Her tale of the vicissitudes of life in the Northern Territory where she lived with her husband at Elsey station on the Roper River, 1901–03, has appealed to generations of Australians and to others like Lord Kintore (1852–1930), Governor of South Australia 1889–1895, who wrote from his London club, remembering his own journey to the Never Never land.*

88. To Jeannie Gunn, 11 March 1909

Dear Madam,

Will you forgive a stranger for intruding a few lines upon you: not merely because he is a Scotchman 'a strange combination of shy reserve and quiet dignified self assurance' (a splendid definition of his race) but also because he passed six of the happiest years of his life in S. Australia, during which time he travelled through the Never Never. He remembers so well all that journey; the hospitality he met everywhere above all. The journeys out from Pine Creek, the Cullen, Ferguson, Katherine and Edith crossings, the heat in the spear grass Country and disappointment at no 3 Well, the Elsey, Warlock, Daly Waters and the rest. Today, driven in by bitter weather, he took up 'We of the Never Never' and has read and appreciated every sentence to the full. It has brought it all back to him so vividly and makes him feel that it was only last year, not 18 years ago, that he was there in a Country which to live in is to love it, and having left it is to 'know that one's heart can Never Never rest away from it'.

Pray do not dream of answering this note but accept my so grateful thanks for the joy your book has given to

Yours very truly/Kintore

Kintore] Sir Algernon Hawkins Thomond became the 9th Earl of Kintore in 1880

William Millar

In 1918, in a letter unexpectedly received from a Northern Territorian, Jeannie Gunn was reminded of the Never Never days on Elsey station and of the harsh indifference of outback Australia to the lives of men. Millar records the fate of some of the men who had served as models for the characters Gunn created in her enduring tale.

89. To Jeannie Gunn, March 1918

To Mrs A Gunn

I have just crossed into the Territory after an Absence of 12 years, having been in the Kimberley district WA. The first Camp I hit in the Territory I asked as usual for literature. I was given We of the Never Never altho' I had read it, I laid down in my Camp & read it again, and in my fancy I lived the old days over again when I used to pass the Elsey & take off my pack under the Shady ti-Trees opposite the Homestead & Mr Gunn Coming down to the Camp & asking us up to the Station in Real Highland Style & of a night listening in the Hut to the Gramma-phone played by H. Bryan or Else Dave holding the floor with some of his oft told Tales. There is a Scatter on the Old Hands Dave dead & buried 3 miles from Ivanhoe Station Jack Brown dead in the Tanami desert Harry Peckham Buried on the banks of the Victoria River Jack McPhee dead & buried between Willeroo & The Katherine Tommy Wakeland I met yesterday on Wave Hill Blacksmithing we had a good old pitch about the Elsey in fact it was Tommy who made me promise to write to you he is looking well and he still goes periodically to the Depot after a cross cut saw. Some time ago whilst going to the Depot he was nearly Speared by the Blacks going thro' Jasper gorge 7 or 8 spears just missed him.

There is a new Element coming into the Territory today I met 6 New Chums Vesteys was sending out to Wave Hill 'parcel post' Embryo stockmen by the way they was bumping in the saddle riding along the road I am afraid when they go Mustering they will fall off.

Owing to labor troubles the Meat works is laid up for 12 months it is a shame as there is over 50,000 good Bullocks in Victoria district & Kimberley that would have been treated in Darwin otherwise.

I noticed the Cave I wrote you about some years ago when I was writing a letter for Dave was explored by Professor Spencer. There is another I know of it is full of Mammoth Bones. I am sorry I did not meet Professor Spencer in Port Darwin I would have told him about it. The blacks will not speak about it as it is tabu to the blacks except the Grey headed niggers it is between the Mary river & the Alligator.

Hoping this letter will find you OK/I remain faithfully yours/W.Millar Tommy did not know your address **but** he said Melbourne will find you if you are as well known there as you are in the **Bush** owing to the books you Circulated

H. Bryan] H.H. Bryant, the model for Gunn's character The Dandy. In later life he lived in South Australia   Dave] David Suttie, Gunn's Dan, the head stockman; died of heart failure on the

Wyndham–Ord River road some time after 1912   Jack Brown] Neaves' mate in *We of the Never-Never*, originally from Victoria; perished from thirst in the Tanami Desert in 1909   Harry Peckham] Henry Ventila Peckham, The Fizzer, originally from Adelaide; drowned in the flooded Campbell's Creek in 1911   Jack McPhee] Jock McPhee or Tam-a-Shanter, a drover and horse breaker; died of thirst in 1910 on the Willeroo–Katherine road   Tommy Wakeland] Thomas Wakelin, 'Little Johnny', drowned in 1924 in the King River crossing   Vesteys] the vast Northern Territory pastoral station at Wave Hill owned by the Vestey family in England   Professor Spencer] Sir Walter Baldwin Spencer, Letters 63 and 86

Tom Roberts

Following the federation of Australia in 1901, a friendship developed between Alfred Deakin and the painter Tom Roberts (1856–1931). Deakin never lost his belief in the importance of the creative imagination or his respect for the aspirations and struggle which motivated artists. These themes recur in the letters Roberts wrote from England in the years when Deakin was a force in the building of the young Australian nation.

90. To Alfred Deakin, 31 March 1910

My dear P^r M^r

It's on my conscience, & now that I write it's on one matter principally, for we go on quietly, in our new house here, with our garden & a fine air and outlook.

I am working hard, & seem to be developing, & have now been getting my works 'invited' to shows, which tells that the efforts to 'get a new skin' are succeeding—at last.

The 'one matter' is this. I've been thinking a lot of late of all of you & your confrères are doing & have done in the beginning of a new nation, & it disturbs me to think that most of you are likely to go on till the inevitable comes, & leave behind nothing that will give the future anything that will show what you all were as men to look at.

Now this is important, and must appeal to you, & it is the duty of the present for the future. I don't need to press this on you or say more than—what would America give for authentic records of its founders?

And, that there is no time to lose. I think there should be head paintings at least of all the first Federal Ministry—the leaders of the different parties & of the first High Court— (of the first Speaker it is already too late for a direct painting & so of Mr Kingston).

After a lot of thinking I make this appeal to you to act in the matter without any delay,

You will say 'Roberts be practical'. Well—I owe a lot to Australia & am at your service thus far—I am getting on (anno domini) & am striving for something here, but will give 6 months to this work as a pleasure, if the paintings of those I mentioned could be kept ready for the Federal House. I am not well enough off to do this unpaid but I think I could come out & pay my passage for £500 & produce a record of great value to the nation in the future.

I have so far offered myself—you know my work & can trust me, & I think at least I can give you portraits with character.

You may not think it wise or necessary to call me over to do the work, that will not matter—only again let me ask you to consider the importance of acting early, & do set the thing in hand, & let these records be painted if not by me by some one you can trust to give faithful representations of the first leaders of the Commonwealth.

I was going to write you a personal letter & another more formal with my suggestion, but you can make this official or not. If the idea could not be a Government one might it not be done amongst yourselves.

You will not misunderstand my 'offer', but I should be proud to have my name on paintings of you & your co-workers, that would be kept for Australia of the future.

Believe me

with every good wish & remembrances to you and the members I know.

Sincerely yours/Tom Roberts.

as men to look at] Roberts' suggestion bore fruit in 1911 when the Commonwealth established the Historic Memorials Committee to commission political and other official portraits for the national collection   the first Speaker] Frederick William Holder (1850–1909), a former Premier of South Australia, was appointed first Speaker of the House of Representatives. He collapsed during an acrimonious debate in the House, 22 July 1909, and died some hours later.   Mr Kingston] Charles Cameron Kingston (1850–1908), a former Premier of South Australia and a prominent advocate of federation. He served as Minister of Trade and Customs in the first Commonwealth ministry.

In January 1913 Deakin had announced his decision to retire from politics. He had suffered a serious breakdown in his physical health and, more worrying, in his mental powers. The following year Roberts wrote sympathetically, affectionately, a letter of comfort and of friendship.

91. To Alfred Deakin, 31 May 1914

Dear Alfred Deakin,

I hope you're better—& will send me a letter saying so.

I see in this week's Weekly Ed. of the 'Times', your word to the Overseas Club, & last week Lord Tennyson & I were talking of you. I am now painting the full length of him, & I feel it an honour to do it for the Commonwealth—& trust to make a fine work, it has begun well & my sitter is very good over it.

I thought you might have come over for holiday & the voyage—it's been, in spite of the cold spells of May, the uncertain, the loveliest of springtimes—our garden here a delight, from the time of the crocuses and daffs—now it's a wait for the Roses.

We've as a family had experiences. The boy picked up diphtheria. I followed with symptoms & went at once to the London Fever Hospital, in a plague gown; it turned out 'gout'!

We're all cleansed painted and disinfected now and going normally once more—

Did you get my notice of a little show in Bond Street? It came off very well—so I started my studio in Sloane St. Strangely I found men put up these shows & rarely get any direct profit out of 'em—so I had the luck of it.

The work was the result of a happy Summer at Como & on the Spluga Pass. 'Twas fine to get amongst the colour there, the glowing sun, fire flies & the courtesy of the people—Echoes of Donizetti—Byron. A Baroness of the family of the Poet's Countess lived next us.

From the soft warmth of the Lake up by Chiavenna to an Alpine village & God's air for energy, & the company of some Alpinisti who claim the love of the mountains to pass that of woman. They had the collector's pride in taking me to 'points'. Climbers with the mania, they always went over a point, by finger nails, rather than take a shepherd's path round it, & laugh & agree it was 'una follia' & teach me Italian expressions as we lay out of the wind behind some rock—high above the pines—& between the peaks, right down the great cleft of the pass—the soft hazy warmth in blue of the Italia they are so proud of. I had four days in Rome, & now there's only Rome & London as cities. I thought before-hand of the things I wanted to see there, lay one day on the Appian Way, & ate at the last inn back past the Coliseum at nightfall. How strangely familiar it all is to us; & I was alone.

Why is St. Peter's such a moving thing just to look at, as you drop out of the tram car? Four days just full. I wouldn't stay to be sight seeing—it was enough for the first time, with never a moment's tedium, the last word I heard was the 'good journey' of the tram conductor as the car stopped at the central R^y station—Rome—What a city. What a big touch in it all.

I wonder if you have Trevelyan's Essays 'Clio'—& if you enjoy them. He brings you back the joy of walks.

Well, I've been on the flute, & pull up now. I wonder when I shall see you. Our best wishes to you & all your family—dear Grandfather. Write me early. I'm working hard—just having a spell this Sunday with a faint touch of gout in one toe, that gets less as I lie quiet & think of a distant friend & old times—

Adieu

Sincerely yours/Tom Roberts

a little show in Bond Street] an exhibition of Roberts' work at Walkers Galleries, New Bond Street, 3–14 February 1914   dear Grandfather] Deakin had become a grandfather in 1906. In subsequent letters Roberts called him, affectionately, Grandfather

·

A joy for Tom Roberts and his wife Lillie was the news in May 1925 that their son Caleb (b. 1898) was intending to return from England to settle permanently in Australia, which he had left as a child of five. It fell to the English-born Tom Roberts to educate his son in the ways of Australian democracy. In Australia Caleb worked as an engineer, becoming, eventually, Chairman of the Victorian Country Roads Board.

92. To Caleb Roberts, 18 May 1925

My dear old Chap (& the 2)

At 10 this morning we got up here, your cable of 16th inst "Intend sail August" I was working in the studio, Mother brought the envelope, unopened to me—Great news it was for us. Mother wept.

When we'd settled down a bit; I went down to the P.O., got a call through & told Jessie the glad news. "Birthday gift to mother" eh

Luce out, Jessie very cheery, & she'll love to tell her mother my message.

I'll write to Mr Calder this evening. Beyond being so glad at the decision, & the idea, as mother says that a small family is better together. I feel the move is right for you 3. You've been thinking for Norah & the grandson very keenly. The dear girl will have a group of dear & kind friends here, all waiting for her. A man can get along in England or another place; for the wife the home & its surrounding are so important. She will like, first of all the experience of travelling & seeing new scenes.

I'm hoping the change will be good every way for you. It's a very different "atmosphere" from the old country; it's all in the making, unfinished. And the people one meets casually, well, I like 'em, & hope you will.

Nobody says "Sir" to you, except perhaps sometimes to me—a reminder of my "old-posser" dom (damme)

I'm sure your experience with the Essex C C will be valuable. We shall be all agog for your letters.

The exchange is against Aust but not quite so bad as it has been. It's better to use the money if possible, one loses on remitting. I hope you'll get quit of little Talisman. Sell at loss. Potter is a good man. The Bank NSW Mr Campbell will advise you well.

We just look forward to seeing you all three. I had begun to fear dear ones I might never see you again. =69 last March, it's getting a near time for me

So cheerio & through comfortably.

We haven't heard anything from Anderson & wonder. Wool has dropped. Happily there have been blessed rains that mean millions to the country; & there is great hopefulness about things.

Au revoir

Your old Dad/Tom Roberts

PS

A note from Mr Calder who will "be very pleased to see you on arrival".

A word at last from Anderson

He & Bullie leave M. for London June 2nd by the "Sophocles" Aberdeen Line.

TR

All proofs of English Employments & any word from chiefs very valuable here
18.5.25

Mr Calder] William Calder, Chairman of the Victorian Country Roads Board   little Talisman] house in Essex belonging to Caleb Roberts

WILLIAM DUDLEY

William Humble Ward Dudley (1867–1932), the second Earl, was appointed Governor-General of Australia in 1908. His sole qualification for this post appeared to be the possession of a large fortune. Alfred Deakin's estimate of him was unflattering: 'He did nothing really important, nothing thoroughly, nothing consistently … He remained … a very ineffective and not very popular figurehead'. His successor, Thomas Denman (1874–1954), 3rd Baron Denman, apparently disregarded the proffered advice, opting instead for a more moderate and accessible vice-regal style.

93. TO THOMAS DENMAN, 5 MARCH 1911

MY DEAR DENMAN

I am very glad to hear that you are to be my successor and I hope that you will like it—. You will find the climate delightful and the people pleasant and friendly but there is very little work to do and the Ministers are very suspicious and jealous of the smallest interference or influence in their affairs—Travelling about visiting country towns and districts is one of the principle functions of the Gov Gen, and there is no doubt that the more a Gov. Gen does that, the more he is appreciated and liked.

On the whole travelling is not uncomfortable. Excellent cars are provided on the railways, especially in N.S.W and one can often live in them certainly on a short trip. The hotels in the country are as a rule clean, but often rough and noisy, with sanitary arrangements usually so inconveniently placed that it is difficult for ladies to stay in them—One can however nearly always find a squatter to put one up and squatters houses have improved wonderfully in the last few years. The two Government Houses provided for the Gov. Gen—one in Melbourne and one in Sydney—are the most charming residences and up to date in every way—In the Sydney house there are a good many pictures and *nothing* is really required except the usual silver ornaments, cushions etc. Here however there are no pictures and the house therefore, being very large, presents rather a barracky appearance. I should advise you therefore to bring out some prints or pictures or hangings to put on the walls of the hall and drawing rooms.—Linen and crockery are of course provided—but you will want your own plate as the ordinary Govt. stuff is very poor and only consists of knives and forks etc. I have written to Sir Charles Lucas about carriages and horses—so I will not trouble you again about them. He will give you my letter. You had better arrange to get your wine—cigars and cigarettes from England. All those are bad and expensive here—Also things like hair-wash, bath scent etc you had better have out. Australians are rather primitive in these ways. You will get plenty of golf—both here and in Sydney—The courses are really quite good. You will want a horse to ride on parade—I have got one you can take if you like. If not you had better get one from the mounted police. They are the only people who make any attempt to break their horse properly—*Do not fail* to bring your own motor or motors. You cannot get good ones here. I should advise you to bring a limousine for town use, and a car with a light touring body and Cape—cart hood for country work—This latter car ought to be as light and strong as possible. The roads are *awful* and a heavy car consumes tyres like an ogre. As regards Staff, you will want a Private Secretary a Military Secretary and 2 ADC's—The Military Secretary is usually Comptroller as well. I have had a Chamberlain also and found it very useful but perhaps you may not think it necessary

There is a very good clerk here whom Northcote used to employ and I kept him on—He works under the Comptroller in Household affairs keeps accounts etc—and also types for the Private Secretary—I pay him [£]100 a year and he is worth the money. His name is King.

As regards servants—I can only say that it is quite impossible to get men-servants in Australia except odd men, stable helpers etc tho' house maids are obtainable. I will get my wife to write to Lady Denman on these things. We have our own laundry with laundry maids we brought out. I should advise you to do the same, the local laundries are abominable—It is very difficult for the wife of the Gov Gen to make friends among the ladies here—and so, if I may be permitted to say so, I think Lady Denman would be wise to bring out some relation or friend with her who would be a companion to her out here. We were lucky in that way because my Military Secretary Sandy Ruthven had a charming wife who was a god send to us all. But there is no doubt that unless the companionship of some English lady of that kind is available—the wife of the Gov. Gen is apt often to feel very lonely and dull.

The gardens here are *quite* charming—and for anyone who is keen about flowers and shrubs there is plenty of interest and occupation in that way. Lady Northcote was a very keen gardener and did wonders here.

I suppose I shall hear soon when you are coming out. You had better send all your luggage and servants here—We shall vacate the house entirely next month—so your servants can come in as soon as you like and get everything ready for your occupation—We shall live at Sydney until I am relieved and the remains of our baggage will go from there directly after we have left.

Let me know if there are any special points on wh. you want information.

Yrs sincerely/Dudley

Sir Charles Lucas] Sir Charles Prestwood Lucas (1853–1931), head of the Dominions Office Northcote] Lord Northcote (1846–1911), Governor-General of Australia 1904–08   Sandy Ruthven] Alexander Gore Arkwright Hore-Ruthven (1872–1955), 1st Earl Gowrie, who served as Governor-General of Australia 1936–45. He was known throughout his life as 'Sandie'.

MARY KERNOT

Henry Handel Richardson (Ethel Florence Robertson, née Richardson, 1870–1946) was living in London when her novel The Getting of Wisdom *was published. She sent a copy to Mary Kernot (formerly Mary Robertson (1868–1954)), her friend from school-days at Presbyterian Ladies' College, Melbourne, the novel's setting. Although this copy did not reach her, Kernot had read the book, guessed the author's identity and written the first letter in what was to be a long correspondence between the two.*

94. TO HENRY HANDEL RICHARDSON, 23 OCTOBER 1911

MY DEAR ETTIE

Your letter quite restored you to my acquaintance—you seemed a very far-off, lost-in-the-blue sort of personage when I wrote I felt rather like a man with a megaphone shouting from a desert island in hopes that a friend some where might answer I am very annoyed that I didn't get that copy of the "The Getting of Wisdom" Is it too late to send another with the same inscription repeated? By the way who did you send it to? Please tell me if you remember—I am a little curious—The College people still ruffle & hump themselves like outraged turkeys when The Book is mentioned—Tibbys awful fear is that her innocent little scholars may read it. We have had great entertainment out of it all—some old Collegian —I think it was Miss Patterson—told my brother that he ought to collect every copy & burn them all—You can evoke the scene yourself—Place the College—the College man bringing stacks of the contaminating volume—teachers in gown & cap (they all wear them now) muttering incantations & the terrified scholars locked up in No I II & III till it was all over—my husband tells me to tell you that you'll never be elected President of the Old Collegians Association—never—

What puzzles me about your book is how ever you kept such sharp clear memories of—well so many years ago My memory is quite fuzzy—or was till your lightening flashes lit up things—You surely must have begun it long ago—How I would love to talk over some things with you. I note your half promise of coming to Australia. I do hope you will—it is not such a terrific undertaking now-a-days If there is at any time any thing I can do for you here let me know & I'll do all I can—Tibbie, teaches English at the college—Cocky is a morning governess I think—Anna I often see she is Sec of a Musical & Literary Association which I grace with my presence sometimes Anna writes little poems some times & is very plain but much more human than the rest of them—Æneas is a cleric married & settled & a'. The silks & satins lady—how well I remember those silks & how we—M.M^cF & I—quarrelled over them—I said in the holidays I thought they dressed unsuitably—it was told to M & a bitter coolness set in—never broken to this day. Well she has just had a divorce granted or no—her husband has divorced her—she went to England with a jackaroo who had lived in the house with them—a decent chap I believe He seems to stick to her so I suppose they can marry in six months time.

"Truth" our scandal paper had them in large head lines—"Squatters Divorce" "Guest in the Home" etc. Her relations are divided, some stick to her I believe. Her first seemed a very nice fellow but I don't think they got on at all. He lives quite near my married sister—Fannie is little changed—her eldest daughter is grown up—went to England—a while ago—a great fat thing Mary Miller—I often see—she is Mary Bawden lives at Macedon—married about 35 & has set up a flourishing family—they go to England in Dec. it will be a sort of pageant they do things with such impressive ceremony Lily Grant I never see but hear of often she has lost her pretty hair & has grown stout—Janet Telford-Cole you know of She is a person of character. I admire her very much—Annie Gibson is married to a cousin & has lost a good deal of her money & her little boy is so delicate I believe—Agnes Bell I still know as well as of old—she lost her mother a few weeks ago & I saw her on the day of the funeral. Her little sister May—now quite a beauty—is to be married shortly & Nick will be alone as she is the only un-married one—She is to me just the same as of old. Alexa Proudfoot made a fight for literary fame but a school keeps her head up chiefly She writes on hens & gardens & geraniums with brilliant adjectives always recognisable to me. The "Argus" took her up for a while but she suffers cruel cuttings—She is very spinster-y now-a-days The Howitts still inhabit Gippsland all married except Mary—

Do you still knaw, no gnaw—the end of your pen or do you find it too expensive as you must be so often "at it" I think of you a lock of black hair over your eye gnawing fiercely—Why did you make your Louise an Australian?—Maurice Guest is the saddest book I've ever read—I don't wonder you puzzled your critics. Did the name Dufrayer stick to you from the girl I used to talk of—I am curious & kept looking for clues in M.G. as I read it. I'm going to ask the "Book Lover" why they didn't review you—I know them a little there—

I have been married 10 years—my husband is an architect—you would like him I think for he is quite delighted with your book, he holds strong views on education & thinks that the College was an awful spot, thinks that we'd have done better to be hoeing potatoes than shut up with only an hours outlet after our days work—I know he thinks that what brain I had was drawn to too fine wire there & I believe it was—now that I come to think about it

How do I spend my days—I really don't know—I potter in the garden play golf—go to Committees— make jam—set hens—visit my mother a good deal—go to & fro a cabin we have in those blue mountains we used to see so plainly from the College—It is a charming spot right on the top—just beside a great primeval forest—100's of years old gum trees roar all round us in the gales & yet we never feel the wind wallaby & rabbits & wild birds are our only near neighbours I will take you there if you'd like, when you come out "Upalong" is its name so far—We have log fires every night & when the wind doesn't blow it is so still that a sudden bird call is like a knife in your ear—

I'd like you to see our garden today At this window guelder roses purple rhododen-dron & pink monthly roses all in a mass & every where roses pink red & white—bushes just a blaze of color You will be in autumn now. We both love the garden—We have no children & feel rather drifting sometimes We have enough to get along simply without my husband's profession so I dare say we will wander again some day—I have not had good health since I married—but am improving with years I think—I am a thin withered up sort of person nowadays—Please write again some time when you can—

If you see Connie give her my love—how I'd like to see her too

YOURS AS OF OLD INFANT—MARY KERNOT

Tibby/Tibbie] Isobel MacDonald was at PLC with Richardson and Kernot; in 1911 she was teaching there   your Louise] Louise Dufrayer, heroine of Richardson's novel *Maurice Guest* (1908)   the Book Lover] a monthly literary review published in Melbourne   Connie] Constance Cochran, on whom Richardson based the character Evelyn Souttar in *The Getting of Wisdom*   Infant] the name given by Kernot to Richardson during their schooldays

VANCE PALMER

Novelist Vance Palmer (1885–1959) grew up in rural Queensland. His early working life included time as a tutor and bookkeeper on a cattle station as well as time in London as a 'Grub Street hack'. In 1914 he married writer Janet (Nettie) Gertrude Higgins in London, after a long engagement. This letter, written from the Isle of Wight to Nettie in Melbourne, reflects the devotion which on her side at least was to endure through nearly half a century of marriage.

95. TO NETTIE HIGGINS, UNDATED [1912]

Its a ridiculously cold evening, come just for a lark evidently, after all those great days, and I've lit a fire and have been looking at the pictures in it ever since supper. It has been a long day, perhaps because I didn't out much and work has consisted of a multitude of odds and ends. I want to write to you a little before I sleep dear. Do you know, dear you've given me a great capacity for feeling lonely. I was just thinking tonight of how I used to go for two or three weeks sometimes without speaking to a soul except Lottie, the half-cast girl and yet I wasn't conscious of any poignant loneliness. But now … well its different, mate. And yet do you think I'd like to recover that careless self-sufficiency again? No, mate: since you've been in the world life's got a deeper happiness even when I'm lonely and ragged at the edges. The truth is I've been wanting you more consciously even than I've ever done before mate. You'll think, perhaps, that its merely because I've not friends handy to talk to: no, you mustn't think just that, dear, though maybe that leaves me more time to think and remember how you've filled my life ever since you came into it: how this little space was coloured by the knowledge that I'd see you in a few weeks time, and that space by the different looks and words you'd given me before you left me. There was such a frankness and trust about all your ways. You never let me remember that we were anything but one body and one soul while you were with me. I think now that everyone else I've known has been a stranger to me, no matter how much I thought I'd given them. There's only one you, mate: I've given you everything that's in me. And if I want you now more than ever, its perhaps because there's a little more of me—a little more steadiness and a little more strength. I love you dear: I've said it often but it will never be an easily uttered phrase. If you were here tonight you'd be as happy as I would, I think, for I could show you all the love that's eager in me and yet won't go into words. Its very quiet for the rest of the house has gone to bed and I'd be ever so gentle if you came, and you'd forget everything but that my arms were holding you and that your cheek was against mine.

Mate: we mustn't keep away from one another for too long. You've got to give your people their share of you and I've got to make things ready but we mustn't let too much time pass. We're ready for one another now and its only outside things that come between us. But I think we must marry as soon as we can even if it means economy of the straitest kind. Work is getting steadier with me, although I don't suppose I'll be in even a modestly comfortable position for many years to come. We'll be able to look that in the face better than most people. Its deadly being poor, but you wouldn't feel it as much, perhaps, in London as in Melbourne where there are people to make comparisons. I'm going to work my fingers off in the next eighteen months or so. I want you with me, my own wife—you who are so brave and fearless in facing things. We've got a long life to live, but we can't spare an hour of it. Goodnight dear. Let me hold you a moment before you go and feel your heart beating against mine.

Lottie the half cast girl] probably a memory of his north Queensland cattle-station days

NETTIE PALMER

While her husband Vance Palmer concentrated on fiction, Nettie Palmer (1885–1964) directed her talents into literary journalism and critical and biographical work. Her strong but discerning praise of Australian writing was a crucial support in the careers of many authors. Most of all, she backed her husband's work and gave him untiring praise and financial support. Although many would now see her contribution to Australian culture as greater than her husband's she appears never to have doubted his superior talents.

96. To Vance Palmer, 28 July [1930]

An overseas mail, & your letter from the Mediterranean somewhere—only a week after the last. I hadn't dared to hope for one so soon. And by way of giving thanks I must, somehow, write & promise not to be so selfish & greedy any more. It must seem to you that I'm a little mad, to doubt your love for me: & yet—can't you imagine that I need some utterance of it? I'll try to explain & then put it all away. Mabel happened to send me an old letter you had written home from London in 1910. It was charming & interesting & friendly & affectionate towards them all: I felt proud of you—all that time ago—writing so adequately. And you speak of being tongue-tied! It was far more explicit about your feelings than your letter to me today. Oh, I can't help it if my demands sound vulgar & foolish, but how can I bear it when you say always you are lonely 'without your family around you'? God knows I'm glad you love the children & I could never be jealous of them; but do you never remember our intimate life together? What different letters I would be writing to you if I had even a hint that you could endure them! Its all very well for you to be so patriarchal & sensible: I don't look on you as the head-of-the-house but as a lover. I'm middle-aged & plain, I know, but then I never had any looks to lose & I oughtn't to be just a woman who runs a house (I'm not very brilliant if that is my calling!) You'll say I'm playing with words & that I must know you better than to dwell on accidental omissions: & indeed I must, or I couldn't write to you so frankly, appealing from Caesar to Caesar in this way. And yet—if I could show you your letters, so … No, I won't go on, though something drives me to write down the very demands that must exasperate you. Burn any of these letters of mine. They are tortured & only half true, perhaps: I'm just feeling towards some truth of expression in a bewildered way. You'll say, of course, that nothing written on a crowded ship should be counted against you. But your letters have been brilliant, (masterpieces Aileen says!) detailed, ironic, observant; only not the letters of anyone who could imaginably be a lover of the person to whom they are written. As for me, you'll say I can't be your lover if I choose to nag & rasp you in this way. Well, I haven't been at ease with you. I find it hard to write down the words that mean so much between us—as if I have always been cloying you with honey.

Have I come back to the same track again, after saying I would leave it? Well here's goodbye to it. No more reproaches! In spite of your silence & evasions (you'll say they are not intended) I'll dare to tell you I love you & want you. And you'll somehow forgive me for my petulant demands. Always it has been like this—always you have had to forgive me. You are better & greater that I am in every way; can't you see that for that reason I must have reassurances from you? It is because I believe in you, your character, your work, your future, that I find it so hard to believe that I am of importance to you. Yet somehow you have called me your mate & I'll count on that, re-reading a letter you wrote on a troopship in 1918 for our wedding-day—no, it can't have been that, but something near it. Forgive me again!

YOUR NETTIE

Aileen] Aileen Palmer (1915–88), their daughter   on a troopship in 1918] Palmer enlisted in the AIF in 1918; the letter may have been for the anniversary of their wedding in 1914

Francisca (Paquita) Delprat

Paquita Delprat (1891–1974), born in Holland, came to Australia in 1898 when her father, mining engineer, metallurgist and industrialist Guillaume Delprat was appointed assistant general manager of Broken Hill Pty Company. Paquita became engaged to Douglas Mawson (1882–1958) shortly before he left on the 1911–14 Australian Antarctic Expedition. After a long separation and much anxiety about the venture, news came that Mawson had survived a disaster, in which two of his companions were lost, and was coming home on the Aurora. *Although the letter was written in expectation of an imminent return Paquita had many more months to wait.*

97. To Douglas Mawson, 17 August 1913

My more than loved Dougelly!

Liesbeth & I are travelling to Melbourne to get ready our house there for Mother & the others. You know ship-life, however short,—it means just longing. Liesbeth is also feeling this & as she is pouring out her feelings in a letter to some one I cannot keep from you. Oh Dougelly is this long long separation ever going to end! On the sea we seem a little nearer. Thought of you fills my whole time—reading is impossible. How I long to hear everything, to feel everything that you have gone through. Douglas, there is so much happiness in store for us. And if there is worry also—I shall help you ever so much better than before you left. I'm afraid I am a very impatient person though I should be nothing but thankfulness. You will not go again, will you? I know you will not. It is not anything for married men to do. I think I am more sorry for Dr Wilson's widow than Lady Scott. But how terrible that disaster was. Come back safely. Oh darling do be careful of your dear dear self. I wonder if you have felt my love coming to you. How happy we shall be when you return. I'm returning to Adelaide in February (if Capt. Davis still thinks it probable you shall land here or Fremantle) & shall be waiting for you. I warn you that I shall board the Aurora on the absolute earliest opportunity. After all these months I claim that! Shall see what I can do with Capt. Creer—he generally meets incoming boats & you'll have to have a pilot. So come *home* at a nice time of day & the first or one of them to greet you will be your own me. Don't be afraid I cannot control myself! I am not the too-often tearful person you know of old! Just to see you, feel that you are really back from that perilous fascinating ice land. Are you frozen. In heart I mean. Am I pouring out a little of what is in my heart to an iceberg? Oh for a few private dear words. Why havent you sent me a few coded words & trusted to my finding it out! Can a person remain in such cold & lonely regions however beautiful & still love warmly? You were not in love when with Shackleton. How I long to hear about all this. That you love me just as much. Lean over the Aurora's side and say it to the breeze perhaps I shall hear it. Don't laugh it isn't a laughing matter I love you to distraction & if when you return you find I am too warm! Well I can't help it. I own now I was rather cold before you left through ignorance of everything. Oh dear lets get to business!

I'm at least going to meet your Mother & Willy & Jessie in September. Am looking forward to it very much. Capt. Davis arrives by the Orontes next week. We shall see him in Melbourne.

Professor Henderson is writing to Prof Masson & Skeats so I shall probably meet them also.

I told you before I think that we were going to move & shall send you a wireless from Campbelltown. That wireless is a boon although it is rather unsatisfactory. I've sent more than I meant to but did it when I was feeling very low & lonely so excuse. I quite understand your not wanting to use it for private purposes though everyone expects you to & always asks "I suppose you hear every week!" Oh soon the need for wireless will be past. Dougelly *Dougelly*

With my whole heart & being I love & want you.

YOURS FOR *always*/*Paquita*

Liesbeth] one of Paquita's sisters   Dr Wilson] Edward Wilson (1872–1912), member of the 1910–13 Brirish Antarctic Expedition led by Robert Falconer Scott (1868–1912) in which Wilson, Scott and two others died   Lady Scott] widow of R.F. Scott   Capt Davis (1884–1967)] J.K. Davis (1884–1967), captain of the Antarctic expedition ship *Aurora*, was Mawson's best man   Shackleton] in 1907 Mawson had been a member of Shackleton's Antarctic expedition   Professor Henderson] George Cockburn Henderson (1870–1944), Professor of History and English Language at the University of Adelaide, raised funds for Mawson's expedition   Masson] Sir David Masson (1858–1937), Professor of Chemistry, University of Melbourne   Skeats] Ernest Skeats (1875–1937), Professor of Geology and Mineralogy, University of Melbourne

JOHN NISBET

Scottish-born John Nisbet (1887–1957) was a member of the Australian landing at Gaba Tepe on Turkey's Gallipoli peninsula on the morning of 25 April 1915. C.E.W. Bean, the official historian of the Gallipoli campaign, concluded that it was on this day 'that the consciousness of Australian nationhood was born'. Nisbet's illicit postcard greeting to his family is a prosaic but remarkable link to that first Anzac Day.

98. TO MRS J.H. NISBET, 25 APRIL 1915

DEAR MOTHER & ALL

Just a line to let you know I am well etc. Am not supposed to write at all, only I can get this away. We arrived at the Dardanells this morning April 25. We are right in amongst it now, warships are bombarding like fun the noise is awful; we are to land under their fire, and drive the turks back everything is ready. I have just had breakfast, we go ashore in an hour. Don't know when you will get this, but knowing I have all your wishes for good luck etc. I remain

YOUR AFFECTIONATE BRO. & SON/JOHN NISBET

Margaret McKillop

Private Albert Edward John Petrusch (1892–1915), a laborer of Terang, Victoria, and a member of the 9th Light Horse, died of his wounds in a military hospital in Egypt. In a brave effort to bring comfort to a grieving family, Sister Margaret McKillop wrote in response to a letter seeking more detail than could be provided in the standard official telegram.

99. To Elizabeth Petrusch, 4 August 1915

Dear Madam

Sgt A Baker received your letter—but as he had not anything to do with your son—he came to me as I nursed your son up till within a few days of his death. I was most grieved to have to hand him over to any one else—but it was for his good—two special sisters were put on to look after him—so that he should never be left & might receive every possible attention. It will probably comfort you to know this—also that the Medical Officer in charge of the case attended to him himself every 4 hours night & day—he also called in other surgeons to consult upon the case & left nothing undone that they could suggest or that he himself thought might ease & relieve the patient.

All this is poor comfort to you—but knowing what loss means—I know it is a comfort to know that care & attention has been spent on those dear to us—& believe me your Son's character was such that there was not one among us who knew him, who did not feel that nothing we could do was too much. Always cheery—never a word of complaint, brave & patient to the last. Medical officers, orderlies, & Sisters. We all admired him for his extraordinary fortitude in enduring pain—more than I can tell you. He is a patient that Sister Weigall (she has already written to you I think) his Medical Officer—Capt Barton & I will never forget. And when Suffering & death come to us may we be given grace to answer the call as he did. You ask if he left any message! Not any definite one—because as he became weaker—he mercifully passed into gradual unconsciousness & just passed peacefully away without pain. But in the morning I was sitting with him & he looked so happy—I asked him Why? And he said 'Sister, I've been at home! True I have! I've been dreaming I was talking to Mother & Father—& it was all so bright & all so real!' And after a while he went on—'It makes you happy to dream like that. I could see them so plainly'. Then he smiled so brightly & said 'I must be going home soon Sister'. And truly he *has* gone home. Be very proud of him—we did not know him as a soldier—but as a man & as such we will honour him as 'One of the Best'. I only wish there was anything at all I could tell you further. The last actual words he said to me were 'I've been a terrible trouble to you two girls' meaning Sister Weigall & me & all we could do was take his hands & assure him it was not so, that we'd been glad to do anything for him. And he smiled & said 'Thank you, that's good'.

I may nurse many men as brave—but never a braver, he is the sort that England & Australia want. Sgt Baker wishes me to tell you that he would gladly have written to you but the only times he ever saw your son was twice when he was X rayed to locate the bullet.

Hoping this letter may be some comfort to you & expressing my deep sympathy for you

I REMAIN/YOURS SINCERELY/MARGARET MCKILLOP/(SISTER).

Mother & Father] Elizabeth Jane Johanna and Ernest August Petrusch

JOHN MONASH

In mid September 1915, after the disasters of the Gallipoli offensive, the remnants of the 4th Brigade, Australian Imperial Force, under the command of (then) Brigadier General John Monash (1865–1931) were sent to rest on Lemnos in Greece. In the welcome lull, Monash took the opportunity to send greetings to the members of his Melbourne walking club which he had joined in 1913.

100. TO THE WALLABY CLUB, 23 SEPTEMBER 1915

DEAR WALLABIES

After 20 weeks of incessant fighting, even the magnificent physique of the Dominion troops has yielded to the strains of constant effort and rough living conditions. No other troops could have endured so long. At last the higher command,—alarmed by the steady increase of sickness due to physical exhaustion—has consented to the five original Brigades of the Army Corps being withdrawn for a short 'breather' in this island—So here we are, sadly reduced in numbers & capacity, but with our spirit unimpaired—waiting for our Convalescents & Reiforcements to help us to again build up our fighting efficiency.—So far as my brigade is concerned, the fighting of the last 6 weeks was the toughest and fiercest & most sustained of any we have had (not including our first landing)—so that it is hard for us to realize the sudden transference from an environment of strife & clamour & the wreckage of war, to this peaceful island with its rolling landscapes, its simple Greek peasantry, the windmills lazily turning in the mild autumn breeze, the flocks of sheep & goats, & the quaint old villages & monasteries.—We have commenced a systematic exploration of the island, & there are quite a number of excellent walks on which I should like to misguide the club. A mob of wallabies tracking across this country side is just what is wanted to complete the anachronism.—Even rumours of war fail to penetrate this Aegean elisium, & by our very presence here 'les extremes se touchent'—Best love to you all.

JOHN MONASH

Thanks for Annual Report & Card of Annual Dinner received about a week ago

J.M.

M.M. WALSH

The deferential tone of this letter from an unknown Western Australian woman suggests that reverence for the gentry remained strong. Mrs Walsh makes her appeal as a soldier's mother. Margaret, Lady Forrest (1844–1929) was the wife of Sir John Forrest (1847–1918), surveyor, explorer and politician, colonial treasurer of Western Australia 1890–1901 and member for Swan in the first federal parliament.

101. TO MARGARET FORREST, 27 OCTOBER 1915

Dear lady will you excuse the writing this letter. I do not know rightly how to address your Ladyship so i ask you to pardon me it is a good many years now that once when you where on a visit to Georgina I was living near with my little family and i often think how the children used to speak about the great Lady that came by train. I have reared a good family some married and gone. Some i got here and one boy gone to the fronts. I have been living in the bush in a tent until this winter and seen plenty hardships and poverty. I want to ask you if you could be kind enough before you left West Australia if you would give me any old black or any old dresses you did not want or old shoes or hats. I have not had a dress for years and if anything happened my poor son I would like a little black to wear. I hope you will be good enough to excuse me been so rude as to write me only of the working class but it as allways been said that your Ladyship as a kind heart thanking you for any and a poor mothers blessings attend you.

YOURS VERY GRATEFULLY,/M. M. WALSH/LITTLE HOUSE NEAR STATION EAST CANNINGTON

VERA DEAKIN

The youngest daughter of Alfred Deakin, Australia's second prime minister, Vera Deakin (1891–1978) worked for the British Red Cross during the First World War. She was one of a team of 'searchers' who worked to discover the fate of those missing and wounded, and many of her compassionate letters to their families are on record. This letter from Cairo reflects the constant reminders of wartime suffering while life's routine pleasures of parties, golf and races went on as usual.

102. TO ALFRED & PATTIE DEAKIN, 2 JANUARY 1916

MY DARLINGS,

I scribbled the last few words to you so as to send the diary off in time for Col Springthorpe & hope you got same. We went to the Races with Mrs Syme & Marjorie & of course the boys. They were held at Gezireh Sport's Club, a primitive course with golfing going on in the centre. Everywhere khaki predominated, even amongst the owners of the horses unto the very jockeys themselves, some of whom were from the Intermediate Base … Every here & there a hospital suit with gay tie proclaimed a patient on holiday. There were certainly a number of smart English officers, our Colonel, Prince Alex. of Battenberg, etc but now & again we saw the too well recognised coloring of the worn soldier lately returned from the trenches. The few women represented nearly every nation & were accordingly costumed. I saw Mabel in the distance & of course Miss Chirnside & Miss Osborne. We left the letters at Ghezireh on our way to tea at the Continental but the Col. was out. Win & I returned to dinner, our New Year one, the room full of soldiers enjoying the festive bonbons etc.

Sunday, 2nd.

A typical morning of tidying & odd jobbing with a hurried lunch & rush to meet Mrs S. & Marjorie at Two. Out to Mena with a tram load of new arrivals. Mrs S, as usual chatting to the men. We found the camp smaller, therefore not such a number to serve. I quite enjoyed a turn at the money window where I could occasionally take a few minutes to chat. As there were others coming we left at 6.30, returned, changed dined at the big table as there was such a crowd & retired after doing odds & ends.

Monday, 3rd.

Letters from dear H.R.B. & E.M.B. strayed in, why so late I cannot say. They were good to get. The whole world seems sad with the news of the Persia's sinking. That makes three large mails in a fortnight. It is the first P. & O. too . . . Marjorie came for her first day at the office. It will be a relief to have her. Lady Barker much improved, in fact up & dressed. Rain, & quite cold. Need of good searchers felt very keenly, as there so many men over here, now who have been the whole nine months on Gallipoli. We retired early as we were too cold to sit up . . .

Tuesday, 4th.

Bitter chill & dreadfully dirty streets. A heavy day in the office as I had to hurry up & finish my report of the work in the office for Mr Knox to take back. Lady Barker read it over & was quite complimentary. I doubt if it will convey much to anyone who has not worked in an Inquiry Bureau. We paddled home in the rain to find a bed covered with treasures from you all. The luggage had arrived & Marjorie had brought it round. What an hour of delight it was opening all the parcels … What did not you send would be hard to tell. How nice were the blouses & gloves, the soap & scent, all the things I wanted. Dear Mrs Johnson added such a useful little present in the shape of an electric flasher, & Marjorie's & Mrs Symes gloves & veil just what I was about to buy. Many thanks for the dress & hat, too. I am so afraid the dust coat was sent by mistake. I shall keep it until I hear from you. Each gift brought you before my eyes . . . & the snaps of Jessie were pure joy. How she has developed, the pet. Many thanks Stella dear for the satchet, it is delicious. I sent the parcel to May & Miss Billings immediately. Lady Barkers, I took myself & presented. She was charmed & intends writing to you. I will give Miss Riggall hers when I next see her. I almost had a guilty feeling to have so much when the men want things so badly. Win had two boys from Benalla, the Pres. Clergyman's sons to dinner. One has just arrived from home, the other from Gallipoli. Both had the knack of graphic description & mimicry one moment we were moved to tears the next to laughter. The older is Secretary to the Bgde of which Mervyn Higgins is Adjutant . . . the costuming of the Adj. is of great importance so we learnt. All the men who have been through the long awful months in the trenches are wonderfully calm & unostentatious about their doings. They seem to have learnt to be stoical, almost fatalists, no hysteria, few horrors, but the long wearing months of suspense seem to have aged them. Quote Othello if you will, darling Daddy, but for real heroism without excitement & sudden glory, for the real test of a real man, give me a Gallipoli hero before the mighty Moor. "We had nothing to look forward to" seemed a small complaint from a man who had faced death so long, but on thinking it over it grows in weight & one realises a little the eternity of a second. Again the Gurhkas were much praised & the N.Z. but the Kitch. Army of Younglings … no. To the door of the R.A.M.C. a great debt of sorrow can be laid it seems. Always an Aust. for an Aust. whether it be in the field, in the hospital or as a friend. I am rambling on in this way as Mrs Reid who is sailing to Aust. by the Moldavia is giving this to Dr Travers who is to be a fellow passenger. Half our forces are at Tel-el-Kebir, so great chatter amongst the idlers at Shepheards, as to what is going to happen. Have no belief in these rumours … it is to frighten the natives & keep the troops out of Cairo till it is time to move them to Salonica perhaps. We have friends all around us, & in high places, where danger would be known. Trust to our being wise & do not worry. Little skirmishes with a few Arabs reads so big in the papers. I have no fear whatsoever, so have none either. *Wednesday, 5th.*

Still wintry weather. Nothing of moment happening in the office, but the usual slackness of searchers. Mr Isbister is much the best, & I hope to send him to Tel-el-Kebir to work down there. Mr Knox came to say goodbye, he did not mention seeing you so I didnt either. He has always been very nice. Home now tapping away. Win is down with the Symes. Both of the poor dears have colds. I throw a kiss to each dear soul I love within the walls of Llanarth Winwick, Airlie & The Elms. Again ever so many thanks for the gifts—& bundles of love. How I long to hug you all Dearest Mother Father & the rest.

GOOD LUCK TO THE WORK & THE WORKERS/EVER YOUR,/VERA.

Col Springthorpe] Senior Physician No 2 General Hospital, Egypt   Mrs Syme] Mrs Holland Syme and her daughter Marjorie   Prince Alex of Battenberg] later Mountbatten   Mabel] probably Mabel Brookes (1890–1975), wife of Sir Norman Brookes, one of the Australian Red Cross Commissioners in Egypt   dear HRB] Herbert Robinson Brookes, husband of Vera Deakin's sister Ivy (see Letter 77)   EMB] Vera Deakin's lifelong friend Elsie Bannister   Lady Barker] young English widow of Sir Digby Barker, and director of the Wounded and Missing Enquiry Bureau of the British Red Cross in Cairo   Mr Knox] Adrian Knox (1863–1932), later New South Wales chief justice, was in Egypt as an Australian Red Cross Commissioner in 1915–16   Jessie] daughter of Herbert and Ivy Brookes   Miss Riggall] Louise Riggall, artist, was a Red Cross nurse in Egypt   Mervyn Higgins] son of parliamentarian and High Court judge H.B. Higgins (1851–1929)   Shepheards] one of Cairo's principal hotels   Mr Isbister] Red Cross searcher from Adelaide   Llanarth, Winwick, Airlie and The Elms] Deakin and Brookes family houses in the Melbourne suburb of South Yarra

ARTHUR DEAN

After graduating in law in 1915 Arthur Dean (1893–1970) enlisted as a Lance Corporal in the AIF. Commissioned in 1916, he served in France until the end of the war in November 1918, having suffered a bullet wound and gas poisoning. This letter to his mother, headed 'Somewhere in France', was written shortly before his battalion fought in the battle of Pozières. Later a Melbourne barrister, a Supreme Court judge, and Chancellor of the University of Melbourne, Dean was knighted in 1960.

103. TO ALICE DEAN, 8 JUNE 1916

DEAREST AND BEST OF MOTHERS,

I feel I have been very neglectful of late, in the matter of letter writing; not in quantity, for I turn out a fairly bulky one every week, but it has just struck me you must sometimes be reminded of that "Flossie's pups" letter of long ago. These must be very anxious days for you, dearest mother—here I am in France—you know I have been here over two months,—you never get any "fresh" news of me—you must have seen in some Casualty Lists names of fellows from our Battalion—and you must be in constant dread lest the postman should bring you a Defence Department letter some day with bad news. And here I am quite well and strong, and yet you worrying day and night—and I confess I feel quite guilty. I wish I could send you a cable every week, but in the first place it is very seldom possible to do so, and in the second my meagre income barely suffices to keep us in a few additions to our scanty rations. I hope to get a cable away before long, for I want to allay your anxiety for a while if I can. Fortunately we haven't been engaged in any action to bring our names into the papers so that you can't read of Australian successes here while you wonder if I have fallen in the engagement. You will be receiving letters by now, describing our gradual advance toward the firing line, and I can imagine how deeply anxious you all must be. You will tell enquirers "Yes he must be in it by now. We should soon hear some more definite news.—and pass on to discuss other things, as if it wasn't the matter nearest to your heart. You're the heroes of this war, mother dear, not we careless fellow who live in a world of work, with a few stray shells for excitement—plenty of life and society and conversation—and scarcely ever a thought— seldom a serious thought—of you all at home. But never mind, now we shan't be long! However, our stay in the danger zone is about up, and by the time this mail closes I should be able to say we are right out of it for some fair time. A cable worded "Well. Resting" might arrive before this if I can manage it. That should cheer you up some, shouldn't it?

It has come to our knowledge that the green envelopes, not being censored as a rule, are frequently detained before despatch. So I am sending by this mail an ordinary envelope letter as well, bearing number "23a" in case.

Mails are not arriving too brilliantly. Since my birthday I have received 3 letters 1 April 4th from Glenys Sleeman. 2 March 15th, from Ida Taylor, 3. April 14th from Miss Darvall—so you can guess they are a bit erratic. The last I had from you was dated March 27th. It is now nine days short of Dad's birthday.

We are working fairly strenuously just at present. March 2 miles each way to work, do 8 hours or less on the job—digging etc among the trenches behind the firing line, home about 5—and no time to ourselves at all. Letter writing is fairly difficult. Possibly before long conditions will be better. One hears all kinds of rumours. With the aid of our pay and the canteen we manage to live fairly well, but issue rations are scarce—unless one fancies bully beef and biscuits—which one doesn't as a rule.

Accounts of the naval engagement of 8 days ago seem to be assuming a definite form in spite of the peculiar first message, which caused the gravest concern here. We get the English papers fairly frequently just now, and are becoming conversant with Imperial politics. The reported drowning of Earl Kitchener—apparently correct—has also occasioned the deepest depression in the army. No one doubts that the war will go on exactly as he had planned, but everyone feels the irony of the fate which has robbed England of her hero and the man himself of the reward of success on the eve of the realisation—for such we believe is imminent—of his long planned and patiently awaited triumph.

I have been having some trouble with my teeth. Yesterday I went to the field dentist a few miles back. He stopped one and pulled another in good style for an army dentist. Jaws are still a bit sore, but I don't anticipate any more trouble—at any rate not from the one I left behind me.

Haven't written any more doggerel—all my spare time goes in letter writing. The few I wrote were immensely popular here, and have been sent home by many chaps. One actually asked me if I intended embodying them in book form! From what I hear a couple may find their way into the Bendigo Advertiser—strictly incog. of course. I did it mostly to amuse myself.

Received a paper tonight—March 4th over three months old. Funny thing—but we have had lots of papers—many more recent, about, but somehow I scarcely glanced at them, yet one sent from home, no matter how old—is read through and through. We get most of the current papers from Australia and England.

Weather very fine, but not too hot yet. The tussaud is handy for fatigue these days, being cool to work in. It is also vermin proof which is a great thing.

Well mother darling, I must stop for the present. Hope this finds all well and is able to allay a lot of your fears for the present. I only wish you could get it tomorrow morning. Mail closes fortnightly here (approximately), the next 5 days before Dad's birthday. Heaps & heaps of love to you and Dad and all.

FROM YOUR EVER LOVING SON/ARTHUR DEAN

Later

Haven't time to send the white envelope letter I promised; but am sending a Field Service Postcard to give date.

AD

nine days short of Dad's birthday] Dean's letters can be dated by his use of the code of family birthdays Earl Kitchener] Horatio Herbert (1850–1916), 1st Earl Kitchener of Khartoum and Broome, was drowned when HMS *Hampshire,* on which he was travelling on a wartime mission to Russia, struck a mine and sank

James Hancock

James McCrae Hancock (1891–1916) was born at Bendigo, Victoria, the first son of the Rev. William Hancock and his wife Elizabeth Katherine (née McCrae) and a brother of the historian W.K. (Sir Keith) Hancock (see Letter 131). He was killed in action at Pozières, 4 August 1916, and was buried at Villers-Bretonneux. His spirited and optimistic letter was written from the 'Firing Line, France' to his fiancée in Melbourne.

104. To Constance McLennan, 2 July 1916

Con darling

A promise is a promise tho' if I had made it to anyone else but you I would be inclined to break it now. I wrote to you yesterday—an ordinary letter just telling you how things were going, & said that I would try to write what I always want to tell my girlie today. But I must just tell you what happened last night for although it was pretty off in many ways it was fine too. A splendid failure took place last night in the shape of a rather disastrous raid made by the—Battn.—N.S Welshmen, who hold that part of the line on our immediate right. The raid was not made in front of their own position but in front of ours for various reasons. Well they had no luck at all for everything seemed to go wrong, the chief trouble being Fritz's barb wire which formed an almost impenetrable barrier. The artillery had evidently not got the range & we must always trust to them for the partial demolition of the barb wire. So when our fellows got over they were hung up, Fritz saw his chance & took it—bombs, machine guns, every damn thing. Perhaps twenty out of twenty eight of the raiders came off scot free. The work of rescue, carried thro under a galling fire & in which our coy & especially our platoons took a prominent part, was fine. The conduct & pluck of the wounded, some hopelessly done for, was just splendid. Not a murmur from one & if ever fellows suffered they suffered last night from the unavoidable jolting of broken bodies & limbs when carried in. One fellow said to me 'Do you think its Australitis I've got mate' ('Australitis' being a general term for any malady which takes a johnny home). When I saw what he really had got—9 hits & some very bad,—I reckoned he would be very lucky if it wasn't some other 'itis'. I guess we all felt proud last night tho' perhaps you cant imagine why when our side got a bit of a doing. However very few 'doings' are going to come our way & things like last night only make us keener. There will be bigger things doing by far than last night & very soon, we know, but I will never forget it for it taught me just what a privilege it is to be an Australian & an Australian soldier.

Con you are my own girlie & I want you to feel proud, not of one soldier, but of old Australia & her soldiers. They say war is off Con & so it is but its fine & splendid too & I'm afraid I am beginning to miss seeing the former point of view under the shadow of the latter. That's rum Con & we really can't analyse our feelings about it all, but anyhow we will be mad with joy when its all over & we are bound for home again. And Con I know you don't worry now & are not frightened at all & that is great and right too, & like my own brave girlie. I just think the world of my Con & now more than ever perhaps, for you always help a johhny Con & there is no one that could do it like you do. I do love you so & just long to see you now & hug you & never let you go anymore. But its grown a very bear-like hug in all these months Con & no doubt will be barred when it comes back again to its owner. Con I want to thank you many many times tonight who has given me the most & dearest & most beautiful—the best girlie in all the world. And Con I really am grateful & never forget for one minute.

We are moving out tonight & wont return to this part of the line again. We are marching twelve miles tonight but I don't know exactly where. We are likely to have a bit of a spell in billets & then—right into it we have been promised. I believe the heads are going to wake up & try a big advance at last.

In one of the last letters Con you asked me to tell you always how my constitootion was. That's not necessary is it Con? we are both pretty strong & fit aren't we & I always think of my girlie as strong & well. and if you think of me like that too, you will always be right, for I was strong enough in Australia & I'm certainly stronger now. With your letters Con I received one from Mrs McLennan & I was most pleased to have it. It told me that your behaviour generally was causing no anxiety at home, that you were still 'attending' lectures (the uncorroborated statement of one—not even an eye witness—so mere here say which is not evidence at all), & that you were 'alright'. as if I did not know you were much more than alright—the dearest & sweetest girlie ever. Must say Goodbye now Con, but can't send you all my love for you have it already now & for ever & ever. But I want to book more big hugs for 'the day' & as many kisses as you can spare for your Jim.

PS. Kindest rememberances to Mr and Mrs McLennan & Joan & strokes to Gug & any stray kittens & dogs etc you may have.

OLAF STAPLEDON

Olaf Stapledon (1886–1950), social reformer and writer, met his Australian cousin Agnes Miller in England in 1913. She returned to Sydney in 1914, just as war broke out. They exchanged an unbroken series of love letters across the world until their marriage in 1919. Olaf, a Quaker and conscientious objector, went to France with the Friends' Ambulance unit.

105. TO AGNES MILLER, 4 JULY 1916

AGNES,

Last night two of us were up at the ruined town where we used to go [illegible] long past. It was a lovely evening, so before turning in we wandered all over the town. It is much more battered than before, having reached just that stage between habitability and a heap of rubbish that is most impressive in smashed towns. The church, once a mighty and solid building is a chaotic mass—whole walls flung down and still intact, here a great mound of ruin overgrown with bright poppies, cornflower, & mustard, and often with patches of oats or barley flourishing on top, self sown. There is still one fine wall and windows standing; and a single pillar stands, with a very beautifully carved capital of acanthus leaves. All round the church is the grave yard, closely packed with beautifully decorated little graves of soldiers. Some are covered with growing flowers mixed with gaudy artificial ones. Some are tiled over roughly with fragments taken from ruined house-fronts, or broken slabs of marble, or a headless statue of a saint, or some unrecognisable piece of marble wreckage. All bear their little wooden crosses & inscriptions, mostly commemorating some Breton marine. Some say simply "Here lies X." One, equally carefully adorned, is the grave of a German. Some graves are fenced in with bits of iron bedsteads. Shell holes are everywhere, and here & there you can still come across a man's jaw bone or ribs turned up by a shell and overlooked by the "sexton". The whole ruined town is a medley of yellow & blue & scarlet & green of flowers & leaves. Tall clover grows in the great square, pushing up between the pavé stones. The houses are all shattered, but some still stand in an almost habitable condition, others are tangled wrecks of beams & brick, gay wall paper hanging in shreds, bent iron work broken glass etc. In one room that had been laid bare we saw a little white iron work cradle, "long since disused." Here and there on plaster walls soldiers have drawn marvelous "works of art", faces people, battle, and subjects concerned with the Frenchman's one joke. Here and there is a rough notice forbidding entrance, for military reasons; here & there a patch of lettuces for some officers' mess. Everywhere there are cellars & dug-outs, and everywhere soldiers. Here a scribbled notice "Very good drinking water", here a shattered wall of pre-war advertisement posters. Here suddenly the nose of a canon pokes out of a window at you. And from the one side of the town you look across fields & a river to the trenches, the first line I mean, for of course there are trenches everywhere. Last night all was quiet, save for an intermittent rifle fire and an occasionally wild bark of a gun next door to our post. All the country side is enriched with loot from that town. Mirrors, billiard tables, pianos, tiles, stoves, all have come from that town. Now in these latter days there is no loot of any value, for countless searching eyes have been over every square foot of rubble. But a shell may sometimes turn up some little valuable that is immediately snapped up by someone near at hand. Last night after our walk we slept in our car, rather than go down into a stuffy dug out. Each of us lay on a seat & tried not to keep the other awake by turning & fidgeting & fighting mosquitos & other vermin. Neither of us slept anything to speak of, because of the wretched insects. And at last in the morning we got a job, much to our relief after that vile night.

Some days later. Having very laboriously and ingeniously mended my fountain pen I can at last write to you. I broke the pen in two ragged pieces in an impromptu wrestling bout. It is now marvelously repaired with sticky tape and bound with cotton. It is as good as new, save that it is rather short, rather bulbous, and to fill it I have to put the nib end in my mouth and <u>suck</u> up ink. Great judgement is needed to know when to stop sucking! There is no news to tell you, save that our hitherto secluded position seems to be becoming unpleasantly central; but I must not say why. Last night from our sand dune we had a most glorious view, yesterday afternoon, I mean. We had all our glasses and telescopes out and saw all manner of very distant easterly objects, and disputed about them with the aid of a map. Some of us had been in said places before the war; the rest wondered whether perhaps we should ever be in them, before the end of the war. To the East also there was a most glorious pile of white cloud, beautifully moulded in great shoulders and buttresses and little delicate roughnesses. Such clouds always make me half drunk, sort of. And when the setting sun gilded them most of us forgot all the famous spires and towers and were amazed at the cloud's beauty. There was also a particularly mad tri-plane that kept reeling and twisting and flying upside down, flashing in the low sun light. The other night I was up in our ruined front town again and amongst other things I prowled round the ruined railway station. The floors of the various rooms were covered with old railway literature and unused tickets. I made a little collection of tickets for souvenirs for friends. I would send some to Waldo, but of course they are censorable, so he must wait. People at home always seem fearfully keen to get hold of any little souvenir, such as here one can't bother to pick up. Souvenirs are too heavy and bulky to take home. I never attempt to collect big things. That railway station must have been a fine hunting ground for souvenirs once upon a time. We slept in my bus in an old brewery yard that night, and got a job at 2.45 AM. After we had gone there was a little bombardment, and two shells fell in the brewery, one of them showered bricks and tiles on the spot where my car had been. I am glad the car was not there, for she would have had her canvas roof torn, & that would have meant much wearisome sewing for me, and I am not a great sempstress! This life does teach one to do odd jobs of all sorts, such as one would never have dreamt of doing before. Do you know what a "gadget" is? I don't know what it really is, but in the FAU it is any little contrivance such as a tool box cunningly made to hold all your tools in neat positions, or a strap screwed into wood-work to hold your shrapnel helmet when not in use, or a dodge for holding your brushes or oiler, or a home made ferule on a walking stick, or any home made or professional little convenience. Some people spend all their spare time making gadgets, or "gadgetis-ing". I seldom do so, having other fish to fry, but sometimes I have a fit of it, and gadgetise solidly for a couple of days and then get fed up. My pet aversion is the making of gadgets officially suggested/commanded. I fear I generally avoid such work, unless it is something necessary and interesting. Your cousin is rather insubordinate and pigheaded and democratically inclined! My last gadget but one consisted of crude tailoring, as a result of which I now appear with khaki shorts & bare knees in Anzac fashion, that dress being now permitted at the front in this glorious weather. We cause quite a sensation with our bare knees, here where there are few British about.

Today I am on duty and must not go and bathe, alas. Tomorrow, Sunday, it is my turn to be orderly and that means a day of hard labour under the supervision of the cook, who is a great oar in his way, & comes from John's, Oxford. Next day I spend in a place where to bathe would be most immodest as it would be in full view of—the enemy. So there is no bathing for me just now.

Here comes someone to borrow my glass to see if he can "see the shell leaving" a certain big gun. I don't think! Not except from just behind it anyhow. There is always something or other to look at here. Now dear, I am going to stop, because lots of people are coming up here and there is much talking. So here ends one more letter. If all our letters were to be read through on end, alternately yours and mine, what a lot they would tell that we had not in mind to tell at the time of writing. They would tell of all sorts of changes and fluctuations and gradual evolvings that we knew nothing of at the time. All the past has proved for the best for you and me. We will believe the present is also for the best, but truly I think we are both ready now. Further waiting seems not able to draw us more together. Well, we have got to wait, and take our chances, while all this great busi-ness gets itself settled. What I keep wondering is whether in the future years I shall be able to persuade you that it was right not to fight. Anyhow, we shall be able to look back on this time and laugh at it kindly. And the world, someday, will look back on this awful time and laugh at it, though grieving over it. For the world is apt to grow out of its wars and grieve over them, & laugh at its past dissentions. Good-bye, dear. This is a short letter, but I am busy just now. I'll write again soon. Perhaps there will be another letter from you soon. Oh, but I love my Anzac girl!

Your own/Olaf Stapledon.

Please excuse this beastly mess. My first attempt at mending my broken pen failed. Please excuse bad writing always. I very seldom have the chance of writing at a table. Excuse smudges for dearth of blotting paper.

ruined town] Nieuport (Belgium)   Waldo] Agnes's brother   FAU] Friends' Ambulance Unit

AGNES MILLER

At a time when bitter controversy about conscription divided Australian families, Agnes Miller (1894–1984), whose father despised 'shirkers', struggled to hold on to her love and respect for Olaf without rejecting her family's values. She voted for conscription in the Referendum of October 1916.

106. To Olaf Stapledon, 7 August 1916

My Olaf,

I have had four letters from you this week end, such a feast. I wanted them to spin out & have two now & two next week, but both mails came together so of course then I forgot what I had wanted before & I rejoiced at having them, so many, all together. But alas there won't be another mail now for a fortnight:—but there are plenty outward, I suppose, correctly homeward bound, so I shall make up for it by writing to you. Your letters came out of order but now that I have them all I can get my bearings. You were very disappointed at not getting your move South after all—at least I suppose it was South—but the actual word was cut out. Hard luck. You are just about as fed up with the flat countries as our boys were with Egypt. But they have got their move now, so let's hope you will get yours soon too. I expect it will mean more shells & things down South, but if you will be glad of the change I must be glad too for you. When I got the first of the four letters on Saturday morning somehow I wanted to weep because you think I am so far away from you in what you think to be right with regard to war & conscription & so forth. I said to Mother "he's got the idea that I'm right at the oppo-site end of the stick—& I wish he hadn't—because really I'm ever so much nearer his end than anyone else's". It's horrid to be even thought so far away & I can't stick it out. (drops one dejected or merely petulant(?) tear). In spite of whatever I may have said I don't believe there's a gulf between us at all. If you think there is don't let it rest at that, talk to me, write to me—because if I am not with you I haven't got a firm footing anywhere. No good to say we'll agree to differ & each be loyal to our own point, because I haven't got a point; poor bewildered me! Come back & give me a hand, an arm. I'm so tired of being without you. As a family, we are much nearer your point of view than other families here—though of course we never hear your point of view discussed in this country; and of this family I am the nearest to you, nearer than Mother in spite of her Quaker traditions. Don't say, dear, or think that, though the war has drawn us together—that it might have done still more if you had been fighting— because I'm sure that is not so. If you had been fighting I should have approved because you were doing what you thought to be your duty—now I approve because you are doing other & useful work which you believe to be your duty. If you had taken no part & no responsibility—then I should not have approved. Nor would you. But you must remember this—I am not one who has held a point-of-view primly for years, & then doubted & clutched violently at another point & clung to it desperately & so on—I'm only a young person who has not had a point of view—& truly I do not believe there are many young persons of my age who have a point of view of their own—unless it be those who have never bothered over it & just taken their family & friends' point of view for granted. I suppose that is what I did until the war and you came & put it to the test; & then when I wanted to stand, I found I was not strong enough;—Only a child after all in understanding, reasoning—mental grasp—though perhaps, & I hope, more of a woman in love & in faith. If you had taken other people for granted you would have done the natural & obvious thing & fought with all the rest; then I should have been quite content—I would not have thought seriously of Pacifism & its handful of ardent upholders—at least I might have marvelled at them but never thought of being one of them. It is only because of you that I have been wakened up at all, & I'm glad—although it is a new & difficult way & I have not yet learned to tread firmly. But I have the feeling in me that it is the noble way & I wouldn't give it up for anything while I have strength & you to guide me. The only reason why your way makes me troubled—& sometimes a little bit ashamed—is because your work does not take you into such dangers as the other boys'—you, & I for you, are not taking the risks of the fighters. But I know it's not your fault, you have told me—I know you would take more, gladly, if it were possible. At present it is not possible, so I shall be thankful while I may. It's when I hear of a lad like Carl being killed in action—oh dear then I must be more ashamed than thankful. Thankful indeed that it is not you—but ashamed that it might not have been. So write to me as if I were one with you dear, for I am really.

Oh I'm cant to say [?]—that when I wrote long ago "you would not make Peace while Belgium is in enemy hands"—I understood that the Germans would still be in possession after the Peace. But everyone says that would not be so. You say they would retire peacefully. Well of course that would be much better than to fight on & on. But it wouldn't be *fair* would it, for them to stick to Belgium because Belgium belongs to the Belgians, not the Germans. A line from our play insists on capping this discourse—in broad Americain twang. "Sentiment is sentiment, but damme justice is justice." This is the night of the Mendelssohn lecture at the YWCA. I mean this is the morning of the night. I have been trying to have influenza for the last three days—an inside headache that makes me giddy, swollen glands—a sore throat—& I have to sing tonight hélas. I can sing more easily than talk because I use only head voice mostly being soprano & rise above my sore throat, but it's beastly to feel stuffy & have to keep your head in one position & walk on tiptoe for fear of jogging it! Do you know that kind of head? I hope not—when the jog comes there's nothing to be done but clench your teeth & exist until the spasm is passed. I think it must be neuralgia. It's less than a week until the play so I must recover my voice by then. Daddy & Waldo both have glands & throats too but I seem to have the monopoly of the head ache.

We had our Seekers meeting on Friday night Miss Messiter revelled to her hearts content & Mrs in native legends & folk lore. When she was settled in her corner near the fire before the meeting began—she beckoned me over & said "Miss Miller—you won't mind if I quote Mr Stapledon? I couldn't help it. He has expressed just what I wanted to say." I was pleased & told her so & out came the quotation near the beginning of the paper—"The spirit of man lifteth up her voice in the chorus (?)—There were no Harmony without her". You were referred to as "the young poet who wrote Latter Day Psalms"—& then at the end of her paper by name—Mr Olaf Stapledon—and I started involuntarily (without turning a hair) & nearly fell through the floor! Miss Messiter thinks the world of your book, my dear, she proclaimed to the company in her characteristic way that she "took it" last thing at night & first thing in the morning. And afterwards she apologized for having talked so much about you & she said that it wasn't a 'put up job' because she didn't know that she was to read her paper at my house. She is such a character; much too well read for me, but still I can appreciate her for herself & her enthusiasm & her funny ways & her humour—& she's full of ideas. She read us some quaint & charming legends. A brilliant & wicked idea strikes me. It is Waldo's birthday this month & I think I'll give him those books of Australian Legends—I want to read them so much myself! That's what we call a "wheelbarrow present" from a similar occasion when Daddy the gardener presented his infant son with a huge wheelbarrow on his 2nd birthday. Waldo loved it of course & so did Daddy!—Besides—Miss Messiter *besought* us to encourage people to take an interest in our own native legends lest they all vanish before we have learned to love them. At the meeting in the absence of Mrs Laing—I had to take the chair! it was only a case of opening the meeting, but it was the first time in my life & I was scared to pieces. Don't you think it was good of me not to refuse? I thought I was awfully brave. Lottie Armstrong "sooled me on". I wonder if I shall ever be able to do such things with ease & grace & sense. You think it funny don't you, old stager? So shall I when I reach your years of discretion.

I ought to be stopping now to write to Beatrice, but my head throbs if I do anything new! I believe Alfred will be married before you get this! We have been consoling each other hitherto & exhorting each other to Patience, but I refuse to be consoled any more now that he has deserted Micawber. I wonder if you will see him before you leave France. Doesn't that sound hopeful, "leave France"? Yes thank you I'd love to go & tour in a nice little fast car with you. You can choose your own make. We'll take along your blackthorn stick studded with tin tacks as a protection against bandits in the high passes of the Alps. I don't want to go to flat countries just at present—not Belgium. I think of endless desolation. I should like the Loire the château country, & I sigh for Switzerland & the Italian Alps specially Italy after reading Vittoria. Take me up the Monte Motterone & all the other Montes from where we shall look down into the sweltering plains—& to the Lago di Garda—& I want to see Verona & Milano. I want to go to La Scala & I shall live through "the night of the fifteenth" hear & see La Vittoria singing her triumph song "Italia—Italia shall be free". But first I want to learn Italian. I am annoyed with you because you know Italian & I don't! So I think I'll pay you out by learning it before I see you again. Anyway I would if I had time.

Goodbye now—I'll keep all the rest of the chatter for next mail. Remember about me & that gulf—& if you still think I'm on the other side, it will be all up! Dearest-my-own

YOUR LOVING AGNES.

The Seekers] a reading and discussion group for women   Latter Day Psalms] poems by Olaf Stapledon, 1914

WILSON TONG

Wilson Tong (c. 1896–1973) joined the New Zealand Expeditionary Force in 1915 and served overseas between 1915 and 1919. This letter, headed 'Some Where in France', is the first of a five-year correspondence with a young Australian woman, whom he was never to meet. It is thought that on his way to war Tong threw overboard a bottle enclosing a paper which gave his name and regimental number, and that this was washed up on the beach at Phillip Island. Edith Harris kept Tong's letters in the secret compartment of a small wooden box with a concealed lock: they were found after her death in 1966.

107. TO EDITH HARRIS, 24 AUGUST 1916

DEAR MISS HARRIS,

As I heard from my Mother that you had picked up my bottle I thought that I might take the liberty of writing to you and I hope that you will not be offended. We have been having a fairly lively time of it since we have been here and it is pretty hot & dusty at times especially on a long route march. We have just come out of the trenches for a rest and it is quite a relief to get away from the sounds of the shells ectc. This place is very decent after Sandy Egypt. We were there about a month and we were not sorry to get out of it as it was very heavy work drilling and marching about in the sand. The heat was terrible and at night we could not sleep for the cold for a while but we got use to it. We than embarked for France and we had a pretty lively time for a while as we were afraid of a submarine attack so we had to wear our life belts allday and it was a nuisance. As soon as we arrived at our destination we were put on the train and we were in it for about 60 hours and we were not sorry to stretch our legs. After training for a while we then went into the trenches and I managed to get over my first time under fire allright.

I was a bit nervy for a while and every time a shell came I would duck down. It is quite natural to do it no matter how far away it is. The first bombardment I was in I was very shaky, for every time I heard one coming I thought it was going to land on top of the dugout but nothing happened. I remember one night I was out delivering a message up in the front line and all at once a shell landed behind me and it did not take me long to get out of the road but my foot got caught in a stick and I made a lovely dive into a pool of mud and water and you never saw such a mess. I was covered in mud just like thick pea soup. At night time the machine guns are allways going and they get on your nervs. It does not pay to look over the parapet as Fritz sweeps the parapet with bullets. Then in the early morning about day break the snipers start and Fritz is no mug at shooting as some fellows have found out to their cost through looking over the parapet to long. The rats and mosquitos are fairly thick and are a great nuisance especially the mosquitos. One of our fellows woke up one night and found a rat chewing his nose talk about a yell it was enough to wake the dead he did look a sight with all his nose scratched. France is a great place the only trouble I find is talking the language it gets me well twisted. The people are all very busy getting the harvest in and they work from daylight to dark young and old. It is mostly done by hand in these parts. The country looks lovely as far as you can see, it is all crops ripening. Well I can't think of any more now so will close hoping this finds you as well as it leaves me I remain

YOURS SINCERELY/WILSON TONG

P.S. If you care to answer this letter my address is
Signaller W Tong No 26/143
14th Batt Signal Section
3rd NZ (Rifle) Brigade
NZ Expeditionary Force
France.

ELIZABETH STEELE

Elizabeth Steele née Brooks (1860–1955) was from a pioneering family at Burwood, Victoria. Her eldest son was killed in an accident only weeks before her second son Walter embarked on a troop ship for Europe. He carried his mother's letter with him throughout the First World War.

108. To Walter Steele, 15 December 1916

MY OWN DEAR SON WALTER,

Just a little message and a mother's blessing as you leave us, responding to your country's call to serve in far off lands. My dear boy, I pray that God who gave you to us, and who in His providence has so ordered your life that we have had you up to the present in our home, giving us joy & happiness, may be ever present with you, as you journey over the deep, & may be in strange & foreign lands, keeping you as the apple of his eye, sustaining you in times of difficulty and perhaps sickness, and as He has in the past made you a blessing to others, may you be made tenfold more so now. We know how you will be thinking of us at home with tender memories, and just now as a double gap is made in the family circle, our hearts will be drawn nearer to each other, and our prayers more fervent. I do not fear for you my boy, as I know you will "play the man", as your trust is in a Divine power. "Be strong and of a good courage for I am with thee." I will *never leave thee nor forsake thee.*

God be with you till we meet again/ever your loving mother/L. Steele

May Gibbs

May Gibbs (1877–1969) worked as a children's book illustrator before launching her own career with the creation of the Gumnut babies and other bushland creatures, including the wicked Banksia men and kind Mrs Kookaburra. In this letter to Fred Shenstone of Angus & Robertson, she pleads for a decision on the first book about her most popular creations. Snugglepot and Cuddlepie: their Adventures Wonderful *was published in 1918.*

109. To Fred Shenstone, 5 June 1917

Dear Mr Shenstone,
When may I hear results of your consideration of the book "Snugglepot and Cuddlepie"? Everything is ready and I'm just longing to get on with it—days are slipping by horribly quickly and I do want it out early!
Yours anxiously!!!/May Gibbs
My apologies for not remembering your initials.

110. To Fred Shenstone, 4 July 1917

Dear Mr Shenstone,
Here are the leaves, and by the way *PLEASE* have the printing of the books *good and clear* this time. I should be glad if you would allow me to see proofs while the printing is going on.
With regard to "Snugglepot and Cuddlepie", I feel that not another moment can be spared. I may be missing all other chances by waiting so long for you—I believe I have a good introduction to Lothian in Melbourne, for whom I've already worked. I feel sure you'll understand how keen I am about keeping the ball rolling. I feel it would be bad to miss this year, so I want you to tell me definitely and quickly what you've decided. Please forgive the hustling note. I'm very fuzzy and half awake with my cold and am seized with terror at the way the months are flying. May I expect an answer from you right away?
Yours sincerely,/May Gibbs
I know it's not your fault things are slow, but you can pull the strings!

ELIZABETH JACKSON

Elizabeth Jackson (1890–1923), daughter of a Methodist minister, graduated Master of Arts in 1914. She was one of the first women to be appointed to a teaching post at the University of Adelaide, and although her career was cut short by illness and her early death, she was an influential figure in university circles. Her letter to her brother Canning, then still in France with the AIF, shows the qualified independence of a woman of her time, as well as a touch of defensiveness about taking a man's job in wartime.

III. TO CANNING JACKSON, 17 JULY 1917

DEAR CANNING,

There are rumours that the Australians are having a rest; we hope you are one of them. And yet I wish their sweethearts were there to look after them. Do you remember Xavier de Maistre's "Voyage autour de ma Chambre", and his comments on la vie. The flesh and the devil take a little struggling with, but I will not believe that our men cannot overcome both, even though they (in flesh etc) are as bad as the Germans.

To turn to an everyday subject: this afternoon Miss George, once head of Advanced School for Girls, gave a tea-party to the teachers of M.L.C., her last school on her retirement. Miss George looked like Betsy Trotwood, and the rest looked like—teachers.

The party was at Moore's, the big drapery place which has become an Emporium. Ella and I looked at the furniture department afterwards. I would like to furnish a house, and live as a man might, but Mother doesn't much encourage the idea. Of course if I had a cottage and a maid there would be no saving done, but why should I "pig it" in uncomfortable lodgings all my youth? True, at present I put everything into the War Loan, and I suppose that course must be continued at present. The Modern Pepys writes in his diary "One man may not give another to drink. This do bring the war home to one"! If saying goodbye to our men did not do that for women, the thwarted desire to shop would. Before the war I hadn't the money, now I have (some) money, & the desire, but not the conscience.

I have been made Tutor in Psychology and Philosophy to the Workers Educational Association—the appointment is from the University—and small as the pay is, it is an addition to teacher's salary, and I hope it will lead to enough advanced work to make school unnecessary in a year or two.

It seems unfair to dwell on a feminine career in these days when men find theirs scattered to the winds, but mine is a very insignificant one, and is at the expense of no man, at any rate of no South Australian, for I have done more in these subjects than any Mr S.A. student.

Of course I was at the Grange on Saturday & stayed till 5.54 Sunday. Grandpa was purring with satisfaction—health, and having mother there. Mrs Lewis, the housekeeper, is a very nice *woman*, but quite brainless. She is helpless; doesn't know how to make jam, boil corned beef, & so on. But that sort of thing appeals to men, I believe. They *like* having their advice asked on the most un-accustomed things. We all do. And her muddling results in something or other to eat. Anyway, Grandpa doesn't want to change, and that is all that matters. He makes the fire, & boils the kettle, & sees that there is washing-up water, with simple pride & even sneaks away to sweep the verandah! It isn't so easy to give orders to a housekeeper as to a maid, and I really think he likes doing these little jobs. He feeds the fowls and looks after the cats, and inspects his little estate. We go solemnly over the vines & the almond trees every Saturday, & agree that they need pruning. And we admire the geraniums and perhaps sit on the verandah seat in the sun and observe that the blinds need mending. And then I get the string-tin and (well under observation and orders the while) mend them.

We have had lots of rain—indeed, my new umbrella is wearing through already. Heaven send we may yet learn to make things as well as the Germans! Also I yearn for some English-made boots. The Bulletin may say what it pleases, Australian-made Protected shoes are dear & nasty & let in the wet. I think it would be much better to let each part of the Empire devote itself to developing what it is characteristically best fitted for, and our job at present is production rather than manufacture.

But I do hope we shall learn to make most things *somewhere* within the Empire as good as anywhere out, although I'm not sure that I like the idea of trying to be self-sufficient to the point of exclusiveness.

I wonder if political ideas change much at the Front? Some of the letters published in the papers as coming from there strike one as being written by exactly the same Pro Bono Publico and Pater Familias we knew of yore. Not much war (or other) new literature comes my way, but "the Confessions of a Soldier", if as honest and complete as Rousseau's, ought to be enlightening if someone would write it. Potboundness is the trouble with most of us, and anything that cracks our old pot and forces us to get another, or, better, anything that stretches our present life, is good.

Goodnight, dear old boy. Love from Elizabeth.

The Bulletin may say what it pleases] the *Bulletin's* nationalist policies included protection of Australian industries from overseas imports

NELLIE MELBA

With the exception of three concert tours of the United States, the operatic diva Nellie Melba (1861–1931) spent most of the years of the 1914–18 war in her home city of Melbourne. The world had changed profoundly. In a pessimistic letter to an old friend, the impresario Henry Russell (1871–1937), Melba captures the mood of the times while shrewdly assessing new opportunities.

112. TO HENRY RUSSELL, UNDATED [c. 1918]

MY DEAR HENRY

I did answer your last letter & am surprised that you did not receive it. I sent it to the Metropolitan—As a matter of fact I only thought of giving opera out here because I thought it would help you & give you breathing time—There is a great field for opera here & I dont see why you should not get it.

Everything is so dreadful & awful now, the world *can never be the same* & I dont know what is to become of us all—There is one thing we Britishers must stick together & help each other along—I wonder if we shall meet in America I hope so—If the war continues I shall return here as England & Paris would be too sad, I could'nt *bear it*. All my friends have been killed or wounded so what is the good of returning. Perhaps you could return with me & perhaps we could do a little business on the way home–Manilla Shanghai etc—(this is entre nous yet). You must know that I shall arrange something for you—Cheer up & dont let your nerves get the best of you—You have many firm friends but none sincerer than

Nellie Melba

Oh if only the war would finish—

WILL DYSON

Will Dyson (1880–1938) left Australia for Britain in 1909, and worked as a war artist and political cartoonist. His wife Ruby (1885–1919), also known as 'Ruby Lind', was a sister of artists Norman, Lionel, Percy and Daryl Lindsay. During her brief career she won recognition as a painter and illustrator. This letter to his brother, writer Edward Dyson (1865–1931), describes Ruby's death from Spanish influenza in the 1919 epidemic.

113. TO EDWARD DYSON, UNDATED [MARCH 1919]

DEAR TED

It is, I think, two or 3 weeks since Ruby died. I have left our house—I could not live in it of course and am here—in the sort of studio Ruby dreamed of surrounded by the best of the furniture that we had acquired. I am living here alone. Betty is with friends in the country till I get a school for her close to me—she to come home to me at week ends. I have not written sooner. I could not face it.

My poor darling went to Ireland to her cousins with Dan 3 weeks before she died. She had laryngitis when she left—she came back after a fortnight—looking more lovely than I can remember her and died 6 days later—on the night of the dance she had hurried back to make a dress for—the first dance since the war. She stayed in bed on the Wednesday and died on the following Wednesday night 12th March. At first it seemed like an ordinary cold taking its ordinary course on Thursday I got the doctor—who treated her till Saturday when she got worse—much worse on Sunday and I got Norah Ferguson out to nurse her & on Monday I got 2 other nurses and had 3 doctors—in consultation all that time until she died in my arms at 10.30. She was fighting for breath for the last day and unconscious 3 hours before she died. She was patient & lovable all through— worrying about minor domestic matters to the end—were the nurses comfortable—why didnt I go to bed, was the house clean. They were giving her raw whisky— when she couldnt drink it all—leaving some in the glass she said—(she could only talk during exhalation) 'You have it Joss—I left some Joss—I have everything.' This was a memory of the time when whisky couldn't be got & she believed I was getting to like a glass of whisky. She thought only of me to the end as she did all her life. God forgive me I didnt give her a better time. I have nothing material to reproach myself with but I cannot forget all the things I might have done. This is positive torture—and I know that actually I was 'good' to Rub and if she could she would not have it otherwise. I know she was proud of me—and sacrificed herself as far as I would let her for both Betty and myself. That she should have been proud of me—she didnt believe much in my beliefs but she was really proud of my refusal to take money by working against them. It was for Rube I worked—this I did not know till she went—but I can do nothing now without feeling it has no object—like an actor ranting in an empty theatre. I can have no sympathy with people who talk of grief as a beautiful or poetic thing—it is being torn by the teeth of dogs. My first feeling at any success was to take it to Rube—now I can see that that was the first sweetness of success of any kind.

She was doing such beautiful work—just hinting at a new development—she was a natural painter & we had plans for living so that she could paint landscapes all through the summer—for which she yearned. We had had a trivial misunderstand 2 months ago and had been brought closer together by it—I think we loved each other more at the end than ever & had made elaborate plans to fit a new consciousness of this. This was all to begin with her return from Ireland. I think it is not accidental on the part of God. She died within a few days of her birthday and Betty had been making elaborate preparations for it—surprises in the way of 'camisoles' pin cushions 'post cards' all of which were to be burst on her morning on the 20th. She said a few days before the 20th & after Rube's death to the people she is staying with 'I do love being here—I dont want to go away but you see I must be home with my Mummy on the 20th—its her birthday. She kept record of the days by coming down first thing to see the papers.

I went down and told her. A dreadful business. I temporised for a while & she began to get frightened and I could only blurt out that "Mummy had gone to Heaven". She immediately went into a wild paroxysm of grief. I could do nothing to comfort her. "Oh daddy I want to die myself" was all she said several times. I did not know she would so immediately link it up with death. The girl of the house whom I called in advised me not to try & comfort her but let her cry. I left them alone & she fell suddenly off to sleep in Miss May's arms—she cried that night & is very quiet but never mentions her mother & does not speak if she is mentioned. I am getting her away among other children at once—a good kind school where she will be able to come to me at week ends.

I am all right in health & so on. I started in the Herald this week—4 a week which will keep me occupied. Thank God for that. My poor darling left as much money as we had when I went to France. She feared for the future if anything had happened to me & she must have lived just as barely as we could. All our money was in her name. I will keep it for Bett. There is something over £1000 in all & I am insured for £2000 so that Betty, unless money loses its significance, will not be penniless.

Give my love to the old people—I will write them next—I cannot face another letter today. I wish I was home.

BILL

I am going to spend £100 or two in doing a little privately circulated book of Rube's work. I may ask for subscription or may not I will see. A poor devil of a publisher here who was Rubes devoted & worshipping slave is doing it with me. More anon. Dan Lindsay when he goes out takes little mementos for all.

Ted its unbelievable. A dozen times a day I have the feeling that perhaps its all wrong with a following relapse into the certainty of the situation.

My poor darling. How she did love things when she loved them. and now the world is people[d] with all sorts of useless & ugly walking corpses that have neither desire for life or——

Ruby made the world the better for being in it. There never was a personality that spread a more generous sense of the goodness of human beings than she did.

Betty] the Dysons' seven-year-old daughter   to Ireland to her cousins with Dan] Dr Robert Lindsay, father of Ruby, had migrated from Ireland to Australia: Dan was the family's name for Daryl Lindsay the Herald] Dyson was chief cartoonist for the *Daily Herald*   when I went to France] refers to Dyson's work as war artist   a little privately circulated book] *The Drawings of Ruby Lind* (1920), published by Cecil Palmer. Dyson's own tribute, *Poems: in Memory of a Wife*, had appeared in 1919, also published by Palmer.

EDMUND BARTON

Alfred Deakin, three times prime minister of Australia and one of the principal architects of the country's federation, died on 7 October 1919. From the High Court his old friend Sir Edmund Barton (1849–1920), who had served as Australia's first prime minister, wrote to Deakin's widow in sadness and recollection. Of this letter, Deakin's biographer John La Nauze observed: 'Neither in lapidary inscriptions nor in letters of condolence is a man upon oath; still Barton was a Judge'.

114. To Pattie Deakin, 8 October 1919

My dear Mrs Deakin

However you may in later days have seen that the day of parting was not far off, such a parting is a harsh severance in the case of those who love, and in your case no one can realise a tithe of its meaning or its effects. But I trust that you will have the strength to bear the burden which your daughters will do their best to make less heavy.

I always looked on Alfred Deakin with a reverent admiration, until better knowledge of him turned admiration into love without effacing in the least my estimate of his greatness of heart and mind. At first his purity & nobility filled my mental vision, but later they shared the field with the tenderness which intimacy made so manifest. And thus his image was before me to the last & still is before me, like the effigy of some noble knight of the days of chivalry.

One wonders whether the present times are, or the times to come will be, such as to give soil for the growth of chivalry among men. The condition we see is such as to extirpate that holy plant.

All my sympathy. Say if there is anything I can do 'which may to thee do ease and grace to me'. My best regards to your daughters as well as to yourself

Yours most sincerely/Edmund Barton

NORMAN LINDSAY

Painter, illustrator, sculptor and writer, Norman Lindsay (1879–1969) grew up in Creswick, Victoria. His brothers Percy, Lionel and Daryl and his sister Ruby (see Letter 113) were also artists. By his first marriage to Katie Atkinson, Norman Lindsay had three sons, of whom writer Jack (1900–90) was the eldest. After the separation of their parents, Jack and his brothers saw little of their father: they lived in Brisbane and their father in Sydney. Norman's overtures to his son did not result in a close relationship: father and son had only sporadic contact in the following years, and much bitterness remained.

115. To Jack Lindsay, undated [late 1919]

My dear old Bunny,

I have long wished and intended to write to you, but have waited till it might be easier for us to communicate without the stress that time and circumstance have forced on our relations. I am sure that these in the end will never affect our sympathy, and now that you are coming to maturity it is much easier for us to meet in a spirit of understanding.

Indeed, I have never doubted that you would retain a memory of me that would put aside the need for evasion or misunderstanding. The little memories of youth are always lasting, because they are the chief element of consciousness we carry forward into life, and I long ago felt that we had established the bridge of communication when you were a laddie, and I, I am afraid, a somewhat irresponsible parent. But indeed, when we are most busy with life we are apt to forget that it is life that is busy with us, and we captain our destiny a good deal at the sport of destiny.

But whatever chance or accident may do with the action of life, it does not alter the structure of our hearts or minds, and so I do not think the interval that has separated us will be ever one of unkindness in thought or misunderstanding of emotion.

Now that the silly impediments that society thrusts on all human relations are more or less removed, I would be glad to take up again the interrupted companionship of your child-hood and my youth, and be again at least a pal to you, if I have not been much of a father.

I was very happy to know that you had got into touch with my old friend Bertram Stevens, who is a man of fine and generous spirit, and of an unimpeachable sincerity. He showed me some time ago a note from you which touched me nearly, and I would be sorry to delay any longer an open return to sympathy. So, old boy, you must write to me as you feel and think and I do not feel there is any need for restraint between us.

Let me know what direction your interests in literature are, and if you have been moved to express your own vision of life or thought. You may trust all expression to me with the assurance that I will understand and sympathize with it, and, I hope, be able to return you a sincere expression of its effect upon me. Perhaps also, in return, you would like me to send you some of my work. If so, I will make up a small collection for you to start with, to which I can add in time. And shortly I shall be able to send you a book which is now being published, in which, under the title of "Creative Effort", I have striven to express all that seems to me serious in the problem of Life and Art. I think it is a work that will be best appreciated by the spirit that will reject it, but to that aspect I am indifferent. I am publishing a small edition of fifty copies merely to ensure preserving it, and the first that comes to hand I will pass on to you.

I speak of this book because I think it may have some message for you in it. Anyway, you will see by it where my thought has arrived, and that will make it easier for you to return me your thoughts on it.

I think, perhaps, my recent etchings might have an element of emotion for you too, and will send you them first. They will help to complete the cycle of thought in "Creative Effort".

Don't suspect me of vanity, Bunny, old boy. The whole difficulty of this earth is the problem of mind meeting mind, and most of our chatter is only to bridge the intolerable gulf of silence that misunderstanding forces on us. If my thought and work stirs you to interest and sympathy, then you will know that I will meet yours in the same spirit, for equal understanding is equality of thought.

And now, old boy, I will launch this very long delayed note, and leave you to answer it as you will. Be sure I have never forgotten my affection for you, and have always looked forward to another meeting. The last was not a very gracious one, was it, and I have always been sorry that your boy hood should have been troubled by the spectacle of your dad, in a high state of physical decrepitude, with one leg over the border today and an imminent expectation of dragging the other one after it tomorrow. I would have been sorry to leave you the legacy of a dismal last impression and would be glad at last to dissipate it for a happier one. With all affection, my dear old Bunny,

YOUR DAD

Bertram Stevens] (1872–1922) editor, was one of the founders of *Art in Australia* in 1916   Lindsay's *Creative Life* was published in 1920

ALAN STOKES

The Australian Inland Mission was established in 1912, its first superintendent the legendary Reverend John Flynn (1880–1951) whose services were offered 'without preference for nationality or creed'. As this letter suggests, the efforts of Flynn and the AIM were dedicated to enhancing the quality of life of the remote communities of central Australia.

116. To John Flynn, 1 January 1920

DEAR SIR

I have been requested by the 'boys' on Hatch's Creek to drop you a line expressing the gratitude of all to the A.I.M. for their most welcome gift of a box of books and magazines etc. The case duly arrived by camel team & when it became known that the case had arrived the demand for literature was keen. The appreciation accorded this gift may be easily imagined when the last *decent* literature the field had enjoyed was contained in the wrappers of a new corn cure and the literary possibilities of the latest brand of jam had been exhausted some time. It was a kindly thought of the A.I.M. to make the present and a particularly happy one in making the present one of literature. Wishing the A. I. M. all the good it deserves

Yours gratefully/Alan H. Stokes/pro The Hatch's Creek Wolfram Miners

P.J. Hartigan ('John O'Brien')

Patrick Joseph Hartigan (1878–1952) was a Catholic priest who worked in parishes of the Riverina district. As 'John O'Brien' he published two volumes of poems, Around the Boree Log *(1921) and (posthumously)* The Parish of St Mel's *(1954). Both use the ballad form; both centre on the lives of Irish-Australians in the country districts of Hartigan's ministry.*

117. To George Robertson, 17 October 1921

My Dear Mr Robertson,

I hope I didn't appear the impostor I felt I was when you were crowding those beautiful books on me last Friday afternoon. I did my best to look as an "author" should, but my wiser self kept whispering, "There are people in gaol for a less vindictive confidence trick than this."

I am delighted that I went down. Mr Jose was extremely kind. He allowed my poor lines to stand in quite a number of instances when his better judgement would have put them out. I know the stuff is not much good, and am aware that it is clumsily put; still, I also know that section of the public on whom the sales depend. I do hope sincerely that you won't fall in over it. "A & R" has not been affixed to anything unworthy yet, and candidly, when I think of the critics, "the wind" I get up assumes the dimensions of a gale. Many times during the past few months I have regretted the vanity which allowed me to be persuaded to submit the dope at all. However, that soft old heart of yours must take the blame.

It is worth whatever happens to have met you. Will you pardon me when I say—with all the sincerity I am capable of—that there is nothing in my life of which I am prouder than having met "G. R.". I am seriously thinking of wearing kilts for ever more.

Gratefully,/P. J. Hartigan

Mr Jose] A.W. Jose (1863–1934), historian and essayist, did editing work for Angus & Robertson

D.H. LAWRENCE

In 1922 the English novelist D.H. Lawrence (1885–1930) and his wife Frieda travelled to Australia, and spent the winter in a rented cottage, 'Wyework', at Thirroul on the south coast of New South Wales, where he wrote Kangaroo *(1923). Lawrence's sense of 'empti-ness' in a new/old continent is a recurring theme in his letters to friends in England, novelist Catherine Carswell and littérateur and translator S.S. Koteliansky.*

118. TO CATHERINE CARSWELL, 22 JUNE 1922

MY DEAR CATHERINE

Camomile came last week—reached me here—the very day I sent you a copy of the American *Aaron's Rod*. I have read *Camomile*, and find it good: slighter than *Open the Door*, but better made. Myself I like that letter-diary form. And I like it because of its drift: that one simply must stand out against the social world, even if one misses 'life.' Much life they have to offer! Those Indian Civil Servants are the limit: you should have seen them even in Ceylon: conceit and imbecility. No, she was well rid of her empty hero, and all he stands for: tin cans. It was sometimes very amusing, and really wonderfully well written. I can see touches of Don (not John, Juan, nor Giovanni, thank goodness) here and there. I hope it will be a success and that it will flourish without being trodden on.

If you want to know what it is to feel the 'correct' social world fizzle to nothing, you should come to Australia. It *is* a weird place. In the *established* sense, it is socially nil. Happy-go-lucky dont-you-bother we're-in-Austrylia. But also there seems to be no inside life of any sort: just a long lapse and drift. A rather fascinating indifference, a *physical* indifference to what we call soul or spirit. It's really a weird show. The country has an extraordinary hoary, weird attraction. As you get used to it, it seems so *old*, as if it had missed all this Semite-Egyptian-Indo-European vast era of history, and was coal age, the age of great ferns and mosses. It hasn't got a consciousness—just none—too far back. A strange effect it has on one. Often I hate it like poison, then again it fascinates me, and the spell of its indifference gets me. I can't quite explain it: as if one resolved back almost to the plant kingdom, before souls, spirits and minds were grown at all: only quite a live, energetic body with a weird face.

The house is an awfully nice bungalow with one *big* room and 3 small bedrooms, then kitchen and washhouse—and a plot of grass—and a low bushy cliff, hardly more than a bank—and the sand and the sea. The Pacific is a lovely ocean, but my, how boom-ingly crashingly noisy as a rule. Today for the first time it only splashes and rushes, instead of exploding and roaring. We bathe by ourselves—and run in and stand under the shower-bath to wash the *very* seaey water off. The house costs 30/- a week, and living about as much as England: only meat cheap.

We think of sailing on Aug 10th. via Wellington and Tahiti to San Francisco—land on Sept 4th. Then go to Taos. Write to me:

c/o Mrs Mabel Dodge Sterne, *Taos*, New Mexico. U.S.A.

—I am doing a novel here—half done it—funny sort of novel where nothing happens and such a lot of things *should* happen. Scene Australia.—Frieda loves it here. But Australia would be a lovely country to lose the world in altogether. I'll go round it once more—the world—and if ever I get back here I'll stay.—I hope the boy is well, and Don flourishing, and you as happy as possible.

DHL

Camomile and *Open the Door*] novels by Catherine Carswell   touches of Don] Donald Carswell, husband of Catherine Carswell   Mrs Mabel Dodge Sterne] Mabel Dodge Stern, later Mabel Dodge Luhan, a wealthy patron of the arts, invited the Lawrences to stay with her in Taos, New Mexico

119. TO S. S. KOTELIANSKY, 9 JULY 1922

MY DEAR KOT:

I had your letter, and the Bunin book next day. But not the Mrs Tolstoi reminiscences. What a pretty cover Bunin has! But the tales are not very good: 'Gentleman' is much the best. Some of Woolf's sentences take a bit of reading. Look at the last sentence on p.71.

You should have had *Sea and Sardinia* and *Aaron's Rod* by now: unless Martin Secker is playing me dodges and not sending out the presentation copies as I asked.—I shall be able to read this famous *Ulysses* when I get to America. I doubt he's a trickster.

We still propose sailing on August 10th by the *Tahiti*, to San Francisco: arrive Sept. 4th. Send me a line and tell me all the happenings. I heard from a friend in Paris that the Bunin book was noticed in the *Times*. What was the notice like? I had Cath. Carswell's *Camomile* here: slight, but good, I thought. What are the notices of that?—By the way, don't you think Secker ought to try that *Shestov* again now? You press him about it, and I'll write him too. It would certainly sell some now.

I have nearly finished my novel here—but such a novel! Even the *Ulysseans* will spit at it.

There is a great fascination in Australia. But for the remains of a fighting Conscience, I would stay. One can be so absolutely indifferent to the world one has been previously condemned to. It is rather like falling out of a picture and finding oneself on the floor, with all the gods and men left behind in the picture. If I stayed here six months I should have to stay for ever—there is something so remote and far off and utterly indifferent to our European world, in the very air. I should go a bit further away from Sydney, and go 'bush.'—We don't know one single soul—not a soul comes to the house. And I can't tell you how I like it. I could live like that forever: and drop writing even a letter: sort of come undone from everything. But my conscience tells me not yet. So we go to the States—to stay as long as we feel like it. But to England I do not want to return.— Though no, I don't think you flatter me. I do think I've got more in me than all those fluttering people, good and bad, in London. Buy they are *antipatico*. They are distasteful to me.

Write me a line, c/o Mountsier—or else just to *Taos* New Mexico, U.S.A.
Greet Grisha and Sonya and the tall Ghita, and starve Fox for one day, for my sake.

the Bunin book] Ivan Bunin's *The Gentleman from San Francisco and Other Stories* (1922)   reminiscences] *The Autobiography of Countess Leo Tolstoi* (1922)   *Sea and Sardinia* (1921) and *Aaron's Rod* (1922)] works by D.H. Lawrence   Secker … Shestov] Martin Secker had published Leon Shestov's *All Things Are Possible* in 1920   the Ulysseans] James Joyce's *Ulysses* was published in February 1922   Mountsier] Robert Mountsier was Lawrence's American literary agent   Grisha, Sonya, Ghita, Fox] Russian *émigré* journalist Michael Farbman, his wife, daughter and their dog

CHRISTOPHER BRENNAN

Christopher John Brennan (1870–1932), poet and scholar, was one of the best known figures in the cafe life of Sydney. In 1897 he had married Elizabeth Werth but, after years of unhappiness, went to live with Violet Singer in 1922. Some of his finest poetry was inspired by this love affair. Singer died in 1925 when struck by a tram. Brennan's letter of loss and mourning is written to the scholar and writer, John Le Gay Brereton (1871–1933), 'after a visit to the grave'.

120. TO JOHN LE GAY BRERETON, 31 MAY 1925

Grief is sometimes blind with the tears that are repressed, because there is a wild and wilful clinging to pain as something too precious to be lost, a foolish distrust of any lull that comes: and the imagination flags and declines on 'a luxury of woe' and sly self-pity creeps in and prompts her lies.

'Unhappy' I am not and never was nor could be from that moment when I went to her who was mine before I went. Love knew from then on that it had ceased to wander and that in her it could go on for ever, having her, finding her, seeking in her only her.

What then is my 'loss'?

Death, legally thrice-certified, has not availed to bring about that change we were taught to consider as its most certain work. Morgue, coffin, and grave-mound have not affected the sacred union of the body. Her gift of beauty was so utter, her delight in my delight so whole and evident—it was and is a perfect plenitude ever deepening and expanding (if even DGR failed in the lines entitled *Possession*, do not expect anything adequate here). It continues, and I can tell her of it as before. It did not suffer a moment's abeyance or suspension. If, as each Sunday came about, I underwent grinding & rending pain, that only proves how much we are one flesh: her death-agony was reflected in me, as the devout Christian makes Christ's passion his own. And now I can welcome it, if it recurs, without forcing it.

So that is not lost, nor anything of all it implies: and that is everything. The depth of affection that matched the vehemence of her passion, and the maternal tenderness infused thro' both—all her love, in short, which these words fumblingly strive to shadow forth, is mine still as she meant it to be.

What is my 'loss'?

The dear companionship of day after day, the sweet foolish trifles of domesticity—after a while I shall settle down and find that they are not so far away. And I shall not always be looking eagerly and in vain among the crowd to tell her from afar by her walk, or, as I did this evening, to see her come up laughing from the gully with the boys about her. No, for this very evening I felt that it would be no wonder if I did.

But still, somehow, I grieve for her sake that she is not there in this world and this life that she enjoyed so well—and perhaps too for the world and the life that no longer have and hold her. To sit and watch her and surprise her happy look and smile, to hear her utter sweet words to me—to want that just because it would tell me that she was happy, and only for that reason: to want to see that gladness and blitheness lasting as it lasted from the first moment on—is there perhaps some subtle selfishness in that? Perhaps: but I must yet find out. Anyhow I think that I have honestly set forth my true grief: else why should I still be haunted by the strange feeling that I might be called to account 'She was given to you: what have you done with her? where have you put her?'—a feeling strangely deeper than my natural resentment at her taking and the manner of it (*e'l modo ancor m'offenda*), and at the contemptible gang whom her invincible good-nature allowed to decoy her to her death, and whom even her forgivingness, against which I cautioned her, would not prevent her from despising for the craven way in which they have lurked dumb and dark, so that her last hours are still a mystery to those who loved her.

Before I have her quite back again I must, I fear, consent to lose her yet, to put aside all rebellious craving and leave the rest to her. And here I will set down, roughly and prematurely, the image which has been and is still growing within me.

She was gone—her voice, her smile, her look. She was gone—but only a little way off. I should come on her, but she would be kept from me by a crystal sphere. And now she sits, for me, within that crystal sphere and it will not melt to let me enter as the moon did for Dante. There she sits and smiles discreetly, but she has not yet looked up. She is waiting for something I must yet do or renounce. Then I shall see her eyes again—and after that I cannot yet tell.

I have tried *ragionar mio dolore*, honestly, to be worthy of the most honest creature I ever knew. You have helped me mightily to do so. Thro' her you have come to mean more to me than ever.

Wolombin June 11

It was hard to hold dominion over the drift of my being: so easy, to sit down and write trifles to her. And so, next day, my fit returned.

I had meant a continuation: it has turned to a meditation on the poets—she would love that. And she would be glad to know that DGR is now the one man.

DGR] Dante Gabriel Rossetti (1828–82), English Pre-Raphaelite painter, poet and designer   *e'l modo ancor m'offenda*] and the manner still offends me. Brennan is quoting from Dante's *Inferno*, 5.102, from the episode of Paolo and Francesca   ragionar mio dolore] to come to terms with my grief

P.R. STEPHENSEN

Percy Reginald ('Inky') Stephensen (1901–1965) was a writer, editor and publisher. Described by his biographer, Craig Munro, as an intellectual and literary adventurer, he was a force in the encouragement of a more vigorous cultural debate in Australia after his return from England in the 1930s. But at Oxford in the late 1920s he was plagued by doubts about his life, his prospects and the direction of his love affair with the dancer Winifred Sarah Venus (1886–1971) (see Letter 152) whom he had met in Paris in 1925.

121. TO WINIFRED VENUS, 24 OCTOBER 1926

DEAR

I am still floating around in the quiet whirlpool, here and there like a water insect, vainly hoping for something not quite within reach.

This is a most important period for me, dear. I am trying to get straightened out on big things so that little things won't matter any more.

No use saying that I'm the same boyish lad you first met, years ago wasn't it? I've got a lot graver and the dreadful searing tragedy of existence has burned into me somewhere in a way I can't as yet understand. It terrifies me at times and at times I can laugh; but bitterly, heartsore.

There is too much trouble in the world, too much of weariness and the strain of mind and body.

The clear shining image of beauty is dragged into mud; nothing simple or partial can restore it. Only great strenuous actions, rough & terrible doings, can shake weary mankind to arise for one more effort towards freedom & beauty.

What happens to you & I in this tumult and whirling of forces?

What use for the sweet gentleness which I feel towards you in a world where I must be hard and ruthless. Is time receding from me & am I left weak and full of pity for myself and all mankind—"a beautiful ineffectual angel beating in the void his luminous wings in vain"?

Dear, these are my thoughts. I love you, love you, but I am too robust, too roaring and mad to bring you the peace which you need. *The peace you need.*

My head is like a flame burning on my shoulders. I *will* not & I cannot be alone, pitying or pitied.

I shall go out on the ramparts, stamping my feet, shaking my hair in the great winds of the Earth.

My love shall destroy and not comfort. I challenge life or I shall die. My love is a tempest shaking the oaks, not a summer breeze murmuring in the reeds.

But I am sad because my caresses are blows, but I shall not be gentle.

And you need gentleness now, the fragile image of a beautiful delicate tender love.

What can we do? I don't know. I can't think. I am running around in closed circles of futility.

I refuse to crush you—poor little bruised flower: but the fragrance of your kiss has made me pause one moment in a mad rushing tumult.

Dare we prolong that moment of dalliance. Dare we? dare you? I love you, I say, but my love will hurt & destroy. Kiss me then think. Goodnight. May the Gods be kind to us.

INKY X

May the Gods be kind to us] although they lived together from the late 1920s, Stephensen and Venus did not marry until 1947 following the death of her first husband. The relationship was happy and enduring. 'Our love affair blossomed till the end', Winifred wrote to a friend after Inky's death

FRANK MACFARLANE BURNET

Sir Macfarlane Burnet (1899–1985), Director of the Walter and Eliza Hall Institute for Medical Research, Melbourne, won a Nobel prize in 1960 for his work in immunology. In 1927, while he was a PhD student at the University of London, he worked at the Lister Institute. His future wife Linda Druce had been visiting the Burnet family in Traralgon, the small town in Gippsland, Victoria, where Burnet spent his childhood.

122. TO LINDA DRUCE, 20 FEBRUARY 1927

LINDA DEAR,

Unless your letter tomorrow stirs me to new efforts you are in for a thin letter this time—its been a grimly uneventful week so far. London has been half fogbound until today when for variety it has been raining and my social existence has been confined to appearing at the Lister tea club at 10 past 4 with regularity. A dreary time when your work is in rather a humdrum groove—quite satisfactory but showing no signs of developing a sudden absorbing interest. So I am quite reasonably lonely and inclined to be sorry for myself which is a disgraceful state of mind to be in.

The coming week however should be more interesting—Florence is returning and if she is foolish enough to let me know of her whereabouts I shall probably force my attentions on her at very short notice. I am simply longing to get out of the rut of abstracting bacteriophage papers at the Lister every night and wandering round London or working during the weekend that seems to have been my lot for the last 3 or 4 weeks. Though most people wouldn't notice it you have made a social animal out of me Linda and one of the pleasantest prospects before me is a wife who has the knack of making friends. You will have to manage that side of the business my dear. I can never develop a social acquaintance into anything more (with one glorious exception of course) but people who are forced to associate with me can generally find something to like and I dont think I'll drive any of your friends away. Except of course that there will be occasional weeks (at least I hope there always will be) when things at the lab are much too enthralling to get home before midnight and social events will be off. On such occasions you will I trust rap your forehead meaningly and say "These scientists" in a suitable tone to let me off the charge of social inadequacy on the grounds of hereditary mental aberration.

London wanderings solus are not very comforting to the soul but you are always finding something new of interest. This afternoon for instance I came across Rodins Burghers of Calais underneath the Victoria Tower at Westminster. I walked round it in the rain and found it immensely satisfying. Then I went along Millbank wondered what a host of piledrivers and concrete foundations next the government offices there portended and found my way into the Tate Gallery.

There were two new Monets there that interested me and once again I was impressed by the extraordinary difference between late 19th century art in England and France. Curiously enough I like them both but you can't get away from the fact that in technique originality and individuality the French painters are in an entirely different world from ours. Monet I'm particularly fascinated by at present but the whole group of that period except Corot who is even duller than Turner after the first half dozen examples you see, is interesting. I may even be tempted to visit Paris again to make their further acquaintance. You see my passion for Rembrandt is now fairly well satisfied and the French school has taken his place as the centre of interest.

But being fundamentally a sentimentalist I cant escape from the attraction of Watts Burne Jones and Rossetti for all their provincialisms. They are so very much nearer to my own mentality than the French. If I were an artist I should want to paint classic myths and allegories just as obvious as theirs.

Getting nearer home I noticed Church St Chelsea and walked down it out of curiosity to see the exterior of the Gibson Young menage that Florence had told me of. It was easily found though what the significance of 'The Hurricane Lamp' is I must enquire later. The windows contained a medley of esoteric art reviews, unfinished looking modern portraits including one of Gibson Young, community song books and a notice that portraits were painted in 1 hour from 2 guineas. It certainly did look the real Chelsea. I was almost tempted to have 2 guineas worth and send the result to you just to see what the interior was like. But perhaps a snapshot will be more recognisable. By the way when the sun reappears (presumably in June) I shall have that snap you asked for taken, but there seems no hope for a long time yet.

Monday—For the first time I opened your letter with just a little trepidation this morning and was greatly relieved to find that the family acquaintanceship was progressing satisfactorily. However I was always confident you would get on well with Anne (Its curious that while I always address said lady as Anne I always think of her as with the extra syllable, for which I humbly beg her pardon). Allan and Margie as I told you I have never managed to know properly but I think they are both interesting people Allan particularly. He can write extremely good light verse for instance and Anne tells me though I haven't seen them that he has some excellent prose sketches of the humorous side of dairyfarming somewhere.

I'm afraid you probably found Mother a little hard to get on with. I know my engagement was far more of a surprise to her than to any one else and reading between the lines I think she was a little bit hurt by it. Quite impersonally—the old "A son is a son till he gets him a wife" feeling and I fancy there would be something of a barrier for you to surmount before she appreciates you as she will ultimately.

Traralgons a pleasant spot isn't it and for all its untidiness the house and grounds are rather nice. Didn't you like the view up to the Calignee Hills along the creek? I'm looking forward to a wander round Traralgon with you Linda. Its a particularly attractive place to me from the fact that I left it when I was 10 or 11 and didnt return for 10 or 12 years then only occasionally so that all my memories are the romantic ones of a small boy not over-grown with those of growing up. There are lots of spots toward which I have extraordi-narily affectionate memories because of some schoolboy triviality and I'd love to show you where I once caught an eel in my hand where I used to catch mussells by pushing a reed into their open mouths in the mud of the creek bottom where I had my one and only pugilistic encounter and where I made the original discovery unfortunately forestalled by Bishop Berkeley that things and time dont exist unless you think they do. That used to help me up tedious hills tremendously for some months after I made the discovery.

Its not so acute now but a couple of weeks ago when I was just getting rid of the flu I had a terrific desire to spend a week in Traralgon sitting on the verandah in the sunshine doing nothing and eating food that was <u>not</u> cooked in a restaurant. It may be only in retrospect and with the experience of nearly 2 years ship and restaurant food, but I have the feeling that Traralgon food is something fit for the gods.

On Tuesday next I am down to read a paper on phage to the Royal Society of Medi-cine at the Lister lab. meeting. It will be practically the same as the one I have just forwarded to be published so there wont be much preparation to do for it beyond making lantern slides and getting a demonstration ready. But of course there will be the usual mental turmoil at the prospect. For all my once eminence as leader in the G.C. debating society I hate standing in front of an audience and invariably have a pulse rate of about 120 and a dry tongue for the first 5 minutes. However this time I shall get my first slide on quickly and when you are in darkness with a pointer in your hand and able to talk colloquially things are very much better. I shall survive.

Today there were actually signs of spring—at least the sun shone occasionally and some bulbs in Battersea park were beginning to appear above ground. Going home at night along the Chelsea Embankment you can hear mallards quacking on the muddy edges left bare at low tide and last night there was actually an owl tu whit tu whooing in the Royal Hospital gardens. When as well you have the Westbourne gurgling under your feet—that is the sylvan brook that gives its name to Westbourne Grove and runs thro' Sloane Sq. station in a big steel pipe—things seem quite countryish and spring like. And of course there are the usual signs of spring on the Embankment seats. However I'm not so cynical about housemaids and guardsmen as I once was.

Had a postcard from Florence this morning conveying the welcome news that she was back in London. I shall ring her up this evening.

I am enclosing this with a little sketch you might possibly like. It was only done to fill in an empty Sunday evening and if you dont like it pitch it in the W.P.B. I thought though that it might help out a very thin letter and tho' I still can't quite realise it I do believe bits of me do seem of some little value to you. So please take it in a forgiving spirit my dear.

Life is lonely but theres plenty of interest in it and the prospect of you someday is not losing any attractiveness. Forgive a very dull letter and believe

THAT I LOVE YOU/MAC

phage/bacteriophage] a virus which infects and may kill bacteria   Anne, Allan and Margie] Burnet family members   G.C.] Geelong College, one of the principal Victorian public schools, to which Burnet won a scholarship in 1913

CHRISTINA STEAD

Christina Stead's (1902–83) long delayed recognition as a novelist came in her late middle age when The Man Who Loved Children *(1940) was reprinted in the USA in 1965 with an appreciative foreword by critic and poet Randall Jarrell. Her expatriate career followed several years of privation in which she all but starved herself to save the fare to England. Her response to London's famous places, in a letter to her cousin, resembles the first raptures of many Australians abroad, but the passion and eloquence are characteristic of Stead.*

123. TO GWEN WALKER-SMITH, 11 JULY 1928

MY DEAREST GWEN,

Thank you for your letter which I was very pleased indeed to receive. I often wish you were here with me when we could fill in the long weekends seeing all that there is to be seen: I saw a young girl like you in the Underground the other day which made me stand still for a moment and there is a girl who has lunch in the place where I lunch who looks something like you but that she is less lively, and she has a pack of wolf-cubs, I notice and is always learning tales to teach them and moral histories and the like. She also takes them out for afternoon outings—I hear her tell this, I don't know her.

I hope you enjoyed your birthday and Greenie came to the front with a bouquet for the star performer, as usual. I hope you are getting some assistance in all that work which is now on your hands and are not working too long and late. When is your holiday? I haven't heard from Nellie, except once on the way over, so if you see her one of these days you had better ask her to write me when she has time. Has she yielded at last to impulse and left the old firm and gone to fresh fields and pastures new? I don't suppose so, but I used to smile to see the seeds of unrest germinating in her mind.

I have nothing much to report at the moment: went to the Russian Ballet—perhaps you have heard about that escapade. Last Sunday I spent the day exploring London on my own—rather an exciting, rather a frightening process. At one moment you feel grand to be there on your own and seeing the sights and treading historic grounds and smelling historic smells and the next you feel like some small sort of insect crawling about miserably waving its antennae and only just out of its chrysalis and a long way from anywhere—which is, I suppose, exactly what insects feel like when they come out. The Tower of London is a curious sight—all built of small stones, with a wide moat and four central towers which are very poor style and toy-like from our modern point of view. The modern style is represented all over the city by huge erections, built up pile upon pile, recessed and 'stepped' (as in New York), with pillars and statues, or else some great pseudo-monolithic place looking like Ancient Egypt. The Tower is positively trumpery—except when you first come on it, and then a thrilling feeling runs through your marrow—no doubt it is your marrow—or it may be your less polite innards. The windows whence looked the aristocratic martyrs now have (fairly) modern catches and curtains, so that it looks quite friendly. The gentlemen at the gates and the sentries wear sensational uniforms of red, black and gold—the porters are dressed in a kind of beef-eater costume which is fascinating until you get close and see a raffish, commonplace mug under the velvet hat and gold braid and hear a scolding, rough voice threatening the small boys issuing therefrom.

The first time I saw one of these scarlet and gold gentlemen on the railway station, I thought he was one of the chorus of the Russian Ballet, which I had just been to see—it took me ten minutes to realise that he was just as and where he should be and that I was the only person surprised. The porters and janitors and the like of the Bank of England, too, have very gay costumes which I will now harrow you by describing. Red, weskits, long-tailed bangers of a pucy-pink which doesn't quite know its own mind, black understandings, top hats. The functionaries in chief, such as Head Janitor and Assistant Head Doorkeeper wear also a long red gown after the style of doctors of medicine, with bits of dog's fur or rabbit-fur in rows, in the most regal style, and a cocked hat exactly like our hero Mr Bumble. It's really queer to keep running up against these old customs in the very centre of a modern city—I begin to have doubts about it all.

We have had a couple of weeks of sunshine and the last few days have touched 84 degrees—everyone is groaning about the heat, but our building is cool in summer (and freezing in winter), so that I only just begin to feel like natural when I have spent half my lunch-hour promenading on the sunny side of all the streets near. Keith is tutoring at Oxford and having a gloriously lazy time in dazzling sun, he says—which makes me painfully envious: I just yearn to be out in the country somewhere—I have seen just a glimpse of the countryside, out by Oxshott, where I went driving with the Unwins (Marie Byles's relatives). London would be unbearable, were it not for the wonderful little providential squares which crop up every two or three hundred yards and are as green as anyone could imagine in Summer, with millions of light fluttering leaves—limes, plane-trees and beeches.

Let me know how you are and what you are doing when you have time.

Much love, as ever,

PEG

Greenie] Walter Greenbaum, Gwen's employer   Nellie] Nellie Molyneux, a Sydney friend and neighbour of Stead's at Watson's Bay   Keith] W.G.K. Duncan (1903–87), whom Stead knew as a Sydney University student, later Professor of Politics at the University of Adelaide

In 1928 Christina Stead worked in a London office where she met her future husband, Marxist, banker and writer William Blake (Wilhelm Blech), with whom she went to Paris in 1929. Although this letter to a Sydney friend refers to wedding plans within the year, she did not marry Blake until 1952, after his long-awaited divorce.

124. TO NELLIE MOLYNEUX, 1 MARCH 1929

MY DEAR SWEET-NELL,

Thank you for your charming letter which gave me great pleasure and reminded me of home, once again. It is kind of you to remember me when you are always so busy and have so many friends. You will perhaps be surprised to see my new address—but I am not sure, you may have heard from the family that I have moved to Paris and also, perhaps, that I expect some time this year to be married to my past and present employer, Mr Blech (you will remember I met him on the first day I started to look for a position in London and was engaged by him then—it's a curious turn of fate). I am in the meantime uncommonly happy and I am quickly feeling myself at home in this great Paris, which is not so much the French capital as the capital of the modern world. I have not yet had much time to use up my long lunch-hours (twelve to two, the usual thing here) in exploring, but Mr Blech has taken me round in great sweeps, which has given me a good notion of the lay-out of the city and of its principal glories. I catch a bus in the morning from the Place Victor Hugo, which is two minutes from my present apartment (in the Rue Mesnil), almost to the Bourse (Exchange), get out in the Rue du 4 Septembre (date of inauguration of the Third Republic) and walk down the Rue de Grammont which runs along the Building Haussmann, where I work. Walking down I have a sight of the white Saracenic domes and arches of the Church of Sacré-Coeur which crowns Montmartre and which is a marvel of beauty in the clear sunny air which has now come up in Paris. Everyone feels that spring is on the doorstep although it is still very cold.

The city is far wealthier, and gayer than London, and in point of beauty they cannot be mentioned in the same breath. London is crooked, narrow, mean, dirty and ill-conceived, Paris is a pearl of delicacy, brilliance and suavity. Its great boulevarded residential districts are grand and imposing in style, with refined ornament in stone and iron. The whole city is subject to the surveillance of a committee of building and to building ordinances according to which every building must be in concord with its surroundings and must have some beauty. This does not prevent them from trying daring experiments in the modern and 'futurist' styles. In Auteuil, near the Bois de Boulogne is a street called the Rue Mallet-Stevens, which was handed over to Mallet-Stevens (one of the most famous of present-day architects who builds entirely in the strange unornamented block style which you see in magazines of German architecture today), with the request that he show his mind according to his will. The result is provoking and has aroused all sorts of criticism: I consider it a first sketch for the Architecture of the future, but I admit that it has some very beautiful members—for instance the glasswork which is done in leaded panes, of different types of glass, frosted, coloured, clear, 'arctic' all put into the one window in small panes in a counterpane pattern which is very fetching. However, it makes the city full of interest. The streets also are a perfect joy: 1. every one is charming and looks like an etching and 2. their names are each a page of history. Wilhelm (Mr Blech, that is) knows their history for he has a memory which is more compendious than Webster (unabridged) and the Encyclopaedia Europa, but their history I do not know. However, it is very agreeable to come upon the Rue Guy de Maupassant, the Rue de Quatre September, the Champs Elysées (Elysian Fields), the Rue de Bac (the oldest street in Paris, was the site of a 'bac', that is a rope bridge whereby things and people are passed over the torrent in a basket), the Rue des Saints-Père, etc. You hail from history yourself, with your French ancestry, and I can't help thinking some cells in your body, with a long memory, would stir themselves, when you saw these things. I am certain, in any case that the boulevards would thrill you, they are so light, so bright, so chic and so charming. The clothes here, of course, are absolutely fetching—by the way the Rue de la Paix is about five minutes from here—it is a very short street, running from the Place de l'Opera to the Place Vendôme, Worth is there, Cartier, Paquin and Houbigant, and all those famous people. The shop-front of Paquin is distinguished in the extreme—he does not deign to show anything but two tiger-skins, as if to symbolise his business rather than to advertise it.

My beloved is coming back from London tomorrow evening, so I must go and have my hair waved, or else buy some flowers to put in the salle à manger, I think the flowers will win. He is a ridiculous person, but how lovely!—he would first of all go to London for a week, for he has a lot of business to transact; then he decided he could do it in four days, then in three, then he said he would return to me on Sunday, but now he rings me this morning that he will come back tomorrow at midday, and he only left yesterday at midday! He is most kind to me and loves me very much: it is surprising to me and I am not used to such a romance, but I am really very happy. I wish you could all see him—he has such charm and is so goodhearted and is so witty.

I hope you have taken your holidays and that the days have been cooler. I hope you really went away for your holidays this time, as you did last time I knew about you (the Federal Territory trip). Let me know how you are and if you went away. I feel almost hungry when I think of some spots in NSW, even in Paris. My beloved says he will take me to Australia in about five years—but it may not come off and in the meantime I become a perfect Continental. I send my affectionate greetings to Mrs Molyneux and Bernard and hope you will remember me also to the others. I am glad you liked the rose: Mother chose it for me, of course, and I am awfully pleased that you liked it. I was very pleased to get your handkerchief and card, as I told you last letter. The handkerchief survives ten changes of address and three laundries, which is nothing smaller than a miracle for me, who am pretty careless.

I am interested to hear of the nuptial roll in Watsons Bay. Yes, Mollie is engaged— Kate told me. Kate is beginning to feel the shades of old age roll down, when Mollie finds it is marrying time! All I ask is that she waits decently a short time until her eldest sister enters the hymeneal fold in due order—the wish has nothing to do with custom or propriety but simply with greed and graft.

With much love,
SINCERELY,/PEG

Bernard] Nellie's brother   Mollie] a neighbour of the Steads' at Watson's Bay   Kate] Stead's half-sister

GEORGE ALLEN

Sir George Oswald Browning ('Gubby') Allen (1902–1989) was Australian by birth but a distinguished all-round English cricket player, captain, selector and administrator. Attacking like a 'flaming fire', his right-arm fast bowling with a classical sideways action often touched greatness. He toured Australia in the notorious 1932–33 'Bodyline' Test series. Allen's letter to his father, Sir Walter Allen, from Adelaide offers the perspective of one of the moderates on the English side.

125. TO WALTER ALLEN, 18 JANUARY [1933]

DARLING DAD

I shall start this now and finish it when I get a chance. I am at present sitting in the press box with Arthur Mailey watching Ames & Verity bat in our 2nd innings. They have put on 89 so far and this is the second time in the match that Verity has astonished everyone by batting like an opening batsman. It has been a most unpleasant match as you will have gathered from the papers. There has been nothing but rows & barracking until I am fed up with everything to do with cricket. As you will see from the enclosed paper, which is only a typical example, that the press & more especially the public are taking their setbacks very badly. Douglas Jardine is loathed &, between you & me, rightly more than any German who ever fought in any war.

Plum is worried to death and says the side may have to return at once to England, but that is rot. Premiers, Bishops and the Board of Control are all up in the air. That famous band of muddlers, i.e. B of Control, have stated that they are preparing a protest against the leg theory which they are proposing to send to the M.C.C. If they do he says he will resign: at least 6 members of the team will cease to try, rows will follow, and several will be sent home.

I have not changed my mind in any way about the leg theory & all the side is aware of the fact. I just hate it & will not do it. All the papers, like the one enclosed, have been very nice to me as have the crowds. You will be amused by the cartoon of myself at L.B.W. The broadcasting men asked me on Monday morning if I had seen in the paper that you had been listening to my innings & I said "Oh, dear and I was at L.B.W. He says I am always out that way". When I was out again in the 2nd innings this cartoon appeared so I presume he overheard my remark or was told about it. I can't imagine who gave away all the state secrets for the article enclosed headed 'English team Not Happy' as all the facts are accurate. There is no getting away from it Jardine is a perfect swine and I can think of no word fit for man to see which describes him well enough. Plum simply hates the sight of him and so does everyone else. I have never had a scene with him in public but I have had one or two on the quiet of which not a soul knows: in fact we are thought to be good friends. Larwood & I bowled better on the Saturday night when everyone said the wicket was dead easy and forecasted a huge score, than at any time on the tour. I had Ponsford missed at slip by Hammond & nearly bowled him twice and Richardson was never at home to me. For the third innings running, though I have bowled about the best of the side, I was not given a shot at the tail-enders: Douglas gives them to the pros to keep their support. So much for cricket, let's talk about something nice for a change. I went to a party last night and in order to keep the conversation off that subject we had a 1/- fine for anyone who brought it up. I now hear the B of Control's protest has gone so I will tell you a bit about that when I hear the details. I am going to stay at Langi Willi with Mrs Black-wood & Jean Russell for the Ballarat match. Freddie Brown is coming too so we go tomorrow night instead of with the team on Friday. I feel I want to get away for a bit and also it would be a great opportunity to go over a big station.

I went down to a place called Victor Harbour on Saturday night after the cricket & stayed with a friend of Joyce Verney's (nee V-Smith) for the week-end and had great fun. It was very cold and I enjoyed it but Sorrento & Moombara are much nicer. I don't think there is any more news. Plum & I have some people to dinner tonight.

Later. I need not give you the words of the B of Control's protest as you will have seen it in every paper. I think they have been very stupid to send it especially without having tried to come to some arrangement with Plum & Jardine, Palairet & Woodfull here first. The side, I understand, are considering sending a cable to the M.C.C committee but, if there is nothing more definite or out of order Wyatt & I are going to refuse to sign it. They are such a collection of half-wits that I doubt if they can word a sensible cable and, if they do, I am sure the M.C.C. will tear it up as Plum is not going to sign it.

Later. We polished them off fairly quickly today and 'things' meaning troubles, seem a little quieter. the cable from the team to the M.C.C. was a very reasonable one so that has passed off all right. What will happen remains to be seen. I came out with 8 for 121 in the match which will give some of the gentlemen (?) of the English press something to think over. I expect they will get their laugh later. I shall be in Sydney next Wednesday morning which I am looking forward to. I think I have arranged with Douglas Jardine to play in Ballarat & miss the Sydney match so as not to have too hard a time before the next test. I forgot to say Woodfull was not at all badly hurt by his blow on the chest but Oldfield had a bone cracked, they think, in the forehead. They both played bad shots when they were hit and were a little to blame. Give my best love to Mum

BEST LOVE/OBBIE

Plum sends his love. I am afraid he is worried but is very pleased that I have bowled so well in the last 2 tests. It is funny that I should have failed in Sydney where I should so liked to have *done well.*

Plum has just handed me a note to enclose.

Mailey] Arthur Alfred Mailey (1886–1967), Australian bowler   Ames & Verity] Leslie Ethelbert George Ames (1905–90), English wicket-keeper and Hedley Verity (1905–43), English bowler Jardine] Douglas Robert Jardine (1900–58), English batsman and captain 1932–33   Plum] Sir Pelham Francis Warner (1873–1963), noted English player and, in 1932–33, joint manager of the English side   leg theory] short bowling aimed at the line of the body and supported by a close field Larwood] Harold Larwood (1904–95), English fast bowler who, applying leg theory, reduced Bradman 'to a mere mortal'   Ponsford] William Harold Ponsford (1900–91), Australian batsman Hammond] Walter Reginald Hammond (1903–65), English batsman   Richardson] Victor York Richardson (1894–1969), Australian batsman   bowled ... best of side] in the 1932–33 Test series, Allen took 21 wickets without resorting to leg theory   Brown] Frederick Richard Brown (1910–91), English batsman   Palairet] Richard Cameron Worth Palairet (1871–1955), English batsman Woodfull] William Maldon Woodfull (1897–1965), Australian batsman and captain 1932–33 Oldfield] William Albert Stanley Oldfield (1894–1976), Australian wicket-keeper

Alexandra Hasluck

Alexandra (Alix) Margaret Martin Hasluck (née Darker) (1908–93) married the jour-
nalist Paul Hasluck on 14 April 1932. Each was to make a distinctive contribution to
the writing of Australian history and literature. Alix shared with her husband his politi-
cal and public career, which culminated in his term as Governor-General of Australia
1969–74. These letters, exchanged in the year after their European honeymoon, are filled
with the anticipation of home-making seen from two different but essentially complemen-
tary perspectives.

126. To Paul Hasluck, 17 March [1933]

Darling, *darling* Paul,

When I watched the postie put no less than *four* letters from you to me in the box, I
cld. hardly get inside w. them quick enough. You were sweet to write so much, and just the
sort of letters you used to. I nearly cried. And when I opened the 3rd & took out a letter in
a strange writing I threw it on the floor in disgust, then going thro' the envelope again, I
found your accompanying letter in wh. you hinted that you thought I'd read the other first!

I'm just dying to hear what happened in Melbourne.

Do you realise that we never arranged where I was to send letters? Its rather difficult, & not knowing your times for being at places either. I'm sending this to the
Melbourne G.P.O. in the hopes you'll look there for it.

I caught a disgusting hay-feverish cold the day after you left & have only just got rid
of it. Have been having breakfast in bed, just as you thought.

My dear, I cant keep it in any longer, & I did mean it to be a surprise to you. *I've got*
a flat!!! For you & me. And paid up till the day before you arrive. Darling, it was too nice
to let escape. I'll tell you abt. it. Its in Claremont, at the corner of Bay View Terrace &
Victoria Ave. In case that means nothing to you, its on the river road, tho' not the river
side of the road. Its part of Castillas' old house, *quite* self-contained, & garage. Lovely big
lounge nicely furnished (pictures awful, but that matters nil) decent sized kitchen w. gas
stove (gas only extends this far in Claremont, lucky to get it.) Bathroom quite roomy
enough, w. *gas heater* & *hot shower*; Dyke & wash-basin. Back to the lounge again. Box-
room, wh. will also be yr dressing-room, or where any stray guest for the night can
undress, sleeping in yr. bed on the verandah while you join me in the double. My dear,
huge bedroom, w. nice suite. I thought a good idea wld. be to make the window end yr.
study w. desk & book-shelves, but you can decide for yr. self. Sleep-out, glassed in &
wired in. Two stray bits of verandah. Does it sound nice? Its only got one entrance, thats
its only drawback, but when you consider that we're getting all this for 35/-, well, I ask
you. And I can always receive the tradesmen at the kitchen window while you sleep.

Plan of Haslucks' Flat
[a drawn floor plan is provided]

And such a nice landlady—grandmother of one of my school kids—Molly Rowe. Forgot to say lovely view of river but only when standing, cos of hedge. Our flat known as "Molde". Norwegian.

Well, darling, I'm terribly enthusiastic, & Mum has been a pet. Bought me kitchen things & sheets & blankets, & given me ¹/₂ her dinner service & lots of little things. I dont think I want for anything—except a large amount of loving husband with nice long eyelashes and a lovely giggle when tickled or pursued with intent to clutch & claw. Honey, hurry up & come home. I do hope no one comes to the train to meet you. I want to bring you home all by myself and show it to you proudly. "Look what I did" sort of.

Freda is spending the night so she can drive me down w. all the crockery. Am moving in by degrees.

I'm so tired. I've been ironing all day. Only I do miss you. And the photo I've got doesnt look like the you I know. Its too young. It hasn't been sick in Paris, and starving in London, and loving in Avignon, and I want the one who has.

I'll have to stop now, as I'm awful sleepy. How sweet of you to go & smell my powder & think of me. Wont it be fun when we have a bathroom—& an open fire, darling. Oooh.

Goodnight. When you get this you'll be on your way back to me. Darling, all my love & a kiss.

Alix

got a flat] one of three flats in a house at 17 Victoria Avenue in the Perth suburb of Claremont Castillas'] Henry Couper De Castilla (d. 1938), a civil engineer whose family would have been known to the young Haslucks   while you sleep] Hasluck was night editor of the *West Australian* which meant that he slept during the day

Paul Hasluck

On returning to Perth by sea from Europe, Paul Meernaa Caedwalla Hasluck (1905–1993) had continued on alone to the eastern states of Australia, which he had not previously visited. This was the couple's first separation after their marriage.

127. To Alexandra Hasluck, 31 March [1933]

My little sweetheart

Love. Pages of it. A week today I shall give you more material evidence.

I lobbed in at Adelaide this morning, and am just scribbling this note for the air mail to thank you for the actuality of your dear letter and for the promise of an unknown something I am to receive tomorrow morning. I don't know enough about mail time tables to know whether this note will reach you before or after the one I scribbled from Melbourne on Wednesday night, but shall trust you to fit them into the proper sequence when you get them.

The journey from Melbourne was only so-so. I had a reserved seat—In a compartment with four fat women and five kids with a tendency to sore faces!!! Imagine my reserve! Imagine spending the night in such company!! I shifted next door, where there was more room, and was fairly comfortable until midnight. Then the reserved seats in that compartment were claimed by some new passengers at Stawell but a kind conductor invited me to another compartment which had been vacated at some earlier period of the night. He also rescued another young man from another crowded apartment. Along we both went. One seat of our new quarters was occupied by a snoring man, stretched at full length. I waved towards the other seat with the true old Hasluck courtliness, inviting my companion to take the choice of corners. He grunted and stretched himself at full length too, leaving me to insert my tender bottom into the six or seven inches of space below his upturned hooves. What a night. Came the dawn and some more people with kids and bananas and biscuits. Darling, Australians and Italians are much the same, except for the garlic. It is not nationality. The truth is that on railway journeys, at least,

> I do not like the human race;
> I do not like its silly face;
> Nor snotty boys who wipe their boots
> All over fellow traveller's suits;
> I dislike sleeping tail to tail
> With total strangers; and I quail
> From meals that are the least/promisc'us,
> Where men suck soup from off their whiskers
> And guzzle down their tea like pigs
> And pick their teeth between the swigs.

Oh, darling Alix, what awful things are these to be putting in a love letter. At any rate, I arrived here safely and found your letter waiting. And that, combined with a shave and a bath, soon restored me to that beatific relation to mankind which, as you must know, little confidante of all my moods, is my normal state. (Rot!!).

My word, the flat seems to be coming into shape. It all sounds too exciting for anything. I want to get back quickly and see it all. You are a darling. I love you. I feel something of what you say in your letter about people's idiotic talking. But do not worry. We are going to try to live like civilised educated beings, with as broad a background of interest as we can have behind us, meeting the people we want to meet and doing together the things we want to do. Possibly the showing off that you noticed in Freda and Vi was only just the fruit of a little bit of envy of you. I have seen some indications that that may worry us a little at first but I think we can keep our friends, and above all, our own happiness in our home. I want home to mean so much to us—not a collection of furniture or a domestic establishment; but a new and separate community where we and those who like us may find refuge from those who do not like us and the things we do not like. Love, my darling little spuggerlugs, Your husband,

PAUL.

ADELA PANKHURST

The suffragette, Adela Constantia Mary Pankhurst (1885–1961), left England and settled in Australia in 1914. She became an organiser in Melbourne for the Australian feminist Vida Goldstein (see Letter 155) and took up the anti-conscriptionist cause. With her husband, the seaman and trade unionist Tom Walsh, she moved to Sydney where she continued to be associated with radical and left-wing causes. After her husband's death in 1943, Adela withdrew from public life.

128. TO ELSA GYE, 5 SEPTEMBER 1936

DEAR MRS GYE

I was very glad to learn that you were entertaining Mrs Pethick Lawrence on the occasion of the 30th anniversary of her first imprisonment. It is also the 30th anniversary of my *second* imprisonment and I should very much like to be with you all. Though so long ago, it seems but yesterday to me—our deputation to the House of Commons—the scene when our little force was driven out and pushed down the steps—to be arrested outside.

To all my fellow prisoners who are still amongst us I send my loving greetings—that those who are gone are still with us in spirit I do not doubt. Looking back on those days of struggle, the completeness of our victory sometimes surprises me. All opposition to our demand, which was once so strong and bitter, has completely vanished and almost forgotten. Mr Lloyd George and his Family Coach are all that remains to remind the new generation of the once immense and powerful Liberal party which sent women to jail, rather than give them the vote!

Now I must say a word to Mrs Pethick Lawrence herself. She will remember, no doubt, that as I came into the Movement at the very beginning as its youngest member, I left it after those hard and strenuous years, still young, but as old and worn, as a woman twice my real age.

Being 'chucked out' of meetings; addressing hostile and semi-hostile crowds; abuse from the Press; blows and violence of a still worse kind, imprisonment; moving from one uncomfortable lodging to one still more uncomfortable; continually preoccupied with meetings, collections and all sorts of drudgery—this was just everyday life to me—I had known so little of anything else. I am, therefore, conscious that I did not fully appreciate Mrs Pethick Lawrence's services when she, to whom life offered so much more, devoted herself to the Cause.

My wider experience since I was with you all, has made me realize how unselfish her services to the Movement were and how much those who worked in it owed to the fact that, having wealth and social prestige to give as well as ability she unstintedly gave it and endured imprisonment and suffering for her fellow women.

Without her help the rest of us could never have created an organization strong enough to break down the forces against us and there is no doubt that all those women who are voters today, and those who are in Parliament, owe very much to Mrs Pethick Lawrence and her willingness to support and take part in the militant tactics, which cost women so dear. I send her now a message of love and gratitude.

People in Australia question me today as to whether the vote was worth all the sacrifice made by all sorts and conditions of women? My answer is *Yes*—a thousand times, *Yes!* Though so far away, I know that you women voters have swept away the sweated industries, which once degraded womanhood; that your influence on politics has done much to sweep away the slums which were the only 'homes' many women knew; that infantile mortality is lessened and women's children are cleaner, healthier and happier because women have humanized politics.

I am not much of a feminist myself—I deliberately chose home and family in place of a political career in Australia and only returned to political work reluctantly—but I know that all we did was well worth while and that what we lost, others have gained.

I shall think of you all at your dinner. My best love to your guest of honor and all brave suffragettes.

YOURS EVER

Mrs Gye] in 1936, the secretary in London of the Suffragette Fellowship   Mrs Pethick Lawrence] Emmeline Pethick-Lawrence (1861–1954), ally in the Women's Social and Political Union of Emmeline Pankhurst (mother of Adela) and her daughter Christabel   my *second* imprisonment] in the suffragette cause, Adela became a seasoned prisoner   Mr Lloyd George] David Lloyd George (1863–1945), later British prime minister and a member of the Liberal government (elected 1905) which opposed women's franchise

MARY GILMORE

Poet, pioneer and social reformer, Mary Gilmore (1865–1962) grew up in the bush and became a teacher in rural schools. She identified strongly with militant working class movements and was one of the group of idealists who founded a 'New Australia' in Paraguay in 1896. In old age she was a much admired national figure; she praised and promoted poets and painters and kept up a network of friendships through her many letters. Poet Hugh McCrae (see Letter 160) was one of her closest friends.

129. TO HUGH McCRAE, 22 SEPTEMBER 1936

DEAR HUGH,

I said 'Blast it!' twice this morning, so the effervescence being a'oot I begin soberly & with propriety. First to enclose a reprint; second to say that I have slowly begun Christina Stead's 'The Salzburg Tales'. What genius! and to think that I remember her father bringing her to me in her later teens to ask if I thought she would make a woman journalist! and when I said NO!! he huffed up & said "But look at what she has written!" (Clipped from the 'S.M.H.') I replied 'It is precisely because of what she has written I say it. That girl is too big to write tea parties & frocks. She will be a publicist and writer of great special articles' (& so on.) But I never dreamed that that lank-haired pallid-faced anyhow-dressed girl would attain to the might—might not mere height—she has done ...

Much or little genius stands alone. You know it; I on the fringes, know it; she knows it and with what a sentence she says it in 'Seven Poor Men of Sydney'; 'A thin heart must always be rubbing shoulders with crowds and sitting in the sun to get a little heat. If it does not exercise daily it is found defunct the next morning of inanition. But a strong passion moves in chaos and associates with death, its foot goes among hermits & ravens'.

When I am dead, Hughie, remember that I said Christina Stead would not make a social page woman journalist and make it my pedestal.

S.M.H.] *Sydney Morning Herald*

A portrait of Mary Gilmore at the age of 92 was painted by William Dobell in 1957 and later presented to the New South Wales Art Gallery. Writing to Daniel Robert Rhys Thomas (b. 1931), the Gallery's curator of Australian paintings, Gilmore recalled sitting for Dobell and her own intervention in a public debate over his style as portraitist.

130. To Daniel Thomas, 31 December 1960

Dear Mr. Thomas,

Hogmanay tonight! Have been too much knocked about by the heat to get at this fully till now. The generous appreciation of my gift to the nation of my portrait by Wm. Dobell is better than any money payment could be. As years go on its value to the nation will increase. In which case the Gallery is the only safe place for it.

About sittings for the portrait. There were only two, one (about an hour) I think in October (Not sure now but it is recorded in my diaries wh. are not to be opened till after my death.)

The second sitting was some months later, and was only about 20 minutes (to confirm the first). It was (and is) a case of the portrait being 'in the eye of the beholder'—and what a tribute in the result to Mr. Dobell! But the ancestry is in it—as I have written more than once, and it is ME, and not just a specification of dimensions in paint. And what a lucky woman I have been to have it done. You can tell Dobell this when you see him again. He has given me futurity in time and Australia as nothing else could have done. The least comprehending mind can look at this and remember it. But *my* work has to be found and read—wh. limits remembrance.

The two sittings were here in my lounge room, in wh. I am now writing. Later on Dobell brought a draft painting with a long bare ugly neck. I told him I did not want a Joshua Smith neck and asked him to put a velvet band or some lace around it to lessen the Joshua Smith resemblance. That was all I saw of the portrait till the final painting was presented to me at the Gallery.

I forgot to say that I first saw the finished portrait at Dobell's Agent's Shop . . . It was there I saw my father's eyes looking at me. And it was there I smashed the leading Sydney Critic's opposition to it. I told him ... that a portrait that did not show the ancestors in it was not a portrait. It was only a photograph in paint. I said much more. He took his already written criticism out of his pocket and tore it to little bits and wrote a full-value one in his paper. At the moment this is not for publication. After my death you can use it, if you like. It is all in my diaries for use then. Again I want to say how glad I am of what you say of the gift and that 'the painting is a master piece'. It is more. It is a light in the convention-ridden darkness of Australian Art that will never go out.

YOURS GRATEFULLY

Private

Sorry that my writing is now so hard to read. Only one eye and that is not much good.

a Joshua Smith neck] refers to Dobell's portrait of Joshua Smith, which won the Archibald Prize in 1943. Two rival painters challenged the award in the New South Wales Supreme Court on the grounds that its elongated style was caricature. Gilmore wrote to the Sydney newspapers in its defence.

KEITH HANCOCK

In (William) Keith Hancock (1898–1988), Australia produced one of its greatest historians and teachers. An important formative influence was his University of Melbourne history teacher, Sir Ernest Scott (1867–1939), acknowledged here, not long before his death, as the founder of Australian history as academic discipline and as pleasure.

131. TO ERNEST SCOTT, 8 JULY 1939

MY DEAR SIR ERNEST

I have many reasons for pleasure in thus addressing you; but to begin with it solves a problem. As I grew greyer and as you and I became closer friends, it seemed stilted and unnatural for me to call you 'Professor'. But it never became natural for me (for I am still your pupil) to call you 'Scott'. Sometimes I almost stumbled into calling you (as I confess I often thought of you) as 'Ernest'. But that would have been too familiar. 'Sir Ernest' is for me the ideal solution.

Apart from this happy smoothing out of a personal problem, there is my delight in the event, and my enthusiastic approval of the judgement of those who caused it. Nothing could have given greater pleasure to Australian University people, and to many thousands of Australians who are not University people. We remember that it was you who discovered Australian history for us, as an object of serious study and as a pleasure. Long may you continue to enjoy it yourself.

I am in the throes of writing, and am loathing it. This particular chapter is Racial Aspects of Economic Policy in S. Africa. A miserable story of fear and stupidity. I am sick to death of the British Empire 1918–1938. Hitler volente, I shall finish the second volume about 15 months hence. That seems a long and weary time. When I have finished it, I shall burn 6 trunks of blue books and go back to the past, and to some meticulous Record Office problem—and, of course, to being more civilised with my students than I have been able to be of late.

Hitler volente? I am very gloomy! I put the chances of war this summer well over 50%. Our chances of winning it, about 50%. But thank God we are not going to abdicate and surrender freedom & decency to Nazi beastliness. In my heart I believe we are really finished with the dreadful weakness and surrenders of the past few years (and the deceptions, too). I heard Halifax the other night. He is all right. And this people has for a long time been better than its government.

Of course I am frightened! Most people are when they think. But like most people I'm in a *carpe diem* mood; that means, here, hard writing and a bathe before breakfast, and walking or climbing, and eating too much cream. This is a Welsh-speaking district. It's pleasant (after South Africa) to be in a bi-lingual country where people who speak the different languages don't spend most of the day wanting to scratch each others' eyes out. And the landscapes are beautiful.

All the same, in my imagination I'm in your big room looking through the window to Mt Dandenong; and imagining it makes me wish that I were there. That loveliness is home for me; these are foreign beauties. What a good job, all things considered, Australians have made of Australia! I'm just reading Wadham and Wood, and am fascinated by it. Sometimes of course we ill-treat the country. I hope that this time we shall [give?] some attention to the bush fire experience. And I wish that we'd replenish the trout!

My congratulations and good wishes go to Lady Scott too. And Theaden's go with mine to both of you.

YOURS EVER/KEITH HANCOCK

This really does shock me. I've forgotten your country address. So I send this to the Club.

in the throes of writing] Hancock was Professor of History 1933–44 at Birmingham where he wrote his magisterial two-volume *Survey of British Commonwealth Affairs*   Halifax] Edward Frederick Lindley Wood (1881–1959), 3rd Viscount Halifax, was Foreign Secretary during the Munich crisis   better than its government] a reference to the policies of appeasement of the pre-war British government Wadham and Wood] the Melbourne scholars Sir Samuel MacMahon Wadham (1891–1972) and Gordon Leslie Wood (1890–1953), whose study *Land Utilization in Australia* had just been published to acclaim   replenish the trout] Hancock was a keen fly fisherman   Theaden] Hancock's first wife, née Brocklebank, whom he had married in 1925

EDWARD DUNLOP

In 1939 Ernest Edward ('Weary') Dunlop (1907–93) was living in London, whence he kept up a stream of letters to Helen Ferguson, whom he had met during his student days at the University of Melbourne. Separation and the shadow of war hangs over this correspondence. The couple became engaged in February 1940 but did not marry until 1945. By then 'Weary' Dunlop had entered the pantheon of Australian heroes for the selfless devotion he had given to the men under his command in the prisoner-of-war camps in Java and on the Burma–Thailand 'Death Railway'.

132. TO HELEN FERGUSON, 31 AUGUST 1939

MY DEAR

I've been such a thoughtless, selfish clumsy person to make you unhappy with miserable & dismal correspondence. Your darling letter made it so very plain that unwittingly and stupidly I must have hurt you rather abominably.

Letters are such difficult things, and it is so horrid to reflect that this letter will reach you nearly a month after yours was written (and even that with luck now)

You are the most sweet and very rare person I have ever met and for me it is almost as much happiness as one should want in this world to know that you do love me in some special way.

Please dont think I have been specially impatient or unhappy—sometimes quite the reverse. It is because I desire your happiness above all things that sometimes I feel acutely sensible as to the non essential things I seem to have fussed about in my letter.

You surely have no doubt that the one secure thing in my life is that I love you absolutely, and darling heart so full of sincerity you've read me a lesson I very much deserve. Love is such a simple and big thing, and I've no doubt let you think I believe you capable of littleness. so very very absurd. How much I long to fold you into a corner of my arms and convince you that the person who sometimes writes you wild letters hasn't altered so very much.

You may guess too that the last two months in London have been a little restless and fateful. It rather reminds one of the sort of situation where one goes on making glorious plans about life whilst sitting on a volcano.

Today has seen the complete mobilization of the last navy, army, and airforce reserves and the children leave for the country tomorrow. London is so supremely calm—galling hesitation is replaced by irrevocable decision. This country is somehow so great that come what may I think they will always play a big part in the affairs of mankind bent as it is on wanton criminal folly.

Darling it is somehow good to be living at this moment, and to feel that there may be big things to do requiring endurance & sound nerves, even for a non-combatant who somehow envies the fighting men. How we all do yearn that our lives be touched with a little nobility even if it be posthumous!

And my pet lest you fear I'm becoming intolerably verbose I shall close, by telling you that I am, surely, the luckiest person living that you should like me a little bit.

The lady with serene brow and beautiful eyes is about to be securely packed ready for my departure. Perhaps I should send her to the country to be safe, but I can't bear that—she so reminds me of someone

GOODNIGHT ADORABLE/EDWARD.

lady with serene brow] a reference to Helen Ferguson's photograph

133. TO HELEN FERGUSON, 3–4 SEPTEMBER 1939

MY ADORED

The ball kicked off today by Mr Chamberlain to the relief of all. One's mind just boggles as to the consequences. There is a curious detachment as to personal affairs as though one were a particle seen from another planet. We must make ourselves believe that someday when all the beastliness is over that some of the beauty will remain.

London of course is taking on the appearance of a fortified city. Evacuation has gone on smoothly, and the organization of it all has to be seen to be believed. Endless sand bags everywhere, the sky studded with balloons and the population being trained to live like rats underground as much as possible.

Preparations have been made for terrible civilian loss, but somehow we surgeons all feel that it wont be surprising if we are on the continent before very long. Defence has a habit of getting on top somehow.

The heat and stuffiness inside at present is a little trying. Every chink must be covered with a black curtain at night of course, and you cant open your window much as the breeze blows the wretched things about. The present arrangement is that my team are to be quartered here just temporarily—soon to transfer to base hospital at Harefield Sanatorium Middlesex.

Letters are an awful problem—the only suggestion I can make at present is

c/- Ministry of Health Emergency Hospital Scheme
St Mary's Hospital
Praed St.
Paddington

But I expect that I will soon be gone from here, and it may be the hospital will have gone too! Soon we'll be settled on such matters I hope, since it will be so hard not to have letters from you. I believe that some attempt will be made to keep air mail going for the present.

It is a little amusing to find the entrance hall of this old hospital rather in a state of chaos, because this war interrupted them in the act of building a fine memorial to the last. Everything is like that—just so pathetic as to be funny.

I suppose the Australians will be flocking to the colours again and that there will be an expeditionary force. You too darling busy as a beaver I'll be bound and no doubt a terribly important person.

4/9/39

Restless night, sleep broken by wailing air raid sirens. We are to work in twelve hour shifts and if not on duty are expected to assemble in one of the 'funk holes' with gas mask and other personal trifles (when these sound). At present boredom is the chief enemy combated on all sides by free doses of alcohol and much card playing—neither of these very diverting things I'm afraid.

One small note of personal regret does intrude persistently. I should give so very much to have seen you again before all this. I am so hungry for the sight of your darling face, and the sound of your voice, and so many lovely things. There are so many beautiful and significant things left unfulfilled and so many thwarted hopes.

None of these things however matter so much as to dim the essential loveliness of the feeling between us, and a sense of gratitude for a divine revelation.

Now that the continued separation I have so feared is definitely to be I feel my faith in *us* stronger than ever before. It is happiness in itself to be so in love with you.

Your ever devoted/Edward.

Mr Chamberlain] British Prime Minister (Arthur) Neville Chamberlain (1869–1940) who, after the ignominious failure of the Munich Agreement, declared war on Germany, 3 September 1939 St Mary's Hospital] since the beginning of September, Dunlop had been the leader of an operating team in the West London sector of the Emergency Medical Service based at St Mary's Hospital in Paddington

C.E. Bean

C.E.W. Bean (1879–1968) achieved eminence as an official correspondent covering the Australian engagement in the 1914–18 war. His reputation is inextricably linked with The Official History of Australia in the War of 1914–1918 *and with the establishment of the Australian War Memorial, officially opened in Canberra in 1941. On more than one occasion Bean declined a knighthood, as he did in this letter of quiet eloquence written to Government House in 1940.*

134. To Leighton Bracegirdle, undated [1940]

Dear Sir,

I deeply appreciate the action of His Excellency and the Government in recommending me for a knighthood, but I have for many years believed that in Australia the interests of the nation would be best served by the elimination of social distinctions, so far as is reasonably possible. Though I have the greatest admiration for many titled men and women and for their work and influence, it seems to me that in practice, despite certain advantages, the system encourages false values among our people, and that our generation needs above everything to see and aim at true values. For this reason, and this only, I have begged to decline this reward, by the kind offer of which I am deeply gratified.

Yours faithfully,/C. E. W. Bean/Official Historian

His Excellency and the Government] The Earl of Gowrie, Governor-General of the Commonwealth of Australia 1936–44; the government was a United Australia Party–Country Party coalition led by R.G. Menzies

W. Bray

While little is known individually of W. Bray, this letter is eloquent testimony to the pain of the disruption and damage to family life through official policies which saw Aboriginal families separated and broken, sometimes permanently.

135. To Protector of Aborigines, Northern Territory, April 1941

Dear Sir

I myself, and my wife, both halfe castes we understand, do not want any of our children removed out of their Central Australia their country.

It would not be fair to us, the loss of them. Also not fair to them, the loss of their parents, causing crying and fretting.

We parents, born Arltunga Goldfields, children also, except one, he being the eldest—Norman. He born Deep well, part of the east-west running James Range.

As we were all born here in Central Australia, we don't know any other parts, and don't want to.

Will you please *place* this *Protest*, as we do not understand any *forcible* removal, of any of us, from this Central Australia, our birth right country.

Yours truly W Bray

Protector of Aborigines] the initial recipient of this letter was Theodor George Henry Strehlow (1908–78), at that time a Patrol Officer in Alice Springs reporting to the Director of Native Affairs in the Northern Territory. Strehlow later held various academic positions in Australian universities.

DAISY BATES

Irish-born Daisy O'Dwyer (later Daisy Bates) (1859–1951) was twenty-four when she was sent to Australia for her health. Nearly sixty years later she was living in a tent on the fringes of the Nullabor Plain in South Australia, among members of an Aboriginal tribe with whom she claimed the status of 'Kabbarli' (grandmother/wise woman). Most of her life was spent in promoting Aboriginal welfare: she published widely, and although her insights may now appear limited and patronising, her work valuably documents tribal languages and customs.

136. TO KILMENY SYMON, 9 AUGUST 1941

MY DEAR KILMENY

How can I thank you adequately for your lovely courtesy in undertaking your 'quest' to find me my beloved Dickens!—the little flowers herewith are my thanks & thoughts. Those paper-covered books! *How* did they come to this country? I had a full 'Household' Dickens in green hard covers & I carried that full edition with me throughout Australia & Tasmania—from the 80s till I lent the last copy which was Edwin Drood & some lighter short stories—None of these copies ever came back to me, but I always had the pleasure of thinking that they had given pleasure to the borrowers! I have read a list of those you have sent & I will keep them in a parcel by themselves & will not lend them & the parcel will be addressed to your dear and thoughtful self—These little flowers are growing round & about my tent—& are a lovely sight to me—all so tiny & yet so alive & growing—I've hurt my writing hand just at the junction of hand & wrist & the muscles have all been affected, especially the thumb which is useless almost at present; but as I have no natives I am taking care of my hand & wrist & the young fettler's wife from whom I make small purchases kindly does little services—I can get a meal from her & she launders for me but I must keep my tent out of bounds & so I have not had any white people (tho' I've only seen 2 white young women at the siding) within the brush breakwind. The delight & comfort of Dickens can only be gauged by a fellow Dickensian & one as keen as I am. I can hear Grandma reading bits to us when we were allowed down among the grown-ups between their afternoon tea & our evening meals—& the grape-covered fruit jug brings Grandma back to mind. I had a habit of imitating her as she read—& as I read now I remember it all so vividly. So curious how one can bridge many years—yet forget yesterday's happenings.

I am sending you a small cheque for your war efforts. You are preparing something I know & I hope it's going to be a big success & that my little sum is the first of its kind towards your work. It is only half a guinea, Kilmeny. Success to your efforts.

I miss my natives greatly, but this is their 'season' for initiation assemblages—& all have gone to the West Coast, Fowlers Bay etc for the ceremonies—mainly orgies as only vestiges of the initiation ceremonies are now practised—it is a pity that they have lapsed—

as they made for discipline of the youngsters—Had a shock when I found that all my young novices had turned into young thieves since I left my camp in 1935 & have been roaming along the line from Kalgoorlie to Port Augusta robbing fettlers, tents & houses—

Thank you again, dear Kilmeny, for your most generous & kindly thought & act. My beloved Dickens!

AFFY YOURS/DAISY M. BATES

I am not crossing the little cheque & Martins or Birks will cash it. I usually cross all my cheques when in camp.

Martins or Birks] Adelaide department stores

KARL-ALEXANDER POLLOK

The plight of artists affected by the wartime policies of the precautionary internment of aliens is strikingly expressed in this letter to Bernard Thomas Heinze (1894–1982), conductor of the Melbourne Symphony Orchestra 1933–53, Ormond Professor of Music in the University of Melbourne 1925–56, and a vital force in Australian musical life in this period.

137. TO BERNARD HEINZE, 14 AUGUST 1941

DEAR MR. HEINZE,

From my new address you will see that we were transferred to an internment camp in the State of Victoria. Unfortunately that does not mean that our chances of an early release have increased. As we have very much time here which we try very hard to spend in as usefull a manner as possible and among my fellow internees there are several musicians I take the liberty to write you to-day on behalf of the musicians here in the camp. The reason of my writing to you is to ask you for scores and music as we have only a few. Our musicians not only work hard to improve their art but try to give as frequent as possible performances to distract their comrades. To give you an idea what music we would like to have very much at the moment I would like to state that that would be music for string quartett and trio (Haydn, Mozart, Schubert, Beethoven, Brahms) and some piano music (if possible the late Beethoven Sonatas which the young and well-known Austrian pianist Peter Stadlen who is here in the camp is very anxious to have) and if possible also some music for four hands. But of course whatever you will be able to send us everything will be very wellcome. I hope you do not mind my troubling you and you will forgive me for doing so but I only dared to do so as I was sure that you will understand how important the matter is for our musicians.

MANY THANKS FOR YOUR KINDNESS. YOURS VERY SINCERELY/KARL-ALEXANDER POLLOK

ROBERT MENZIES

Sir Robert Gordon Menzies (1894–1978) held office as Prime Minister of Australia 1939–41 and again for a record seventeen years, 1949–66. In 1941, facing a treacherous backbench, he resigned his leadership of the country and of the United Australia Party. As Prime Minister, he had enjoyed an impeccable relationship with the Opposition Leader of the day, John Curtin.

138. To John Curtin, 29 August 1941

My dear John

I have ceased to be Prime Minister and we shall therefore no longer be opposite numbers at the table.

I want to thank you for two years and four months in which my task, always difficult, has frequently been rendered easier and at all times rendered more tolerable by your magnanimous and understanding attitude.

Your political opposition has been honourable and your personal friendship a pearl of great price.

Yours sincerely,

JOHN CURTIN

As leader of the Australian Labor Party, John Curtin (1885–1945) had been Leader of the Federal Opposition during the difficult period of the declaration of war. While maintaining a principled and conscientious opposition to the government of the day, he had given constructive support to the national war effort and to Menzies' role as a wartime Prime Minister. Curtin himself later carried the burden of the wartime administration of Australia when he was commissioned as Prime Minister on 7 October 1941. He died in office on 5 July 1945.

139. To Robert Menzies, 1941

Dear Bob,

Thank you for your letter. I appreciate it more than I can say. On my part I thank you wholeheartedly for the consideration & courtesy which never once failed in your dealings with me. I wish you good health & fair going. Your personal friendship is something I value, as I hope and know you do, as a very precious thing.

Yrs Faithfully/John Curtin

HEPHZIBAH MENUHIN

Pianist Hephzibah Menuhin (1920–81), born in San Francisco into a remarkable family of musicians, made her professional debut in 1934 in a recital with her violinist brother Yehudi (see Letter 173). In May 1938 Yehudi married Australian Nola Nicholas, whose father George Nicholas had made a fortune from the 'Aspro' patent; two months later Hephzibah married Nola's brother Lindsay. This letter to a Melbourne friend reflects Hephzibah's wish to be an ordinary Australian wife; her interest in the work of her husband's sheep property; her professional confidence and a rebellious instinct which surfaced when she felt her gifts were being used by 'capitalistic ladies'.

140. To Joan Levy, 11–12 September 1941

Dearest Joanie,

It seems such a long time since I've seen you that even a one sided conversation with you will be more satisfactory than utter silence both ends of the meridian. That's why I'm writing, but I would have written before if I'd have had as much leisure as this afternoon. The point is, for one who possesses a more delicately balanced mentality than digestion, a perfect adjustment of routine takes longer than it should, just another proof that frailty and the resultant impression of femininity and grace, are far from being a virtue in terms of practical returns.

However, I am now more than just comfortably installed, and my newly established routine revolves about me in perfect accord with time allowing for duty and rest. Mozart is playing his (and Wal's) favorite Kleine Nachtmusik, while Krony gets on and off his bow wow on wheels and reads maturely all the canine literature he has assembled during his earthly sojourn. What could be more delightful? I know Lin is happy, classing his stud wool after a good lunch, looking forward to our wonderful evenings together. As often as not, we go to bed for dinner, and having now reduced our nightly intake of food to soup and fruit, we start upon our twin occupations of music and reading. The controversial element as personified by your good husband, has been missing since "those days", and though we miss it, indubitably makes for earlier nights! We now know Brahms' fourth symphony almost as well as God Save the King, and the better we know it, more terribly do we want to hear it. They say that one is either indifferent to this great man's music, or else madly impassioned by it. I feel that if all music lovers had Lindsay's remarkable perseverance and studied sounds with such profound concentration, there would be none unmoved by Brahms.

I have been catching up with the Times Literary Supplements and reading learned reviews on the still more learned books England and America are publishing in spite of war and bombs. One Professor says that political nationalism is incompatible with international trade.

In fact none of them say anything that we haven't already said—or at least thought.

I've had a letter from Nola, in which she sounds none too consoling about the old matters of family feud, which like all bad things threatens to overrun the earth and exclude man, unless man ploughs and ploughs and plants forever, every time spring comes. At least Nola has Yehudi's support whereas she used to stand alone. And so I can afford to feel sorry and sad for Mother now, because she can't hurt Nola any more. The less her bitter sorrow touches others, the unhappier of course she'll be. It's terrible to be like that, and terrible to think that on account of pride, a thing that literally doesn't exist, because like inflated money, it has no real matter behind it, she is willing to kill all happiness and stifle the sweetest things in life: love for love's sake and the expression of it in so many precious ways.

Anyhow, she says that they all loved my pompadourish (or is it Edwardian?) upsweep, as portrayed by Shirl's artfully concealing and cleverly revealing photography. All that Mother said was I looked like anyone at all and had a smile full of teeth such as she had seen on every Australian face she had ever met, a smile full of cheek. Well, if that isn't discernment …! I certainly do look like a human being, and what's more I feel like one for the first time in 21 years, and try as hard as any Australian to be cheeky without hurting, and to do as I like without appearing to want to be different.

By the way the concert is off. I started coming undone when Madame used methods of persuasion not entirely kosher, and got Lindsay's upright passions all furiously aroused. She wanted us to believe that the A.B.C. had stipulated that the concert was to be for no other proceeds but to add extra beds for soldiers' wives having babies at the Queen Victoria Hospital! For one thing, morally speaking, men going off on active service shouldn't be encouraged to leave their penniless wives pregnant. So there. Besides, in spite of herself, it soon came out that it was the Committee not the Commission, the Committee being headed by Lady Brookes. Now my idea is too naughty to be any good; it only partly aimed at rubbing these capitalistic ladies the wrong way. What I would really like is to play the Rachmaninoff III for the benefit of the Russian Red Cross at a concert which these most certainly anti-communistic ladies would feel socially compelled to attend. If I practise hard, as I am doing nearly every morning, perhaps the Lord will reward me!

I must now take Krony out for a walk, as the weather seems clear, after days and days of rain.

My love to you both, and hoping that the quantity X is daily becoming stronger and more like a baby—and has it fluttered its wings yet? I send you Lindsay's and Krony's greetings as well. Krony still says bow-wow when he enters your room! What a genial memory!!

Always your/Hephzibah

Friday Sept. 12th

Since I missed the mail this morning I'll just add this bit of news which will most likely interest Wal: old Bob Williams, the rabbiter who was living all alone way out down

Darcy's Lane, was found dead in a paddock yesterday afternoon, while his dogs were standing all about him, some having jumped two fences over to where Mr. McLean was riding, to tell him their poor master was gone. An inquest is being held at Mortlake this afternoon and the poor chap will be buried at Camperdown tomorrow. Although he died the kindest and quickest death possible they think—he must have felt sad to die alone, unloved and unhelped. Perhaps he liked it better that way?

And what about our new U.S. minister? Isn't he a jovial looking chap?

Was it Miss Lanaway's writing by the way, on the envelope containing the article on Crimea? Thanks so much for sending it; Lin and I read it with great interest.

MUCH LOVE AGAIN—DEAR JOANIE,/HEPHZIBAH

Wal] Joan Levy's husband   Shirl] Shirley Nicholas, stepmother of Lindsay and Nola   Krony] Kronrod, elder son of Hephzibah and Lindsay Nicholas   Lady Brookes] later Dame Mabel Brookes (1890–1975), see Letter 102

JESSIE MILLER

War, drought and heat provided the backdrop to the wedding of Grace Miller and Tom Black, celebrated on the property Stranraer, 265 miles west of Brisbane in 1941. The story of this special day is told by Jessie Strathearn Miller (1876–1943) in a letter sent afterwards to her brother and daughter. Jessie Miller was born in England but as a young woman had settled with her family on Queensland's Darling Downs.

141. TO ERNEST MCCLURE AND JESSIE HOCKING, 14 NOVEMBER 1941

MY DEARS

I promised to let you have an account of Grace's wedding so here goes, I will do my best but the insects tonight, as every night are driving us mad. I have a large basin of water beside the lamp and have caught hundreds but there are hundreds more.—A break occurred here, a beetle flew into my ear & for a while things were hectic as the family rushed round trying to get it out & it continued to sting & flutter. No more writing that night. Now Sunday morning & will have another go at it.

The weeks before Grace's wedding should have been weeks of steady getting ready. But the drought was terrible & Grace was kept busy riding with Hugh watching & shifting the cattle. The dust, heat & wind put cleaning quite out of the question. We dare not clean up the dry grass in the garden because of fire so most was left to the last ten days when we just had to do what was safe to do as all hope of rain to help us had to be given up. However we tried to forget the weather & set to work until the house looked fresh & bright. The gardens we cleared of the dead grass & would you believe it phlox seed had taken root amongst the grass in the hard ground & was budding. We carefully left it & on the wedding day it was lovely—a carpet of red, pink & white flowers for Grace to walk over. The honeysuckle too was a sight with hundreds of flowers. My creeper up the telephone pole had just shed its mass of flowers which was a pity but the guests wondered at the garden in such weather. On the Thursday Sheila & Grace erected & iced the wedding cakes which had been made by Teddy Walker. It was a day of much love & laughter & backaches. Icing a tall cake is hard work with blistered hands. When finished it looked well & I was very proud of the girls first attempt.

On Friday Grace decided the front room would be improved by giving the doors & wainscot a coat of paint which she did. Presents were arriving & the house was alive with the family all weekend. Monday was a hectic day. All furniture from sitting room made the front verandah into a lounge (by the way Grace washed down the front of the house & verandahs previously. The piano was put into the breakfast room. Hugh had a hectic day erecting the tables on his verandah & made long forms which he covered with rugs down each side. Cooking went on in odd moments. That night Tom went in to town & collected the minister Rev. J Blake of Dalby, and Mrs Cleeland and a sack of bread, more presents, boxes of bouquets & boxes of flowers, the latter from our Jean & sundry other things. Dad had gone in with Tom & then our first tragedy happened. Dad sat on the sandwich loaves & you should have seen them, but worse things are happening at sea. The minister was a delightful man & a pleasure to have in the house. If ever I have time I think I must write an article entitled 'Parsons I have entertained'. It would be an eye opener about the cloth. After supper Mr Blake & Dad yarned while Grace & Essie sorted out the flowers & plunged them into buckets of our precious water. I suggested at one time that all the guests should bring a billy of water. Finally all was done that could be done & we all went to bed and slept. Tuesday morning Sheila came in early bringing Hilda Morrison with her. We had a busy but happy morning. Tables were set & food prepared & covered & protected from ants. Grace arranged the flowers in all the rooms & by mid-day the whole place looked lovely. I managed just to run across & see the tables & they were a picture with lavender & pink sweet peas & asparagus fern. The cake looked perfect & from it waved the precious little flag that David sent home from Palestine. Above the places set for Grace & Tom Hugh had fixed the big Union Jack. I had been busy in my kitchen too & thanks to Nunks I was able to prepare grape fruit for fifty & jugs & jugs of orange drink. These I put out on a table on the verandah lounge also a water bag. And how the guests appreciated the grape fruit & drinks when they arrived. The distances varied from 25 to 100 miles that they had come & the temperature was 102 degrees on the verandah. By 1.30 p.m Dad & I were dressed & ready to receive our visitors who began to arrive at 2.p.m. Hugh & twins & Norman & Jennifer were with us to help. The three babies looked lovely & of course attached themselves to Grandma but they helped me carry on as by this time I felt sort of breaking up. Jennifer wore a lovely little frock, white silk, that Mrs Mawley had given to her. Lesley was in pale green georgette & Billy in grey pants & pale green top. Of course the ladies went dilly over the three babies who kept so close to me & were such good children. (They dont know the three like I do but they did behave well—overawed. By 2.30 all the guests were here &

such a happy chatter was going on. By 2.45 Tom & his parents had arrived. I had not seen Grace since 1.30. She with Essie & Shirley were dressing over in Essie's assisted by Sheila & Hilda Morrison. Then came a chance to escape for a minute & I went over to see & say goodbye to my Gay. She looked very lovely in her simple frock made by Esther, with Nunks gift veil & the orange blossom coronet from Mrs Mawley & the lovely bouquet. I must confess I broke up a bit after I left her but Teddy Walker was as another daughter to me & I was soon ready to face everybody again. Hugh was a good son & watched over me all day. The time had arrived & Dad went across the garden to fetch Grace. Hugh turned on Rosamunde & the chattering of the 50 guests was hushed to a silence you could feel while Grace & her attendants came slowly across the flower studded drought stricken ground. The guests formed an avenue through which Grace passed & so into the room to where Tom & his best man were waiting. The guests filed in & the music ceased. Grace & Tom gave a searching look at each other & a smile. The service began & was very simple, then the register was signed at Dad's desk & then as the Wedding March was played they came amongst us all and everyone was happy & noisy. I must tell you of Esthers & Shirley's frocks. Esther made her own of cyclamen coloured georgette & carried a bouquet in same colour & her hat was cream, she was matron of honour & Tom gave her an opal ring. Shirley was a lovely little bridesmaid in a long frock of pale green georgette, a little bouquet of roses cream & on her head a green net cap that did not hide her lovely hair. To her Tom gave a green manicure set.

It is now Monday night & the beetles are a plague but I have both ears filled with cotton wool To continue my story.

In a little while Sheila slipped away with Hilda Morrison to finish the table & make the tea etc. Pat Griffin & Betty Walker also lent Sheila a hand. Then soon everyone was seated at the table. Jean had sent the place cards from Thursday Island, made by a friend & all taken away as souvenirs of a happy day. The feast was a merry one & notwithstanding the great heat the folk were hungry & terribly thirsty. The Rev. J Blake made a splendid chairman & was as jolly as the rest. Every one was surprised to learn there were sweets & macaroons from so far north & sweets, fruit, almonds, raisins & chocolates from so far south but appreciated the fact that although so far away you both were with us. We had several toasts & God Save the King was sung lustily. The speeches were all short but satisfying. Then Grace cut the cake assisted by Esther. Everyone thought the cake was a wonder & all had to be told the story of the Little Flag. The same little flag has become known all over Queensland & the papers had it in a special little framed paragraph, how the story got to them is a mystery but it was well noted as we know by the folk ringing up Mrs Cleeland about it not knowing she had been at the wedding. Peggy had found it & no doubt discussed it with her mates at the Technical. Well! the tea party came to an end & then folk drifted about talking, looking at presents etc. admiring our honeysuckle & Grace & Tom mingled. Then Grace disappeared with Betty & others & reappeared in her travelling rig out & she looked lovely and sparkling. Her dress was dove grey, very simple, navy shoes, navy belt, navy fringed georgette hanky in invisible pocket, white hat with navy & red twisted ribbon, white gloves, navy handbag & she wore my little red brooch. We looked a good crowd out at the cars & such a storm of confetti. Finally they went off in the best man's car, destination unknown to themselves or us. We heard they went to Dulacca & on to Brisbane next morning by the early train. Then on to Coolangatta where they appear to have had a happy holiday.

And so ended our last wedding and I have folded up my fourth weeping handkerchief & laid it away in naphthalene (not lavender) with the other three in my little memory box. Each has a different story to tell me. The last one to go has left the biggest gap as her going has left Dad & me quite alone. I cannot see it makes much difference to dad as life goes on the same for him, his pipe, his papers, his patience, his odd jobs & tea at intervals. To me the loneliness with the work to do alone that we used to do together & how I miss Gay's companionship. But I will get used to it & the twins are always in & out.

Looking back on the wedding there were many mistakes but no one knew. Sins of omission & commission that we laugh over,—Sheila, Esther & I. But it was a day to remember & stands out for happiness & simplicity amid war drought & heat. Another boat left the mother ship to sail the Great Seas of Life. What does the future hold for Tom & Grace. Happiness I hope, much hard work I know. That is the lot of everyone in this struggling world.

They have settled down in Tom's bachelor abode & are working out plans of the home they intend to build round it with our family gift of 5000 ft timber. I will try & remember their presents now.

Several cheques & Nunks 5 pound note.

3 cut-glass salad bowls (one from Mr & Mrs griffin & one from Mrs Cleeland).

cut-glass jug & goblets from Tom's sister

tea set from Jean & family

silver entree dish Mrs McLennan & Mavis

lace mats & powder bowl Mrs Lloyd of Sydney

fruit spoons & server Aunt Flossie

3 cases of tea spoons one from Ruth (beauties)

Quilt from Eileen, Amy & Nell

Several pyrex from Walker family

Pyrex in silver stand. two casseroles

3 crystal vases. Crystal sugar & cream from pat & Clive Griffin. English china
    teapot from the McLachlans

Carvers, tablecloth, suppercloth & napkins

pretty cups, saucers, plates, butter dishes

China supper set, china vases, several towels

I cannot remember any more at present. I remember cheques came from Mrs Mawley, Tom's father & mother, his sister in Ayr, his brother, Mr & Mrs Alexander.

And so ends my chronicle of a Bush wedding & there are things I could tell but cannot write. Much love.

MOTHER & SISTER/JSM

Hugh] Hugh Miller, Jessie Miller's son   Sheila] Jessie Miller's daughter   Dad] Jessie Miller's husband, William Robert Miller   David] David McClure, brother of Jessie Miller

JAMES McAULEY

Poet James McAuley (1917–76), later editor of Quadrant *magazine and Professor of English at the University of Tasmania, was working in a military intelligence unit in Melbourne when he sent this letter to writer Donald Horne (b. 1921), a friend of Sydney University days, author of* The Lucky Country *(1964) and co-editor of* Quadrant *1963–66. McAuley's contempt for the modernist verse published by Max Harris as editor of* Angry Penguins *found expression also in the Ern Malley hoax (see Letters 146 and 147), which belongs to the same period as this undated letter.*

142. To DONALD HORNE, UNDATED [1943?]

DEAR DONALD

Miller sends me an issue of Honi Soit with your Hooton remarks. He tells me also that you think I find that letter-writing is an affair something like indecent exposure; and asks me Is This True?

Which has prompted me to write an overdue letter to you instead of a reply to Miller. To hell with Miller, I hear on the bamboo wireless that he is engaged again but I cant bring myself to find out. Whether you are right about my attitude to letter-writing I don't know. I usually find when I come to the point that I have no great desire to say anything about anything very much, so you may be right.

I admit I did let Harry down fairly lightly—although I wont have it that I applauded him half-seriously. There is nothing serious in my applause of Harry, even if I didn't deal with him strictly on his merits. Actually, I was more dissatisfied with the review I gave the other two. The words about Hope are just literary words, and those about Lyle are not nearly nasty enough—he is worse than Harry in being obtuse and incompetent without being a joke. Harry is at least a joke.

I've been looking at the last sheaf of guano dropped by the Angry Pangwungs. There is an article on Baudelaire which contrasts his images, ["loose, tawdry ornaments, decorative enough at times, but rarely inspiring"] with those of Max Harris ["deftly chipped and polished"]!

There is some reely wunnerful stuff about how art and the workers must get right in pitching for the anti-fascist war. One article is by J.D. Blake who is somewhat wildly described as a "labour leader"—he lets us know that "our art must be armed with the most advanced and humanitarian ideas". Whaddya know? Whaddya know?

And there is Max himself. The moments when he showed earlier that he could write are disappearing under the frightful mass of silliness. He seems to have completely abandoned any interest in poetry as craft of words, with the result that he gets sound-effects which have no relation to the poem:

revere the ovoid of the night
for the glass of its velvet in her hand

Probably Max didn't even notice the V's. What are they there for? Even in prose you don't do that sort of thing unless you're writing carelessly.

Norma is in Melbourne with me now and we've found a fairly suitable lodging. She is going to find employment outside of teaching, having had a belly full of school life. So far as I can foresee I shall be permanently based in Melbourne. Hugh Gilchrist has not left for New Guinea yet but he is going up shortly to have a look at the army through the other end of the telescope.

Stewart continues to write. I have a typed copy of his Phoenix poem and others. It's amazing how much better they are when not read in his awful handwriting. he remains intermittently ill in a sub-clinical fashion, a bit neurotic about it but not as badly as he might be.

The Melbourne intelligentsia contains some good people to drink with but they're almost completely subjugated by a quite infantile Stalinism. Even those like Brian Fitzpatrick who know something about it take good care not to say anything. Melbourne is still in the roaring 30's when if you weren't a member of the party what the hell were you—a Fascist you rat? However there's gonna be some changes in the party now that the old politicals can no longer beat the next over the head with the authority of the latest directive from Moscow. Probably the union leaders will fight it out with the Dixons & Sharkeys.

I don't much care. The 30's are over for me and I feel a certain relief that they never got as far as my written work even if they got in the way of my thinking. I can read my Herrick without a guilty feeling that I should be reading about the wrongs of the workers with less silliness if I want to. The blackmailing of artists to damage their art in "good causes" is finished. The newer blackmail to stop all this nonsense of talking sense and the surreal or apocalyptic is not nearly so effective. There may even be a chance of art recovering a more general appeal now that people have stopped talking about Art & The People. To hell with Art and The Unconscious—you don't have to invite The Unconscious in on the party, its always been there. To hell in fact with Art and Anything, including Art and The Ivory Tower.

Yours /JIM

Miller] J.D.B. Miller (b. 1922), later Professor of International Relations at the Australian National University   Honi Soit] the students' journal, University of Sydney   Hooton] Harry Hooton (1908–61), Sydney poet and journalist   Hope] A.D. Hope (b. 1907), Canberra poet and academic

Lyle] Garry Lyle, Melbourne poet   Angry Pangwungs] the *Angry Penguins* magazine   labour leader] J.D. Blake was a Communist Party member and activist   Norma] Norma McAuley, wife of James McAuley   Hugh Gilchrist] (b. 1916), Australian diplomat   Stewart] Harold Stewart (1916–95), see Letter 189   Fitzpatrick] Brian Fitzpatrick (1905–65), historian, radical socialist   Dixons and Sharkeys] Communist Party activists   Herrick] Robert Herrick (1591–1674), poet, who proclaimed 'Art above nature'

ETHEL TURNER (CURLEWIS)

Ethel Turner's son, Adrian Curlewis, was taken prisoner by the Japanese in 1942 and spent seven months in forced labor on the notorious Burma–Thailand railroad before being sent to Changi prison camp in Singapore. Although Ethel Turner (1872–1958) (see Letters 55 and 74) had never stopped writing to her son, this is the first letter written with the knowledge that he was alive to read it.

143. TO ADRIAN CURLEWIS, 20 JUNE 1943

MY DARLING BOY,

And still there are miracles! I was alone in the house—a common thing now-a-days—and as I had some plants to set had just decided the telephone could mind itself—nothing is likely to come that is of any importance. I don't hear the bell even when I am in the hall but as I passed the telephone table I put my hand on it and a vibration came through it so I picked up the receiver and it was Betty—in office hours. "Can you hear me?" she said, have you got a good battery? We just had a radiogram from the Red Cross. Talk about vibration—body and soul were alive. "My dearest—she read "I am very—and am having good treatment so don't worry "Sick" was the word I got for that blank. My mind kept saying "sick"—malaria—wound—oh, a thousand things, but even so I felt a chastened rejoicing all day to have heard anything. As Betty could not come home till 8 she said I could tell the children (I was leaving it for her to tell the news) Two lustrous eyed children—silent from sheer surprise. Then Philippa had a happy thought "Why, they may send him home in exchange", she said "Oh he may be here quite soon—lots are coming." When Betty did come in and handed me a radiogram it was my turn to be lustrous eyed. "Not very sick, but very fit"! Can you imagine the new vibrations?

Darling I have been walking on air ever since. All through the days I keep giving a little skip mental and physical. "Fit, he's very fit! Fit!, fit!, fit! I tell you, you little donkey to hear so badly. If we had been allowed to radiograph a reply. But no, the Red Cross said "only a letter may be sent"." The broadcast news this morning said there were three internment camps and gave their names. Perhaps we shall hear more. Perhaps—oh perhaps the Japanese will let there be a communication before very long between heart-sick wives and Mothers and their boys.

A bitterly cold day today, with a cold bright sunshine over the garden side, and icy winds the garage side. I am quite alone, the elderly women who are all who offer—not allowed, if young enough for munition work—are infinitely less use than the worry and expense they give, so I am trying it with casual labour when I can get it. Fortunately I am next door to being a vegetarian and that is—I eat a chop or little fish twice a week, so I don't have many cooking worries. I'd live on an egg one day, some milk, an apple and bread and butter—and keep in good health too, but where my egg order used to be 4 or 5 dozen a week today I think it good if I am given three eggs in 10 days. At the same time no one here is really short of food.

All my love my darling, darling "fit" boy. Keep well. Ever and ever thy Mother.

Betty, Ian and Philippa have written by this—all three are very well.

Betty] wife of Adrian   battery] refers to Ethel Turner's hearing aid   Ian and Philippa] son and daughter of Adrian

MARTIN BOYD

Martin à Beckett Boyd (1893–1972), the novelist member of the Boyd family of artists, served in the First World War as a pilot in the Royal Flying Corps, and took part in bombing raids. The thought of having almost certainly killed civilians as well as combatants weighed on his conscience; and in the Second World War, living in England, he was appalled by the British Government's policy of bombing German cities, with the certainty of heavy civilian casualties and the destruction of countless homes.

144. TO WILLIAM TEMPLE, 5 AUGUST [1943]

TO THE MOST REVEREND THE ARCHBISHOP OF CANTERBURY

Your Grace is reported to have said that our post-last war blockade of Germany was one of the greatest crimes of history. The British Government is now contemplating an even greater crime, the blotting out of Berlin and reducing it to the condition of Hamburg.

The sense of shame and despair which comes upon one in the moments when the imagination glimpses what this means is insupportable, and it is made worse by the fact that the Church, in which one has been nourished and which should provide a safe home for the spirit, to whatever depths unredeemed mankind may sink, is identified with the government in its policy. It is impossible to contend that to bring desolation to the countless homes of a great city is in accord with the Will of Christ.

I believe that members of the Church have the right solemnly to charge their leaders in the Name of God that they shall not betray the faith they are appointed to preserve, and even if it is too much to ask them to proclaim the message of Calvary, at least they should keep to the moral level of an honorable pagan who knows that it is better to be dead and defeated than to corrupt his own spirit.

MARTIN BOYD

William Temple (1881–1944) was Archbishop of Canterbury 1942–44

145. TO WILLIAM TEMPLE, 12 AUGUST [1943]

YOUR GRACE

I must thank you for your letter of Aug. 9 in reply to mine about indiscriminate bombing. I am sorry to intrude again on your attention, but I think your reply is not quite to my argument. I fought in the last war and, although I have strong sympathy with the pacifist point of view, I did not write from it, nor do I expect the Church to adopt it. I only ask that she should not sink below the traditional level of Christian chivalry. I believe that the Church's support of the war should be limited and conditional on the state's committing no atrocity which could be repudiated by any civilised man of the past. The blotting out of a great city is such an atrocity. In Hamburg the explosions were so terrific that they set up a whirl wind which spread the flames through the city. Corpses hung from the tree-tops and women rushed about, driven insane. It is an affront not only to one's intelligence to be asked to accept this as a necessary Xtian preliminary to the setting up of God's Kingdom.

Your Grace writes: 'The one thing that is certainly wrong is to fight the war ineffectively.' Surely the one thing wrong is to put any other necessity before the necessity of obedience to Christ? Is there no point at which the Church will withhold her approval? If it were possible to capture a number of German children and induce the German Govt. to surrender by crucifying one a day until they did, would the Church endorse this as part of the supreme duty of 'stopping the German war machine'? Yet this is virtually what she is doing when she approves of the bombing of great cities, when thousands of children are tortured to death. There is no authority either of Scripture or tradition, for the easy personification of evil within the bounds of one nation, nor for the Church's giving carte blanche to the state to oppose that evil by whatever means it finds most effective, however monstrous.

There is another aspect to this. A naval captain, by no means a pacifist, speaking in the Union here last term said: 'You say this is a war for Xtianity but you use the most abominable methods to prosecute it' and there was no dissentient voice. I know of several cases of young airmen who have repudiated their padres who approved their activities, saying: 'What we do is not Xtian, but we are not Xtians.' So the Church is making it impossible for these men ever to return to God, at any rate under her guidance.

I realise that it is easy to criticise those who bear the terrible responsibilities of high office, but if I may do so without impertinence, I should like to make a constructive suggestion. It is that the Church should privately inform the Govt. that it will dissociate itself from the war if no attempt is made to preserve the traditional minimum of honour and humanity, and that it should withdraw now from use those collects which ask for God's blessing on the activities of airmen, or approve them by implication.

When it is over, 'we have got to find a way of showing both justice and mercy'. St. Augustine prayed: 'O God make me chaste, but not yet.' Is the Church now to say: 'O God, make me Xtian, but not until I have paid full tribute to Mars.'

YOUR GRACE'S MOST OBEDIENTLY/MARTIN BOYD

'ETHEL MALLEY'

'Ethel Malley' was the creation of poets James McAuley and Harold Stewart. The letter in her name was sent to Max Harris (1921–95), editor of the modernist magazine Angry Penguins: *with it came a selection of the poems allegedly written by her late brother, the mechanic and insurance salesman Ern Malley, also invented for the occasion. McAuley and Stewart later said that they had concocted Malley's 'life-work' in an afternoon. Their motive for the hoax was to demonstrate 'the decay of meaning and craftsmanship in poetry'. Harris was caught, as were many others when he published the Ern Malley poems in a special issue of* Angry Penguins. *See Letters 142 and 189.*

146. To Max Harris, October 1943

Dear Sir,

When I was going through my brother's things after his death, I found some poetry he had written. I am no judge of it myself, but a friend who I showed it to thinks it is very good and told me it should be published. On his advice I am sending you some of the poems for an opinion.

It would be a kindness if you could let me know whether you think there is anything in them. I am not a literary person myself and I do not feel I understand what he wrote, but I feel that I ought to do something about them. Ern kept himself very much to himself and lived on his own of late years and he never said anything about writing poetry. He was very ill in the months before his death last July and it may have affected his outlook.

I enclose a 2¹/₂d stamp for reply, and oblige,

Yours sincerely,/Ethel Malley

147. To Max Harris, undated

Dear Mr Harris,

Thank you for your letter of reply and your kindness in giving your opinion of Ern's poems. I am very glad to know that you think they are so good.

Please find enclosed all the rest of the poems I can find. They were in a folder with the couple of sheets in his own handwriting which I am sending you also. The ones I sent you before I got out of the folder too. Just to be sure, I have added another sheet of paper which he must have been writing on when he was in bed. It wasn't in with the rest of the things and I don't know whether it is any use to you but I am sending it in case.

Certainly you may publish any of them you like in your magazine. I had no idea they might be good enough to publish overseas. I suppose as he numbered the pages he intended it to be published as a book. It is a pity he did not leave any instructions about what he wanted done with them. I am very much obliged to your kind offer to publish them in a book. Do you think it would be a paying proposition? I don't want any money from them myself because I don't feel that they belong to me. I would be very grateful if you would let me know if your partner agrees to publishing them.

You asked me for some details about Ern's illness. I didn't mention in my last letter that his death was due to Grave's disease. If he had only taken better care of himself it need not have been fatal. But while he was away from home he neglected his health. When he was called up for his medical exam the doctors evidently told him what was wrong with him, because he was rejected. But I don't believe he saw a doctor again until he came home last March though I found out later he had been dosing himself with iodine and the doctor said that must have kept him going. He was terribly irritable and hard to do anything for. I was anxious for him to go to hospital where he could be properly looked after, but the doctor said it would be better for a person in his condition to stop at home. The doctor spoke of operating at first but when he refused to have it done the doctor said it would be better not to which I thought was strange.

You asked me also to tell you something about Ern's life. Well, my brother's full name was Ernest Lalor Malley and he was born in England at Liverpool on March 14th, 1918. Our father died in 1920 as a result of war wounds and the family came out to Australia where mother had relations. We lived for many years in Petersham where Ern went to the Petersham public school and the Summer Hill Intermediate High. He did not do very well at school although he was good at other things. Mother died in August 1933 and I could not stop Ern from leaving school after that as he was set on going to work. I have always thought he was very foolish not to have got his Intermediate but he was determined to go his own way. He got a job as a mechanic in Palmer's Garage on Taverner's Hill for a couple of years. He was always clever with mechanical things and I thought he was settled and had got over his wildness. But when he turned seventeen he came home one day from work and said he had given up his job at the garage and was going to Melbourne. I did my best to persuade him but he went. After that I did not see much of him or hear from him as he did not write, but some-one I knew met him in Melbourne and told me he was working for National Mutual selling insurance policies. They said he was living in a room by himself in South Melbourne. I remember I was worried at the time whether he was looking after himself properly because he was never very strong. I wrote to him but he did not reply for a long time. Later, in 1940 I think it was, I did get a letter from him saying that his health was better and that he was making a fair amount of money repairing watches and doing other work on the side. I did not hear from him again until the beginning of this year I found he was back in Sydney. I got him to come home and it was only then I realized that he was ill but even then I had no idea of how bad he really was. He was amazingly active for his condition. Finally he told me that he knew what was wrong and I managed to get a doctor to him. The weeks before he died were terrible. Sometimes he would be allright and he would talk to me. From things he said I gathered he had been fond of a girl in Melbourne but had some sort of difference with her. I didn't want to ask him too much because he was nervy and irritable. The crisis came suddenly and he passed away on Friday the 23rd of July. As he wished he was cremated at Rookwood.

As I said in my last letter I never knew that Ern wrote poetry. He was a great reader and he told me he did a lot of study in Melbourne. He said he often used to go to the public library at night. I wouldn't have thought Ern was interested in architecture and art as you say. If he had brought any books back with him you might be able to tell more from them. I still have the only book he brought with him though he was mostly too sick to read much, it is called Theory of the Leisure Class by Thorstein Veblen. He did have a coloured postcard pinned up in his room which I haven't included because the writing on the back seems to be personal, but if you think it would help I will send it to you.

I am sorry I can't tell you much more about Ern, but as I said before he kept very much to himself. He was always a little strange and moody and I don't think he had a very happy life, though he didn't show it.

If there is anything else I can do to help please don't hesitate to let me know.

Thanking you again for your interest and kindness,

I remain, /Yours sincerely,/Ethel Malley

E.W. Tipping

Edmond William (Bill) Tipping (1915–70) was one of Australia's most talented journalists. His byline and his column 'In Black and White' in the Melbourne Herald *had instant recognition and immense influence. His crusade on behalf of mentally retarded children did much to improve conditions in public institutions. He served in both the AIF and the RAAF during the Second World War. This letter to his wife, writer and historian Marjorie Tipping, shows the journalist's wartime world as well as Tipping's gift for friendship.*

148. To Marjorie Tipping, 20 June 1945

Dear Marjie,

Well, I got your letter yesterday—the one you sent through Reg Smithers. It was a thrill, especially to get it within a week or so. I'll be here for a few days longer (in Manila or roundabout) so I'm hoping I may get another. Great to hear things are going so well and that you're really enjoying yourself, happy that I'm getting the best background any journalist has ever got. (I've just been reading Time, June 12 edition, printed here in Manila, about how Alexander Woolcott first made his mark as editor of his college newspaper and later as a writer of frontline stories for Stars and Stripes, a troops' magazine like Wings, in World War I.). To date I've sent Broggo four good stories. I've taken time over them, making the most of the opportunity for writing them under more or less civilised conditions here and I'm leaving the other stuff which is not so good (on which I don't want a by-line) till I feel like it. I did a good one on the Borneo landings, another on the mail run, a third on what a big base Morotai has become (which, incidentally, has to go to about six different people for approval—I have to submit all my stuff through the GHQ censors) and a wow, which I sent yesterday .... I got an interview with General Arnold, the biggest shot of all the combined US and British heads, the head of all the Allied air forces. He's touring the Pacific sizing up what forces should be sent over now the show in Europe is over. It was a first class interview—you know, General Arnold tells Wings RAAF will have role in final onslaught against Japan stuff. I got four foolscap pages of it.

On Sunday I also met and attended a press conference given by General Uncle Joe (or Vinegar Joe) Stillwell. It was an interesting experience but not much good for a story. He had very little to say, was very guarded as you can imagine. At the moment I'm waiting still on Gen. Kenney, MacArthur's air chief. They say I'll get him sometime but he's working night and day at the moment—Arnold's visit has complicated things a bit. Still if I don't get him at least Arnold should be good compensation, probably better than Kenney.

I was disturbed to hear you disappointed about my not writing more often. Actually I thought I'd been doing pretty well. Perhaps you changed your opinion when a couple more letters arrived. Getting back to yours, I think I'd really forgotten we had the outstanding child of the century till I read about him sitting up etc and gurgling. He's going to be a happy child, don't you think. I'm also bucked about your getting the new suit (sounds very snappy) and the other things. There must be kick left in you yet. Perhaps you are not going to become dowdy after all. As soon as I get back this time we're going to dine out, do a show and wind up at the Embassy. I think I've got sufficient war background now to look anyone in the eye. I think it will be time for us to get back in social circulation. (You probably think I'm going off my rocker.) Anyhow it's been great living with some of these blokes—had grapefruit (tinned) for breakfast this morning and two eggs yesterday, a welcome change from the usual cursed hot-cakes or pancakes. Here are a few of the blokes I've met—Lachie McDonald, as I've told you—with Jack Percival my best buddy here—Pat Flaherty, famous NBC commentator, Bill Gray (Time), Carl Mydans (Life), Victor Jurgens, March of Time, Lindsay Parrot (NY Times), Frank Kelley (Herald Tribune), Guy Richards (NY Daily News—a good buddy, he was with the Marines at Guadalcanal and also at Ballarat and we have had some great reminiscing chats. He thinks the Aussies are marvellous, Melbourne probably the nicest city he has ever been in. But I have a list of correspondents here and I'll be able to tell you lots more when I get home.

We've had pictures here the last two nights, first class shows both of them. We saw an American documentary called "Fighting Lady" which tells the story of an aircraft carrier in the Pacific operating with Task Force 58 from Truk to attacks on the Jap mainland. The shots of the death battles between the Hellcats and the Jap Kamikazis are unbelievable. If it comes to Melbourne in my absence don't miss it whatever you do. The other feature film was Fred McMurray and Claudette Colbert in "Practically Yours". A first class comedy. Last night we had easily the best murder who done it I've seen in years.

(That should have been whodunit). A thing called Laura with a magnificent performance by a bloke called Clifton Webb, a New York stage star of note, who, my American friends assure me is a friend of Coward's and also a pansy. They were first rate shows.

Before I forget—I haven't bought you a thing and I'm not going to. Prices are breath taking. Lachie McDonald and Jack Percival say I should buy you one of the big floppy Panama beach hats a bloke has been retailing around here at 30 pesos. They have been buying them up, as many as they can get, saying they're an excellent buy. There are smaller ones, not so floppy for 20 pesos but I'm not going to buy that price. They are no use except for the beach and you know how often we get to the beach. The same applies to everything so I'm not buying a thing and I hope you won't be too disappointed. The same applies to those Yankee bags, like Jock's. They are about £5 but I don't think they would be much use in civilian life (a suitcase is probably better) and besides how the hell could I get your mother's case back from here. We got an issue of 4 cartons of cigarettes the other night and six cans of American beer (had to pay six pesos). Helps a lot. We have a can for a cocktail after our pre-dinner shower each night.

Incidentally those photos I mentioned. John Harrison has developed them on negatives but there's a paper shortage around here and he doesn't want to bot too much from the Americans so he's not printing them till we get somewhere where he can. The negs show, however, that they are excellent. The one for your mother—me with the luscious American piece on the plane behind me—is a wow. There's a good one of me looking operational too, headphones Mae West and all, looking out the side of the Liberator as I came back from the Borneo show. I'll send them as soon as I can. We're going up to Clarke Field from here and down to Leyte for the Cats and we'll probably stay on for the next "do". That shouldn't put me more than a couple of weeks behind by original schedule, however. Have to confer with Broggo first. Will let you know later. I think it's best to make the most of my opportunities on this trip.

Actually, for two pins I'd whiz across to Chungking and be damned to Broggo, McDonnell and the lot of them. It can be done. I would but my Chinese pal Eddie Tseng says I might have trouble in getting back. You are apt to be stranded for weeks, even months. So I guess I'd better not. Wouldn't it be marvellous if I could?

Anyhow, keep at it, cleaning out the mouse cupboards and tidying the books—you don't mention having swept the carpet yet I notice—and tell Paul I'm getting very anxious to see what he looks like again. Tell him to keep in practice with his dribbling and so on. I'll write again in a couple of days. (I wrote to Dad on Sunday). You'd better not bother writing after this unless I tell you too. We won't be here many days more.

Incidentally, I nearly forgot. I went across to where Reg Smithers and co. live for mess on Sunday night and met a frightfully nice fellow, a Law graduate of Sydney Uni. and former editor of Hermes about the year you did MUM. He'd heard of both of us. Gough Whitlam is his name. A most cultured bloke, terrifically interested in newspapers and journalists. He's navigator in the plane the Air Commodore boss has to tootle round. We had some great discussions with Reg who is very keen to get into politics (he was a

Melbourne barrister) and doesn't know how to do it via the Liberal Party or Labor—over half a bottle of Black and White (Scotch). I had three—long ones in iced water—they were very nice.

I haven't spent any money much beyond what I pay for meals—only on chewing gum. I'm a great gum fan now. However, I did draw some pay. Because old John Harrison is honorary commission and can't and he has been buying all the things around the place, boots, bags, shirts, pants, singlets, towels etc. He owes me £5 Australian and 40 pesos. He will give me a cheque in Townsville on the way down.

That's about all I think. Look after the old man of the sea, and see if he chortles when you read that out. As for you, buy up lots of slacks and things (what color are they?). How's the old tummy. Sounds as though it must be just about back to normal. Notice once again how I'm keeping off what I generally talk about at this stage. No, it isn't the Filipino girls. I can't understand how the Yanks can go for them, although some have beautiful bodies. Gosh, am I sick of American accents. It's undoubtedly the worst language in the world. I realise I haven't told you much about this place but there are lots of restrictions. Sorry Broggo seems to think my movements are a sort of super military secret but I think you'll be able to follow me round.

Lots and lots and lots of love to/you both,/Your Tip.

Reg Smithers] Sir Reginald Smithers (1903–94), judge of the Victorian Supreme Court   Woolcott] Alexander Woollcott (1887–1943), American critic and essayist   *Wings*] Tipping was writing for this RAAF journal   Broggo] Stanley Brogden (b. 1913), editor of *Wings*, and author of a history of Australian aviation   Stillwell] Joseph Warren Stilwell (1883–1946), US commander of the American and Chinese troops in the China, Burma, India theatre of wartime operations   Kenney] George C. Kenney (1889–1977), US air force commander who took up his appointment with Douglas MacArthur in Australia in August 1942   MacArthur] Douglas MacArthur (1880–1964), US general who in April 1942 was appointed Supreme Commander of the South West Pacific Area   General Arnold] Henry H. 'Hap' Arnold (1886–1956), a member of the US Joint Chiefs of Staff and Allied Combined Chiefs of Staff throughout the war   child of the century] the Tippings' eldest son Paul, b. 1945   the Embassy] Melbourne nightclub   Lachie McDonald] the London *Daily Mail*'s Pacific War correspondent   Jack Percival] *Sydney Morning Herald* war correspondent   also at Ballarat] invalided out of the AIF, Tipping was sent to the same hospital in Ballarat, Victoria, as the Marines who had been at Guadalcanal   McDonell] Wing Cdr Leo McDonell, director of RAAF public relations   Chinese pal Eddie Tseng] correspondent for the *Chungking Daily*   Gough Whitlam] see Letter 183   Hermes] University of Sydney student magazine   MUM] *Melbourne University Magazine*, co-edited in 1940 by Marjorie McCredie, later Marjorie Tipping   Coward] Noël Coward (1899–1973), English actor, dramatist and composer

PAUL HASLUCK

Before commencing a successful political career in which he held senior Cabinet portfolios, Paul Meernaa Caedwalla Hasluck (1905–1993) was a diplomat in the Department of External Affairs. In 1945 he travelled to England as a delegate to the Executive Committee of the Preparatory Commission of the United Nations Organization meeting in London, a city dulled and wearied by the long years of war.

149. To Alexandra Hasluck, 15 August [1945]

Darling Alix,

I wrote one double letter (two airmail letters in series) just after my arrival and, as our committee meets tomorrow, I am scribbling a few more lines before we become immersed in affairs. Today has been declared a general day of rejoicing at the end of the war. Renouf and I started out fairly early to go to the office but were caught up in the crowd waiting to see the King drive to the opening of Parliament and perforce had to stand with the crowd in the drizzling rain for about three quarters of an hour as it was impossible to get through the barriers. We saw nothing, for the throng was really enormous but did our bit of celebrating by hoisting to our shoulders an enthusiastic little WAAF who happened to be standing alongside us with her father. She had a good view and, I suppose, a comely pink cheeked girl of 18 or so, weighing less than six stone, is just as good to wave in the air by way of celebration as a coloured flag or a bunch of streamers. Daddy and daughter thanked us most courteously and we went on to the office. The crowd in London today is thick. There is some singing, mostly rather flat, and some clattering of mechanical noise-making devices, but I am still struck by the joylessness and lack of high spirits of these people. They fire off crackers occasionally and sometimes shout and cheer but there is no animation—animation is the word, for it evokes the idea of "animal" and it is lusty animal spirits that these people lack. They mostly trudge around waiting for someone else to do something extraordinary or for someone important to drive by so that they can rush to look at him and then congratulate themselves on having seen what no-one else has seen.

Our committee seems likely to get away to a fairly slow start and things may be a bit difficult at first, without a great deal of help at this end but we shall manage. I feel a bit homesick at the moment; first, because my tummy is not good (just the usual) and, second and more important, because today of all days is the one I should like to spend at home, with the people I love, celebrating the victory with the people to whom it means the same as it means to me. Such days, spent in foreign countries, make one feel more a stranger than ever, more an Australian than ever.

Give my love to all, particularly dear Rollo and dear Nicky. Goodnight sweet girl/Paul

Darling, I had better wish you a happy birthday in each letter now, hoping that one arrives at the right time.

Renouf] Alan Philip Renouf (b. 1919), Australian diplomat and later Secretary, Department of Foreign Affairs, Canberra, 1974–77   Rollo, Nicky] Rollo John Darker Hasluck (1941–73) and Nicholas Paul Hasluck (b. 1942), the sons of Paul and Alexandra Hasluck

May Sands

In Australia, as in so many countries, the vagaries of war played cruel tricks. Writing from Melbourne in 1945, Mrs May Sands (1888–1972) talked to her son George, 'missing in action', of her hopes for his return and of the progress of family life and affairs. In January 1946 she received official notification that he had died in action on 1 March 1942.

150. To George Sands, 2 October 1945

Dear George

I am writing these few lines to you hoping they find you well, as this leaves us all well at home.

Phil is in Borneo now & he is expecting to be home in a few weeks time now & I will be pleased to have him home again & as for yourself, well George nobody will ever know how pleased I will be to see you home again & thank goodness your time will be up in the Navy & we will all be happy again. I have a great surprise for you. Albie is married & he & his wife are still living with me waiting for yourself & Phil to come home to me again & then they are going to take a house on their own.

Dorrie has three children now. As you know, there is Raymond George 6 years last June 7 Lorraine May 3 years last March as you know & since then she has had another boy Gary Philip & he is 6 months old & they are three beautiful children. I wish you could hear them pray for your safe return every night & I can promise you a big surprise when you see them & I hope it wont be long now before I hear the good news that you have been found. George the suspense of waiting is awful, but it must be double hard for you poor chaps, but I thank God it is all over now & we are all looking forward to seeing you soon.

I forgot to mention that Albie's wife (Dot) is going to have a Baby & if it is a boy she is going to call him (George Christopher) they were married last Xmas.

The Dairy is much the same except for cream there is no cream now. That is a luxury. Phylis Nathan has got 2 children now. Christy died while a P.O.W. & Paddy & Midge & Samboy are all away at different places. Sammy is in New Britain & Midge is in Brisbane & Paddy is in Victoria somewhere.

Uncle Pat & Agnes are keeping well. Well George I think that is all for the present & still hoping to see you soon with love from all at home.

Your loving/Mother xxxxxxxxx

A. R. Nankervis, Royal Australian Navy

151. To May Sands, 1945

Dear Madam

Since the termination of hostilities in August 1945, an exhaustive investigation, which included enquiries made from repatriated Prisoners of War, has been conducted in an effort to obtain news of personnel who were Missing as the result of the sinking of H.M.A.S. "PERTH".

This investigation has now been completed and it is with deep regret I have to inform you that no hope can now be held that your son A/Stoker Petty Officer (temp.) Patrick George Thomas Sands, O.N. 19703, is still alive.

The evidence indicates that your son was in a portion of the ship which received a direct hit and there seems little doubt that he was killed at that time. After careful consideration, the Naval Board have reluctantly concluded that he was killed in action on 1st of March, 1942, and have accepted this date for official purposes.

The Minister for the Navy and the Naval Board can fully realise the grief this sad news will bring after many anxious months of waiting, and they desire me again to convey to you their sincere sympathy.

Yours faithfully/A.R. Nankervis/Secretary

Miles Franklin

A prolific correspondent, with a wide circle of friends, Franklin (1879–1954) wrote as readily on domestic affairs as on literary or political concerns.

152. To Winifred Stephensen, 11 February 1946

My dear Winnie

Alas, I have few recipes for jam as in all my family households the women came out of the Ark knowing all there was to know by constant practice and experiment and I took to it like a duckling on the home pond and it was in our heads—now all the heads but mine are dead and I'm forgetting.

We never made crab apple jelly because crab apples were fish I never saw till I went to USA. Of course you can't risk sugar in experiments these days but I shd think crab apple wd jell well being a barbarian fruit.

Normal jam-jellies are made by choosing fruit not too ripe and fresh off the tree. Boil till soft enough to strain first through a collander and then through cheesecloth.

Guava might be a model. For that we used to crush the fruit and to every four quarts of fruit add one pint of water, boil till soft, strain as above then add one pound of sugar to every pint of juice and it took only about 45 mins to jell when boiled.

For gooseberry jelly you do the same and put a cup of sugar to a cup of juice and it takes a long time to boil. You have to keep trying it with a bit of stuff on a plate in the wind to see when it is just right.

You would use all the fruit of crabapples—core and pith—as that helps to jell, but of course cleaned of whiskers or grubs or dust etc. You may need a little extra sugar for crabs and a lemon carefully skinned and cleaned of every particle of that bitter white pith but the pips left in will help with jelling.

Once upon a time there had to be brewer's crystals or pure cane sugar we thought beet sugar was no caste but living abroad I found out whole nations doing very well with the beet article who had never heard of cane sugar's superiority.

I so love making jam that I'd boil some in a top hat if I had no other way. I've just finished about 40 pots of fig. Friends who don't drink sugar in tea contributed sugar. I had to use some 'raw' sugar which gives a coarser flavor and makes my aristocratic Portugese figs taste like the common colored figs which are found in some of the bought preserve. Wish you were here and I'd give you some.

I had forgotten all about the MS at Mrs Lang's. Will go for it and answer your letter etc when I get it.

The crabapples won't wait so I get this off.

Love/

JOY HESTER

The writer Janine Burke has noted that the letters of the artist Joy Hester (1920–60) and her patron and friend Sunday Reed (1905–81) draw a picture of their life and times. On Hester's side, the letters cover 'flows and breaks in creativity, struggles with illness and poverty, losses and gains in love'. From the late 1940s Hester's life was shadowed by Hodgkin's disease. The account she gives of her first major treatment for her illness in Sydney in 1947 is, perhaps, an allegory of the modern age—vaguely sinister, threatening, uncertain.

153. To Sunday Reed, undated [May 1947]

DEAR SUN

I have been thinking of you. Last night Gray brought in a book of Spender's poetry or rather it was an early anthology of those boys, Auden etc. with a lot of Spender in it—seems quite odd to read them now—thinking of the time when we read Spender when a new poem of his came out, and how excited we were—Gray bought this book for 1/- at a funny little second hand book shop over here where I saw some books Nolan would like and when I'm out of this confounded place I'll go and have a look [at] what there [is] for him. It's quite a quaint old shop.

Had my gland taken out on Monday & they'll take the stitches out Friday. I had another sort of anaesthetic not ether, no lovely dreams. I was disappointed it just put me out of it and no sensations at all. Not even aware I was going to sleep. They are keeping me here for a week while they start me on the therapy ray treatment. They did not remove the lump in my throat, only took 1 gland from there. It hurt for a couple of days & made me feel sick but I had a terrible time today. I was taken into the "ray" room which looks something like a H.G. Wells picture. A huge wall that looks like a Nazi wireless wall & big things in the air like this [sketch] and this [sketch] quite terrifying and they lie you on a bed in this square padded room, lie you staring at all this apparatus in the air and a large sheet of black glass above you & a thing sticking onto your gland & weights on your head to stop movement & cover your head practically all of it with rubber & the stifling "cramped in" feeling & then they leave you in this room alone, shut a huge iron door behind you & "turn it on"— terrific buzzing & burring etc. lights & numbers jump up & down on the dial & you are supposed to stay there 11 minutes. Well, you know what I'm like in a square car, something I can move about in—I panic[k]ed, my heart beat like a threshing machine my throat seemed to nearly choke & I yelled my head off—at last after 4 minutes yelling they came & saved me (from myself) & I was booing & beside myself, & feeling very ashamed & I'll have to have 11 minutes of this a day ad infinitum or at least until something happens.

I'll be alright tommorrow I hope. I'll have to be. Because of the scene I only had 4 minutes today—God I have not been so frightened since I was a little girl alone in the dark. It was not exactly fear but a sort of panic caused by [the] thought of all the power of unknown things harnessed in that room—the final diagnosis has not come through yet of what is wrong with me. But meanwhile, & what ever it is, they can only reduce the glands by ray & they have to do that first. Apparently Littlejohn had mentioned Hodgkins Disease to them as both McCallum & Lovell said they agreed as far as they could go with Littlejohn that it was that but still they may find out that it's all due to tonsils or something equally silly. After all this I hope they do—It is the most perfect weather over here & would you believe it, it's too hot even in the hospital & hospitals are usually cold, even in summer.

I feel very lonely in here with things happening to me & seeing Gray for 1/2 hr each day & the long hospital nights with people groaning etc. (including me at times for my neck is sore still). So much has happened since we've been here that I've forgotten all Melbourne things except one or two personalities, everything else seems never to have existed—the mind is curious. How things can happen to it & we have little or no control over those things. The mind flips this way & that & the only thing we can partly control, & its remote control, is what happens to the things we think. Sages of the east, in fact the eastern mind, is of a much more advanced stage than us in this respect—& it seems not only the more intelligent ones but the masses too have this control. But we are too young, Australians I mean. We'll have to learn it.

Write and tell me what has happened to the firm and how you all are—What will John do?

I find it very hard to write a letter since I have been here. I find I have forgotten what I said in the last letter & forgive me if I say the same thing each time. In fact life seems to have been very disjointed & I seem to have been over conscious of physical things owing to this blasted treatment etc. I just started to write to you when I was whisked off for another "ray" treatment. I am not frightened now & I am going home from hospital for the weekend and I come in again for Monday & Tuesday & then get discharged & have to come back each day for ray treatment. It'll cost me 1/- a day in fares and God knows how long in time. I s'pose knowing how hospitals muck you round it'll be the best part of half a day.

Elizabeth Bay in the moonlight mist is like no place on earth, a bit of Capri, a bit of Sydney & mostly dreams. It's like visiting a dream coming in & interrupting from the outside. The other night it was bathed in a soft misty silver and the Chinese fishermen were mumbling in the dark below us and scraping their fish—there was an island shining like Tristan in the distance & lights looking starlike in the mist. I will go there again this weekend but I'm almost afraid to go. Surely it can't be really as lovely as it looked that night. I shall never go in the daytime for fear of destroying the unreality of it. I'm sure it must be plebian in the daylight. Sydney is a wonderful place at night. I would have loved you or Nolan to have seen Elizabeth Bay that night for it shone like Nolan's painting of Heide in the mist.

I have not done any more drawings as I have been in this death chamber where life stands still—even though I suppose some of the greatest human dramas are enacted in hospitals they seem devoid of all emotion & sterile in every way.

Thank Nolan very much for the paper which I received OK and was very glad to get it. You cannot buy any over here. Gray has been doing paintings on it as there is no board of any sort either.

It is very funny, our lives together because I get exhausted & have to lie down & cannot walk far at all these days before I have to rest. The business before I left Melbourne seems to have left me exhausted somewhere & then all this doctor business etc. so when I feel good oh Gray gets sick & visa versa but I think it is rather funny for us both to be together and somehow out of it all, we want it that way. When Gray gets a migraine I usually draw or write & when I feel exhausted he feels good & paints. It really works quite well as the kitchen is the only room light enough to work in & we couldn't both do things at the same time in that tiny little room.

At night when we open the back door there is a blaze of neons [that] smacks [you] in the face & silhouetting the only tree in the district & it's in our yard. [Sketch of Hester & Smith's home with yard and tree]. Our poor little leafless tree. That's just about the shape of the tree. Can't tell what sort it is until it gets leaves. In this little yard one feels as though one is in the centre of a huge metropolis like New York & [it] never fails to give me a shock.

I'll post you these poems written in hospital between pans & thermometers & nurses mucking around, so forgive them.

Love to you all & Heide must be looking wonderful if its nice autumn weather.

Did I tell you David Boyd has gone to Tahiti to go into partnership with a Tahitian (not native) potter or something?

Gray] Gray Smith (b. 1919), painter who married Joy Hester   Nolan] painter, later Sir Sidney Nolan (1917–92), in the 1940s a central figure in the life of Sunday Reed   the firm] the publishing firm of Reed & Harris, which had been run in partnership by Sunday Reed's husband John (1901–81) and Max Harris (1921–95)   Elizabeth Bay] inner Sydney suburb near Kings Cross where Hester and Gray Smith lived for a time at 61 Bayswater Road   Heide] home of Sunday and John Reed overlooking the Yarra River at Heidelberg, Victoria; the original house adjoins Heide Park and Art Gallery   Gray gets sick] Gray Smith suffered from grand mal epilepsy   David Boyd] Boyd (b. 1924), potter and painter, travelled to New Caledonia in 1947 with the writer Hugh Atkinson

FLORENCE JAMES

Florence James (1904–93) was the New Zealand-born collaborator with Dymphna Cusack (1902–81) on Come in Spinner, *first published in 1951 and winner of the 1948 Sydney* Daily Telegraph *competition. The book was largely written in Australia but work continued on it when James went to England in 1947. James and Cusack were part of Miles Franklin's large and cherished circle of correspondents.*

154. TO MILES FRANKLIN, 14 DECEMBER 1947

MILES DARLING,

Your letter dropped right into the middle of grinding out the extra Spinner wordage and cheered me along the way no end. "Miles can do 10,000 words in a day," I said sternly to myself and the typewriter, "why the hell can't you do a couple, you constipated pair." Well, for better or worse the extra wordage took wing to Nell last week and here I am with a couple of days to get off a few greetings. I'm afraid I've resorted to a round robin for general news, but I know friends would rather get a bit more in that form than a few extra words each. The account of the wedding was written as it was with a view to a very dear Aunt's susceptibilities. You will understand the lack of comment. Actually, I never cease to be surprised at the enthusiasm of all classes and the tremendous personal feeling it has inspired. I've listened in buses and the underground: I've talked to professional women and shop assistants, business men and the old gardener burning the leaves in our little park. And, every one of them, without a single exception, takes it as personally as though it was a wedding in their own family, with those of wider interests adding a foot-note to the effect that we'll show the world that England isn't falling apart yet whatever sort of mess we may be in financially, politically or any other way.

I had a letter from Mrs Ogden saying that she is sailing for sure on the 20th Dec. from Liverpool. I'm very glad for her as from the few letters that have passed between us I know she's had long enough away from her folk in Australia; I'd love to hear her reaction now that the longed for trip is over—and just whether the old country came up to the memories of her youth and the rosy glow of family affection that surrounded it.

No Miles, I'm not taking root here. I know more surely with every week that passes that my home is in Australia. Why, I can't sit down at the typewriter and write a story about anywhere else. My characters only have to open their mouths and no matter where they're supposed to have come from they speak like Australians. And I belong to the new world, right to my very marrow. Our antipodean point of view is peculiarly our own and it's not the slightest good trying to make other people understand it through statement or argument; the only way we can present it is artistically. And for that, the novel is the most satisfactory medium, because it is a popular imaginative art and if we are good enough artists we shall be able to give other people the means to understand us through our common humanity. I am sure this is all so clear to me because this is my second visit. On my first visit I was coming to the heart of culture straight from an ex-patriate education in an Australian University. And I was young too with plenty of respect for cultural authority. Well, now the position is reversed. It is true that here is the home of the culture of our race, but it must be looked at historically not absolutely. There's a wealth of museum culture here, old customs, old traditions and academic and popular roots going deep. But to my southern eye, England badly needs a blood transfusion from the New World. We have as good writers, as good painters & as good dramatists if only they had a theatre,—I do not know enough of music to include that—and they're doing so much fresher work than the work done here on the whole. And now that this paper shortage has hit the great publishing capital of the world, there is little experimental work coming out of the presses. Publishers are playing safe with their precious paper and filling the shops with reprints, anthologies and new books by established names.

I haven't been on your quest to Australia House yet, because I haven't been in the city since I received your letter; but I have an introduction to the manager of Shakespeare Head (Aust. variety) here and I shall go to Aust. House and to him in pursuit of the same information for you as soon as Christmas is over. The children break up from 16th to 6th of Jan. which will tear me away from the typewriter, so we'll go out on our quest for you. I'm so glad you got at least 50 pounds from the Newcastle paper—but my God that's only a beginning for a book by Miles Franklin. Who is going to publish it?

I did drink out of your Waratah Cup, but I remember now that I didn't inscribe the book so I'm surely coming back to do that! May be next year, there is nothing like setting one's heart and mind on a thing to bring it off. The children are as keen as I am and I'm going to keep them that way so that they get the utmost of England but still have their roots in Australia. I'm afraid this is the limit of the half oz. allowed. Christmas greetings & love from us all—Florence

Many thanks for your thought of us with parcels, but it is fine we have friends sending to us and we'd much rather you went where there are no other Australian contacts.

Happy Christmas from us all—Darling dearest—from Joy, Fran & Tess.

the wedding] HRH Princess Elizabeth (later Elizabeth II) had married Prince Philip, Duke of Edinburgh, on 20 November 1947   Waratah Cup] in 1940, the botanist Richard Baker (1854–1941) had given Miles Franklin a cup and saucer set with a waratah design. Tea was served from this set to favoured guests who were also invited to sign a red-covered album originally presented to Franklin by the Sydney feminist Rose Scott (1847–1925) in August 1902

Vida Goldstein

Vida Goldstein (1869–1949) grew up in Melbourne and was active in the movement for women's suffrage from 1899. She was a witty and accomplished public speaker and a role model for younger feminists, including Miles Franklin. Goldstein's pacifism and her commitment to an international sisterhood developed during the First World War are seen as strongly as ever in this letter written in the shadow of atomic warfare.

155. To Miles Franklin, 22 December 1947

My very dear Stella—

Here I am bobbing up at the last lap, as usual, to send you the season's greetings, & what I find most useful in the kitchen. White dishcloths always get such an abominable colour, so I make them of coloured cotton; they are satisfactory and durable. I would draw your attention to the stamp on the envelope that carries this letter, the twopenny one I mean, with the head of George V. It was to have taken one of the many letters I have *intended* writing you through the years. I am sorry my friends have to take my love for granted; they get mighty little proof of it. Well what do you think of our postwar world? Doesn't Hitler seem to have won the war? He said something to the effect that if he didn't win it, he would bring civilisation down with him. As you know I have not a fraction of sex antagonism in me, but one is almost driven to think that men are absolutely unfit to govern. They seem incapable of thinking & acting on other than belligerent lines. War, war, war—either fighting wars or trade wars. Humanity their last consideration. The Atomic Bomb doesn't kill off enough human beings quickly enough, so now they turn their attention to bacteria to accomplish their devilish ends.

But what about women also? I feel they, too, have failed humanity in 2 world wars. They proved their ability to help their country in a time of national crisis, but have done nothing to help prevent crises recurring. Where are the women's demands & organisations for a practical humanitarian programme, a 'fighting' programme, to make the world a fit place to live in? I marvel at the silence & inaction of women. Why don't they rise & war against war, call it by its right name, *mass murder*, strip it of its 'glory', expose the vice, the political & economic & financial corruption that go with it; and above all the trade policies which make war inevitable? Sometimes I wish I were 30 years younger, & could have a say & do again on behalf of the common people!

LOTS OF LOVE FROM/VIDA

DAVID MARTIN

Hungarian-born writer David Martin (1915–97), the former Ludwig Detsinyi, visited Australia in 1949 and decided to remain. Not long afterwards, he entered the circle of Miles Franklin's 'Congenials', as she called her correspondents, and began to test his European impressions of a new country against the values and perceptions of a native-born Australian.

156. TO MILES FRANKLIN, UNDATED [1950]

DEAR MILES

I owe myself a letter to you. I was in town some ten days ago but too rushed to go out to Carlton. There was a festival of art for Peace in which I had the honour to participate in a humble way. Time will be when Peace will be taken for granted.

Out here in the bush, summer has arrived. I am still astonished every day at the luminous quality of an Australian summer day: there is more light in the sky than in the Mediterranean countries, though the sky somehow is paler. Richenda thinks the bush is full of grandeur while England is sweet and lovely in a more domestic way. to me the bush seems not 'grand' but essentially homely. Why is it that Australia has not fame as one of the world's most beautiful continents and countries? You see, I am beginning to develop the right instincts …

Spiegel has been finished some little time ago: it is a poem of about 1,900 lines and I am pleased with it. 'The Stones of Bombay' was published in London on the 20th and the first reviews are beginning to trickle in. Not discouraging, so far. I shall send you a copy when it arrives here. Though, I am sure, you will probably feel that as a novelist I am missing my métier. I am actually thinking of a little novel about Putty and Singleton to occupy me for the next few months. But I don't know if anything will come of it.

I think I wrote to you that we had been offered a flat in Melb. for the next six months, but nothing quite firm has yet come through. The idea is quite attractive though we shall leave a piece of our hearts (that's a teutonism) in the bush. It is said that if one does not leave Australia within the first two years of one's arrival, one is likely to remain here for good. Our two years are fast running out. Gradually I am changing and correcting my impression about this country. I think Australia can learn almost nothing from the old world. Her contribution will be completely her own. Perhaps the time is not so far off when Australians will realise that they can and must look only to themselves. Of all the British nations the Australian is the one to develop along lines most its own. In a few generations, when people will say 'Australian' they will (I hope) think of something and someone with such marked and specific characteristics as distinguish a Greek from an Irishman.

What stands out as the basic Australian characteristic? I suppose a certain and typical kind of courage—guts. And it is an unproblematical, cheerful courage—so people think it's dumb. But it is merely unselfconsciousness. 'Culture' and self-consciousness have always gone together in the old world, but need it follow that it must be in the new one, too? Courage is, after all, the basic quality: greater than love or intelligence, for with courage all others can be gained and, without it, all others are quite barren. While that is there, everything is possible. Then there is the ability to see things as they are. That is an ability which comes out in the naming of objects. 'Swampy Creek' 'Bacon and Eggs' (a bush flower, as you know). Most unromantic but the heart of the matter is in it. Just add to it the inevitably growing weight of corporate experience and you get something new and solid. Aussies don't have to comfort themselves with pretty names.

As long as Americanisation can be resisted! That curse of the western world in this century! Or rather, as long as we can have ice-boxes without the ice-box mentality! I think that is possible, because Australians, more than the English, 'can't be bothered' with sweating for their comfort—they like to take it where they can find it which is more human. A great pity that the Government is satisfied with being an American camp-follower. But that does not penetrate deeply. The blunt refusal of young Australia to be rail-roaded, black-mailed and panicked into uniform is a healthy sign. Only the decadents look upon it as decadence. (By the way, I was surprised by your use of the term 'draft-evader' in a recent epistle. Explain, please: what did *you* mean? is this a sound Australicism that I have missed or merely a jingoistic term out of the paper armoury of Norman Lindsay? It smells of 1917: but I daresay in 1917 the draft evaders had often more courage than the draft enthusiast. (As to myself, I am occupied with trying to be an overdraft-evader).

As the Country circulation library does not send out fiction, I have been thrown back on biographies and factual works for the last 15 months, and am glad of it. Novel writing is one thing, novel reading another. Jan is developing a taste both for words and for reading. But there seem to be not many interesting books for clever young chaps of 6½. The good ones cater for those from nine years on. Richenda's school term is coming to an end. It has been a lot of sweat and concentration for her, but the results are very good. Of course, out of ten kids there will always be some two or three duds. It seems to me that the bright kids are also the happy kids.

Which is a good note on which to end this. We all hope that you are well and in good spirits. The holidays are coming and we only wish we could have you here for a bit. But, believe me, our place is *too* b----- rough. We're broiling under the corrugated. It is an indication of Putty's interest in education.

Yours,/David

Richenda] David Martin's wife, née Powell, a school teacher and writer   Spiegel] *Spiegel the Cat*, published in 1961   Putty] New South Wales country town where the Martins first lived in Australia. Later they moved to the outer Melbourne suburb of Boronia and finally to Beechworth in rural Victoria Jan] David Martin's son

KEITH MURDOCH

A powerful figure in the Australian newspaper world, Sir Keith Murdoch (1885–1952) began his career in journalism at the Melbourne Age. *He later worked in London and the United States. His controversial despatches from Gallipoli brought him into promi- nence, and in 1920 he was appointed managing editor of the Melbourne* Herald. *Always a newspaperman as well as a magnate, he hired young reporters himself, invited them to his house and kept a paternal eye on their progress. One of the most gifted was E.W. (Bill) Tipping (see Letter 148), who took up a Nieman Fellowship in journalism at Harvard with Murdoch's encouragement.*

157. TO E.W. TIPPING, 15 JANUARY 1952

Dear Bill Tipping,

Your splendid letter of 12 December has had the appropriate circulation in the office. I find that most of the boys know about your activities and are watching them with quite an enthusiasm.

I must get off a quick reply to you. I have let much time pass before getting down to this particular lot of correspondence.

It is good news indeed that you are comfortable; that your family is happy and well; that Mrs. Tipping is finding so much interest in life; that she has got an appropriate little job; and above all that you yourself are acquiring so much first-class experience and knowledge.

The bad spot is, of course, the little boy. I had heard all about this and Lady Murdoch is sorry also and we sympathize with you all in your anxieties and fears.

We have had deep anxieties in our family, including one desperate illness of a child. But we have got through and are still united. I fear, however, that parents must regard fami- lies as not easy to rear and "count their blessings" as the old-fashioned people used to say. My mother, in the days when children had many diseases to get through, lost three fine boys; two had grown to manhood. But she found full happiness in the remainder of them.

It is certainly all right by us that you should write over there and we would, in fact, approve of all you are doing and give you a full-hearted blessing.

Occasionally you should manage something for us. I am out of touch at the moment as to whether you have done something or are going to do something. We are always glad to hear from you and would be pleased to receive an occasional bit of writing.

Rupert came home for his vacation. He got a concession fare—very cheap! So, he spent four weeks with us here and on Friday set off again for Oxford where he will arrive to-day. He is getting through his examinations with great torture of mind. His interests are so scattered and he has been elected to the executive of the Oxford University Labour Party and is Associate Editor of its journal! He talks with many young friends, reads a diversified lot of stuff and on the whole I have cause to be proud and thankful about it.

ALL GOOD WISHES, BILL./YOURS SINCERELY,/KEITH MURDOCH

the little boy] refers to the illness of one of Tipping's sons   Rupert] (Keith) Rupert Murdoch (b. 1931), whose present media holdings began with his inheritance of the *Adelaide News*, his father having retained few *Herald* shares and having left a comparatively small estate

HILDA DALE

Hilda Esson (1887–1953), widow of playwright Louis Esson, married John Dale in March 1951. Lovers for many years, they could not marry until Esson's death in 1948 was followed by Dale's divorce. Dale was health officer to the City of Melbourne and Hilda one of his medical graduate assistants. The Dales, then in their sixties, were travelling in Europe when Dale was killed and Hilda injured in a car crash in Venice, after only six months of marriage.

158. To KATHARINE SUSANNAH PRICHARD, 30 DECEMBER 1952

DARLING,

I was desolate when I rang on Sunday, and found you had flown. I hadn't rung before as I didn't want to disturb your family party, and also because I was helpless with grief and loneliness. It is the first Xmas for twenty-five years without John, and I had dinner with Viva in the room that echoed last to the laughter and triumph of our wedding party. John was so excited, so proud, so happy; and that last night he seemed to be hiding in the shadows, heart-broken and alone, so that I could barely move or breathe with the pain of it all. As I begin to come to life, it is quite intolerable and often I blame myself for being so heartless as to be alive when he, who loved the sun and the wind and the song of birds—a magpie greeted me heartbreakingly one morning,—is blind and deaf and condemned to eternal darkness. All my control and philosophy seem to be the most futile subterfuge and hypocrisy, and there will always be times when I can't bear it at all. Then I tell myself that I am proud and blest beyond words. But it is all so vivid, it is cruel! Really, I have never left Venice and we're standing by the Grand Canal and one hand tucks mine under his arm, and with the other he throws kisses to the young moon—as he always did when he was away from me, so that I should feel them floating down to me when I looked at her. And now the treacherous moon has taken him from me—The Gods were jealous!

We always—or for some years—went camping in the holidays by a river where he fished, and we bathed naked, rejoicing in each other. On our honeymoon we had supper under a great tree by the gleaming river in the moonlight, with dark mountains in the distance and great stars, and the light almost as bright as day. The thousands of days and nights pass before me like a pageant, and every word, every movement, every tiny inch of him lives again in my ears, under my tender hands—so dear so familiar, so eternally with me that I seem to lose all touch with the world, and lie cold and lifeless, scarcely breathing. But you know all this. It just helps a little to tell you because there is absolutely no one to talk to. Grief is a private thing—it isn't fair to expect anyone to share it. Your love and understanding comfort me, and your wisdom and courage sustain me and help me to look forward to a future infinitely rich in memories, sweet and bitter, but to be lived out till the end as worthily as possible.

I am really better physically. My last X-rays were re-assuring and the doctor who helped me through my long illness says that I can forget about the old trouble. When I demurred he said 'No—there is no easy way out for you; but you will go on and face things and be active and interested again.' and so on. I don't want to, but personal sorrow seems a small thing with so much in the world so infinitely more important.

Helen came to see me—very charming, and most interesting and enthusiastic about her trip. The Chinese spared no effort to tell them of all their activities, education, music, literature, drama and the enthusiasm of the people in their new life. She is very bright and working hard, and Longman's are to publish a social history of Australia that she is writing for children of from 12–14 years old. She teaches part-time and does research at the Mitchell Library. Nettie is coming to see me on Thursday. She is doing the O'Dowd memoir. Bernard had promised it to Victor Kennedy altho' Nettie had collected a great deal of material which she generously handed over. Then he died about a year ago, and after some hesitation she agreed to do it. I really do admire their hard work and enthusiasm—envy it too, I'm afraid. I feel so empty and futile at present.

Bee tells me you will be away for a month. Please take things as quietly as possible. I'm very anxious about you—I'm wondering if perhaps, after so many plans for it, I might go over to you next Spring. John and I looked forward so much to seeing you at Greenmount, and wandering through the places in the West that he had loved.

I am still terribly weak and exhausted, can only walk about for at most ten minutes then the pain forces me to rest again; but it is less severe, and I feel stronger and at most times calmer, and even begin to make plans. The worst of all is the feeling of utter incompetence and disinclination to make any effort, that I can't talk over with him even if he didn't particularly approve. His strength supported me for so long—I thought I was independent and did everything myself; but I realise now what it was to have his wise and loving help. My darling—be careful of yourself. You are so infinitely precious.

ALL MY LOVE, HILDA

Viva] Hilda's sister Vivienne   Helen] Helen Palmer, daughter of Vance and Nettie Palmer

KATHARINE SUSANNAH PRICHARD

Katharine Susannah Prichard (1883–1969) was the author of a stream of novels, plays and stories including Coonardoo *(1929). From her home in Western Australia and while travelling, she was another who enjoyed a correspondence with Miles Franklin. Prichard's son, Ric Throssell, has noted that while his mother valued the friendship, admiring Franklin's grit and determination and the wry cynicism with which she saw herself and the people about her, he thought they had little in common apart from 'temper democratic, bias Australian'.*

159. TO MILES FRANKLIN, 2 DECEMBER 1953

MILES DARLING

Safely arrived, & chewing over my lovely time with you! Such a treat just to hear you talk. I do love the wit & play of your so original mind. Nobody makes me laugh so much. And I've had Dodie & Ric chortling over some of your bits & pieces—so delightfully Miles, gay, intrepid & unique!

Only hope you weren't too tired by my being there, & having things to do about meals—and so on. Hate to think of having impeded your work, or destrained on your time. Although, those days with you will always be a precious memory for me.

Karen was rejoiced with her cake—& is making a drawing for you to say thank you: she had to go off to school this morning before it was quite finished—and made me promise not to post my letters until her work of art is finished. There's something quite fey about the little person. Whatever happens, I feel sure she'll be something quite unusual.

Quite warm here to-day, which pleases me; feel as if I'd never get this last winter out of my bones. Do wish you cd have come for a visit while I'm in Canberra. The place itself is such a smug, un-Australian version of all that it ought to be. Only the blue divine mountains, & the gums still undisturbed on Mt Ainslie behind us, assuring me that this is still Australia. Out & away from the neat suburbs & stucco of official buildings there remain the rounded sunburnt hills, & the Molonglo—by its very name, though shrouded in willows, reminds us of the earth and a tradition deeper than the fantasy of the federal city here. The earth & the tradition are part of us, belong, at least—though filched from the aborigines.

Love to you—my dear, incomparable Miles—and thank you again for so much stimulus—and the happiness of being with you.

KATHARINE

The little bottle of skin perfume is to refresh you on hot days—& make you think of me. K.S.

Safely arrived] Prichard had arrived in Canberra to stay with her son and his family for Christmas, a brief respite in the course of a libel case she was fighting against the *Sydney Morning Herald* and federal parliamentarian W.C. Wentworth   Dodie & Ric] Dorothy, Prichard's daughter-in-law, and Ric Throssell (b. 1922), a noted playwright and at that time a member of the Department of External Affairs Karen] Prichard's granddaughter

Hugh McCrae

Although Hugh McCrae (1876–1958) is best known as a lyric poet he is also remembered for the distinctively handwritten and illustrated letters which his friends cherished for their visual as well as verbal artistry. His letters to his sister Helen reflect his strong family ties and depth of feeling as well as his whimsical comic sense. Written when his health was failing, this letter mourns his wife Nancy and meditates on his own death as well as hers.

160. To Helen McCrae, *c.* 1954

nice }
NICE }
NICE}
Helen!!!!

"Mick *jacet*" … your conclusions, on the deaths of people we've known, quickened me; and, looking at my marriage certificate, I saw that, of six signatories, I am the solitary one left … George, Gussie, Cecil, Nancy, Herbert Taylor; all of 'em safely stowed. The joke is on me (by myself) a 'oldin' of me breaf wiv bofe 'ands, on a ship, sinkin'—an' nuffin to do but wait, 'n' wait 'n' wait 'n' wait 'n' WAIT.

Death's good medicine: it cures every pain, mental and physical … besides, we have the anticipation of being "stiffs" at God's Circus in a row. Everybiddy invited. The McCraes, the Joshuas, the Ow!thwaites, the Hellikers, the Blighs, the Sandringham Shark's Own Self … even the little Martins … *though far away from you* (I shan't say in the Pit! but, anyhow, in a place they deserve).

Becos people, down to their roots, don't accredit God, is a chief reason why they balk and skip at every tombstone by the road.

God's jolly. God likes us, too, to be jolly: to laugh, to stretch our legs, to run without hitches, manifesting the Toy-Master and giving him joy of his skill.

"He went up with a Merry Noise!" (God did) So shall I—if I'm sure I shan't fall; I shan't come down again. People aren't happy (I found this through experiment) unless they belong to the Club of God … lots of whom you'd never guess to be members by their clothes or surroundings: but, you find it in their minds.

Old women (like Mrs M …) with church-bells in their ears, are only pseudo-elect. Smell their eau-de-Cologne, on Sundays; and watch 'em elevate their noses while they make wide sweeps round the Joneses, going (if the Mrs M's only knew) with invisible Jesus, up the same steps. It's their SINS and SOULS they care about—the hierarchy of heaven interests them in no way except as a wash-house, to job-wash linen they have dirtied all their lives.

Vive Dieu!

"For He's a jolly good fellow!" and a cunning one, too.

I remember Father Taylor's ecclesiastical gymnasium; its bruised windows, its coconut matting; and miserable groans of constipated Christians squeezing out thrippenny-bits, one at a time.

God strolls out by the vestry-door, the moment the *cretins* leak in: and I've met him, since I grew up, not always in expected places; but, *mostly*, where there's lots of sin. *I want to die.* I'm in a hurry to jump into the next paddock, as we used to jump into the Hamilton's one, when we were young, to gather "Gentle Annies" . . . presage of Nancy, my darling, in the shape of a flower I've never seen since.

Only one thing that stops me from cheerfully "seeking my own salvation" (SHAK.) is terror of Death—and of M.I.O. . . . the latter, in case she might be encouraged to follow, too closely after. God helps me every minute. If I want a necessary gadget at

a hopeless moment, it always $\begin{cases} un\text{miraculously} \\ \text{naturally appears.} \end{cases}$

Item: While I write "God", I'm not taking his pen-name in vain. I choose it, becos it has only 3 letters to it; needs less ink; is spoken at a breath . . . and, though a same word, doesn't signify Old Testament Jealousy who "visits the sins" etc. *My* God is a very great and true God, revealing himself, every day.

I've seen Nancy twice since she died; both times while I wasn't thinking of her. She appears in peoples' faces, superimposed; *actually*.

It first happened, while I was one night, alone, with Mrs Crookston, N's particular friend. We had stopped talking; and Zoe, seated on a sofa, opposite, had her eyes closed, when her countenance became Nancy's all over. The change lasted a moment; but, in that moment, she had beamed towards me, and I went home happier than I had ever thought to be.

On another occasion, visiting Smee at 7 o'clock one evening, I asked where my favouritest grandchild, Margaret was? Smee said she had a headache and was in bed on the sleep-out: but that I might see her if I didn't stay too long. The sleep-out was in darkness, and, although I had no prevision, beams of light rayed out from Margaret's (Nancy's) face; and both, radiantly excited, waved hands to me. I kissed them, together; and presently only Margaret remained. These happenings show that Nancy, without collaboration on my part, has succeeded in getting through to me, so that I'm assured now that everybody's life continues in another world. I'm a nonentity and don't count: but most *great* men have been sharply aware of God. It puzzles me how the ruck of people can't believe in Him, by Him I don't mean the sheep-faced gentleman with a prize beard & a passionate desire for the smell of burnt offerings—but an indescribable element (beyond our power of understanding) creator of the world, of all beauty and some ugliness: the ugliness not fixed but in a state of evolution . . . creator of man, too; think of *his* architecture; of woman; think of *her* architecture . . . the baits used to induce us to propagate children: without which no children should ever have been.

Dunderheads, confused, think they, as well as the sun, moon, wind, rain, flowers, are products of accident. The seasons? I feel a bewitchment every time I watch a star.

Nancy teaches me. She is closer to me in this house, called after her name, than anywhere in her life-time.

Mendelssohn, or it might have been Haydn, dedicated his musick to God.

Your exquisitely written caricature of Vicky leaning out of "the gold bar of Heaven" across the stomach of Albert the Good has brought this sermon on your head: a sermon, sensible—not mad.

LOVE TO YOU ALWAYS,/HUGH

Next week—my latest marital adventure: not meaning a 3rd!

'Mick *jacet*': *hic iacet*] here lies, the traditional tombstone inscription   George, Gussie] McCrae's parents, his sister Helen, his brother Cecil, his wife Nancy and the Reverend Herbert Taylor, Vicar of Christ Church Hawthorn, where McCrae was married   The McCraes, the Joshuas] family and friends present at his wedding   Smee and Margaret] McCrae's daughter Georgiana Rose and his granddaughter Margaret

CYNTHIA NOLAN

Cynthia Nolan (1913–76), sister of art patron and collector John Reed, published two novels before her marriage to painter Sidney Nolan in 1948; later she published another novel and several travel books. She had connections with various groups of writers and artists in 1940s Australia: many of these were to leave for Europe in the 1950s. Pat Flower and her husband Cedric wrote film scripts and television plays. In 1956 the Nolans rented a house on the Greek island of Hydra, where writers George Johnston and Charmian Clift were living (see Letter 175). The Flowers had left Hydra late in 1955.

161. TO PAT FLOWER, MARCH/APRIL (?) 1956

MY DEAR PAT,

So delighted to hear all goes well and you are both content to be back. I always fear a moment of revulsion, but you seem to have avoided this. No wonder you both loathed Greece, I understand this completely. Its the most difficult country and the people the strangest to adjust to of any I've been in. Apart from this your little anxiety dear was enough to turn your stomach what utter misery. And living with other people is a penance a mortification, an impossibility. Then Hydra in summer, full of myths I could never raise more than a yawn over, preferring my case histories contemporary, with the name of Brown. Nor do I swoon over shards, pieces or pillars. Nor readily accept fleas, lice and bugs. But it is winter and we live in this great house that stands alone, rising three stories out of the bare hill behind Carmini. Everything is charming, the beds heavenly comfort, a puller when one bothers to pump water, a basin and taps here in my bedroom, from every window scenes from some book of hours, eight great terraces, wild with olives and almond trees (now in bloom) with plate cacti, blue hyacinth, single stock, geraniums, cyclamine, white daisies and scarlet poppies. All surrounded by great thirty foot high stone walls. Its dead quiet. Only sometimes in the evening goat bells, or the sound of a distant mouth organ. We have had, true, the tail end of some of the blizzards, but many many days to sit outside in, and two last week when I sunbathed naked. You know what this means after London also I regret to admit it, but after all the small rooms, the discomfort, the other peoples houses, the stove by the la and the bath under the bed, I am happy, content, relaxed, at home as I haven't been since eighteen. There is no hope. I thought I'd beaten all that, its just waiting till I had a taste to stick out its tongue. Unworthy am I, and thats the way I am. As to local food, its quite all right now, fresh fish of several varieties every night except storm times, good salads as they come round, lamb that melts. The citrus better than I've had anywhere, extraordinary. I tell you I like it all, the white two story houses that have a blue haze for that twenty evening minutes, the kites that jerk up into the blue and white sky, the brilliant mainland you can touch across the satin ribbon blue, or pewter or yes wine red Aegean, the naked mountains that glow and stand up like cardboard cut out against a primrose cloud. Sorry, I am in love again, besotted, swooning, unable to embrace enough. Every day my madness grows. It is true I have no ambition, I have always wanted to pull out, not to give it a go. Cities, unless one can live in sheltered luxury, disturb me. Walking along those crowded pavements, into those pushing shops. The noise of the gutters and horns, the smell of petrol and people, the anxiety on every face. J J J J J J J J J J J go my rhthms. Buses, undergrounds, smoke, voices. j j j j j j j j. But not S. who is a city man, stimulated, as one should be I'm sure, by all the sights and sounds, longing to get in, to compete, to give it a go. No matter how flyblown the cafe table, he will want to sit with me, for one or two or more hours, over some piece of some- thing, watching and thinking and perhaps expounding. I long to flee. So although he has enjoyed his bits of Greece (God and Delos singing out of the sea, Delos with its carven lions, frail pillars, and scent laden dew. We had the whole island entirely to ourselves). and finds the myths utterly fascinating, not to say hilarious, he would die of boredom if he was confined to any island, while I could spend my days within just such walls which would fill my hours with meditative scrapings and weedings, with all the great steps that have uncovered from their years old overgrowth, with creating a garden that would become one of the wonders of the world. And I mean this. Undoubtedly what talent and desire I have lies here. Such a garden is my thing. One over which I dwelt a lifetime, and which would take other lifetimes to grow entirely to perfection. Quoth the raven, not only nevermore but never, never, never. Little bits I'll do, scraps, a tree here or there—nothing. But I stand and contemplate and think what could go where, slowly putting the place together. Woniora Av of course one could only do so much with. But this place is something else.

As to the Johnstones. Charm is admirable truly. As her hour approaches I think some or most of the bitterness and frustration and anguish have gone. She swings along, shoulders back, great smile working, although I know she must be deadly tired, by now. I've seen thousands of pregnant women, and strong ones who delighted to be bearing a baby, but I can't remember one who bore herself with such verve, with such an air. I view her having it here with the local midwife with the greatest timidity. Fine, if all goes well. Or not all that fine, without any drug whatever. You know how mad she is on the Greek way of life—without I may say knowing a lot about it—and its been a joke to see her horror as more and more Greek dames shes met in shop or side street tell her not to worry, they will be along from the first pain, they will sit with her, and keep her company, throughout! Yes one feels this is as it should be, but we, want to never so much, can't act natural within another culture.

The Johnstones new house is the last bargain on Hydra, and really quite a dream. I expect they have told you of it. But whatever their usual exaggerations, this is tops. I fear George will bugger it as nearly as he can as I note his preparations with his treasures from the trunks—sets of prints beautifully framed by himself in black pas pt. etc. George and I have certain qualities in common, that he would not admit to. We both are in a way gregarious but detest most people. George more than I, dislikes, I would say, everyone outside his immediate family, and this in spite of wanting awfully to love the whole world and more so, have the whole world find him the greatest mate going. We both like to talk. And if we lived in the same house it would be a matter of who could get to the carving knife quickest. I can say this with you still understanding that I like George, hes good fun in short doses. I think he probably dislikes me intensely. Certainly we have often to maintain great control not to attack the other. I dont know but can guess what he has stopped himself from telling me. I know I have just managed not to say that the Sea and the Stone is the most revolting rehash of Steinbeck and Hemingway, and the Greek characters as unreal as Hemingways Spanish ones in For Whom the Bell Tolls, without the book having any of its merits. One doesn't care what is done in this way, its a good way to live and make a living, writing what one can sell well and decently and having a pleasant life. But I will not say what he wants to hear, that he is a brilliant writer. And if asked I will say that if he wants to write something a bit better he'll have to go to what he knows—Elwood, Melbourne, and the shoddy flats of third rate journalists, the newspaper rackets, the big time boys. Australia. And NOT be afraid of treading on the toes of some mate who will one day cut him in the Hotel Australia bar—and who really he hates like shit anyhow.

Well all this because there is, I suppose, a lot of writing talk in the air. The other couple, living in Lilys house, are irish writer and aus-jewish painter or anything you please (Nancy has infinite ability for making dough, she could I know take a restaurant or photography business and turn it over almost immediately, has done in the past). Anyhow, Patrick the husband is Protestant Irish, an orphan, educated at a school for distressed gentlefolk. He is I should think a good teacher—they have made a mint between them at british instit. abroad—but will kill himself, Nancy told me (I don't see any signs) if he doesn't write. He has been writing short stories for years on the side, I mean about six short stories and six articles, and one turned down novel. And not only will he not be the great writer he thinks he is, he wont even be a writer who will sell, unless he pulls his head in. I get frank even though I have the best intentions, because everyone gives everyone else their things to read and wants to know what they think (thank God there is nothing of mine or Mr Nolan would be passing that round) and each in turn says Wonderful out of one side of their mouths and Crap out the other. I got tight the other night and told Patrick his was one long whine, and complaining was good if you could do it like Faulkner, Dostoevski, Kafka, but a whine was neither good nor saleable. How can I get out of that one? When S. and I are sitting at a large table in one of the cafes and the others come in to join us I always notice a rush as they hasten to bring chairs and place them jammed tight around S. while I sit in lonely state with three quarters of the table to myself. As S. says, theyre in a panic. However we really all get on rather well. Its fine not having any more. Did you know that horror english painter Vere? Frightful trouble maker, almost managed to get S. and George at each others throats. And Carol I didn't go for really, the foreign accent and upturned eyes—a bit of a nuisance with men around. Sooner or later there would always be trouble where she was, as S. said, because thats what she wants.

I think I have said too much now. Love and to Cedric. S. gets madly homesick for Aus. I shall really wither if I get my roots pulled up much oftener. Hugs.

PS April.   Have left this open until now to give news of the baby. Jason arrived at 6 a.m. within three quarters of an hour and with the aid of Zoe and the midwife. The latter crooned over Charm. and rubbed her stomach with alcohol during the event, and gave her two tumblers full of ouzo after. The time must have been hell without any drug, nevertheless she is a damn lucky girl and I tell you I heave a great sigh of relief. Fortunately all this family seem so strong (spit spit). This way seems so much the best under the circumstances. Jason is very like Charm., same build, and big mouth and bone formation of face—but the longest fingers I've ever seen—what does this portend? and I'm not sure he isn't going to catch George's nose—George reports also, with what satisfaction you can imagine, that he has a large cock. Knowing what an adoring mama Charm. is I think she is now all pride in this third wonder. The poor girl has certainly had a bad time of resentment and rage behind her. George is absolutely thrilled. Shane so relieved it's not another girl . . . and Martin watching over his mother, sitting beside her all the first afternoon while G. was elsewhere, and reading five chapters of The Iliad without stop—aloud. The old crone—once procuress, remember, insisting on coming in the second day and spitting—and I mean spitting, three times first on Charm. and then on Jason. You can imagine this old nursies blood pressure.

We were terribly thrilled to hear your wonderful news Cedric! May it go on better and better. And that you both have a good flat quick. More and more good times and beautiful money! and quick building with your cottage at T. address is co Bank of NSW, Berkeley Sq., W1

LOVE C.

I find one can get as much of every kind of Barbital etc. at the chemist as one asks for!

S.] Sidney Nolan (see Letter 153)   Charm] Charmian Clift (1926–69), writer   George] George Johnston (1912–70), writer and husband of Charmian Clift   if he wants to write something a bit better ...] Johnston's best known work, *My Brother Jack* (1964), followed Cynthia Nolan's advice 'to go to what he knows'   Lily] Russian wife of Christian Heidsieck, potter   Nancy and Patrick] Australian Nancy Dignan and her Irish husband Patrick Greer   the baby] Jason Johnston, born April 1956   every kind of Barbital] in 1976 Cynthia Nolan killed herself with an overdose of barbiturates: Charmian Clift had done the same in 1969. Pat Flower took her own life in 1977.

V. Gordon Childe

When the Australian prehistorian Vere Gordon Childe (1892–1957) died in a fall in the Blue Mountains near Sydney in 1957, it was assumed he had met with an accident. In 1980, his colleagues at the Institute of Archaeology in the University of London released the text of a letter and an enclosure which Childe had prepared during his stay at the mountain resort of Katoomba. These were addressed to Professor W.F. Grimes (b. 1905) who succeeded Childe as director of the Institute. Many have accepted this statement as confirmation of Childe's suicide.

162. To William Grimes, 20 October 1957

Dear Grimes

The enclosed contains matter that may in time be of historical interest to the Institute. But now it may cause pain and even provoke libel actions. After ten years it will be less inflammable. So I earnestly request that it be deposited in the archives and be not opened till January 1968 supposing that year ever arrives.

Yours sincerely,/V. Gordon Childe.

The progress of medical science has burdened society with a horde of parasites—rentiers, pensioners and other retired persons whom society has to support and even to nurse. They exploit the youth which is expected to produce for them and even to tend them. While many are physically fit to work and some do, others are incapable of looking after themselves and have literally to be kept alive by the exertions of younger attendants who might be more profitably employed otherwise. And in so far as they do work, they block the way to promotion against younger and more efficient successors. For all in all persons over 65—there are of course numerous exceptions—are physically less capable than their juniors and psychologically far less alert and adaptable. Their reactions are slowed down; they can only gradually and reluctantly, if at all, adopt new habits and still more rarely assimilate fresh ideas. I am doubtful whether they can ever produce new ideas. Compulsory retirement from academic and judicial posts and from the civil services has of course done something to open the rewards of seniority to younger men, and has rescued students and subordinates from inefficient teachers and incompetent administrative chiefs. In British universities the survival of the old system during my lifetime has provided cautionary examples of distinguished professors mumbling lectures ten years out of date and wasting departmental funds on obsolete equipment. These instances probably outweigh better publicized cases of scientists and scholars who in their colleagues' opinion are 'forced to retire at the height of their powers'. But even when retired, their prestige may be such that they can hinder the spread of progressive ideas and blast the careers of innovators who tactlessly challenge theories and procedures that ten or fifteen years previously had been original and fruitful (I am thinking for instance of Arthur Evans).

In fact if the over-age put 'their knowledge, experience and skill at the service of society' as honorary officers or councillors of learned societies, public bodies, charitable institutions or political parties, they are liable to become a gerontocracy—the worst possible form of leadership. In a changing world their wisdom and maturity of judgement do not compensate for their engrained prejudices and stereotyped routines of behaviour. No doubt the over 65s are competent to carry out routine investigations and undertake compilations of information, and may be helped therein by their accumulated knowledge. Yet after 65 memory begins to fail, and even well-systematized information begins to leak away. My personal experience is confirmed by observations on senior colleagues. And new ideas, original combinations of old knowledge, come rarely if at all. Generally old authors go on repeating the same old theses, not always in better chosen language.

I have always considered that a sane society would disembarrass itself of such parasites by offering euthanasia as a crowning honour or even imposing it in bad cases, but certainly not condemning them to misery and starvation by inflation.

For myself I don't believe I can make further useful contributions to prehistory. I am beginning to forget what I labouriously learned—forget not only details (for these I never relied on memory), but even that there is something relevant to look up in my note-book. New ideas very rarely come my way. I see no prospect of settling the problems that interest me most—such as that of the 'Aryan cradle'—on the available data. In a few instances I actually fear that the balance of evidence is against theories that I have espoused or even in favour of those against which I am strongly biassed. Yet at the same time I suspect this fear may be due to an equally irrational desire to overcome my own prejudices. (In prehistory one has to make decisions on inadequate evidence, and, whenever I am faced with this necessity, I am conscious of such opposing tendencies.) I have no wish to hang on the fringe of learned societies or university institutions as a venerable counsellor whose authority may slow down progress. I have become too dependent on a lot of creature comforts—even luxuries—to carry through some kinds of work for which I may still be fitted; I just lack the will power to face the discomforts and anxieties of travel in the USSR or China. And in fact though I have never felt in better health, I do get seriously ill absurdly easily; every little cold in the head turns to bronchitis unless I take elaborate precautions and then I am just a burden on the community. I have never saved any money, and, if I had, inflation would have consumed my savings. On my pension I certainly could not maintain the standard without which life would seem to me intolerable and which may be really necessary to prevent me becoming a worse burden on society as an invalid. I have always intended to cease living before that happens.

The British prejudice against suicide is utterly irrational. To end his life deliberately is in fact something that distinguishes *Homo sapiens* from other animals even better than ceremonial burial of the dead. But I don't intend to hurt my friends by flouting that prejudice. An accident may easily and naturally befall me on a mountain cliff. I have revisited my native land and found I like Australian society much less than European without believing I can do anything to better it; for I have lost faith in all my old ideals. But I have enormously enjoyed revisiting the haunts of my boyhood, above all the Blue Mountains. I have answered to my own satisfaction questions that intrigued me then. Now I have seen the Australian spring; I have smelt the boronia, watched snakes and lizards, listened to the 'locusts'. There is nothing more I want to do here; nothing I feel I ought and could do. I hate the prospect of the summer, but I hate still more the fogs and snows of a British winter. Life ends best when one is happy and strong.

Colin Clark

Throughout a long and distinguished career, London-born economist Colin Clark (1905–89) was a strong voice in Australian economic and social policy. As Director of the Centre for Research in Agricultural Economics at Oxford, Clark maintained his interest in Australian affairs. Writing to his son Gregory, Clark commented on the Western Australian Rhodes Scholar (later Australian Prime Minister) Robert Hawke (b. 1929), whose thesis he had been asked to supervise.

163. To Gregory Clark, 25 November 1957

Dear Gregory,

Nick has heard that he can get permission to enter the 2nd year of the Engineering course in the University of Queensland, but he is having some difficulty in getting a passage, as the boats all seem to be full.

I must say that I think Hawke is showing some effrontery. He turned up in Oxford with an I-know-it-all-already attitude, and thought that if we just showed him one or two more tricks of the trade he could be a complete authority on wage fixing. We found, not only that he did not know any economics at all, but that he was far too stubborn to learn any. So we got him to drop his thesis and transferred him to Wheare, to write a thesis in the sub-faculty of politics, which we thought would be easier. Hawke's principal interest was cricket. If he succeeds, I shall regard it as proof that Australian labour leaders, like British, are now beginning to produce a hereditary governing class—and I shall regret it.

I see that the Ambassadorship in Washington has gone to Beale. I believe that in political circles he was regarded as a more outstanding liability to his party than McBride, who after all does appear to have been a man of integrity, though very awkward in his demeanour. I have no objection to political ambassadorships, especially the Washington ambassadorship, like the High Commissionership in London, but it is a bad look out if it is to be used as a dumping ground for political failures.

I regard trouble with the external balance of payments as a chronic or indeed normal state of affairs for Australia now, and the excitement and relaxation over temporary rises in wool output and prices in 1953 and 1957 very dangerous wishful thinking. The balance of payments crisis comes about through a long run factor, the persistent neglect of agriculture, and will only be remedied through a reversal of that policy, which will not come in a hurry.

I think I saw in the Gazette that your degree was granted, but I will confirm when I see McKay tonight.

Will you make up the account and let me know how it stands.

Yours/CC

Nick] Nicholas Clark, son of Colin Clark wage fixing] Hawke proposed a thesis on the the development of the Australian arbitration system Wheare] Kenneth Clinton Wheare (1907–79), Australian-born Professor of Government and Public Administration at All Souls College, Oxford Beale] Sir Howard Beale (1898–1983) was the Australian Ambassador in Washington 1958–64 McBride] Sir Philip McBride (1892–1982), Minister for Defence 1950–58 your degree] Gregory Clark's degree, MA (Oxon.), had been officially gazetted

Owen Dixon

Sir Owen Dixon (1886–1972), Chief Justice of the High Court of Australia 1952–64, was the Court's longest serving judge, having been appointed in 1929, and the one whose reputation still stands highest for erudition and clarity in judgement. During the Second World War Dixon was released from legal duties to take various administrative duties associated with the war effort. His shrewd sense of the personal element in political matters is reflected in his letter to United States Supreme Court Justice Felix Frankfurter (1882–1965).

164. To Felix Frankfurter, 14 January 1959

My dear Justice

My wife and I were indeed sorry to learn that you had been ill and in hospital. The source of our information was a letter from Mrs. Erwin Griswold to my wife but I have since seen Maxwell who is one of the representatives of the London Times in Washington and who called on me at your instance. I do hope that you have fully recovered. If, as I gather, it was some heart condition, for goodness' sake observe medical advice without deviation. I do not know whether I ever told you of Starke's medical history. It is true that he is now dead but he did not die until he was over eighty-seven, and although I am beginning to regard that as premature it is not a widely held opinion. He had a very serious cardiac breakdown some twenty-five years before his death. He had always been notorious for his refusal to conform with any rule of any description but to our astonishment he made an exception after his illness in favour of medical instructions. In his eighty-sixth year he remarked to me that I should tell some lawyer who had had a coronary occlusion that he should follow medical advice with punctiliousness, that even yet he (Starke) had found it necessary to do so, and added that he could not hurry. I know your abounding energy and I know that it comes very largely from the mind but even the mind can be controlled.

Of news from Australia there is nothing really to interest you. The election results were a little surprising to many. It had been believed that the Government would return to power but that they would have so considerable an increase in their majority was not foreseen by many. Menzies himself afterwards told me that he knew that a very favourable result was certain after he had addressed two or three meetings, one in Sydney, one in Melbourne and one, I think, in South Australia. He remarked that he might not know much but he had had sufficient experience to guess what people were thinking from their attitude at an election meeting. He said that he took no credit to himself for anything he did during the campaign except on the negative side. On the other hand he said that the only period when he had any apprehension was when his opponent became ill. Menzies himself seems very well, better than I have seen him for two or three years. He ascribes the improvement of his health to the removal of his tonsils but anyhow I do not think there ever was very much wrong with him except a tendency to catch colds.

Barbara Ward and her husband Robert Jackson are at the moment in Melbourne. They have been spending a holiday in Queensland. So far as he was concerned it was interrupted to go to Delhi and attend Nkrumah during his visit to Nehru. His report is that Nehru seems in pretty good form and appeared very interested in Nkrumah. So far as he was able to observe, however, conditions of life in India are probably more distressing than ever. At all events Bombay was not in a satisfactory condition. I do not know whether you noticed in the London Times or elsewhere news of a television broadcast given by Attlee. I took a most adverse view of it. It included purposeless and irresponsible criticism of the life and works of Jinnah. Whatever one may think as to the policies of Jinnah and of Nehru, their stature seems to me to be undeniable. I never met Jinnah but of the Pakistanis he seems rightly placed in the position of a national hero if nations must have heroes. Why an ex-Prime Minister of Great Britain should for the purpose of television broadcast insult the national hero of an eastern country in completely friendly relations with England I cannot understand. Yet when I met Attlee I was very much impressed with his care and caution and anxiety to get things right. But that is now eight years ago and he has been out of office for a very long time. Barbara Ward's explanation sounds too cynical for her. It simply is that Attlee must earn money to live and that he was simply seeking to be interesting when the B.B.C. offered him an opportunity of appearing.

Our Court is in vacation at the moment. We have arrears of judgments which are occupying the judges and they ought to be occupying me most of all but I am afraid that I have allowed myself to be drawn aside one day after another during the last week. Poor Dudley Williams whose health seemed to be restored by his retirement and who therefore began to regret it very much, has now had the misfortune to lose his wife. He very much depended upon her.

The new Attorney-General, Barwick, whom you met is entering on his work with great energy. But his inclusion in the Cabinet so early in his Parliamentary career seems to have caused somewhat of a flutter. The Deputy Prime Minister, Holt, is a Melbourne man. It was taken for granted that he would succeed the present Prime Minister when the time came. There is a member of the Cabinet, a solicitor living in Sydney named McMahon, who regarded himself as the leading Minister from New South Wales. As you will see in the case of each of them there are thus grounds for jealousy of Barwick. However, Barwick has not had political experience, is untried in Parliament or for that matter in the Executive, and notwithstanding his recognised abilities he may not be so dangerous to these aspirants as they fear.

I have seen very little of Casey since his return and I know the curious operations of his limitations, that is to say that outside the limits which he lays down for himself he seems to think that all is irrelevant. But for myself, I would have thought his energy and his capacity within those limits make him a better successor to Menzies than those I have mentioned, if any succession were in question which it does not yet appear to be. However, I have known Casey a long time and this may be partiality. He and Menzies do not appear to understand each other. I have always felt that the quality of humour was the cause. That may seem a strange statement. But Casey has none and Menzies too much and that always appears to be a barrier to the mutual understanding of men.

Denning has been in India to the meeting of the International Commission of Jurists. He is reported to have gone very far in his statement of the judicial function in making law. His statements are reported as if he treated it as an arbitrary act, which I find it hard to believe. On the whole controversy, which in England now seems to centre around him, I have felt that it is unwise for a judge to speak publicly. He ought to appear to believe that he has some external guidance even if in his ignorance he regards it as untrue. In the Darwinian processes of adaptation to environment such a bird as the honey-sucker ought not consciously to enlarge his bill by stretching it even if reaching for the honey causes him to do so. In any case law-making ought not to be regarded as honey.

I hope that Mrs. Frankfurter is better and that you have not resumed your own work too quickly and in any case that it is not too heavy.

WITH KINDEST REGARDS,/YOURS SINCERELY,/OWEN DIXON

heart condition] Frankfurter served until 1962   Starke] Sir Hayden Starke (1871–1958), Justice of the High Court of Australia 1920–50   the election results] the Menzies Government was returned to office in November 1958   his opponent] Dr Herbert Vere Evatt (1894–1965), leader of the Australian Labor Party   Barbara Ward] Barbara Mary Ward (1914–81), English journalist and broadcaster, later Baroness Jackson of Lodsworth   Robert Jackson] Robert Gillman Allen Jackson (b. 1911). Australian-born official of the United Nations who married Barbara Ward in 1950   Williams] Sir Dudley Williams (1889–1963), Justice of the High Court   the new Attorney-General] refers to speculation that Sir Garfield Barwick (see Letter 184) would succeed Menzies in the party leadership: it was, however, to be first Harold Holt (1908–67), then John Grey Gorton (b. 1911) and William McMahon (1908–88), who became Prime Minister   Casey] R.G. Casey (1890–1976) later Baron Casey of Berwick and Westminister, was seen by some as an alternative to Menzies   Denning] British jurist Alfred Thompson, Lord Denning (1899–1977)

HAL PORTER

Hal Porter (1911–84) published novels, poems, plays and an autobiographical trilogy beginning with The Watcher on the Cast-Iron Balcony *(1963). His friendship with Beatrice Davis (1909–92), commissioning editor at Angus & Robertson, was crucial to his career. This letter, following a visit to Sydney, dates from his time as municipal librarian at Shepparton, Victoria, when he was working on the collection of stories* A Bachelor's Children, *which he dedicated to Davis. In 1961 he became a full-time writer.*

165. To Beatrice Davis, 10 September 1959

Dearest Beatrice

First of all, of course, I thank you for all your wonderful hospitality, and your unfaltering personal gaiety and forbearance. Between the moments of fantasy and grog-craziness my instinctive geiger was able to pick up much gold … more, in fact, than ever before, and more than I was capable of picking up ever before. I had sensed long before I left Shepparton that a dangerous line had to be crossed—I'd rather pictured myself crossing it utterly alone and too defiantly. In retrospect I am astounded by and humble (me!) before the love of my friends, and you especially. No-one can have behaved so outrageously, so almost diabolically and been forgiven so wisely. For me this has been less a salutary and chastening experience than an exciting revelation. One feels like saying one is not worthy—one finds oneself inspired to prove one's worthiness. In short, I have, I think, become 'human' at last. Somewhere I wrote 'love, the last barrier between two people, is down'. Something of that sort has happened to me—it reveals, not as I thought, an exquisite dreariness but a childlike world of exhilarating dimensions and clarifies far beyond what I'd allowed myself to see before—stubborn bastard. There were, for example, so many unhappy people about—each one was sweeter to me than I should have thought possible. It is all to make an immense difference to me and, *cela va sans dire*, to my writing. Naturally, I still faintly suspect this seeing- the-light, and mutter superstitiously 'Its a seventh year *and* middle age'—but conviction of my extreme good fortune goes too deep to accredit such flip evasions. No more, I fear, can be said except 'Thank you' until the proving time comes at its proper moment. Keep faith, little one—I'll still need it.

Now, to reportage

After you left, Ray and I boozed on talking of you, and were finally (nicely) ejected to not trap taxicabs but to walk to his place where Mena Kashmiri Abdullah waited with Indic nervousness. Ray quickly burnt some steaks for us, M.K.A. drank brandy, I drank some Lorenzini claret wine, Roger and children arrived, in less time than it takes to listen to four cheap songs we were at Newport and into the vodka. Here I draw a veil. Morning, and we were off—the trip to Shepparton was commingled absurdity and fantasy including rows in pubs, a night sleeping in the car (never before and never again), Roger getting the lowdown on Frensham from the school chef in a bar, a session with Kellaway at Wangaratta (he wore the same fancy dress as at Folly Point) and a raddled entry into Shepparton where the cottage alterations were only just begun and the place looked like one of those *untidy* Dutch interiors (Teniers??). I shouted Roger and Tony rooms in our posh hotel and passed out. This week has been guilt-letting with a vengeance but I've already caught up with work—largely because of the carpenters who rage into the house each morning at 7 so that I am at work by 8 to escape their shattering din and shouted platitudes. Daffodils, primroses, hyacinths, boronia were all in their proper places in the garden and burgeoning properly. It is, in fact, good to be here again with my usual pick-ings of nostalgia, regret and sorrow—it is wonderful to have really learned something and, instead of jettisoning it on the way back, to have carried back what I've learned.

It was wonderful of you to let me see dear Rosemary and Alec, Judy, Thea, Christo-pher Koch et al—most exciting was to meet Ray Mathew. It was a good time to meet him … more than any other writer (and, indeed, any man) I've met did he have the sort of value I cherish … the precision plus the wildness, the direct attack plus the brilliant gaiety, the wordy wit plus the gentle humanity (Jesus! there's that bloody word again!). Ah sure love that man.

Roger proposes bringing him here for a few days within a few weeks—whether the proposal was vodka and restlessness or a further nice gesture or a wild statement I can't assess. if they do come why not, dearest Beatrice, come with them, and see me when I'm a working man. You'd be quaite surpraised. I should *naturellement*, go into an ecstasy. You'd enjoy the contrumpery pub as my guest, and I'd see that your name went into the *Shepparton News*!

I continue shaving away at the stories—largely a matter of destroying old gods, and replacing words that had become measles (*dazzling*, was one, *vaudeville, indubitably, even* etc.). I've thought this, and should like your A&R opinion: a collection rather than a selection because this will (already has) finished my first creative period. Should it turn out to be a bit larger than a book-sized book I'll be perfectly happy to pay the extra—what else to do with the dough except get my children of the first marriage out of my hair. It'll give that extra fillip to the next period's writing drive—there's something untidy about orphans tugging at one's coat-tails. Chronological, you think? I do (Or did *you*?). I tried that last night—it seems very interesting.

I've not written sooner because I wanted to send your pen with this— the nibs seem to me superb, a steel nib that behaves like a half-fountain-pen, and lives in its well on a fascinating chain. I've one for Dick which I'll send him when I can track down that ruddy quotation—frankly it sounds like Dante or the Waddell creature herself.

I've told Ray Mathew to look after you. You look after him. Turn down an empty glass for me, and don't say anything of me except the most malicious truths or the most enchanting lies.

Dear Beatrice—I know that too much courtesy is discourtesy, but—thank you Always yours,/Hal.

Ray] playwright Ray Mathew (b. 1929)   Mena Kashmiri Abdullah / M. K. A.] writer (b. 1930): co-author with Mathew of a volume of short stories, *The Time of the Peacock* (1965)   Roger] Roger Jennings, lawyer and friend of Porter's   Kellaway] Frank Kellaway (b. 1922) poet and novelist   Rosemary and Alec] poet Rosemary Dobson (b. 1920) and her husband, editor and publisher Alec Bolton (1926–97)   Thea] Thea Astley (b. 1925) novelist (see Letter 172)   Christopher Koch] (b. 1932), novelist   that Waddell creature] Helen Waddell, medievalist and translator

JOYCE GRENFELL

Joyce Grenfell (1910–79), English actor, writer, comedian and musician, visited Australia four times, winning the hearts of audiences with her one-woman shows. A lively account of her impressions of Australia is given in the diary letters she wrote to Virginia Graham (1910–93) in England. Friends from the age of seven, as adults these two women maintained almost daily contact, by telephone when in London and by letter when separated. In 1977, leaving Sydney for the last time, Grenfell wrote of the wrench of parting: 'You know how I put down roots and they have had a footing [in Australia] ever since the first visit …'

166. To VIRGINIA GRAHAM, 13 JULY 1959

DARLING VIRGINIA

Another glorious morning. I'm off to the theatre soon to unpack my props and settle in. the revue running there closed on Sat, so now I move in. Last night I was on T.V. in "Meet the Press". It seems to have been rather a big success. *Very* nice reaction. What amuses me is the constant amazement when they say "But you are so *natural?*" What else can one be?

After the prog. we went—the panel and chairman and me—to the chairman's house near here for a drink and Danny Kaye came in. Pale tweeds and those extraordinary space shoes we used to see in N.Y., remember. Very clumsy but obviously bliss for the toes. He was cordial and guarded at the same time! We sang close harmony on a sofa for about ten minutes and he said I'd been very good on telly. He'd seen it. He's having a huge success here. I find him a little scaly—lizard like—but not bad. At least he plays friendly this time. When I met him with Ginette and Paul Emil he was *so* bored at meeting another entertainer. It was quite funny.

Yesterday Nola Dekyvere gave a Sunday lunch party for me. Very nice people—twelve in all, and we sat out in the sun before and after lunch. Small charming white house right on the water facing the harbour. You never saw such a lovely situation and it's ten mins. from central Sydney.

I've suddenly tumbled on a truth I really should have discovered before. Namely that the Australian accent is *not* a class thing. We equate it with suburbia because of our home associations, but it means nothing here and one suddenly hears erudition, wit, quality talk in that accent and realises one has been *unconsciously* feeling slightly superior! I was appalled when I realised this. And ashamed.

After the lunch which was delicious but went on rather, I was driven back by a man called Inglis who is to do with the business side of the D. Telegraph here, and he showed Bill B. and me his flat in another superb position. He and his wife are our sort of age and she obviously has great taste. I was surprised (!) by this and again humiliated to think how clumsy one can be. Such pretty things—books—colours. I grow increasingly ashamed of the way we all treat Colonials, not discriminating at *all*. And they sense it. I've been able to talk pretty freely to one or two people and it's interesting. This is a good country and I am longing to see more of it—the country places.

No more now. I'm hoping for mail today. None since Thursday so it should have piled up. Darling, such a happy hol. I don't know when you'll get this? Are you having mail forwarded. If not you'll get a pile when you get home. Much love and to old To.

LOVE FROM JOYCE

Danny Kaye] Danny Kaye [David Daniel Kominsky] (1913–87), American-born comedian   Nola Dekyvere] Nola Laird Dekyvere (1904–91), charity and community worker, society hostess and (in 1959) a member of the Board of Directors of the Phillip Street Theatre   Inglis] Antony Gordon Inglis (b. 1917), Manager, Australian Consolidated Press and Managing Director of the Shakespeare Head Press   Bill B.] William Blezard (b. 1921), pianist and composer, accompanist to Joyce Grenfell   To] Antony Frederic Lewis Thesiger (1906–69), husband of Virginia Graham

167. To Virginia Graham, 9 September 1959

DARLING VIRGINIA

I wrote to you on Mon. rather late at night and I left the letter on the round-ish table among my papers and forgot it. Solly.

Such blinding rain this a.m. and Princess A. arrives at 12.30. I feel a terrible personal responsibility for Sydney. It should be all sparkling and lovely. Spring is here and the gardens are gushing full of gerania, cineraria, roses, hibiscus, phlox and all manner of local flora. And the harbour looks like Loch Ness on any Scottish summer day. So sad.

Almost nothing new to tell you. I've written a lyric for Bill to put a tune to as a surprise for the last night. They make a big thing of last nights. It's just a thank you song to Phillip St., which I really do love so it's easy to say. It's the nicest theatre I ever played in.

Yesterday the Overseas League lunch. Such dear funny British faces under the funniest Australian hats. they all (hats) look as if they'd been made in a mould and I rather think they have. The felt has a sort of solid look even when, as mostly, it's fuzzy. And all in bright colours with something to shine somewhere. a buckle or three infinitesimal diamonds sewn in on front. Never a lapel without a sparkler. And the teeth are always borrowed or else gold filled. Not very pretty. Rugged faces but nice. There were about 100 there, 95% women, sitting on those pile-up tin chairs eating sandwiches and acorn coffee. A chord on a pale yellow upright piano, not remotely in tune, and everyone stood and belted out the Queen. Somehow remarkably moving as well as comic. I fought a lump and giggle equally, and mastered both.

It is absolutely fascinating and I think thrilling that the tribute paid to me is 'We left the theatre feeling *so* much better than when we came in!' 'Such a sense of happiness' and *never* 'You are such and such!' I think that's entirely as it ought to be from a C.S. p. of v. and it lifts the burden. I know *I'm* not that good so it all falls into place, and the success of the thing ceases to be anything that could make me conceited. (I'm not honest. Really). I'm just grateful it all works and apparently gives real pleasure.

Here endeth the lesson.

A gleam of sun. Oh I do hope it continues. 2 and a half hours to go. The hairdresser asked to trim Maud yesterday rather overdid it and she's so brief. All love darling.

JOYCE.

Princess A.] HRH Princess Alexandra of Kent (b.1936) visited Australia 14 August–26 September 1959 to mark the Queensland centenary   C.S. p. of v.] Christian Science point of view. Grenfell and Graham were both brought up as Christian Scientists and their letters constantly refer to this perspective.

PATRICK WHITE

The claim of Patrick Victor Martindale White (1912–90) to Australian celebrity rests on his prodigious literary output and his award of the Nobel Prize for Literature in 1973. His biographer David Marr has emphasised another aspect of White's writing career, the habit of keeping in touch by letter, drummed into him as a little boy, which stayed with him through life.

168. TO FATHER XMAS, DECEMBER 1918

DEAR FATHER XMAS
Will you please bring me
a pistol, a mouth organ
a violin
a butterfly net
Robinson Cruso
History of Australia
Some marbles
a little mouse what runs across the room

I hope you do not think I am too greedy but I want the things badly
YOUR LOVING/PADDY

David Marr has observed that in speaking his mind, as he did in letters, White was a wise man who could be stubbornly wrong. In a letter to the young Barbara Fisher (later Miechel), the daughter of a friend, he scolded the child for a chance remark about chives, but made a large point about the importance of cultural diversity in Australia.

169. To Barbara Fisher, 23 February 1960

Dear Barbara,

Your remark about not eating chives because you wanted to be an Australian continues to haunt me. The chives in themselves are an unimportant detail (though I consider them one of the minor pleasures of life); it is the attitude which horrifys because it is so false & mistaken.

I know that a great many ignorant native-born Australians (and nothing can be more ignorant than certain native-born Australians) go out of their way to encourage New Australians to drop their own standards and traditions in favour of our dreary semi-culture which exists here at present. However, there are also a great number of civilised Old Australians who are hoping that the migrants from European Countries will bring something of their own cultures with them, so that we can incorporate them into what will some day be a true civilisation of our own.

The best advice I can give you two girls is to learn as much as possible about the traditions of your parents & grandmothers while there is still time, & to make the most of what you learn. That way you will give far more pleasure to others than if you model yourselves on suburban nonentities of the conventional Australian pattern.

I am sending you a little book on herbs, written by a woman who lives at Castle Hill, which will show you that some Australians do eat chives, & which contains all sorts of wise and useful information besides.

Yours sincerely/Patrick White

One of White's great set-piece letters, his sharply observed account of a luncheon attended on the Royal yacht Britannia *in 1963, was written to the painter and designer Desmond Digby (b. 1933) who designed stage sets for several of White's plays. A month earlier Digby had himself been a guest on the* Britannia *in Auckland but 'only for drinks!' so White was perhaps indulging in some oneupmanship.*

170. To Desmond Digby, 8 March 1963

Dear Desmond,

How are things at the El? Pretty wet, I'm afraid, after reading about the Royal Progress yesterday at Coolangatta. Here it rains, but only in a mild drizzly way, and I am able to run about between showers and start another fire in the incinerator; my desk is being turned out for the first time in five years.

I managed to get to the Luncheon on Monday after a dreadful Sunday night, when I started a kind of bronchial complication and vomitted up everything besides. However, I took everything. Manoly took me to Parramatta and I went in by train, looking like a waiter going on duty, as my only presentable and cool suit was a new black one I had bought to wear to the theatre and concerts in the summer. There was quite an amiable atmosphere in the Sydney streets for once, and I hung about the Circular Quay for a bit waiting for them to approach. Finally they did, standing up in a very leisurely car. She was all in blew, he in a kind of tweedy number the colour of dry cowshit. After a bit I approached the yacht in fear and trembling, and ran into the Utzons, who had received a summons in the air on their way from Tahiti, and had been rushed straight from the plane. In our nervous condition we ganged up quite a lot, and he promised to show me over the Opera House. His wife is of that plain, dank-haired mermaid kind one sees from Denmark, very pleasant. As her English is a bit vague, she smiles. Then we went on board, up a red carpet, with sailors slapping their rifle butts, and were received by I don't know how many members of the household: a tall, toothy, elderly man in a lounge suit, and glamorous young Navy and Army equerries among them. The Army equerry, who was Australian, appeared to have read some of my books, and told me that other members of the household were "very interested". In fact, he said, the copy of VOSS had disappeared mysteriously. (I should think the Juke had probably thrown it out the porthole after reading half of Chapter I.) The guests were very oddly chosen indeed, and I couldn't think for the life of me why I had been asked. I had imagined there would be other artists of various kinds, but Doris Fitton and Murray Rose were as close as we got to that—with of course the Utzons as a last minute inspiration. Otherwise they were all business tycoons (that Kirby, looking like a purple fig about to burst, Warwick Fairfax, Hallstrom) civil servants, and an admiral and general or two. We were lined up on either side of the saloon for the introductions to Ma'am and the Juke. There were drinks before and after, good stiff ones too, and one needed it. Mary Fairfax was tottering and using her smelling bottle before other drink was produced, and the headmistress of Cheltenham High, a nice hearty old thing with whom I had conversation, confessed that she was petrified. Doris, of course, was in her element, doing all that *grande dame* stuff she'd learnt in rep, tremendous curtsey while Lady This and Lady That were tottering and nearly falling under their chiffon hats. Lunch was really very good—rolls of smoked salmon with scrambled egg at the side (it's worth remembering), tournedos on foie gras with a salad, and *profiterolles* with chocolate sauce. I have never sat at such a long mahogany table. There were some rather ugly gold urns down the centre, and vases of yellow and white flowers. *They* sat on either side, and I was at the lower end, so could look right down and observe. I was between Murray Rose, who is a most civilised young man, able to talk about things, and a Mrs Parbury, a youngish woman with heavily loaded eyelashes, who is a niece of the Duchess of Gloucester. She came out here originally to be with her auntie, and fell for Parbury, a tall dark handsome Australian of family. I used to know his great-aunt (now dead) and aunt (now crazy, but at large—she was always a thin spinster drifting from park to park, for no wrong reasons, just to pass the time, and now poor thing she is so mad she no longer knows which park she is in.) My mother used to know the Parburys in her youth on the Hunter and I can remember her telling me in shocked tones that whenever the Parburys wanted to go for another trip they sold off a paddock. I used that in connexion with the Goodmans in the AUNT'S STORY. However, I couldn't tell the Hon. Mrs Parbury any of that at the luncheon. I couldn't find out any of her interests, only that she has two children whose education is worrying her. I told her to send them to the ordinary schools, but she is afraid they would develop split personalities. I replied that I had developed one at the best of schools. That didn't get us very far either, nor the fact that one of her relations is one of my oldest and closer friends. After lunch we stood about in the saloon again for coffee, and I spoke to Admiral McNicoll and his wife. He is the brother of the bastard on the *Telegraph* who is one of the leaders of the opposition to my books. I think the admirals would show themselves to be of the opposition also if the politenesses were down, but we were soon led up to Ma'am, who began to discuss with McNicoll the oiling of stabilisers. She is fed up because the stabilisers in *Britannia* are apparently of an old-fashioned variety, which have to be taken out for oiling, while the latest can be oiled in position. After they had been through all this another lady who had been led up, all coffee lice and chiffon hat, spoke about the Barrier Reef, so I thought I had better put in a word as obviously a word wasn't going to be put to me. I told Ma'am she must make a point of seeing Fraser Island one day, and about the interesting wreck which had taken place there, and of the Nolan paintings which no doubt she had seen. At which she gave a shriek, or as close to a shriek as she could come, and said: "Ohhh, yurss! The Naked Lehdy! We saw one in Adelaide." Poor girl, she might loosen up if one took her in hand, but as it is she struck me as being quite without charm, except of a perfectly stereotyped English county kind, and hard as nails under the Little-Thing-in-Blew appearance. I suppose it's just as well that she's tough. One wasn't led up to the Jokey Juke—he approached, and I think he made up his mind early on that he was going to keep well away from anything that might be an intellectual or an artist.

When all this was over I went up to the Cross and had a long gin session with Jack Lee, the English film director, whom I liked, and with whom I have a feeling I may get together over something eventually. He is here to make a film of THE DELINQUENTS, and is going to marry a woman in Adelaide, so I expect he will be turning up quite a bit on and off. His brother is Laurie Lee whose book CIDER WITH ROSIE won the W.H. Smith Award the year after I won it with VOSS.

Last night the dinner at the Dicksons' took place. I liked the sister. She has a strong, rather refreshing personality, I thought—Australian in the best sense. Poor Wendy faded away into being the shy little flower, and also seemed to be doing most of the cooking. The Robin Lovejoys were also there. He talked with great authority. I could not agree with all of it. I wonder how many rows we should have.

Very depressed a couple of days ago. Stefan Haag rang up and tried to coax me to agree to let them put on SARSAPARILLA at the *Tote*! I said it would be a physical impossibility. We are back at the same old stumbling block: how to get the Royal for long enough to make a production pay. Still, it wouldn't pay at the Tote unless it ran for a couple of years, and then I should think the actors' salaries would still be running away with any profit. Hopeless! I can't see any place for my plays in the Sydney theatre.

Have written to Sumner, and told him you are coming, but haven't yet received an answer. Hope the weather isn't too awful, and that you are both happy

Yours/Patrick

the El] The El Dorado Motel, Surfers Paradise, where Digby was staying   the Utzons] Danish architect Joern Utzon (b. 1918), designer of the Sydney Opera House, and his wife Lis Fenger   Doris Fitton] Doris Fitton (1897–1985), founder (1970) of Independent Theatre, Sydney   Murray Rose] (b. 1939), Australian Olympic swimmer and actor   Kirby] James Kirby (1886–1970), machinery manufacturer   Warwick Fairfax] (1901–87), newspaper owner   Hallstrom] Edward Hallstrom (1886–1970), maker of refrigerators and benefactor of Sydney's Taronga Park Zoo   Mary Fairfax] (b. c.1920) wife of Warwick Fairfax   Admiral McNicoll and his wife] Alan McNicoll (1908–87), later Australian Ambassador to Turkey; and Frances, a former correspondent for *The Economist*   poor Wendy] Wendy Dickson (b. c. 1939), designer of three of White's plays   Stefan Haag] (1925–86) opera producer and one-time Executive Director of the Elizabethan Theatre Trust   the Robin Lovejoys] Robin Lovejoy (1923–85), actor, designer and artistic director   Sarsaparilla at the Tote] a mooted production of White's play *The Season at Sarsaparilla* at Sydney's Old Tote Theatre   Sumner] John Sumner (b. 1924) founded (1952) Union Theatre Repertory Company, Melbourne, which became the Melbourne Theatre Company

171. To *Time Magazine*, 17 February 1974

Dear Sir,

It isn't my habit to write to papers after reading reviews of my books, but after coming across Martha Duffy (whoever she is) on my novel *The Eye of the Storm* where she refers to me as "living in Sydney with several dogs and a male housekeeper" I feel I must draw your attention to an incorrect, and I should have thought gratuitous, biographical detail. The distinguished, and universally respected man who has given me his friendship and moral support over a period of thirty-four years, has never been a housekeeper. *I* am that, and shall continue playing the role at least till I am paralysed: it keeps me in touch with a reality often remote from those who dish up their superficial, slovenly pieces for *Time Magazine*.

Yours sincerely,/(Patrick White)

The distinguished ... man] Emanuel (Manoly) George Lascaris (b. 1912), who met White in 1941; they remained together for fifty years

THEA ASTLEY

One of Australia's most distinguished novelists, Thea Astley (b. 1925) is known for her wit, humour and flair for social comedy as well as for seriousness of vision. Her letter to Thelma Forshaw (b. 1923), journalist and author of short stories, reflects the Sydney literary scene at a time when Patrick White's reputation was reaching its height and his personality drew fascinated attention.

172. TO THELMA FORSHAW, 14 JANUARY 1963

Thelma Chum, I laughed till I literally wept over this latest. Thank you, you silly chump for making a manic depressive laugh. Tell George he is bloody wrong and I observe you no more closely than I observe anyone and certainly have not the slightest intention of using you in a novel. So there. Doesn't he approve of me. I am not a grand seducer and do not intend for you to deceive him, me, us, all pronouns, objective case. I simply enjoy your company, your sympathy and kindness as any bloody normal manic depressive would. Geez, does he want me to mix solely with bottlers and pavlova makers? Gotta have a few red corpuscles traipsing across the grey grey hinterland of my mental life. In fact his implication has made me cross, and the next sentence is addressed to him. Dear George you are *wrong* about me. I merely crave an intelligent buddy. Can't talk Vogue patterns and ninety ways with a meringue (That's Patrick's joke) all the time.

The dinner at Saint Patrick's was yummy, But felt Manoly slightly effer so slightly antagonistic. To punish him I helped Saint P do up the zipper on his windbreaker. Wow! (My dear, any time you need it renewed simply to ask …) There was cold soup in cups and I disgraced everyone by prolettishly attempting to use a spoon instead of quaffing the muck like tea. Then there was delish meat in rice served with yoghurt. (his ideas!!!) then peas served separate cooked in lettus then cherries and raspberries or something. Coffee in the lounge under the shade of expensive abstracts. P has just discovered Texta colours, the old poppet, and produced his first abstract, a gay series of squiggles called Joy. He and Manoly have been losing thousands on the stocks and shares poker machines so should be bitter, but P was the most genial I have seen for a long time. And suddenly, tho I love him dearly, I DON'T CARE ANY MORE. I mean the friendship suddenly seems easy-pleasant. I don't have mental post mortems, duzze want to be pals or duzznt he. Nice this way.

Saw the do over review in the Bully this morning of Coast to Coast and think Ray must have been omitted maybe. Should Amy be glad or sad over the things he says? Glad, I guess. She is away in a caravan with hubby and child. Laurie has gone. He has returned Jack's tie that he borrowed to wear to Dogwoods and then forgot to remove. I nearly got away with HIS expensive looking cashmere jumper the same way but conshents made me coff up. The bulder is hammering at the front putting on rooms. Soon, soon. A jazzy wackydo Coast to Coast party with frothings of beer and turgidities of gin. Please to come George and Thelma.

It's on. Tonight I will start me new nun book. Did you see that fabbo play on Canal Two last night with Helen Hayes as Mother Superior still pulsating with sex and femininity under the old habit. Play called The Velvet Glove by a Rosemary Case. Her Bishop wasn't too good, but does she know her nuns! Thelma, have just thought of the most delicious book for us to write together only I don't think my letters would be good enough. How's about a series of notes exchanged by two convent school girls, Thellie and Theie (other names, of course), just busting out all over with gamps and coifs and throbbing inuendoes going on under the veils. Could be a gimmick. Don't think any one has tackled that line. Maybe we could be in separate convents, parted for the semester, smuggling some letters through and some not. Faint story line, developing hinted at scandals of appointment, dominance of horsey nuns and so on. We could work out details and then work roughly to a plan, actually sending each other the letters, waiting for replies, and getting spontaneity that way. Do I hear you throwing up? Is this crummy? Think it has possibilities myself. Nothing like it done here or elsewhere as far as I know. Then we will rush gloriously neck and neck into print with Faber or Secker and Warburg who love off-beat thingos. No illustrations by request and it will sell like Franny and Zooey, I know it.

Listen, Forshaw, I read your letters and they are literally flashing opal mines of wit. You are seriously one of the funniest, no, THE funniest woman I have ever met. All I could do would be the stodgy chummo who sparks off the old unpredictable. Think it over, chook. Could be therapeutic as well!

LOVE, YOU OLD CLOT,/THEA

George] husband of Thelma Forshaw   Saint Patrick] Patrick White (see Letters 168–71)   Manoly] Manoly Lascaris (see Letter 171)   the Bully] the *Bulletin*   Coast to Coast] anthology of Australian short stories, published annually 1941–48 and biennially 1964–70   Ray] Ray Mathew (b. 1929), playwright and poet   Amy] Amy Witting, pseudonym of Joan Levick (b. 1918), novelist and short story writer   Laurie] Laurence Collinson (1925–86), poet and playwright   Jack] E.J. Gregson, husband of Thea Astley   Dogwoods] home of Patrick White and Manoly Lascaris   nun book] The proposed 'nun book' was never written   Canal Two] Channel Two   Helen Hayes] American actor   Faber … Secker and Warburg] British publishers   Franny and Zooey] novel by J.D. Salinger

YEHUDI MENUHIN

Yehudi Menuhin (b. 1916) is acclaimed as one of the world's great violinists. This letter of congratulation was written to Joan Sutherland (b. 1926), the Australian operatic soprano, after her performance as Amina in Bellini's La Sonnambula *at Sadler's Wells Theatre, London, on 26 June 1963. Sutherland specialised in Italian and French opera of the nineteenth century and excelled in the roles of the* bel canto *repertory.*

173. TO JOAN SUTHERLAND, 27 JUNE 1963

DEAR MISS SUTHERLAND

You transported me last night: I have never heard such beautiful singing—your voice would be the dream of any string player, as in addition to the most wonderful articulation each note seemed to carry a warm weight as it were, as if your bow arm was drawing the sound out of the vocal chords in a way which makes me feel both inspired and discouraged at the same time.

I came backstage hoping to express some of my feelings at least, but as Princess Margaret was due back and there were so many formalities I left the message with Ronald Anderson, hoping that at some future date I might have more propitious occasion to speak to you.

SINCERELY YOURS/YEHUDI MENUHIN

ROBERT MENZIES

Sir Robert Menzies (1894–1978) wrote of cricket as 'one of the great loves of my life'. He was also a consummate public speaker. On the eve of the 1964 Australian Test tour to England, he was approached by the new Australian captain, Robert Baddeley Simpson (b. 1936) for some guidance in the preparation of the speeches to be delivered as an unavoidable part of a Test captain's obligations. Menzies prepared a careful response combining a sense of inherited tradition with a clear expression of his identity as an Australian.

174. TO ROBERT ('BOB') SIMPSON, 25 MARCH 1964

MY DEAR BOB

I enclose a few copies of things that I have spoken and written which may help you in your tasks as Captain of Australia.

But I really think that the best thing I can do for you is to set down in this letter a little broad advice, based upon much experience.

On the occasions when you will be called upon to make a speech in England, your audience will represent a pretty fair sample of English cricket-players and cricket-lovers, with, every now and then, somebody quite famous from Prince Philip and the Prime Minister down.

Don't make the mistake of striving for effect. Just be yourself; speak your own mind and use your own natural language. I learned long ago that the English are more disposed to judge a man on his own merits, and accept him if he rings true, than almost any other race on earth. You will not encounter snobbery among intelligent people. Nor will they seek to patronise you. The only social embarrassment you are likely to encounter will arise from that fact that, as you are a Captain of Australia, you will find yourself prominent on some occasions when your own modest instincts would make you wish to be obscure.

There are some silly and snobbish Australians (very few, I am glad to say) who think that the right way to recommend themselves to their English hosts is to conceal or apologise for their own country. They defeat their own ends. In England there is a growing interest in Australia as a country quite different from England. Don't hesitate to tell them about your own country and background. Tell them about our Grade and Sheffield Shield competitions, so different from the incessant County cricket over there. Tell them of the excitement that a young batsman experiences when, playing for the first time in the first eleven of his Club, he finds himself facing the bowling of a famous Australia Eleven Star! Explain how this develops our promising players early and quickly.

As you know, I believe that there is something historically special about playing for Australia against England. It was your own ambition, and is that of many others. For England was the cradle of cricket. It gave cricket to the world, and to Australia in particular. Say this. It is true, and it will be warmly received.

In England they are a little worried about the decline in the attendances of County Matches, and are tempted to feel that only repeated visits from the West Indies can save the game. Nothing could have a better effect on their spirits than for you to express your own belief that the game will go on, and that your own team will help in its growth. Speak about your young and comparatively untried players, and say that you believe that they will make a great contribution to the immortality of the game.

Have something to say about the beauty of England, of the thrill of playing at Lords or the Oval, or Trent Bridge; of meeting the great players of yesterday; of being in the land of our ancestors, from which the good and great things in Australia are derived.

CHARMIAN CLIFT

Charmian Clift (1923–69), novelist and journalist, married writer George Johnston (1912–70) in 1947 and went with him to London in 1950. In 1954 they moved with their first two children to Greece where they lived at first on the island of Kalymnos, later on Hydra, where their third child was born (see Letter 161). In 1964 Johnston went back to Australia for the publication of his autobiographical novel My Brother Jack: *Charmian and the children followed some months later. Her letter to literary agent David Higham gives her response to Australian life after the long absence. Its buoyant tone belies deep unhappiness and instability: she ended her life in 1969.*

175. To David Higham, 10 September 1965

Dear David

Sorry about the long silence. This has all been so new and so invigorating in a mad sort of way. I think I like it. At least it is a country where you can still make things happen instead of waiting for them to happen. I have been making my own sneaky little revolutions, first, by writing essays for the weekly presses to be read by people who don't know an essay from a form-guide, but absolutely love it, and second by barging into television with a ten part serial of *My Brother Jack* that is getting rave notices from astonished critics who didn't seem to know that we could make good television in Australia. All this has been tremendous fun and tremendous hard work and all in the first year back, so at the moment I am taking stock and considering what to do next. Here I am high-priced help and greatly valued and I suppose I could go on writing television or start pushing a film or turn to straight theatre (which I'd like to do, actually). On the other hand I have a half-finished novel which I'd like to get done—excepting that there's so little from novel writing in the way of daily bread, let alone jam or gravy, that I don't know whether I can afford to. I don't know whether you know that George is back in hospital with a recurrence of the old wog and will be there probably for six months on present prognosis. It's rather a blow just at this time, but at least they say they can cure him really this time, and I suppose we must regard it as time to be used to the best advantage possible. He'll be able to work, although not under any pressure—I hope he will get on with the novel, but I suppose that depends on his emotional climate (he is even more disillusioned about novel-writing than I am, and I know the Elizabethan Trust want him to write a play). Anyway, we'll see. The most important thing is for him to get well again. Bruce Hunter has written me saying Hutchinson are going to abandon "Honour's Mimic" (what stocks are left) to a cheap edition to get rid of them. See what I mean about novel-writing. So I would like you to get me the rights back, David, and also the rights to "Walk to the Paradise Gardens", as quickly as possible. I have "Mermaid Singing" and "Peel Me a Lotus", don't I? Hutchinson in Australia might as well be non-existent as far as selling anything of mine is concerned, which seems a little ridiculous when my name appears in the leading newspaper in every capital city every week and my weekly mail runs to hundreds of letters. Perhaps they don't read the papers. Oh well. Greece seems far far away and I haven't had time to miss it yet. This is nice too, and just as foreign. The children have adjusted rather well (excepting perhaps for my daughter, who thinks Australian men crude beyond belief and swears she's going back to Europe as soon as she can raise the fare). But the eldest is on his way to Sydney University with (on present marks) a Commonwealth Scholarship to see him through, and the youngest is as happy and busy as a small boy should be, and nobody is really pining. MBJ is still getting the most amazing publicity, particularly since my telly serial has started—and at the moment we are all praying the BBC is going to buy it and give it another boost in England. American sales are, as usual, disappointing. Love, David. George I'm sure will write to you himself.

CHARMIAN

essays for the weekly presses] Clift wrote a regular column for the *Sydney Morning Herald* and contributed to various other newspapers and magazines   ten part serial] Clift adapted Johnston's novel for television   they say they can cure him] refers to George Johnston's tuberculosis which was to kill him a year later   my daughter] Shane Johnston   the eldest] Martin Johnston (1947–90), writer   MBJ] *My Brother Jack*

MICHAEL DRANSFIELD

Michael Dransfield's (1948–73) natural talent as a poet was impressive, if not fully matured. Rodney Hall has written of Dransfield's uninhibited embrace of his literary calling and his enthusiasm for a mixed cultural heritage ranging from medieval traditions of courtly love and heraldry to the Buddhist transcendence of the individual. The dreamer and romantic in Dransfield responded to the dramatic story of the incarceration of the writer Peter Kocan (b. 1947) in a mental institution following his attempt on the life of Australian Labor Party leader Arthur Calwell.

176. To Peter Kocan, 1 December 1967

DEAR PETER

It was so wonderful to have your letter this morning. Last night was perhaps the most cataclysmic and terrible hour of my life, tho' shot through mostly with bright colours and smiles and a flame of roses that burnt for two hearts in the ashes of hope. And today is grey—the sullen sky has sent me neither rainbows nor butterflies and I am very sad here. Then to receive your letter. To know that I had a companion. For though mountains and two great rivers and many miles and more walls than you could know of, separate us, our hearts beat, I know, as as one for we love the same things.

I sit here at an old desk in my house. Shall I describe the room? There is a window with, just outside, two great trees, one a maple higher than the roof of the house.

Summer shows me her green leaves, winter bars me with bleak bare branches. There are more than a thousand books in my room. I have collected and studied and loved them. Ten of them I have written. I have some paintings here—two are portraits of my forebears, a third is a 19th century picture of a German castle, Stoltzenfels am Rhein. A fourth is a painting done by an ex-friend, of two other of my ex-friends. It was done for me in 1965 when even they, those few of my generation, yet cared about Art. In the corner of the room by the door, are some artefacts—my violin, my Winchester rifle that an uncle gave me, and another pile of books. On my desk, an hour-glass, a marble bust of the finest and most poetic of all composers, Frederic Chopin (1810–1849). Also a bottle of Kirsch, a brass candelabra which is 170 years old, an inkstand, a model of H. M. S. Cossack that I made years ago when inspired by the deeds of her gallant crew, an empty box of Gauloise cigarettes, a pair of dark glasses, a few silver shillings, and the spidery ghosts of letters that have been written on this desk before I was born, or that I have writ. On a table in the corner, is a little stereo record player my parents gave me. I am listening to Rachmaninoff's Second Concerto. Then I shall play some of the compositions of Chopin. What else?—a little chased-silver coffer, holding some medieval and crusader coins I collected once—a small copper-and-glass candle lantern, a bust of Apollo, god of music. This then, Peter, is my cage, my retreat, my study.

In other rooms—a piano by a window, antique furnishings of the Jacobean and Queen Anne eras, and a garden of shrubs and great trees and tiny flowers. It is all ghosts.

Your poems were lovely. The sonnet is excellent, and yet perhaps 'A White Seagull' is dearer to me, already, because in its fragmented and aghast lines I hear the cries I myself have uttered—it is a better poem really. One minor change I would suggest—in line 5, change 'breathlessly' to 'breathless'. And in line 4 of 'Sonnet' remove either 'wrinkled' or 'autumn' to fit the metre. Beyond this, they are faultless.

Oh, how glad I am that you too love 'The Innocent Moon'! I hoped you would. That you are familiar with the work of Francis Thompson too, that you have read Shakespeare's 'The Life and Death of King Richard II' too, and A. E. Housman (do you know this quatrain of his),

> Here dead we lie because we did not choose
> To live and shame the land from which we sprung
> Life, to be sure, is nothing much to lose,
> But young men think it is, and we were young

Because, Peter, I have on my shelves, frequently read aloud as the litanies and incantations of the night-hours, the poetic works of these—Brooke, Housman, Henry Kendall, Swinburne, Francis Thompson as well as other Romantics you may not have read: the German poet Rainer Maria Rilke (1875–1926), the sad Italian poet Salvatore Quasimodo, who was awarded the Nobel Prize in 1959 'for his lyrical poetry which with classical fire expresses the tragic experience of life in our time'. And Gerard Manley Hopkins, and Dylan Thomas, and Guillaume Apollinaire, and Rimbaud, and the rest.

Now, as to your enquiry. Whether Williamson's other books are as beautiful, let me say this—I have read & reread eleven of his books. All are unbelievably lovely. Do you remember Willie Maddison? Williamson has written a five-volume sequence called 'The Flux of Dream' about Willie, from birth to death, just as 'A Chronicle of Ancient Sunlight' is about Phillip. But I feel—and I hope you will give this some thought—that each of the fine writers I love, Williamson, Elizabeth Smart, J. R. Salamanca, Goethe, and W. H. Hudson—that each of these has written one book, told one story, which excels his other works and I feel it may be better only to read and love that one story, than to search for other works by the same writer which, though *almost* as wonderful yet have not the magic, the first, the holy. I have read Williamson's other books; J. R. Salamanca's other book 'The Lost Country' etc. etc. and though they are marvellous in their own way they are not so dear to me as the first. So I say it is best only to read the holy books, the best work, of a writer, and not to search for their complete works. Perhaps I am wrong.

Now, on the gramophone, I am listening to a guitar concerto by Joaquin Rodrigo, Spain's greatest composer, the world's greatest living composer. played by Andres Segovia. It is called 'Fantasia para un gentlhombre' which means Phantasy for a Courtier (or Gentleman). So rich it is, and the sad slow notes of the guitar, and the poignant rippling melodies and tunes like rills of mountain rivulets falling over hillsides into the dreadful chasm. I wish, I wish you were here and could listen with me, could hear the wind's murmur in the trees outside.

'Ilex'. It is a collection of poems I wrote about a year ago. The poems have names like 'Autumn's Sylphs'; 'Forest Girl'; 'On a theme of Taktakishvili'; 'Song for an Anonymous Survivor'; 'Sea'; 'Dido'; 'Tarantella'; and 'Images transcribed from Debussy'.

When you write—let it be soon, for I long to hear from you, you are my only friend now—tell me of David Lawson-Bowman, and tell me if there is anything you need or want that I can have sent to you. And I should like to read The Battle of the Villa Fiorita if it is possible to arrange.

I shall close now, my eyes are full of tears, it is a melancholy day. How I feel—I shall show you—a quotation from (a translation of) Tasso's poem 'Canzone'

> O my rough song, seek out some cavern or
> grot among these verdant cloisters; and do not go
> Where there are gems and purple

See if Morisset holds a copy of 'The Idiot' by Fyodor Dostoevsky. If not I shall try to send one. It is a long but lovely book and you will feel an affinity with the main character, Prince Myshkin (as I do). Bye for now.

LOVE/MICHAEL.

shot through … with bright colours] presumably a drug-induced sensation   Your poems] since the 1960s Kocan has built a substantial literary career as poet, playwright and novelist. He won the New South Wales Premier's Literary Award in 1983 for his novel *The Cure*   David Lawson-Bowman] the name, possibly assumed, of a prisoner Kocan met in Long Bay Gaol, Sydney, while awaiting trial for the attack on Calwell. Lawson-Bowman spoke of Rupert Brooke's poems and set Kocan reading these and other literary works.

Barry Humphries

Dame Edna Everage, the best known character in the repertoire of actor and writer Barry Humphries (b. 1934), made her stage debut in Melbourne in 1955. She has evolved into an outrageous international superstar. Her creator's concern for her integrity as a vehicle for his satiric intent is explored in this letter to entrepreneur Harry M. Miller (b. 1934), who for some years represented Humphries in Australia.

177. To Harry M. Miller, undated [c. 1971]

Dear Harry

I was pleased to hear that the rough samples of Edna worked. Certainly I think a rousing ragtime theme is essential whatever length or format we settle for. *May I make one point clear.*

Edna Everage is my most famous character and she has never before been prostituted in commercials. As you know, Massius Wynne Williams are the only other people considering this potential at present with their product 'COFFEETIME'. I would love to do a daily radio show using the character but obviously I would never be happy if the character herself became secondary to the product and thus permanently identified with it. Money is the prime factor here, and I dont have to tell you that she is only available to the highest bidder. In thinking of texts for her daily Arnott's homily I found myself digging into themes which she would use in the theatre or television. Here is the danger. Radio segments such as this *eat up material.* Three minutes a day of Edna for a hypothetical eternity kill her future on the boards. Thus, I wish to feel completely happy with whatever commercial destiny we settle for Edna. The PUBLIC must be charmed or astonished by her in *her own right.* The commercials must be prestige ones, not obvious hack work. I know the Australian public and I know how fickle they are. If once they suspect their beloved housewife figure is selling out, they'll never accept the character as a satirical force again. I state these profound reservations merely to emphasise two things:

1:   I work for the joy and exhilaration of it and couldn't successfully present an Edna programme that cut against the grain.

2:   I want to keep a valuable creation exclusive and expensive. She's the product of fifteen years of slog and my name is not yet identified with the razzle dazzle rat-race of ultra-commercial TV.

Barry

PS Edna has been approached many times in the past with derisory offers to sell people's stuff. She's an obvious winner, and they know it.

Massius Wynne Williams] Australian advertising agency   Arnott's] Australian biscuit-manufacturing company

The Humphries' wit has delighted in sending up the cherished values and institutions of his native Melbourne. In 1981 Richard Allen was a member of the Council of the newly co-educational Geelong Grammar School. Clyde House, attended at that time by one of Humphries' daughters, had been established to accommodate female students at Geelong. The tennis court was eventually constructed.

178. TO RICHARD ALLEN, 4 DECEMBER 1981

DEAR MR ALLEN

Thank you for inviting me to subscribe to a fund to build a tennis court for the students at Clyde House. Regret that I am unable to do what you so kindly propose since I am deeply opposed to all forms of sporting activity, which I have always felt receive far too much emphasis in our "better schools". I always found it tiresome at dinner parties in Australia finding myself seated next to ladies who think of little else but sport, and I think we parents should do all in our power to prevent another generation of muscle-bound, bone-headed girls from infesting society.

The dangers of encouraging tennis have been forcibly brought home to me in recent months by the disclosures about the life of the American tennis star Billie-Jean King, who has admitted to the press that the game of tennis contributed to her grievous sexual disorder. Under these circumstances, I am very sorry that I cannot be a party to this scheme, although I would always be happy to make a generous financial contribution to any proposal which involved the dismantling of Geelong Grammar's sporting facilities.

May I wish you the compliments of the season.

SINCERELY YOURS/BARRY HUMPHRIES

NEIL DAVIS

Tasmanian-born Neil Davis (1934–85) built a reputation as the bravest and most distinguished Australian combat cameraman and war correspondent since Damien Parer in the Second World War. For over twenty years he covered civil and international conflicts in South-East Asia; he died filming an attempted coup in Bangkok. A record of the remarkable career of Neil Davis is contained in the letters he wrote to his aunt, Lillian Davis (1891–1973). Through this correspondence Davis kept up with family news and the achievements of his beloved Clarence football team.

179. TO LILLIAN DAVIS, 14 NOVEMBER 1972

DEAR AUNTIE

Almost forgot I had a typewriter sitting in front of me, and that's certainly much easier for you to read than my usual scrawl. Received your last letter a few days ago from Hong Kong. I wish the so-called peace moves would result in something, as I can see myself waiting here in limbo for a long time. I think maybe the North Vietnamese and Nixon will sign a separate agreement shortly. The Americans will stop bombing North Viet-Nam, and take up the mines blocking their harbours, and also withdraw all American and Allied troops (now largely the Koreans, who with nearly 38,000 troops outnumber the Americans) from South Viet-Nam. In return, the North Vietnamese will send back all POWs, and maybe agree to work towards a peaceful settlement with the South Vietnamese. About all that will mean will be a temporary lull, and then the Northerners and Southerners will get to it again with a vengeance.

However, the psychology is interesting. Everybody wins something—and save their faces—very important in Asia. North Viet-Nam win because they prove to their people they have defeated the great Americans, and forced them to halt the bombing, take up the mines, and get out of Indo-China. The Americans win because they force the North Vietnamese to give back all the prisoners, and they have assisted the South Vietnamese to remain independent of Communist rule—all they have to do is point to the Saigon regime still being in power, and point out that their job is over—the South Vietnamese still are free. And the South Vietnamese win because President Thieu has already gone on record a few days ago as saying that what should happen is that there should be two peace agreements—or even three. He can tell his people how strong he is, and how the North Vietnamese and Americans both acknowledged what a great statesman he is by taking notice of his advice. But at last it means that things are inching just that little bit closer, and certainly means that direct American involvement is over. Most people think that will mean that the South Vietnamese will crumble—but I don't think it is as simple as that.

I've had more good film lately. One was a sad and bloody piece—but at least it brought home the human element, which is so often missing. Most people don't understand that the South Vietnamese and North Vietnamese soldiers fighting and dying are nice, simple people with human faces, and thoughts. I joined a section of five soldiers moving very close in to North Vietnamese positions just outside a small village north of Saigon—about 16 miles away. I was an old battlefield friend of one young guy. You know, many people one meets are that kind of friend. Over the years one continues to see the same faces—and then they're there no more. However, I quickly recognised this guy, and decided to go in with his section, because not only did I know him, but I knew he would be very close. You see, he was a grenade-throwing specialist, and he would strip off his military gear down to pants and shirt only, and then crawl forward under fire until he was only yards away from the Communist positions. His friends covered him from 20 or 30 yards back. Then he would hurl his grenades and crawl back—all of which makes good film. The North Vietnamese this time were dug in an overgrown graveyard.

I was able to film Phuc (the grenade-thrower) crawling forward, then standing up behind an old tombstone he used for cover, then hurl his grenades, see them exploding a few yards away, then see him crawl back under fire, with his friends covering his retreat. He did that three times, and the last time actually stood and scampered the last few yards very cockily. I was half-laying behind a tree, and Phuc stood in a shallow trench laughing and excited about it all. There had been many bursts of gunfire into our position and another one came in at that moment. I ducked my head, and when I looked at Phuc I could see he had been hit. He just said one word—"Chet" which means "dead"—and he meant "I'm dead". And then he fell forward. Well, I suppose it was a reflex action, and I started my camera running on him. And it was such a difficult decision to make, because the inevitable question I will be asked later—in the future— will be … "how could you just lay there and film your friend in that situation?" All I can say is that many, many things raced through my mind—and obviously large in my mind was this fact. But also I knew that Phuc was well aware of battlefield chances, and a whole world unknown to those that haven't been there exists under those circumstances. Contrary to many thoughts about this is the lack of hatred for the man trying to kill you from a few yards away. He's very much like you, and with the same problems—and he might die at any time, just the same as you. And I knew that if I showed the shock of his suddenly dying it would impress people, and bring home very graphically to them what it was like just to be a common soldier out there—no matter what side one is on. And so I ran my camera, and Phuc lifted his head, and it was obvious he was dying quickly. He died with dignity, and quietly, and slumped forward without another word about 10 seconds later. And that was the end of the film. The film has received enormous praise, but they really miss the point I think. They see it rather as a piece of film taken in unusual circumstances, and not as I see it—intended to bring home the awful reality of war—particularly on a personal basis. However—it's done, and there's little doubt I won't ever do it again.

All the world seems pretty excited about the prospects for peace, but it rather seems here like the eye of the hurricane—fairly calm, and with little actual optimism, just talk. They'll believe it when it happens—and then they realise it will most likely last only a short time. No, I haven't done any more yet for the Herald. They had to cut the last one a bit to allow room for Arthur Calwell's memoirs! Only thing is that they cut a couple of the better parts out—however, that's editors I suppose.

Seems Rosny is changing again—somehow, I wish the old days of the golf course were back—it was such a nice break in the countryside there. It was only for the favoured few, but maybe they could have made it into a nice parkland for everyone to enjoy. Glad Teddie, Raef, and family are all well—tell Reg I'll write him if he writes again—I think he wrote me one letter this time, but I've left it at home in Phnom-Penh or somewhere.

My wounds are healed ok. Had secondary infection for a while, but the Americans treated me, and finally it cleared—saw the doctor for the last time yesterday. Only bad for a couple of days really, and didn't miss any working time. I guess John arrived with the tape at last—he has lots of scandal to tell me these days. Anyway, it keeps John alive—he's never been happy unless he had a nice piece of scandal to keep him going!

Give my regards to all—hope Mrs Button is keeping well, as well as all the family: regards to Kaylene & family, Barb, Darrel, Mary & their all …

Take care,/Love/Neil

one young guy] Nguyen Van Phuc (d. 1972), a member of the ARVN 25th Division. Davis had been friendly with him for over four years   Rosny] a suburb of Hobart, Tasmania   Arthur Calwell's memoirs] *Be Just and Fear Not*, the autobiography of the Australian Labor politician Arthur Augustus Calwell (1896–1973), published in Melbourne in 1972

'It's Time'

Possibly no other election in Australian federal history ushered in so great or concentrated a period of political, cultural and social change as the election of 1972 when Edward Gough Whitlam (b. 1916), leader of the Australian Labor Party, won office as Prime Minister. The 'It's Time' public letter, signed by an array of distinguished business, academic and cultural names, was one indicator that a decisive shift was taking place in the electorate.

180. To the *Age* (Melbourne), 23 November 1972

Sir,—

We, the undersigned, who are not members of any political party, believe that Australia's interests will be best served by a change of Government as a result of this election.

Our democratic system works properly only when each of the major parties has the chance to govern. Each benefits from the responsibilities of office. Each gains from the freedom of opposition.

Some of us think the Liberal–Country Party coalition has had a productive, as well as long period in office. Others of us are less enthusiastic about its record, especially in recent years.

But we all agree that today, after 23 years in office, it needs new ideas and has problems of long-term leadership which can be best worked out in opposition.

Although we do not subscribe to all the Australian Labor Party's policies, we see no over-riding reason for continuing to exclude it from office.

It is Australia's oldest and biggest party. It represents aspirations in our society which cannot be ignored. It has prepared itself for office and needs only a moderate swing in its favor at this election to take power.

If denied office any longer, the Labor Party is in danger of disintegrating as a force in Australia's political life.

We believe a change of Government will benefit both the major parties, on which the vitality of our political system depends.

The ultimate beneficiary will be the Australian nation and its people.

Signatories to the letter: Professor R.R Andrew, Professor Macmahon Ball, Professor Hedley Bull, Sir Macfarlane Burnet, David Campbell, Professor Manning Clark, Sir Walter Crocker, Professor R.I. Downing, Dr Frank Fenner, Leonard French, Bruce Grant, Sir Keith Hancock, The Rev Dr J.D. McCaughey, Kenneth Myer, Patrick White, and Judith Wright

GIOVANNI ANDREONI

Born at Grosetto in Italy, teacher and writer Giovanni Andreoni (b. 1935) arrived in Australia in 1962. An academic, he is also the author of the semi-autobiographical novel Martin Pescatore *(1967). In this letter (translated by Andreoni himself) to his mother Maria Bertocci Andreoni (1904–85), he distils the experience—and dilemmas—of many of Australia's post-war immigrants.*

181. TO MARIA BERTOCCI ANDREONI, 2 JANUARY 1974

MOTHER,

I have decided to become an Australian citizen. "Tempus fugit" and I don't want to miss the chance of participating in the rebirth of this vast and beautiful land.

For many years the detached observer within ruled my life finding faults and ridiculing colonial Australia. It was indeed an easy task! At the theatre one had to stand up and be afflicted by the sound of "God Save the Queen". In every public building small and large effigies of Elizabeth II harrowed the poor visitor. I don't mind the photos as much as the portraits of Her Majesty in regal attire—her selection of artists is as pedestrian as her choice of hats.

You know all this from my letters, full as they are of humorous and not so humorous details illustrating the dullness of colonial Australia. You also know I was trying to hide from you my anguish at the realisation that my only function was to serve and be grateful. At the University I am constantly reminded that, being a wog, I have overstepped the mark by working there.

No reasonable person can blame me for not wishing to be assimilated. Assimilation is the dehumanising scheme of colonial Australia. Migrants will be educated into accepting proper roles assigned to them by their masters: wogs and dagos can grow vegetables and sell fish, Huns work as mechanics, blacks as farm hands. Their children will soon forget the old culture and think and act like happy little Australians. What a squalid and destructive policy.

Well a huge man stood up in Parliament, his name is Gough Whitlam, and behind him there is an unruly mob of dreamers and reformers. Down with assimilation—they shout—let us accept and respect each other for what we are, let's build the new Australia together.

Now Mother, control yourself, I know you are going to quote "il vecchio Machiavelli". I too remember his words: that reformers will always come to grief, because they face an unrelenting opposition from all those who benefited from the old system, and only lukewarm support from those who might benefit from the new order. I am old enough to be able to survive the possible failure of this dream of "Egalite, Fraternite, Liberte". But I am also young enough to feel the elation of these Promethean days. It is grand to partake of such historical events.

Write to me soon. I must know what you think.

I miss you.

GIOVANNI

ELIZABETH JOLLEY

The writer (Monica) Elizabeth Jolley (b. 1923) settled in Western Australia in 1959. Encouraged by Ian Templeman (b. 1938), foundation director of the Fremantle Arts Centre, Jolley taught creative writing and literature at the centre, which published her first book, Five Acre Virgin, *in 1976. Jolley and Templeman have maintained a long but intermittent correspondence, their letters a kind of extended ongoing conversation.*

182. TO IAN TEMPLEMAN, 4 AUGUST 1975

DEAR IAN,

Thank you for the delightful evening we had with you. For me it was the kind of rest I hardly ever have and I think, for the others, it was what they needed too. You were the provider, *thank you.* I started to read *Ted Hughes* as soon as I came home, thank you. *The Rain Horse* is the only story I have read so far, I'll read it several times, it would be a good one to read in the class for many reasons. I have never read anything of his before and must thank you for the introduction.

I'd like to go back to something we were saying at the Centre about the children. I do understand so well the difficulties that you have, I feel sure that your sons will emerge very whole people and will find their ways of facing the world. Children often (from my experience) turn away from the enrichments which would come from their parents, 2 of our children are very reluctant to allow themselves the pleasures of reading and music because these don't seem to fit with the people they have to be with, this is just an example. It's a pity. Your children receive a picture of you from your parents as well as their own picture when they come to your place. Though in some ways this has its difficulties it has *advantages* towards their wholeness later on. I admire you very much for your way of managing or appearing to manage. We all have to appear to manage of course. I have found family life very hard at times. I've never lived alone, family, boarding school, institution (2 hospitals) marriage part of the time sharing part of a house (poverty) continuing marriage children d'you see, its a struggle to have a room to oneself, to do this, without hurting some one you love and who loves you.

You are quite right when you say it needs time to make a friendship, a deep whole exploring "relationship" with another person and of course people don't have this time and, as you said, Fathers/Mothers often live their whole lives without a friend. It's a pity we all have to live in this way where it's not possible to really know a few people. I thought our talk last night reached some interesting depths and I hope we didn't talk too much (fear of not keeping up required good manners). Because I want to write I stay up late at night, and because I need to find out about myself and other people I've had a rather troubled life (apart from children) and I suppose after a lot of years I am fortunate to have the kind of husband I have. My work at the Arts Centre has shown L. that it is possible for me to be absorbed in something without causing him the kind of "suffering" he might be afraid of. So thank you for that too. (Mark F for lack of proper paragraphs) sorry to write such a long letter. Very much love to you. Elizabeth. I hope you enjoy the rest of the holiday. I really love your house, it's charming and restful, I felt really happy there.

P.S. I think people went away from the writers week end well pleased, such a good thing to be able to provide this.

Ted Hughes] Jolley had borrowed a copy of Ted Hughes' *Wodwo* (Faber, London, 1971), a collection of poetry and prose   the children] Templeman was widowed shortly after the birth of his twin sons Nicholas and Paul   L.] Leonard Jolley, husband of Elizabeth Jolley   your house] in 1975 Templeman was living in a house in the Perth suburb of Mount Pleasant overlooking the Canning River

GOUGH WHITLAM

Both in and out of public office, Edward Gough Whitlam (b. 1916), Prime Minister of Australia 1972–75, has been drawn irresistibly to the display of wit, erudition and, sometimes, pedantry. In this letter his sparring partner is Clyde Cameron (b. 1913) who held two portfolios during Whitlam's term in government.

183. To Clyde Cameron, 23 September 1975

My dear Clyde,

I so much enjoyed your letter on the accentuation of kilometer that I was nearly moved to reply in iambic tetrameters or pentameters, the classic form of satiric verse. When, however, I read the text in the popular press, I realised that you had merely signed a letter prepared by your Department and that your personal staff had released it in the normal way. Hence I am sending this prosaic instead of prosodic response; it is more a letter to a Minister for Science than a letter from a Minister for the Arts.

Whether the accent falls on the penultimate or antepenultimate syllable normally depends on whether the penultimate syllable is a long or short one; if it is a long syllable, it bears the accent while, if it is a short syllable, the accent falls on the antepenultimate syllable. All English words ending in 'meter' or 'metre' derive from the Greek word 'metron' in which the penultimate syllable is short, the letter 'e' in English reproducing 'epsilon' not 'eta' in the Greek.

Accordingly all such words in use before the Parisian urban guerillas introduced the metric system have been accented on the antepenultimate syllable, whether they are literary words dear to me, such as tetrameter or pentameter, or scientific words familiar to you, such as perimeter (first identified in English in 1592), diameter (1602), thermometer (1633), barometer (1665) and chronometer (1735).

Your advisers have, I suggest, been influenced in their preference for the accent on the penultimate by a desire to reproduce the French pronunciation of metric units of distance. One might as well accent the penultimate in all the words in the preceding paragraph on the ground that they have a corresponding French form. One does not accent any of the scores of other words subsequent to the French Revolution, such as altimeter (1847), just because the French have also used a corresponding word.

One of your abiding concerns has been consideration for our migrants. You of all people should know that our migrants from Italy, Greece, Spain and now Timor accent the antepenultimate in metric units of distance. This pronunciation should come readily to you, for I have myself heard you consistently attest your brute strength on the ergometer (1879), your staying power on the pedometer (1723) and your vigilant velocity on the speedometer (1904), invariably stressing the antepenultimate.

I shall send copies of this reply to the same Ministers as you sent copies of your own letter. Your staff might see to its wider dissemination. Some member of a Caucus committee in which you have influence might even ask a question permitting us to table correspondence on which we clearly set so much store.

YOURS SINCERELY/E. G. WHITLAM

GARFIELD BARWICK

If the election of Gough Whitlam's Labor government in 1972 was hailed as a watershed, the manner of its demise, dismissal by the Governor-General invoking the largely untested reserve powers of the vice-regal office, has been described as the most dramatic event in Australia's political history. Crucial in the action taken by the Governor-General on 11 November 1975 was advice tendered in writing by the Chief Justice of Australia, Sir Garfield Barwick (1903–97), on the afternoon of 10 November. The terms of this advice and the propriety of the Chief Justice in providing it remain the subject of constitutional debate.

184. TO JOHN KERR, 10 NOVEMBER 1975

DEAR SIR JOHN,

In response to Your Excellency's invitation I attended this day at Admiralty House. In our conversations I indicated that I considered myself, as Chief Justice of Australia, free, on Your Excellency's request, to offer you legal advice as to Your Excellency's constitutional rights and duties in relation to an existing situation which, of its nature, was unlikely to come before the Court. We both clearly understood that I was not in any way concerned with matters of a purely political kind, or with any political consequences of the advice I might give.

In response to Your Excellency's request for my legal advice as to whether a course on which you had determined was consistent with your constitutional authority and duty, I respectfully offer the following.

The Constitution of Australia is a federal Constitution which embodies the principle of Ministerial responsibility. The Parliament consists of two houses, the House of

Representatives and the Senate, each popularly elected, and each with the same legislative power, with the one exception that the Senate may not originate nor amend a money bill.

Two relevant constitutional consequences flow from this structure of the Parliament. First, the Senate has constitutional power to refuse to pass a money bill; it has power to refuse supply to the Government of the day. Secondly, a Prime Minister who cannot ensure supply to the Crown, including funds for carrying on the ordinary services of Government, must either advise a general election (of a kind which the constitutional situation may then allow) or resign. If, being unable to secure supply, he refuses to take either course, Your Excellency has constitutional authority to withdraw his Commission as Prime Minister.

There is no analogy in respect of a Prime Minister's duty between the situation of the Parliament under the federal Constitution of Australia and the relationship between the House of Commons, a popularly elected body, and the House of Lords, a non-elected body, in the unitary form of Government functioning in the United Kingdom. Under that system, a Government having the confidence of the House of Commons can secure supply, despite a recalcitrant House of Lords. But it is otherwise under our federal Constitution. A Government having the confidence of the House of Representatives but not that of the Senate, both elected Houses, cannot secure supply to the Crown.

But there is an analogy between the situation of a Prime Minister who has lost the confidence of the House of Commons and a Prime Minister who does not have the confidence of the Parliament, i.e. of the House of Representatives and of the Senate. The duty and responsibility of the Prime Minister to the Crown in each case is the same: if unable to secure supply to the Crown, to resign or to advise an election.

In the event that, conformably to this advice, the Prime Minister ceases to retain his Commission, Your Excellency's constitutional authority and duty would be to invite the Leader of the Opposition, if he can undertake to secure supply, to form a caretaker government (i.e. one which makes no appointments or initiates any policies) pending a general election, whether of the House of Representatives, or of both Houses of Parliament, as that Government may advise.

Accordingly, my opinion is that, if Your Excellency is satisfied in the current situation that the present Government is unable to secure supply, the course upon which Your Excellency has determined is consistent with your constitutional authority and duty.

YOURS RESPECTFULLY,/(SGND GARFIELD BARWICK)

John Kerr

Not long after 1.00 p.m. on 11 November 1975, Sir John Kerr (1914–91) as Governor-General of Australia handed a letter to Gough Whitlam determining his appointment as prime minister and determining the appointments of all the ministers in the government. Attached to the letter was a statement of reasons for a decision which divided political and constitutional opinion. At the election which followed, the caretaker Prime Minister John Malcolm Fraser was given a decisive mandate by the people, a result which some have argued was John Kerr's vindication. Others maintained that the means by which Kerr brought the country to this outcome were flawed in conception and execution.

185. To Gough Whitlam, 11 November 1975

Dear Mr Whitlam,

In accordance with section 64 of the Constitution I hereby determine your appointment as my Chief Adviser and Head of the Government. It follows that I also hereby determine the appointments of all the Ministers in your Government.

You have previously told me that you would never resign or advise an election of the House of Representatives or a double dissolution and that the only way in which such an election could be obtained would be by my dismissal of you and your ministerial colleagues. As it appeared likely that you would today persist in this attitude I decided that, if you did, I would determine your commission and state my reasons for doing so. You have persisted in your attitude and I have accordingly acted as indicated. I attach a statement of my reasons which I intend to publish immediately.

It is with a great deal of regret that I have taken this step both in respect of yourself and your colleagues.

I propose to send for the Leader of the Opposition and to commission him to form a new caretaker government until an election can be held.

Yours sincerely,/(sgnd John R. Kerr)

KATHLEEN FITZPATRICK

Former colleagues, historians Kathleen Fitzpatrick (1905–90) and Manning Clark (1915–91), kept up a correspondence about books and ideas after Clark had left the University of Melbourne for the Australian National University. Fitzpatrick retired early to her house at Lorne, Victoria, to complete a book on Henry James but it did not find a publisher. Her autobiography Solid Bluestone Foundations *(1983) is a classic of its genre: elegantly written, ironic, perceptive.*

186. TO MANNING CLARK, 5 JANUARY 1977

DEAR MANNING,

Thank you for your most welcome Christmas letter and also for your Boyer lectures. Oh dear! I wasn't serious in describing you as a 'product of the Melbourne History School'—I knew well 'nough that you didn't think of yourself, nor wish to be thought of, in that light. It is too late in life for me to give over the habit of intellectual larking. My friends must just bear in mind that I am among the comparatively rare birds one encounters in academic life—one of the Micks. I suppose that during our centuries of oppression we learnt the trick of expressing our more subversive thoughts by stating their harmless opposites and, in general, of the resort to verbal obliqueness. (I never heard my father use the words Yes and No—if absolutely forced to commit himself to an affirmative or negative he would say—'That is so' or 'That, I believe, is not so.') I expect mine will be the last generation of expatriate Micks to use the double-talk and just as well, too, because out of context it leads to misunderstandings.

I was particularly pleased to receive the Boyer lectures because, owing to the awkward hour at which they were given, I had heard only the first. Now I have read them all, with very great interest and pleasure. I have been brooding on that remark of Sainte-Beuve about 'the whole acquires after the event a semblance of reason which is deceptive' and have concluded (and now I *am* talking seriously) that it is one of those remarks which looks intelligent at first sight, but is really superficial, because precisely the opposite is true—if a whole is created its parts do not merely seem to, but in fact actually do cohere. You state (p. 16 of the Boyer lectures) precisely what the 'reason' which in fact does make a unity of your *History of Australia* is—I mean 'I wanted to paint the human heart in all its complexity'.

What a theme for the Australian historian lies ahead when the time comes to analyze the results of the great migration of our time. When I was a child it used to be said that we were 98% British in origin—now 40% non-British and the figure seems likely to go higher. What will the Anglo-Turkish and Irish-Greek Australians be like and who will tell their story?

It is glorious at Lorne this summer. My chief occupation is gazing at the Southern Ocean breaking on the beach. For entertainment I am writing an account of my recollections of the year 1914—not the 1914 famous in history, but the one I spent as a boarder at Portland Convent. For self-improvement (in which I am persistent although so little has ever rubbed off on me) I am wrestling with the thought of Teilhard de Chardin. It is almost completely beyond my intellectual capacity, but every now and then I hear a great rustling and feel a stir of air from the beat of unseen wings and experience, as dear H.J. says, 'a very strong sense of something or other'.

Enough, enough, or you will never write to me again.

WITH LOVE,/KATHLEEN

Boyer lectures] a series given annually on ABC Radio by a distinguished Australian. Clark gave the 1976 series, entitled 'A Discovery of Australia'   My recollections] Fitzpatrick's *Solid Bluestone Foundations*
Teilhard de Chardin] controversial Catholic theologian   dear H.J.] Henry James

MANNING CLARK

Charles Manning Hope Clark (1915–91) taught history at the University of Melbourne and was Foundation Professor of History at the Canberra University College, later the Australian National University. He is best known for his six volume work, A History of Australia, *published between 1962 and 1987. He played a decisive role in making Australian academics take their country's history seriously and in bringing its study to a wide popular readership.*

187. TO KATHLEEN FITZPATRICK, 22 JANUARY 1977

DEAR KATHLEEN,

Thanks for your letter. I agree that the remark by St Beuve is itself deceptive. I came across his work when working on de Tocqueville—not long after that decisive event in Bonn early in November 1938 when the sight of what the Nazis had done to Jewish property the previous night led, there and then, to a painful re-examination of the hopes about the future, and the ease with which they could be achieved.

Yes—I agree too, that there are moments when I believe there is a 'something, somewhere'. I also ask that 'something' for strength—but have not got further than that though have wanted too. Am two-thirds of the way through the third and final writing of vol. 4. Some of it, I hope, says something, and some of it is very flat and lifeless.

Yes—there must be a something in a work which give it a coherence. That is why it is a mistake to press on when one's heart is as dry as the sands of the desert.

I hope you are at *it* again. I think of you always as someone who has something to say—as an appreciator, a person who feeds on life, a person for whom the light in the eye would fade if that gift were to disappear and cease to be.

My love to you. I hope you will write again.

EVER,/MANNING

R.F. Brissenden

Robert Francis Brissenden (1928–91), academic, poet and crime writer, was a pioneer with David Campbell, Rosemary Dobson, A.D. Hope and others of what has been called the wine poem. Such poems were written during the 1970s and 1980s for the Annual Poet's Lunch held at the Australian National University with wine merchant Jim Murphy. Brissenden's absence abroad in 1982 saw him exploit the letter to honour his poetic commitment to the 'Company Assembled'.

188. To James Murphy & the Company Assembled, August 1982

Dear Jim: I see the time's come round again
For me to take glass, bottle, paper, pen
And turn a verse or two in celebration
Of wine and friendship for that rare occasion,
The POETS' LUNCH—a gathering which this year
I'll sadly have to miss: RESEARCH, I fear,
Has brought me here beside the River Arno
Where Dante wrote his epic *The Inferno*,
And Byron wrote another called *Don Juan*.
Each points the reader down the road to ruin,
But Byron's hero finds his way to Hades
By happily seducing all the ladies
While Dante's view of things is grim and tearful.
So when I feel the need of something cheerful,
I take my Byron, lay aside my Dante,
And pour myself a fresh glass of Chianti.
To be more accurate I should have said
'I pour myself a glass of local red
—The one we bottled in the good old way
Out on our kitchen terrace yesterday.'
Here on each hill the olive and the vine
Still flourish: every village makes its wine,
Presses its oil and turns out fresh cheese
From sheep-milk—as it's done for centuries.
Does it sound too idyllic to be true?
Well, in some ways it is: only a few
Small farms remain—abandoned houses stand
On every second ridge: 'ill fares the land',
The village is deserted. Factory farms
Spread like a giant blight across the charms

Of Tuscany's old landscape. True—but still
The shepherd trails his flock across the hill
Each day, and from my window I can see
The vines that grew the grapes, the winery
That made this red I'm drinking. If the bad
New ways are winning, at the least I'm glad
To see the old that last: and so I raise
My glass, though absent, with you all to praise
The OLIVE and the LAUREL and the VINE:
Our joy and comfort: POETRY and WINE.

HAROLD STEWART

At the time of writing this letter to poet and academic Dorothy Green, Stewart (1916–95) was living in Kyoto, Japan, having left Australia permanently in 1966. He became a member of the Shinsu Buddhist sect, and published haiku translations as well as other poems which show his strong interest in Chinese as well as Japanese culture. He is perhaps best known in Australia for his part with James McAuley in the Ern Malley hoax (see Letters 146 and 147). In spite of the concern about his health expressed in this letter, Stewart lived for another nine years.

189. TO DOROTHY GREEN, SEPTEMBER 1986

MY DEAR DOROTHY,

With unexpected suddenness I find that my life seems to be drawing to a close. I have just been discharged from hospital after a month of tests by the latest in medical technology, which has showed that my heart is tired, old, worn out, and diseased. The aorta is enlarged and 90% blocked up with atherosclerosis; there are three lesions in the right ventricle; and the left ventricle's main vein is congenitally twisted. There is some myocardial infarction near the septum and blood cannot be expelled and leaks back into the heart, resulting in insufficiency of oxygen—hence the anginal pain. Among other tests I had an anginograph operation which revealed the above sad facts. The prognosis is therefore bleak : I may last hours, weeks, months, but hardly years. I had hoped to go on into my seventies (I shall be 70 in December) even if not eighties. But this now seems infinitely improbable. This is what comes of being a lifelong non-drinker, non-smoker, vegetarian, celibate! Now the new epic will never be completed, though I shall go on writing it to the last day. I added sixty new lines while in hospital : what better place in which to write about the tortures of the damned? Tomorrow I see my lawyer about my new Will in English and Japanese, to comply with the laws of both countries. I have made him joint-executor with Bishop Hillebrand, an Australian friend of twenty-six years' standing. Before resorting to open-heart surgery, the doctors here decided to try every possible medication, to which I am responding positively, so at least I am not in pain any more. But my clockwork orange could stop ticking at any time—I hope for preference in my sleep, though one is supposed to be conscious in one's last moments in order to recite the Name.

Thank you for letting me know the sad news about Ken. I had heard already through a friend-in-common, and had written to him as soon as you told me that he was seriously ill. But my letter may never have reached him in time, as was the case with the letter of the friend-in-common, which arrived too late and was returned by Ken's executors. I feel that the stab-in-the-back delivered by Lady MacRyan contributed to his early demise, since he had invested so much intellectual and emotional capital in *Hemisphere* and worked so hard to keep it afloat and to develop it into such a fine magazine. His dismissal, having to sell up his home and leave Canberra, and to go job-hunting at sixty may have driven him to the bottle, always an occupational hazard with 'journos'. One more example of how Australia shows its gratitude to its benefactors. Yes, so many of the old leaves are falling off the tree this autumn—I, too, have lost several, and even younger friends are ill. It is *mujo* or impermanence, one of the three basic facts of life in the Buddha's view, which no one can deny.

May I take this opportunity to say once again how much pleasure and profit I have derived from our long correspondence? Though it now seems unlikely that we shall meet again in this life, I hope that our friendship by post as well as personally has been as fruitful for you as for me. Heartfelt gratitude, dear Dorothy.

The weather here at present is of a divinity, and makes me regret having to leave Kyoto, with which I have had a long love-affair. Among my other regrets is that you never managed to come up here while we were both young and active enough for me to show you a few of the beauties in art and nature that this city preserves. I regret, too, not being able to see my last two books, already completed, through the press before leaving. Carmen Blacker has recently given the Mss. of *New Phoenix Wings* to O.U.P. in Oxford but they are terribly slow to decide and I may not even hear the news of its acceptance or rejection. *Over the Vermilion Bridge* is still held up for want of the illustrations and so I cannot send it to Tuttle, who may or may not accept it. While in hospital I have been going through many old papers, dating back even to the 'thirties, destroying everything that I do not wish to fall into the hands of the biographical ghouls, psychological beachcombers and editorial illiterates. This will also save my Literary Executor much trouble. No, I did not appoint you to that thankless task, knowing how conscientious you are and how already overloaded with literary chores. An old friend of 40 years, Peter Kelly, who was a professional editor for many years with Anguish and Robbery and later Melbourne Univ. Press, will guard the remains like Fafnir coiled around his gold—or in this case iron pyrites! When he dies the papers will go to the National Library, though it is doubtful if anyone would be interested in perusing them. Ern Malley represents the level above which Woz kulcha seems unable to rise, along with Ned Kelly and Phar Lap. I do hope that your hips are behaving and that you are in no pain. With every good wish,

HAROLD

sad news about Ken] Kenneth Henderson, former editor of the Canberra journal *Hemisphere*   Lady MacRyan] Senator Susan Maree Ryan (b. 1942), Minister of Education, had closed down *Hemisphere*   Anguish and Robbery] A well-known nickname for the publishers Angus & Robertson

KYLIE TENNANT

The writer Kylie Tennant (1912–88) died after a battle with cancer. Among her best-known books are Foveaux *(1939) and* The Battlers *(1941). She wrote sympathetically of the dispossessed and the underprivileged. In an open letter published in several Australian newspapers not long before her death, she expressed with a fine poetic sensibility a deeply felt case for voluntary euthanasia.*

190. To 'A Friend' (*Sydney Morning Herald*), 6 February 1988

The last letter to a friend—from Kylie Tennant

One night my friend Hans, a song composer who lives at Blackheath Mountain, came out on his front doorstep in the dark and his little moustache encountered something soft.

It was the nose of my daughter's black mare Princess who had crept up to the open door. They blew on each other quietly, then Princess went away.

As all my friends know Death and I have for the past few years had these close looks at each other. Thanks to devoted doctors, nurses, friends, relatives, hospitals, I have managed to finish a couple of books while Death looks in at the doorway.

I have no complaints, but the cancer cells have gnawed out my rib cage and the bets on how long I can last must be called in anytime: As Housman says:

"And I will have to 'bate my price for in the grave they say/Is neither knowledge nor device, nor fourteen cents a day."

If I were stronger I would be filling notebooks with statistics, facts, collections and scraps of research on the desperate social problem of the aged and terminally ill and the way our stupid laws keep such people alive and put compassion of doctors, nurses and helpers within the realm of criminal prosecution should any attempt be made to shorten the agony of sufferers.

Of course this absurdity of our laws is circumvented by those not too timorous or self-regarding. But why should such a responsibility be placed haphazard?

My friends flinch away from any discussion of death or cancer. These words never pass their lips until they are right up against the desperate social situation of the dying.

What is needed is a change in the Australian people's attitude. Decades of evasion, looking the other way, do not favour your acceding to my last request—to investigate, raise a cry, insist on action. "Oh well, everyone knows that perhaps, in 20 years time maybe"—but you are brave as well as lazy, my friend. I'm only asking you to do what you *can* to bring to public notice our absurd injustices to the aged and ill.

We recoil from the alarming unknown, but Death needs only a legal bridle and halter. Collect, advise, find out, keep a record of material for social change in this *one* area. Do something—not necessarily form a committee and forget it. Do what you can with all honour to help change the social attitude to the terminally ill tucked away as a home for Lost Pills and left to endure their end.

So, you know, you yourself will feel the soft nose of Death and hear the breathing on your doorstep. Before then accept my legacy and do some thinking and working on this problem.

With all affection I commend you—my friend—heart up—its only Princess in the dark.

BRETT WHITELEY

In September 1988 the Sydney arts journalist Janet Hawley published a moving last interview with the painter Lloyd Frederic Rees, then in his nineties and with the sands running close to their end. In response to this news, many friends and admirers took the opportunity to say farewell to one of the great figures of Australian art. The painter Brett Whiteley (1939–96) was one of these. From Endlessnessism, his studio in Sydney's Surry Hills, he wrote a letter which paid homage to the old man and acknowledged a deeply felt debt to Lloyd Rees' example and influence.

191. To Lloyd Rees, 21 September 1988

DEAR LLOYD

I received a sad telephone call from Janet, the journalist from Good Weekend magazine a few days ago, she had recently been with you in Hobart and she brought me the inevitable news that it didn't look as though you had much time left …

'rage, rage against the dying of the light', and since our telephone call a month or so ago, which I enjoyed so much; there are a couple of things I wanted to tell you which I have never quite sorted out in my own mind, but now realizing that time is finite and that there is a finality to everything, I put pen to paper and indeed, attempt to sort out these feelings I have carried for years but never expressed.

I wanted to convey to you just how important an influence you have been on my life and my art, how one event in 1953 or 1954 had a profound effect upon my under-standing of what painting was and could be, and that the realization of that day has continued to influence and inspire me to this day.

I was a 14 year old school-boy in a cadet uniform attending Scots College, when after school I visited for the first time a one-man show of your landscapes at the old Maquarie Gallery next to the Savoy Theatre. I had been drawing and painting since early consciousness and had shown signs of precousity but had no real idea of a direction, like most youngsters I worked in a cat & mouse manner, pounching on any new influence and imitating everything I liked.

The thrill of discovery walking into that little gallery and seeing for the first time. Landscapes, big & tiny, that looked to me as though they had every influence in the world in them. I had noted already that Dobell and Drysdale produced visions, but I could see that they were grafted from two or three other visual sources. But these little pictures signed in the corner L. REES, seemed to have filtered and sometimes dredged the whole of Europe through them. They were paintings that showed a sort of visual code, as though 15 artists had miraculously been brought to bear on the one picture, still with the feeling of incredible unity, but at the same time fertile in 15 different ways. They contained nature AND ideas, they contained naturalism but seemed also very invented, and the adventure of them, was that they *showed* the decisions and revisions that had been made while they had been painted.

I had never seen anything like that before. My understanding till then was that one set up an easel in front of nature and rendered it in one mood, one style, one principle—you simply covered the canvas until you couldn't make it look any better.

Now here were pictures that had for me an Einsteinian leap forward, for it showed just how flexible & wide the implications of painting could be, and it set me on a path of discovery that I am still on today—namely that change, and particularly change of pace in a painting is where the poetry gets born. What I saw that day was your genius for knowing when & when not, to put paint, where and how onto a canvas. When to edit, and when to leave. When to invent and when to mimic. was it you Lloyd who said that 'God was a wonderful creator, but He never learned how to paint'?!

So essential was it that I further understand what was nature, and what was you, I set about at the age of 17 to paint 'The Harbour from McMahon's Point' setting up my easel in the exact same spot you had a few years earlier, and although I produced a 'homage to Lloyd Rees' I learned practically how the critical facility of your mind worked. I learned how to use the rag for accidents, and when to get the fine sable out and sew mass together. I learned when to use meat and when to use turpentine. But mostly I learned how to adventure in and to risk, and from that came what I can only describe as tough freedom.

Later on I acquired from William Scott a taste for the unexpected, and from Francis Bacon, the mystery in flesh, and how to capitalize upon a mistake, how to 'order' an accident. From Picasso—ambiguity. From Bob Rauschenberg—irony … and so on … but what I learned from you, was to be influenced by everyone, and to extract out of everything I looked at and every corner I went around, the 'critical mass', and to put it in my spiritual pile, my optical repertoire, later to be amalgamed and dealt out like a humming bird deals honey.

It really is difficult at the 11th hour to try and summarize how in so many ways you have been my role-model and mentor, without sounding patronizing or sentimental, certianly your whole vibration and presence as a person—your manner, your morality, your kindness and enthusiasm, has affected a lot of people and I know Lloyd I will continue to be influenced by you until the day I too, come up to giving in and giving over; and I know someone will pick up on something of what I have done, and carry the mantle on into the 2000s, whatever shape and form that will take, so the profound thread, that leads its way back to Leonardo and on through the millenium to Egypt, that wonderful line, the most precious club in the world, that occasionly gets new members, and bids farewell to those whose innings of dreaming, are done.

My love/and/adieu/brett whiteley

Dobell and Drysdale] Sir William Dobell (1899–1970), one of Australia's most celebrated portrait and genre painters (see Letter 130); Sir (George) Russell Drysdale (1912–81), Australian painter who brought new vision to the subject of outback Australia   The Harbour from McMahon's Point] one of Rees' best known works (1950), held in the Art Gallery of New South Wales   meat] thickly applied paint   Scott] William Scott (1913–89), painter of Irish and Scottish descent   Bacon] Francis Bacon (1909–92), English painter   Rauschenberg] Robert Rauschenberg (b. 1925), American painter, sculptor, printmaker, photographer and performance artist

LLOYD REES

Lloyd Rees (1895–1988) wrote a response to Brett Whiteley's letter which was as dignified and courteous as it was touched by the emotions which Whiteley had put down in words. Rees dictated a letter from his son's home at Sandy Bay in Tasmania where his efforts were concentrated still in the making of art. He died on 2 December 1988.

192. To Brett Whiteley, 23 September 1988

Dear Brett

During the course of a long lifetime I have received a few letters with outstanding qualities of understanding and, I believe, love also. But one received from you today is beyond all others in depth of feeling and depth of understanding. It overcame me because I did not realize that my work could bring forth such wonderful feelings regarding my status as an artist and even more, if possible my status as a human being. I can only send you, Brett, a simple thankyou from the bottom of my heart. It took quite a while for me to realize the meaning of several letters from you of which this one is the climax.

Yes, Brett—I think old Mother Nature has called a halt to my creative life, but I have two pictures—one a gossamer-like dawn, the other a lithograph depicting the wildness of our rain forest areas. I wont write in detail of either of them, but I would be very happy if they touched you in the manner that my better work seems to have done.

The litho is to be a gift from Fred Genis—it was his suggestion, in fact—and myself (we combined—he to do all the printing, and me, the picture) to the Wilderness society to be sold to raise funds for them at an exhibition to open at the Australian Galleries in Melbourne next month.

I hope I'm not wrong Brett, but I have no reason to use my illness as an excuse for the quality of my work, and I get a certain glow of happiness to think my last two works may be worthy of my general standard.

It is a bad crash I have suffered and I'm afraid I have to fight to contain my patience with a slow period of decline. I look upon you, Brett, as a beacon light that will reveal aspects of Australian creativity hitherto unknown in the years ahead.

Go forward, my dear warrior, and take with you my love and deep thanks for what you have already given us.

LLOYD

Fred Genis] (b. 1935), Dutch-born master lithographer who worked closely with Lloyd Rees in preparing printed editions of his work   Wilderness Society] the conservation body which had campaigned vigorously to protect Tasmania's wilderness and heritage areas

GWEN HARWOOD

Gwen Harwood (1920–95) is best known as a poet but she was also a brilliant and prolific letter writer. Born in Queensland, she spent most of her adult life in Hobart. Although she felt the limitations of a small society, her sociability and her generous spirit are reflected in the spirited comedy of her letters. These kept her in touch with friends in distant places, as well as those close to home like Father William Paton, former rector of All Saints' Anglican Church, South Hobart.

193. TO WILLIAM PATON, 3 DECEMBER 1990

DEAR FR PATON,

I was planning to write you a long letter today, the grass being too wet to mow and the car being away for some constitutional reform; but the day proved to be one of constant interruptions and matters needing attention in the mail, so Pelagius will have to wait. You'll be pleased to know that Blessed City won the Age Book of the Year Award. My friend and editor Alison Hoddinott and I were flown (she from Armidale NSW) to the luncheon at the Hyatt in Collins Street. We felt like provincial Goths in Imperial Rome. The Hyatt is all Pompeian pink marble and interior waterfalls and hanging gardens, not to mention a great Savoy Room where we had the lunch under ceiling mirrors. The judges and speechmakers were on a stage lit in a golden diffused glow; they sat in a row at a trestle table. It looked like a Renaissance Last Supper (the irreligious couldn't decide whether Dinny O'Hearn of the SBS Book Show or the poet Kevin Hart should have the main role.) Alison and I, two grandmothers in sober dress, sat at our publisher's table. A book distributor on my right, who seemed to wonder why we were there, said he didn't often come to Tasmania, and added 'but my grandmother deceased in Burnie.' The main course was oddly trinitarian: three small fillets of lamb; three small potatoes; three small carrots; three pieces of tomato interleaved with zucchini slices. Plate after plate of these threesomes went by. It reminded me of the time when my children were very small and I had to count the grapes, the sardines, the strawberries, the pieces of meat, the toast fingers. Alison and I, who rarely see one another, were souls in bliss. We got a cheque for $3000 which we are sharing, and a leather-bound copy of Blessed City (dull coffin-brown leather, though the gold title on the spine looks impressive). The book distributor cheered up and promised to 'keep us on the shelves.' Alison and I tried to spend some money in Collins Street but couldn't—we belong to a generation that saves money for football boots, higher education, extreme old age.

Kevin Hart, a fine poet, is working on the RC liturgy; he was distressed because his committee wanted to render 'and was made man' as 'and became very human.' Terribly human, one might say.

Fr Mills, who has endeared himself to us, is soon to go. He preached a lengthy anecdotal sermon on death and judgment (you probably know the story: a king gives his jester a cap-and-bells wand saying 'Give this to a greater fool than yourself, if you ever find one.' The king, at the point of death, reveals that he has made no preparation for the Great Journey. The jester hands him guess what.) I was deeply touched, especially as my problem is not free will but the resurrection of the body. *What* could survive physical dissolution?

This week my youngest son and his wife are expecting a child. 'And the prayer thou hear'st me making …' Pray for its safe delivery. I put a notice on the prayer board this morning (the ancient ones remain). My favourite is still the one asking that you win Tattslotto, although I like one in S Peter's Eastern Hill: 'Pray that Mum doesn't get rough with me for being home late.'

I HOPE ALL IS WELL/YOURS/GH

Pelagius] British theologian (fl. AD 4000), taught that mankind can achieve perfection; this was seen as a heretical denial of original sin and God's grace   Blessed City] a collection of Harwood's early letters, *Blessed City: Letters to Thomas Riddell, 1943*, edited by Alison Hoddinot, was published in 1990   Fr Mills] Anglican priest who deputised for Father Paton during his illness   S Peter's] St Peter's Anglican Church, East Melbourne

194. To William Paton, 18 July 1991

DEAR FR PATON,

What bliss, half an hour to spare. I've just returned from the 102nd birthday celebrations of the Hamilton Literary Society. As the Governess was coming (not to mention the Lord Mayor) we all had to assemble 30 minutes before the expected arrival of the official party. I'd been asked to write A Poem for the occasion (I've become a sort of lady laureate); I was rung up three times by three different office-bearers while I was having breakfast to make sure that 1. I had in fact written it; 2. I wouldn't forget to bring it to read; and 3. it wasn't too long. There were other readers too but they put me at the end just before arvo. Everyone had gone to extremes with The Plate they brought, no doubt hoping their Plate would end up on the official table for Lady B to cast her eyes on. The president assembled at the very last minute a truly impeccable pavlova which remained (heavily veiled) in the kitchen; but the other Plates were put on a trestle table and very inviting they looked as the time wore on. There were guests from other literary and artistic bodies. We sat and sat and finally the official party arrived (I should have liked to hear The Arrival of the Queen of Sheba by Handel; there's a dazzling oboe duet played at great speed). At these formal meetings I remember Peter Bennie's response when I'd been arguing over some trivial point of liturgical practice and said to him 'I've had enough of this; I long for the discipline of Rome.' To which Peter replied, 'As an Arizona coyote might long for the decorum of a drawing-room in Washington D.C.' Irene Isles, wife of a long-ago vice-chancellor, is also a member. She rebuked me for turning her over to Lady B for the regulation chat. 'Gwen, you know I can't make small talk.' I said 'Irene, you made it for years and years at the vice-chancellor's lodge.' 'Yes,' she replied tartly, 'but then the boot was on the other foot.' I think I've told you about the time when she came up to me in full sail at a meeting and said loudly, 'Ah, we haven't had you and your husband at the lodge for a while. But that's because we've had so many important people visiting.' The luscious pavlova, as we all foresaw, went straight to the vice-regal table; but we had a happy feast. Berenice (that most decorative of All Saints' ladies—pure pre-Raphaelite) was there as a guest. She says Louis is back from Sydney.

I'm off now to the launching of Cassandra Pybus's book Community of Thieves, all about the Pybus family and their early days on Bruny and Snug, and the aborigines, and the Crowthers. Once after an enormous spring tide I found a sort of Crowther midden: shards of old Victorian dinner services and pottery chemists' jars and crockery oddments. I had an enjoyable evening with Cassandra's book & will send it down if you'd like to read it. This letter is really to say I hope you are home again, and feeling better. Marjorie Eagle rang to say she & I have been invited to lunch at S John Fisher College next week to meet a Russian novelist. Hot ziggety, as they used to say in the old movies.

Yours/GH

I just rang the hospital & learned that you are still there

Literary Society] the Hamilton Ladies' Literary Society, Tasmania, the oldest literary society in Australia
Lady B] Lady Bennett, wife of the Governor of Tasmania   Peter Bennie] Fr Peter Bennie was a curate
at All Saints' Anglican Church, Brisbane, during the Second World War, when Gwen Harwood was
church organist   S John Fisher College] the Roman Catholic college at the University of Tasmania

Marmburra (Banduk) Marika

In 1988 the print maker Banduk Marika (b. 1954) and her partner Mark Alderton commissioned Glenn Murcutt (b. 1936), one of Australia's finest and most innovative architects to design a house on her traditional community lands at Yirrkala in Arnhem Land. The Marika–Alderton House was completed at the end of 1993. Murcutt's design paid special attention to the requirements of Aboriginal culture, the way of life of the Yirrkala community and local climatic conditions as well as the usual practical needs of any domestic client. In this letter to the Northern Territory Minister for Lands and Housing, Marika argues the case for a more sensitive approach to Aboriginal community housing projects.

195. To Maxwell Ortmann, 5 December 1991

YOUR EXCELLENCY

As a member of the Yirrkala-Dhanbul Community Council and senior member of the major land-owning Rirritjingu Clan I had the pleasure of meeting you during your recent visit to Yirrkala. I was able to briefly express to you how important I feel it to be for Aboriginal people to be involved in their Community Housing projects. House construction is world-wide traditionaly a man's activity, but women should none-the-less not be excluded from questions concerning our living conditions.

My family have for the last 50 years shared our homes and culture with a wide range of professional people from all over the world and have a deep understanding of European values and how they are different to our own. Sadly we have been greatly disrupted, socially and psychologically by various experiments in Aboriginal Housing often undertaken by people who had no prior notion of our needs. It is my personal struggle to create a design whereby myself and my family can live in a healthy and dignified way and so express our true worth as Australian citizens. Over the last three years I have worked at my own expense in close collaboration with Mr Glenn Murcutt, one of Australia's most highly honoured architects on a Coastal House design (category 1 cyclone), with the approval of the Yirrkala-Dhanbul Council, for Yirrkala. Mr Murcutt researched at great length the history of Aboriginal Housing and spent many hours speaking with me, recording my views. In August 1990 Mr Murcutt stayed with myself and my family to experience first-hand the cultural, topographical and climatic particularities of Yirrkala (Gamarrwa Nuwul). He expressed a willingness to discuss all questions relating to Community Housing with Mr T. Bullamore and J. Hopkins during his stay. Both these men were new to our Community at that time. In April 1991 Mr Murcutt produced a design which has already received much critical praise from his professional peers. I too am regularly hearing references to our design and feel very honoured to have been associated with it. For the past 9 months I have been further involved in all areas of the building industry in an effort to get the best quote possible for the complete construction package 'as per the architects and engineers specification', including the use of Australian timber only. The use of high-grade hardwood (necessary because of the high salt, sand and water combination) from northern New South Wales has proved to be the major reason why the project has run over the acceptable cost limit for a Community House. The quote here-enclosed is the result of many months of work by the two men involved and includes no preliminary charges as a sign of goodwill to myself. Experts in the building industry have suggested to me that a design proto-type is always more expensive than those which follow on from it. I wish to continue in good faith to this end with the architect and engineer and to further research all the possibilities in materials choice to save costs but still retain the design.

For the last two years the Yirrkala-Dhanbul Community Council has endorsed my application for a house. I am presently first on the list for a house to be constructed in the remainder of this financial year 1991–92. Even though detailed financial information has been witheld from me it is common knowledge that as much as $135,000 was paid out to contractors to build a house in Yirrkala last year. This year I have been told that the community is to receive $240,000 from Lands & Housing for the construction of two (2) houses but have not been shown any documents.

I am well-known in Australia as a professional artist, public speaker and member of the Council of the Australian National Gallery, Canberra. I have every reason to hope that in the next six months I will be able to secure enough sponsorship to complete my house.

I am requesting that you intervene as the Hon. Minister for Lands & Housing on my behalf with the Yirrkala-Dhanbul Housing Dept. and Mr Terry Bullamore to secure for me the sum of $120,000 so that I can make the necessary contractual agreements without undue delay. These men are employed by Yirrkala-Dhanbul Community to work in the best interests of ourselves, and not to delay our development.

As a senior member of the Rirritjingu Clan, daughter of Mawalan (d. 1967) I see no logical reason why I should not be able to finance a part of my building costs myself on land to which I have title under the Aboriginal Land Rights Act and am prepared to take this principle to court.

Aboriginal people are being encouraged to depend less on Government support and to determine our own economic development plans. Those of us who believe in this are never-the-less often driven to hopelessness because of the binding nature of the conditions of funding agreements between Communities and Governments.

Please assist me to assist myself, my children and grand-children in this matter.

YOURS SINCERELY,

Your Excellency] Hon. Maxwell Henry Ortmann (b. 1941) was a member of the Northern Territory Legislative Assembly 1990–94 and Minister for Lands and Housing 1990–92.   My family] Banduk Marika is a member of a family of distinguished artists which include her father Mawalan and her sisters, the bark painters Banygul (b. 1927) and Dhuwarrwarr Marika (b. 1949).

KATE LLEWELLYN

Katherine Jill Skye Llewellyn (b. 1936) is a widely published poet and writer of fiction. An enthusiastic writer of letters, Llewellyn values the intimacy they offer and the pleasure of conversing with friends across time and space. Her friendship with writer Jerry Rogers is of long standing.

196. TO JERRY ROGERS, 19 JUNE [1992]

DEAR JERRY

Thank you for getting the tickets to Rustifali..here's a guess at what I owe you for them … many thanks …

Hugh and Cathy are coming up tonight … he says he must retrench 53 next week...he has got special counsellors in to help the people deal with the horror …

It is icy blue … 4 degrees (but snug in here). I just relit the fire. Bill is due any moment it is 7.30am … he is finishing off the dining room (painting) and it looks fresh as you would say…

I ride to Katoomba with a series of 5 stories I have done and a woman, very sweet and obliging … weighing about 20 stone types them well for me … off they go, not to Tim, but to any one I think will pay. *Simply Living* got *Country Shows* … I enjoyed doing that one … *Friends* went to *New Woman* (more of that later). *Neighbours* will go to *W. Weekly* I think … and *Funerals* is going to *New Woman* or *H.Q.*

The funny thing is *New Woman* took *Friends* at once and I got the letter offering 500 dollars for it from the chief Editor (as Jillian Mcfarelane with whom I deal and who commissioned me in the past has gone … god knows where or why … another sad tale possibly … so, with my heart in my teeth I wrote and rejected the 500 explained that I never got less than $1,250 and could not go backwards … and, in fact, my agent would have asked for more. Now I wait … will I miss out altogether? I am fed up with Tim and as he takes *so long* and lost my story *Birds* and the photos, and as I said, only now has sent it to out to *The Bulletin*, I feel I must act on my own behalf or go under..

Today, and this is what made me think of writing to you at once, I saw your red and blue and green parrots embroidery almost *exactly* as I walked from the bathroom … one hung upside down from my back railing … the partner sat in the branch hanging above … so exact and lovely..like an omen of course …

I have got Varuna for 1st July to 21st July … what a thrill. Jocelyn Scutt and Amanda Lohrey were to be there too, at that time, which I would enjoy … but this is now doubtful as J.S. has to go to a court case in Melb …

I will hold the writing weekend workshop July 24th here and Marion Halligan says she will come and I await to hear from Drusilla and Barbara Brooks and Susan Hampton … she is farming in Vic.

Forgetmenots are in sweeps of green everywhere so abundantly … it will be a good spring. Tim is supposed to get the consul for NZ onto my trip and to get Collins to advance some money..if they have any … so maybe in spring I will go … but I think I should see some islands, others I mean as the title is not a pulling one … *Islands* though is … I must get to the Cook Islands for the Sth Pacific Dance Festival if I have to swim … That's in Oct. would you like to join me for that … It will be grand and nobody knows its on except, I suppose, a few anthropologists in sandals …

I had lunch with the Czechoslovakian Ambassador and a publisher as I said last Sat. The former was a thin 50 year old woman with husband to match...it was like talking to an oyster … a khaki woollen frock, grey hair, no colour anywhere, no lipstick … cold. grey. elegant, been everywhere, smoking, khaki skin. eyes like cold stones, … I felt so defeated in my scarlet outfit I decided to try to get some reaction … the man was half dead … he is either a womaniser on his best behaviour in front of his wife, or has committed a crime wherein he is utterly in her power as a result … nobody spoke to him for hours and if it had been the other way round, and she the wife of the Ambassador it would have seemed outrageously rude and sexist … and I think it was … he sat like a grey lizard basking in the cold … I spent the next day in bed recovering … I was kindly treated … the food is very mediocre … it was called Echoes, the place … not in Lillian-fels but next door … owned partly by Tom Keneally … the taste of the cassoulet was as queer as the people I dined with and took hours to leave, too …

Rita, the naturopath with whom I went, gave the women flowers and the ambas-sador acted as if they were a baby in the most touching and deprived way..held them to her chest … (just a little bunch of wildflowers—) in the photos session on the balcony … and would not put them down for ages and then wanted them in the car away from any heat … it is as if she came from the north pole … and the seals had been hunted out … what a pair … the woman who was the host, Barbara someone, is a friend of Leo Schofield's and names fell like jewels onto the table … I felt quite bewildered and I suppose I got kindly collected but I am not sure … nobody talked literature but it was excruitiating chit chat of what will grow in the garden here … much ill informed and I did not argue … well, enough … I do not expect to hear well from Random House..I think that was a hook to get me to lunch … yet, the woman was warm, warm, warm and even ingenuous and most hospitable … what can one make of it?

I have 3 books Angela Carter's last … Spalding Grey's Somebody, the one who wrote *Swimming to Cambodia* … his first novel this … looks great … and C.Stead's letters … really, a wonderful book … she is a wizard … so queer, mad, right, sweet, hopeless … not unlike Jean Rhys in some ways...you know, the hopeless, feckless, blighted genius who good things avoid in spite of her almost starving … but gracious, always gracious … a bed-sitter, no money … Basically, Christina is a woman who married her father and who was man mad as you know and a funny kind of genius to boot … cruel to women, feminist and scathing of that same thing … feminist in liking freedom, but vile to most women … fawning to men in a way that is quite painful to read in the letters ... but generous, encyclopaedic, lusty, and full of paradoxes ... Bill Blake was in the fur business for a time ... can you believe it ... and she left her money to the conservation foundation ... plus had white mink coat ... Basically, Bill was a wonderful, loving brilliant man whose books did not sell and who had a wife and child for 30 years of their life (his & Christina's) together while she longed to marry ... sound familiar ...? that (the latter, Father part, I mean).

I was interested to see the definitions of your dream Jerry..Facts..facts..are you overwhelmed by facts?

I think still fish are sexual ... call me one-eyed if you will but I think others think this also ... what have you made of the dream so far?

Here is my poem from last weeks effort ...

I hope your garden is now thoroughly stuffed with good things for spring ...

MANY THANKS AGAIN/LOVE/JILL

Rustifali] a Georgian dance troupe   Hugh and Cathy] Llewellyn's son and daughter-in-law   Bill] Llewellyn's neighbour   Tim] Tim Curnow (b. 1944), the Sydney literary agent.   Varuna] house at Katoomba in the Blue Mountains west of Sydney, formerly the home of the writer Eleanor Dark (1901–85) and now a residential centre for writers   Jocelynne Scutt] (b. 1947), lawyer and writer   Amanda Lohrey] (b. 1947), Australian writer   Marion Halligan] (b. 1940), Australian writer   Drusilla] Drusilla Modjeska (b. 1946), English-born Australian writer   Barbara Brooks] (b. 1947), Australian writer   Susan Hampton] (b. 1949), Australian writer   Collins] the Australian publisher, Harper Collins   Lillianfels] a resort in the Blue Mountains   Tom Keneally] Thomas Keneally (b. 1935), Australian writer   Leo Schofield] (b. 1935), restaurant critic and artistic director of festivals in Sydney and Melbourne

DAVID WILLIAMSON

Playwright David Williamson (b. 1942), in charting the manners and morals of his audience, has been a defining influence on the direction of Australian theatre. His sense of his country as a kind of earthly paradise is reflected in this letter to novelist Peter Carey (b. 1943). At a time when many were predicting that facsimile and electronic messaging would bring an end to the intimate exchanges represented by the letter, Williamson welcomes what he finds to be the immediacy and spontaneity of such exchanges.

197. TO PETER CAREY, 10 JUNE 1993

DEAR PETER,

Re: Life, The Meaning Thereof, and Other Profundities.

It was so good to hear you this morning on the phone, if for no other reason than to remind us both what a dear and valued friend you are. (I could never say this verbally which is why the fax is sometimes such a wonderful invention.) Frankly both Kristin and I were a little worried and guilty that we didn't respond in a more open and communicative way, getting bogged down in a wealth of platitudes, self promotional news bulletins, and other inanities. The truth is that we were both deeply touched, both that you phoned up out of the blue and that you felt such an obvious and endearing nostalgia for things Australian. The Spanish extroversion reminding you of home, and the Australian Ambassador being so warm and friendly seemed to carry to us a barely disguised subtextual message that you hadn't yet managed to throw off the last vestiges of that deep rooted and irrational tribalism which is so much a part of our own psyche. As I get older the love of this country, like your own, starts to focus more and more on the landscapes. I have a dream of living in a beautiful Australian environment far out of Sydney and to the north. Possibly in the area of Port Douglas which I think is one of the earth's most beautiful regions. I find increasingly that the prickly ambition, which drove me so hard in my earlier years is fading, and I just want to wander amongst tropical plants and marvel at my luck that one sperm out of millions hit the egg and gave me the chance, albeit briefly, to marvel at the interlocking weave of life forms around me. This condition is sometimes called wisdom, more often senility. I am still doing the project for Altman, my play is working wonderfully, but I couldn't really give a fuck. I still want to keep writing plays, but in a leisurely and considered way that allows time for thinking, reading, reflection and tropical splendour. We can't of course move until Rory is finished at school, but the thought is there in both my own and Kristin's mind with a strength that indicates that it's not just a geriatric fantasy.

If you and Alison ever get to the point where the tawdry baubles of ambition cease to beguile, we should settle within visiting distance of each other somewhere up there and enjoy the incomparable landscapes and each other's company. We did enjoy the time when you were only a stones throw away in Louisa Road, and this is a wonderful country, something that as my brain cells deplete becomes more and more obvious to me. I sometimes feel as if a benevolent but mischievous god gave our forefathers the use of a land they tricked up as hellish, then slowly revealed to us, their descendents, that in fact we had been given Paradise. If you think I'm off my nut and blind drunk, (I am), wait until you see Far North Queensland.

Thanks again for the call. We miss you all a lot.

DW.

Kristin] writer Kristin Williamson who married David Williamson in 1974   Altman] With Robert Altman (b. 1925), American film producer, director, and screenwriter, Williamson was working on a script about the First World War spy Mata Hari   Alison] Alison Summers, wife of Peter Carey. Carey and Summers now live in New York

LES MURRAY

Alexander (Alec) Thorley Bolton (1926–96) was a distinguished Australian publisher and founder of the Brindabella Press in Canberra where, from 1973 until his sudden death, he produced a steady stream of fine editions. At the Brindabella Press, his skills and experience were joined in the search for the making of the perfect book. In this letter to Bolton's wife, the poet Rosemary Dobson, fellow poet Leslie Allan Murray (b. 1938) salutes a master printer.

198. TO ROSEMARY DOBSON, 22 NOVEMBER 1996

DEAR ROSEMARY

I took pleasure in knowing Alec: I'll miss his warm shy smile and our quiet conversations. I'll also miss his deeply perfected craftsmanship, his unique editions which so honoured those whose work he chose to present. The last printer is dead, it strikes me, the last true master of the old silvery-black metal. Condolences, I've noticed, aren't usually much good to the bereaved when they first come, but they have a cumulative effect even then, and can be a help when recalled later. In that spirit I offer you ours. We greatly hope you and your children find comfort and peace—and I've always liked the Trappist epitaph *Laudabiliter vixit*, which the late Thomas Merton translated as 'he did good'

YOURS SINCERELY/LES MURRAY

NICK JOSE

Nicholas Jose (b. 1952) is a former academic who has published stories, essays and translations as well as five novels. His friendship with the painter Mandy Martin dates from their student days in Adelaide where they both grew up. Their exchange of greetings makes use of electronic mail. At the end of the twentieth century the evolution of technology has given new life and form to the letter, which for many, with the advent of the telephone, had ceased to be other than an incidental or formal means of keeping in touch.

199. TO MANDY MARTIN, 14 JANUARY 1997

DEAR MANDY,

[Re: Back O'Bourke]

Thanks so much for sending your catalogues. I've sent one on to Simon. They're now back in NY. Lanyon sent one too with dates for your show there. I really look forward to seeing the works in the flesh, so to speak. They look quite wonderful. So dramatic. Congratulations. Saw your Flying Dutchman print gracing the Opera House wall the other night when we went to Ariadne, also wonderfully dramatic. If only Ludwig Becker were alive to see his legacy revivified.

I've just finished final copyediting of my new novel The Custodians which also traverses some of that territory. Becker gets a mention and there's a whole drama of land custody played out between the group who were on the bus out of Adelaide in the 1970s. I'll love to know what you think of it.

Look forward to seeing you soon. Thanks for inviting us all to the red earth. Simon and Ginny would have loved that.

I've no doubt Simon will be back with his pen in hand, so maybe another time.
HAPPY NEW YEAR AND LOTS OF LOVE/NICK

your catalogues] a reference to the catalogue for Martin's exhibition *Tracts: Back O'Bourke* curated by Peter Haynes and presented at the Nolan Gallery in Canberra 7 February–17 March 1997   Simon and Ginny] Simon Schama (b. 1945), the author of *Landscape and Memory* (1995) and his wife Virginia Papaioannou   Lanyon] the Nolan Gallery is located at Lanyon, a historic property near Canberra   Ludwig Becker] German-born artist (1808–61) who accompanied the ill-fated Burke and Wills Expedition and whose work has provided a point of reference for an important series of landscape paintings by Mandy Martin   The Custodians] Jose's novel was published in 1997

MANDY MARTIN

Mandy Martin (b. 1952) is a noted Australian painter who trained at the South Australian School of Art, and is now a lecturer in painting and drawing in the Australian National University. She is represented in the National Gallery of Australia and in most of the Australian state galleries as well as in private collections in Australia and overseas. Her painting Red Ochre Grove *(1988) was commissioned for the Australian Parliament in Canberra. Her E-mail letter to Nicholas Jose was written from a remote corner of north-western New South Wales on Australia Day 1997.*

200. TO NICK JOSE, 26 JANUARY 1997

DEAR NICK,

Subject: More Red Soil

It was a delightful surprise finding your email in Canberra last week when I was there for a few nights. I realize why we all like email so much now, it is because we all always liked letters more and now we can get them there instantly, we do not need to suffer the let down of the postage system, so voila instant converts! You and Christie are such great letter writers too—I always regret that in my miff over Vicki I destroyed my letters from you despite the fact that I knew you were destined for great things! So here I am again in the utter solitude of a hot Sunday cooking corned mutton and wondering still whether there is anything that can be done in a painting with a gumtree—the whole wired-in verandah becomes a studio here and at present I have 15 or so of these problematic little paintings spread about in various stages of dress and undress—I figure the key is in how I get it down and I'm reminded of an article on Albert Pynkham Ryder, where the writer described him as a great groper, searching after light from within the canvas, I'm groping about on the treeline and it all seems a pretty fundamental search. That's the art side of things and on the theoretical side I'm grappling with new ideas on Ecocriticism which brings together the Arts, Ecology, Ethics and Criticism. This is what I've been up to the past few years but it always feels quite good to know that what one is doing does have a name, I guess! I have the mental space and time to read and write up here—it took forever to read "Lie of the Land" but it was pertinent, I'm a fan of Paul's even though I think his work is probably hopelessly flawed by its own enclosure act—I feel reasonably justified keeping on with my own little enclosure acts played out on canvas after I have read one of his massive follies.

Anyway your comments have given me a shot in the arm, maybe I need my head read even attempting gumtrees—as I say this I think I am betraying them because after all they are Coolabah, Gidgee, Blackbox, Quinine Bush and so on.

Thanks we all need feedback and yes my eyes will be out on stalks when your new bomb is let loose on the bus escapees! Just tell me when and where! I finished Robert Drewe's "The Drowner" the other day and think it admirable if a little worrying, I'm reserving judgement at present although I have felt compelled to relate some of his book in conversation with people out here which must mean that it hits a nerve.

It would be great to see you, Clare, Simon with pen in hand and Ginny and any multiple or single permutations if there is a window of opportunity some time. We come up here regularly, it is a long way but it needs to be to be far enough away. In fact we have talked of getting a place even further out. You should receive an invitation this week for the Canberra opening of Tracts, if by chance you will be down let me know in advance, you can email us at Wapweelah this week and we will be back at Pennyroyal near Cowra, Friday night. It is evening now and time to go out drawing then pick Guy up off the grader, he is 20 kms away grading tracks, this place is 150 square miles so there are a lot a miles of track to do. On this morning's drawing sortie, when Guy was fixing the bore-drain, we saw the pair of brolgas who breed here every year, their undersides were Naples red-yellow with the reflected light from the red-soil of the low sand hills. More red soil. With love Mandy.

Christie] Christina Hamilton (née Slade), an academic in Canberra and an Adelaide contemporary of Martin and Jose   Albert Pynkham Ryder] (1847–1917), American painter   "Lie of the Land"] Paul Carter's *The Lie of the Land*, 1996   Clare] Claire Roberts, Curator of Asian Decorative Arts and Design, Powerhouse Museum, Sydney; partner of Nicholas Jose   Wapweelah] pastoral property north-west of Bourke, New South Wales, where Martin has prepared much of her recent work   Pennyroyal] pastoral property at Mandurama, New South Wales, home of Guy Fitzhardinge and Mandy Martin   Guy] Guy Fitzhardinge is a pastoralist and environmental consultant. He and Mandy Martin married in October 1997.

SOURCES AND ACKNOWLEDGMENTS

1.   DL MSQ 140, State Library of New South Wales, Printed by permission of the Library Council of New South Wales.

2.   ML C830, State Library of New South Wales, Printed by permission of the Library Council of New South Wales.

3.   ML C213, State Library of New South Wales, Printed by permission of the Library Council of New South Wales.

4.   Private Collection. Printed by permission of the owner and with the kind assistance of Derek McDonnell Esq., Hordern House, Potts Point, New South Wales.

5.   ML MSS 5934, State Library of New South Wales, Printed by permission of the Library Council of New South Wales.

6.   ML ZA 1677-2, State Library of New South Wales, Printed by permission of the Library Council of New South Wales.

7.   ML ZA 2908, State Library of New South Wales, Printed by permission of the Library Council of New South Wales.

8–9.   *Letters and Papers of G.P. Harris 1803–1812*, ed. Barbara Hamilton-Arnold (Sorrento: Arden Press, 1994). Reprinted by permission of the British Library, London, United Kingdom.

10.   Archives Office of Tasmania, NS 123/1. Printed by permission.

11.   *Portrait with Background*, Alexandra Hasluck (Perth: Fremantle Arts Centre Press, 1990). Reprinted by permission.

12–13. *The Letters of John Bede Polding, O.S.B. 1819–1877*, ed. Sr. M. Xavier Compton *et al.*, 3 vols. (Sydney: Sisters of the Good Samaritan, 1994–96). Reprinted by permission.

14.   Collection of Bathurst District Historical Society Inc. Printed by permission.

15.   *The Correspondence of Charles Darwin, 1821–1862*, ed. Frederick Burkhardt and Sydney Smith, 10 vols. (Cambridge: Cambridge University Press, 1985–97). Reprinted by permission.

16.   Australian Manuscripts Collection, State Library of Victoria, Gipps-La Trobe Correspondence (Boxes 71–73). Printed by permission of the Library Board of Victoria.

17.   *An Emigrant's Letters Home,* Henry Parkes (Sydney: Angus & Robertson, 1896).

18.   In the possession of Major William Spowers, Windlesham, Surrey, United Kingdom. Printed by permission.

19.   National Library of Australia, MS 4253. Rex Nan Kivell Collection (NK 6451). Printed by permission of the Council of the National Library of Australia.

20.   *Westralian Voices*, ed. Marian Aveling (Perth: University of Western Australia Press, 1979). Reprinted by permission.

21.   Australian Manuscripts Collection, State Library of Victoria, MS 10241 Box 1055/3. Printed by permission of F.A. Walker Esq., Bombala, New South Wales, and by courtesy of the Library Board of Victoria.

22.   Australian Manuscripts Collection, State Library of Victoria, MS 9356 Box 1045/2a. Printed by permission of F.A. Walker Esq., Bombala, New South Wales, and by courtesy of the Library Board of Victoria.

23.   *The Letters of F.W. Leichhardt*, ed. Marcel Aurousseau, 3 vols. (London: Published for the Hakluyt Society by Cambridge University Press, 1968). Reprinted by permission.

24.   In the possession of Rodney Davidson Esq., Melbourne, Victoria. Printed by permission.

25.   Archives Office of Tasmania, GO 33/57. Printed by permission.

26.   Marion Amies and Martin Sullivan, 'Three Letters from Christina Cuninghame to Agnes Cochran-Patrick describing life in the Port Phillip District' in *La Trobe Library Journal*, vol.8, no. 30, December 1982.

27.   *Tenants No More*, ed. P. Frazer Simons (Melbourne: Prowling Tiger Press, 1996). Reprinted by permission.

28.   DL MS 235, State Library of New South Wales, Printed by permission of the Library Council of New South Wales.

29.   National Library of Australia, MS 1395. Printed by permission of the Council of the National Library of Australia.

30–31. National Library of Australia, MS133/1/11–12 and MS133/1/1–3. Printed with permission of Angela Neustatter, London, United Kingdom and by courtesy of the Council of the National Library of Australia.

32–33. *Letters from Menie: Sir Henry Parkes and His Daughter*, ed. A.W. Martin (Melbourne: Melbourne University Press, 1983). Reprinted by permission.

34.   *Papers and Correspondence of William Stanley Jevons*, ed. R.D. Collison Black, 7 vols. (London: Macmillan for the Royal Economic Society, 1972–81). Reprinted by permission.

35.   ML A63, State Library of New South Wales, Printed by permission of the Library Council of New South Wales.

36.   Australian Manuscripts Collection, State Library of Victoria. Exploration Committee, Royal Society of Victoria, Box 2076/2. Printed by permission of the Library Board of Victoria.

37.   ML MSS 272/1, State Library of New South Wales, Printed by permission of the Library Council of New South Wales.

38.   ML MSS 2229/9, State Library of New South Wales, Printed by permission of the Library Council of New South Wales.

39.   Australian Manuscripts Collection, State Library of Victoria, MS9504. Printed by permission of the Library Board of Victoria.

40.   DL MS Q313/2, State Library of New South Wales, Printed by permission of the Library Council of New South Wales.

41–42. Alexander Turnbull Library, National Library of New Zealand, qMS 1086. Printed by permission of the National Library of New Zealand.

43.   ML MSS 342, State Library of New South Wales, Printed by permission of Mrs Nan Gill, St Ives, New South Wales, and by courtesy of the Library Council of New South Wales.

44. Beinecke Rare Book and Manuscript Library, Yale University Library, New Haven, Connecticut, United States of America.

45. *Clyde Company Papers*, ed. P.L. Brown, 7 vols. (London: Oxford University Press, 1941–71). Reprinted by permission.

46. Australian Manuscripts Collection, State Library of Victoria, MS 10840. Printed by permission of the Library Board of Victoria.

47. In the possession of Mrs Moira Peters, Toorak, Victoria. Printed by permission.

48. Cudmore Papers, Mortlock Library, State Library of South Australia. Printed by permission.

49. *No Place for a Nervous Lady*, ed. Lucy Frost (Brisbane: University of Queensland Press, 1995). Reprinted by permission.

50. National Archives of Australia (Vic.), (CRS) B 313/122.

51. ML A849/4, State Library of New South Wales, Printed by permission of the Library Council of New South Wales.

52. In the possession of Mrs Judith Deakin Harley, South Yarra, Victoria. Printed by permission.

53. In the possession of Mrs Philippa Poole, Wellington, New South Wales. Printed by permission.

54-57. Public Record Office of Victoria (VPRS), 3181/201(Town Clerk Employment Records).

58. *Letters from Smike: The Letters of Arthur Streeton 1890–1943*, ed. Ann Galbally and Anne Gray (Melbourne: Oxford University Press, 1989). Reprinted by permission of Oliver Streeton.

59. ML A2478, State Library of New South Wales, Printed by permission of Oliver Streeton and by courtesy of the Library Council of New South Wales.

60. *Westralian Voices*, ed. Marian Aveling (Perth: University of Western Australia Press, 1979). Reprinted by permission.

61. *Colonial Voices: Letters, Diaries, Journalism & Other Accounts of Nineteenth-Century Australia*, ed. Elizabeth Webby (Brisbane: University of Queensland Press, 1989). Reprinted by permission of University of Queensland Press.

62. *Dear Robertson: Letters to an Australian Publisher*, ed. A.W. Barker (Sydney:Angus & Robertson, 1982). Reprinted by permission.

63. *'My Dear Spencer': The letters of F.J. Gillen to Baldwin Spencer*, ed. John Mulvaney *et al.* (Melbourne: Hyland House, 1997). Reprinted by permission of Hyland House Publishing.

64–65. National Library of Australia, Leopold Podraghy Collection, MS 2647. Printed by permission of Pamela, Baroness Vestey, Coldstream, Victoria and by courtesy of the Council of the National Library of Australia.

66–67. *The Correspondence of G.E. Morrison 1895–1920*, ed. Lo Hui-Min, 2 vols. (Cambridge: Cambridge University Press, 1976–78). Reprinted by permission of the publisher and by courtesy of Alastair Morrison Esq., Hughes, Australian Capital Territory.

68. Public Records Office of Western Australia, AN24 Acc.527 file no.3371/97.

69–71. *Bushman and Bookworm: Letters of Joseph Furphy*, ed. John Barnes and Lois Hoffman (Melbourne:Oxford University Press, 1995). Reprinted by permission.

72–73. National Library of Australia, MS4653. Printed by permission of Professor Maev O'Collins, Campbell, Australian Capital Territory, and Mrs Moira Peters, Toorak, Victoria, and by courtesy of the Council of the National Library of Australia.

74. *The Camp at Wandinong*, Ethel Turner (London: Ward Lock n.d.). Reprinted by permission of Mrs Philippa Poole, Wellington, New South Wales.

75–76. *The Letters of Sidney & Beatrice Webb* ed. Norman MacKenzie, 3 vols. (Cambridge: Cambridge University Press, 1978). Reprinted by permission.

77. National Library of Australia, MS 1924/1/230. Printed by permission of Mrs Jessie Deakin Clarke, Hawthorn, Victoria, and by courtesy of the Council of the National Library of Australia.

78. *Family Fresco*, Nancy Adams (Melbourne: F.W. Cheshire, 1966). Reprinted by permission.

79. National Register of Archives, (S) 888/554, Hopetoun Papers Trust. Printed with the gracious permission of Her Majesty The Queen and by courtesy of Lord Linlithgow.

80. ML C 752, State Library of New South Wales, Printed by permission of the Public Trustee Company Limited, Sydney, Trustee of the Estate of the late Miles Franklin and by courtesy of the Library Council of New South Wales.

81–82. Australian War Memorial, Canberra, 3DRL 3834. Printed by permission of the Australian War Memorial Council.

83. Queensland State Archives, COL/14402/12740. Printed by permission.

84–86. The Grainger Museum, The University of Melbourne. Printed by permission.

87. *Barbara Baynton*, ed. Sally Krimmer & Alan Lawson (Brisbane: University of Queensland Press, 1980). Reprinted by permission of University of Queensland Press.

88. National Library of Australia, MS 83/38. Printed by permission of Lord Kintore, Inverurie, Aberdeenshire, Scotland, United Kingdom, and by courtesy of the Council of the National Library of Australia.

89. National Library of Australia, MS 83/58–59. Printed by permission of the Council of the National Library of Australia.

90–91. National Library of Australia, MS 1540/15/981–4 and MS 1540/1/3277–79. Printed by permission of C. Peter Roberts Esq., Hawthorn, Victoria, and by courtesy of the Council of the National Library of Australia.

92. In the possession of C. Peter Roberts Esq., Hawthorn, Victoria. Printed by permission.

93. National Library of Australia, MS 7694–8. Printed by permission of Lord Dudley, London, United Kingdom and by courtesy of the Council of the National Library of Australia.

94. ALS ML MSS 325, State Library of New South Wales, Printed by permission of the Library Council of New South Wales.

95–96. National Library of Australia, MS 1174/1/777 and MS 1174/1/3649–57. Printed by permission of the Equity Trustees Executors and Agency Limited on behalf of the E.V. & J.G. Palmer Estate and by courtesy of the Council of the National Library of Australia.

97. Mawson Antarctic Collection, The University of Adelaide. Printed by permission of The University of Adelaide.

98. In the possession of Val Miller Esq., Curtin, Australian Capital Territory. Printed by permission.

99. Australian War Memorial, Canberra, PR 0057. Printed by permission of the Australian War Memorial Council.

100. Australian Manuscripts Collection, State Library of Victoria, MS 13020. Printed by permission of Mrs Elizabeth Durré, Kew, Victoria, and by courtesy of the Library Board of Victoria.

101. *Westralian Voices*, ed. Marian Aveling (Perth: University of Western Australia Press, 1979). Reprinted by permission.

102. In the possession of Mrs Patricia Sharp, Hawthorn, Victoria. Printed by permission of Mrs Judith Deakin Harley, South Yarra, Victoria.

103. In the possession of Mrs Ursula Whiteside, Toorak, Victoria. Printed by permission.

104. Australian War Memorial, Canberra, PR 84/123. Printed by permission of the Australian War Memorial Council.

105–106. In the possession of John Stapledon Esq., Heswall, Wirral, Merseyside, United Kingdom. Printed by permission.

107. In the possession of Dr Jan Bassett, Kew, Victoria. Printed by permission of Mrs Margaret Tong, Waiheke Island, New Zealand, and by courtesy of Dr Jan Bassett.

108. In the possession of Bruce Steele, Esq., Balwyn, Victoria. Printed by permission.

109–110. *Dear Robertson: Letters to an Australian Publisher*, ed. A.W. Barker (Sydney: Angus & Robertson, 1982). Reprinted by permission of The Northcott Society & The Spastic Centre of NSW, C/- Curtis Brown (Aust.).

111. National Library of Australia, MS 1354. Printed by permission of Pamela, Baroness Vestey, Coldstream, Victoria and by courtesy of the Council of the National Library of Australia.

112. Australian Manuscripts Collection, State Library of Victoria, MS 10617/3. Printed by permission of the Library Board of Victoria.

113. Barr Smith Library, The University of Adelaide, Papers of Sarah Elizabeth Jackson, SD 92J 142 Series 1 Printed by permission.

114. National Library of Australia, MS 1540/23/27. Printed by permission of Ann Macintosh and Bettina Rankin-Reid, Sydney, New South Wales and by courtesy of the Council of the National Library of Australia.

115. ML MSS 742/25, State Library of New South Wales, © Jane Glad. Printed by permission of Barbara Mobbs on behalf of the Estate of Norman Lindsay and by courtesy of the Library Council of New South Wales.

116. National Library of Australia, MS 5574 Box 167. Printed by permission of the Council of the National Library of Australia.

117. *Dear Robertson: Letters to an Australian Publisher*, ed. A.W. Barker (Sydney: Angus & Robertson, 1982). Reprinted by permission.

118–119. *The Letters of D.H. Lawrence*, ed. J.T. Boulton *et al.,* 7 vols, vols i–iii (Cambridge: Cambridge University Press, 1979–93). Reprinted by permission of Laurence Pollinger Ltd., the Estate of Frieda Lawrence Ravagli and Cambridge University Press.

120. ML MSS 281/3, State Library of New South Wales, Printed by permission of Angus & Robertson and by courtesy of the Library Council of New South Wales.

121. ML MSS 1284/122, State Library of New South Wales, Printed by permission of the Library Council of New South Wales.

122. University of Melbourne Archives, Burnet Papers, Series/File/No. 2/10. Printed by permission of Mrs Elizabeth Dexter and by courtesy of Melbourne University Archives.

123–124. *A Web of Friendship: Selected Letters (1928–1973), Christina Stead*, ed. R.G. Geering. Reprinted by permission of Professor Margaret Harris, Sydney, New South Wales on behalf of the Estate of Christina Stead.

125.   State Library of New South Wales, ML MSS 5571. Printed by permission of the beneficiaries of the Estate of Sir George Allen, and by courtesy of the Library Council of New South Wales.

126–127.   In the possession of Nicholas Hasluck Esq., Claremont, Western Australia. Printed by permission.

128.   National Library of Australia, MS 2123. Printed by permission of Susan Hogarth, Leichhardt, NSW, and by courtesy of the Council of the National Library of Australia.

129–130.   *Letters of Mary Gilmore*, ed. W.H. Wilde and T. Inglis Moore (Melbourne: Melbourne University Press, 1980). Reprinted by permission of The Public Trustee, Sydney on behalf of the Estate of Dame Mary Gilmore and Melbourne University Press.

131.   National Library of Australia, MS 703. Printed by permission of the Council of the National Library of Australia.

132–133.   Australian War Memorial, Canberra, Dunlop Papers. Printed by permission of the Trustees of the Estate of Sir Edward Dunlop.

134.   Copy in the possession of Mrs P. G. F. Henderson, Yarralumla, Australian Capital Territory. Printed by permission of Mrs Anne Carroll and Mr Edward Le Couteur, Sydney, New South Wales, and by courtesy of Mrs P.G.F. Henderson.

135.   National Archives of Australia (N.T.), (CRS) F126 Item 33.

136.   Barr Smith Library, The University of Adelaide, MS 0015/5. Printed by permission of Dr David Symon and the Barr Smith Library.

137.   Australian Manuscripts Collection, State Library of Victoria, MS 9824. Printed by permission of the Library Board of Victoria.

138.   In the possession of Mrs P. G. F. Henderson, Yarralumla, Australian Capital Territory. Printed by permission.

139.   Copy in the possession of Mrs P.G.F. Henderson, Yarralumla, Australian Capital Territory. Printed by permission of Mrs Elsie Macleod, Cottesloe, Western Australia.

140.   In the possession of Mrs Joan Levy, Sydney, New South Wales. Printed by permission of Clara Menuhin-Hauser, France, and by courtesy of Mrs Joan Levy.

141.   Copy in the possession of Jennifer Wallace, Braidwood, New South Wales. Printed by permission of Mrs Kay H. Davidson, Southport, Queensland on behalf of Mrs Grace Black.

142.   ML MSS 3525 Folder MLK 2132, State Library of New South Wales, Printed by permission of Mrs Norma McAuley, c/- Curtis Brown (Aust), and by courtesy of Professor Donald Horne, Woollahra, New South Wales, and the Library Council of New South Wales.

143.   In the possession of Mrs Philippa Poole, Wellington, New South Wales. Printed by permission.

144–145.   National Library of Australia, MS 6812/1/2. Printed by permission of Mrs Phyllis Boyd, Sandringham, Victoria, and by courtesy of the Council of the National Library of Australia.

146–147.   *The Ern Malley Affair*, Michael Heyward (Brisbane: University of Queensland Press, 1994). Reprinted by permission of Curtis Brown (Aust) on behalf of Mrs Norma McAuley.

148.   In the possession of Dr Marjorie Tipping, Melbourne, Victoria. Printed by permission.

149. In the possession of Dr Marjorie Tipping, Melbourne, Victoria. Printed by permission of Dame Elisabeth Murdoch, Langwarrin, Victoria.

150. In the possession of Nicholas Hasluck Esq., Claremont, Western Australia. Printed by permission.

151–152. In the possession of Bob Lewis Esq., Malvern, Victoria. Printed by permission.

153. ML MSS 364/39, State Library of New South Wales, Printed by courtesy of the Library Council of New South Wales.

154. Australian Mansucripts Collection, State Library of Victoria, MS 13186/1/5 CPT 1. Printed by permission of the Trustees of the Estate of John and Sunday Reed, Ms Fern Smith, Ainslie, Australian Capital Territory, and by courtesy of the Library Board of Victoria.

155. State Library of New South Wales, ML MSS 364/30. Printed by permission of Professor Julie Bailey, New South Wales, and by courtesy of the Library Council of New South Wales.

156. ML MSS 364/30, State Library of New South Wales, Printed by permission of Harper Collins Australia and by courtesy of the Library Council of New South Wales.

157. ML MSS 364/41, State Library of New South Wales, Printed by permission of Mrs Richenda Martin, Beechworth, Victoria, and by courtesy of the Library Council of New South Wales.

158. ML MSS 364/21, State Library of New South Wales, Printed by permission of Ric Throssell Esq., Ainslie, Australian Capital Territory, and by courtesy of the Library Council of New South Wales.

159. National Library of Australia, MS 6201/10/3. Printed by permission of Mrs Marjorie Esson, Toorak, Victoria, and by courtesy of the Council of the National Library of Australia.

160. *The Letters of Hugh McCrae*, ed. Robert D. Fitzgerald (Sydney: Angus & Robertson, 1970). Reprinted by permission of Mrs Janet Hay, Newport, New South Wales.

161. ML MSS 3865/4, State Library of New South Wales, Printed by permission of Jinx Nolan, Boston, Mass., USA, and by courtesy of the Library Council of New South Wales.

162. Institute of Archaeology, University College, London. Printed by permission of Professor David Harris.

163. In the possession of Professor Gregory Clark, Tokyo, Japan. Printed by permission.

164. In the possession of the Dixon family, Melbourne, Victoria. Printed by permission of J.D. Merralls Esq., Melbourne, Victoria, on behalf of the Dixon family.

165. National Library of Australia, MS 3956. Printed by permission of Jack Porter Esq., Bairnsdale, Victoria, and by courtesy of the Council of the National Library of Australia.

166–167. From *Joyce and Ginnie—the letters of Joyce Grenfell and Virginia Graham*, edited by Janie Hampton, Hodder & Stoughton, London, UK, 1997. Printed by permission of Janie Hampton, Temple Cowley, Oxford, United Kingdom.

168. ML MSS 5717, State Library of New South Wales, Printed by permission of Barbara Mobbs on behalf of the Estate of Patrick White and by courtesy of the Library Council of New South Wales.

169. In the possession of Dr Andrew Fisher, Camberwell, Victoria. Printed by permission of Barbara Mobbs on behalf of the Estate of Patrick White and by courtesy of Mrs Barbara Miechel, Mt Waverley, Victoria.

170. In the possession of Desmond Digby Esq., Scotts Head, New South Wales. Printed by permission of Barbara Mobbs on behalf of the Estate of Patrick White and by courtesy of Desmond Digby Esq.

171. *Patrick White Letters*, ed. David Marr (Sydney: Random House, 1994). Reprinted by permission of Barbara Mobbs on behalf of the Estate of Patrick White.

172. MS 3431, State Library of New South Wales, Printed by permission of Thea Astley, Nowra, New South Wales and by courtesy of the Library Council of New South Wales.

173. In the possession of Dame Joan Sutherland and Richard Bonynge Esq., Les Avants, Switzerland. Printed by permission of Lord Menuhin, London, United Kingdom and by courtesy of Dame Joan Sutherland.

174. National Library of Australia, MS 4936/22/13. Printed by permission of Mrs P.G.F. Henderson, Yarralumla, Australian Capital Territory, and by courtesy of R.B. Simpson Esq., Strathfield, New South Wales, and the Council of the National Library of Australia.

175. Harry Ransom Humanities Research Center, The University of Texas at Austin, Austin, Texas, USA. Printed by permission of Barbara Mobbs on behalf of the Estate of Charmian Clift and by courtesy of the Harry Ransom Humanities Research Center.

176. Australian Special Research Collection, Australian Defence Force Academy, Canberra. Printed by permission of Mrs Elspeth Dransfield, Neutral Bay, New South Wales, and by courtesy of Peter Kocan Esq. Tuggerawong, New South Wales, and the Australian Special Research Collection, ADFA.

177. MS 798 Box 98, National Library of Australia, Printed by permission of Barry Humphries Esq., London, United Kingdom, and by courtesy of Harry M. Miller Esq., Kings Cross, New South Wales, and the Council of the National Library of Australia.

178. In the possession of Richard Allen Esq., Toorak, Victoria. Printed by permission of Barry Humphries Esq., London, United Kingdom, and by courtesy of Richard Allen Esq.

179. Australian War Memorial, Canberra, PR 00223. Printed by permission of the Australian War Memorial Council.

180. *Age*, Melbourne, 23 November 1972.

181. In the possession of Dr Giovanni Andreoni, Armidale, New South Wales. Printed by permission.

182. In the possession of Ian Templeman Esq. Deakin, Australian Capital Territory. Printed by permission of Australian Literary Management on behalf of Elizabeth Jolley, and by courtesy of Ian Templeman Esq.

183. *The Whitlam Government 1972–1975*, Gough Whitlam (Melbourne: Viking, 1985). Reprinted by permission of Penguin Books Australia.

184–185. *November 1975: the inside story of Australia's greatest political crisis,* Paul Kelly (Sydney: Allen & Unwin, 1995). Reprinted by permission.

186–187. *Dear Kathleen, Dear Manning,* ed. Susan Davies (Melbourne: Melbourne University Press, 1996). Reprinted by permission of Melbourne University Press.

188. *Suddenly Evening: The Selected Poems of R. F. Brissenden,* ed. David Brooks (Melbourne: McPhee Gribble, 1993). Reprinted by permission of Curtis Brown (Australia).

189.   Australian Special Research Collection, Australian Defence Force Academy, Canberra, Papers of Dorothy Green. Printed by permission of Mrs Marion Riley, Whale Beach, New South Wales and by courtesy of the Australian Special Research Collection, ADFA.

190.   *Sydney Morning Herald,* 6 February 1988. Reprinted by permission of Mrs Mavis Cribb, Maitland, New South Wales, on behalf of the Estate of Kylie Tennant.

191.   In the possession of Alan and Jancis Rees, Northwood, New South Wales. Printed by permission of Wendy Whiteley, Surry Hills, New South Wales, and by courtesy of Alan and Jancis Rees.

192.   Copy in the possession of Alan and Jancis Rees, Northwood, New South Wales. Printed by permission of Alan and Jancis Rees on behalf of the Estate of Lloyd Rees.

193–194.   In the possession of Mrs Josephine Denne, Bruny Island, Tasmania. Printed by permission of Dr John Harwood, Blackwood, South Australia, and by courtesy of Mrs Josephine Denne.

195.   Copy in the possession of Ms Banduk Marika, Nhulunbuy, Northern Territory. Printed by permission.

196.   Australian Special Research Collection, Australian Defence Force Academy, Canberra, G 29 Box 44/288. Printed by permission of Ms Kate Llewellyn, Wonona, New South Wales and by courtesy of the Australian Special Research Collection, ADFA.

197.   National Library of Australia, MS 7378/381. Printed by permission of David Williamson Esq., Marcus Beach, Queensland, and by courtesy of the Council of the National Library of Australia.

198.   In the possession of Rosemary Dobson (Bolton), Deakin, Australian Capital Territory. Printed by permission of Les Murray Esq., Bunyah, New South Wales, and by courtesy of Rosemary Dobson, and Robert, Lissant and Ian Bolton.

199.   In the possession of Mandy Martin, Mandurama, New South Wales. Printed by permission of Nicholas Jose Esq., Surry Hills, New South Wales and by courtesy of Mandy Martin.

200.   In the possession of Mandy Martin, Mandurama, New South Wales. Printed by permission and by courtesy of Nicholas Jose Esq.

Index of Writers

INDEX OF RECIPIENTS